THE NEXT REALIGNMENT

THE NEXT REALIGNMENT

WHY AMERICA'S PARTIES ARE CRUMBLING AND WHAT HAPPENS NEXT

FRANK J. DiSTEFANO

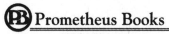

Prometheus Books

59 John Glenn Drive
Amherst, New York 14228

Published 2019 by Prometheus Books

Cover design by Liz Mills
Cover image of Cracked American Flag © Argus/Shutterstock
Cover image of Buttons © PhotoStockImage/Shutterstock
Cover design © Prometheus Books

Trademarked names appear throughout this book. Prometheus Books recognizes all registered trademarks, trademarks, and service marks mentioned in the text.

The internet addresses listed in the text were accurate at the time of publication. The inclusion of a website does not indicate an endorsement by the author or by Prometheus Books, and Prometheus Books does not guarantee the accuracy of the information presented at these sites.

Inquiries should be addressed to
Prometheus Books
59 John Glenn Drive
Amherst, New York 14228
VOICE: 716–691–0133 • FAX: 716–691–0137
WWW.PROMETHEUSBOOKS.COM

23 22 21 20 19   5 4 3 2 1

Library of Congress Cataloging-in-Publication Data

Names: DiStefano, Frank J., 1973- author.
Title: The next realignment : why America's parties are crumbling and what happens next / by
    Frank J. DiStefano.
Description: Amherst, New York : Prometheus Books, 2019. | Includes index.
Identifiers: LCCN 2018045604 (print) | LCCN 2019000834 (ebook) |
    ISBN 9781633885097 (ebook) | ISBN 9781633885080 (hardcover)
Subjects: LCSH: Political parties—United States—History.
Classification: LCC JK2261 (ebook) | LCC JK2261 .D576 2019 (print) |
    DDC 324.273—dc23
LC record available at https://lccn.loc.gov/2018045604

Printed in the United States of America

To my parents,
whose unwavering support made this book—
and every project I have ever done and will ever do—possible.

CONTENTS

CHAPTER 1

INTRODUCTION:
THE NEXT REALIGNMENT IS COMING

Americans are alarmed about their country's politics, and for good reason. Each week that goes by brings another stunning event in a long ongoing trend—the gradual but consistent shattering of one assumption after another about how politics in America works. With each new surprise and with each norm broken, American politics becomes progressively angrier and more unsettled. Americans no longer know what to expect next from their government. New movements keep butting into the public square and more and more of the unwritten rules that governed American politics for decades are falling away. Increasingly worried about their future and their country's future, many people are anxious. They should be. America's parties are in the process of breaking apart and everything we think we know about how its politics works is about to change. We're preparing for the next realignment.

Political realignments are part of a cycle built deep into the political structure of the American republic. They're much like earthquakes that occur on known fault lines in the earth—the places where two of the continental plates floating over the planet's surface rub against each other. We can't predict exactly when a quake will happen but, because quakes are part of a long naturally occurring cycle, we know how they will happen, why they will happen, and approximately where they will happen. We watch the pressure build for years as massive tectonic plates grind up against each other. As they press, their hooks and grooves inevitably catch and tear. All the while, the people who live on these floating continents go about their lives. People go to work, buy groceries, and play in the park, forgetting all about the powerful force slowly building underneath their feet. One day, the pressure becomes too much. The two great plates rip past each other, rending the earth above. Structures topple, bridges fall, and the landscape is reconfigured. In a moment, lives get disrupted and the entire shape of the earth is changed. Then, the pressure gone, the plates rest comfortably once more. With time, people forget it even happened—until the cycle repeats and it happens again.

Having lived our entire lifetimes inside a stable part of a larger cycle of destruction and rebirth, we mistakenly believe the world we know has always existed and will last, unchanged, forever. In fact, this stable system of two parties built around familiar ideologies is now in the process of collapse. That's why American politics has become so turbulent. That's why new movements and ideas have been crowding uncomfortably into the national debate. That's why America's parties are struggling with feuding coalitions no longer willing to put aside their differences for a common agenda. That's why it's been so long since anything important in government has gotten done, leading to the never-ending complaints about how American politics is broken. The next realignment is coming. It will reorder everything we think we know about America. That's what this book is about.

WHAT'S A REALIGNMENT?

For the entire life of virtually everyone alive today, American politics has meant the same old war between Democrats and Republicans. As far back as we all remember, the fundamental battle lines of American politics haven't changed. Democrats have championed the ideology we call New Deal liberalism—that expert-driven reforms can create national progress to benefit ordinary Americans and the least well off. Republicans have championed the ideology we call modern conservatism—that the Democrats' agenda of New Deal liberalism is "big government," violating liberty and undermining the nation's virtue. The specifics of this never-ending war have changed from time to time, as political warfare moved from field to field. Issues, policies, and political leaders have come and gone. States painted red on political maps shifted over time to blue, while blue-colored states became red. Yet as far back as most of us remember, Republicans and Democrats have each essentially represented the same ideologies, attracted similar coalitions of people, and advanced consistent agendas of ideas. It wasn't always thus; nor will it ever be.

Just on the other side of our historical memories lie other versions of major American parties unlike anything we've ever known. These parties were neither liberal nor conservative in the way we now use those terms. They united coalitions of people who, to our minds, come from opposite poles of the political "spectrum." In fact, America has had five distinct sets of political coalitions over its history, each completely unlike the others. During their long reigns, these parties would sometimes win and sometimes lose. Demographic groups, or even entire bases of support, might switch allegiance with the ebb and flow of issues and candidates. Ideologically, however, each party during each era remained consistent, invoking the same principles and promoting the same ideology. Then, over a short period of time, each of these stable party coalitions burst and two new coalitions emerged from the chaos. Some parties outright collapsed, as with the traumatic disintegration of the Whigs or the sad whimpering away of the Federalists. Some parties the people cruelly abandoned, such as the Depression-era Republicans. Some became infected with new people and ideas, like the Democratic Party that a populist third party captured in the late 1800s. Whether by collapse or renewal, when the upheaval ended America had two major parties that stood for different principles, attracted different coalitions, and advanced different agendas than their predecessors. American parties change in sudden and catastrophic bursts.

Scholars call these sudden changes in America's parties "realignments." It's a term that's often misunderstood. People like to say a shift in loyalty by some demographic group from one party to the other is a "realignment"—they might call rural voters trending to the Republicans a realignment, or northeastern voters trending to the Democrats a realignment, or the recent monumental shift in the "Solid South" from a virtual lock for Democrats to a virtual lock for Republicans a realignment. Political realignments aren't about this kind of shuffling of voters from one political team to its opponent. Nor are they about which party wins more elections or controls which offices or institutions. They're a total remaking of the existing two-party framework, redefining America's parties from their foundation as factions and interests abandon old alliances and struggle to find new partners to chart new paths toward political power. Realignments reorder the most basic political divides in America, changing how we see ourselves and how we define the national tribes that make up our nation. In realignments, ideas, principles, and ideologies are tossed completely up for grabs, and the parties that emerge look nothing like what came before. The next realignment won't be good or bad for Democrats or Republicans, nor for conservatism or liberalism. It will destroy them all as new parties with new beliefs viewing our problems in new ways spring up from the ash.

It's remarkable so few people know about political realignments because they're a well-established part of political science scholarship. The idea goes back to a 1955 essay called "A Theory of Critical Elections" by Vladimir Orlando Key Jr., one of the most famous political scientists of the first half of the twentieth century.[1] Key was writing in the aftermath of Franklin Roosevelt's New Deal, which had just dramatically ripped open America's politics, and he realized the transformation of America's two major parties in the 1930s was hardly a unique event. He noticed a similar pattern in the election of 1896, in which William Jennings Bryan brought the populist movement into the Democratic Party, launching America's energetic Populist and Progressive Era. Key theorized that American parties don't change gradually over time. They change in sharp and noticeable breaks when one national election suddenly creates stark new divisions in the electorate.[2] Soon after, the scholar E. E. Schattschneider echoed Key's work and the theory of political realignments was born.[3]

In the years that followed, more scholars built on Key's work. They too noticed that America always has two strong national political parties, each within striking distance of a majority. For generations, these parties stand for a consistent set of principles bound into established party ideologies. They attract similar voters and advance similar policies. Then something happens and that stable system rapidly falls apart and gets reforged. Walter Dean Burnham, who became something of the adopted father of the realignment theory, proposed a progression of distinct "party systems" punctuated by one of Key's critical elections.[4] Each of these American party systems, Burnham found, had stable voting patterns with little deviation until a critical election arrived, bringing high intensity, increased polarization, and transformations in the agendas of the parties. In other words, although people assume great change must always come gradually, that's not how American political party systems change at all. They snap, triggering an explosive national upheaval. According to Burnham, "eras of critical realignment are marked by short, sharp reorganizations of the mass coalitional bases of the major parties which occur at periodic intervals at the national level."[5]

In 1973, James Sundquist, a former speechwriter for Harry Truman turned scholar at the Brookings Institute, provided the final important piece to the theory of realignments in his book *Dynamics of the Party System*. Navigating through the history of three American party systems to explore how they rose and fell, Sundquist found what mattered most was issues and ideas:

> In each of those three periods of political crisis—the 1850s, the 1890s, and the 1930s—the existing rationale for the division of voters between the parties gave way to a new one. One or both of the major parties was radically changed in composition and character. The voting blocs that came together as coalitions to make up the major parties were rearranged. Thus the line of party cleavage sliced through the electorate in a new direction, shifting the party structure on its axis. When things settled down, the change had been so profound that in retrospect, as noted earlier, a new party system can be said to have replaced the old.[6]

From all these scholars, and the many others building on their works, we know several things about how American political parties operate. For long periods of time, political parties stay basically the same, attracting similar coalitions and standing for a consistent set of ideas. Then they suddenly break, whether through one sharp "critical election" or a longer period of disruption, unleashing an unstable era of turbulence and change. New parties arise in the turmoil, attracting different coalitions and standing for different ideas. Most important, what defines these parties and the breaks between them is the rise of new issues and ideas.

It's generally agreed that American politics has moved through five distinct party systems punctuated by four realignments. There's some disagreement on precisely where to place the dividing lines, but there's rough agreement on what each of these five distinct party systems are. America's First Party System arrived when President George Washington's treasury secretary, Alexander Hamilton, and his secretary of state, Thomas Jefferson, discovered they had clashing visions about what the new republic was supposed to be. Hamilton and his partisans, the Federalists, wanted to build a strong commercial republic with a strong central government to rival the great powers of Europe. Jefferson and his supporters, whom we now call Democratic-Republicans, thought America ought to be an agricultural nation of independent yeoman farmers with decentralized authority closer to the people. What Hamilton thought essential—banks, a national currency, a strong army—Jefferson believed were threats to republican government. By Thomas Jefferson's presidency, the American people effectively concluded America could be both. Its debate essentially resolved, the First Party System fell into decline until a weakening Federalist Party blundered, lodging a collection of overzealous demands during the War of 1812 that got it branded a pack of traitors and secessionists, resulting in the party's swift collapse.

After a brief "Era of Good Feelings" in which America attempted to function without parties or partisanship, a Second Party System emerged after the messy election of 1824. The nation split once more into two camps, one group supporting John Quincy Adams and Henry Clay and another coalescing around Andrew Jackson. Jackson was a rough man of the people and military hero who raged against banks and elites and believed America ought to be a popular democracy that empowered ordinary Americans using common sense. Adams, Clay, and their supporters feared Jackson was an uneducated tyrant and demagogue whose rowdy populism threated America's modernization and national greatness. Jackson's followers became the Democrats. The Adams and Clay faction took on a name honoring the patriots who fought against British tyranny during the American Revolution, the Whigs. In the decades that followed, Democrats and Whigs sparred over banks, modernization, tariff policy, and western expansion, but as proxies for another great debate. Was America meant to become a dynamic and meritocratic republic of industry and progress? Or was it to become a popular republic in which ordinary people using common sense charted their destiny without deference to elites? As America entered the 1850s, it resolved that debate too. America was both a popular republic and a dynamic one, a republic of the people that eagerly embraced modernization, building, growth, and reform. At the same time, a new debate rose as the nation expanded west and religious revivals erupted. Was it moral to allow slavery to expand further into new territories? In 1852, a Whig Party now divided over slavery collapsed. The electorate battered the Democrats two years later. America plunged into nearly a decade of turmoil, violence, and scary new movements like the Know-Nothings. Eventually a new party organized around fighting slavery's spread emerged, the Republican Party. Over the next few years, this new party built strength until, in 1860, it won a presidential election. America spiraled into a civil war. A Third Party System began.

As America emerged from that civil war, the Third Party System settled in. Republicans now represented the interests of the North while Democrats represented those locked out of power—mainly Southern business interests, farmers and laborers particularly in the South, and new urban immigrants locked out of the Northern Republican establishment. These parties debated issues like tariff policies and the patronage system that traded federal jobs for political support. These were again proxies for another great debate—resentments still lingering in the war's aftermath.

Over the following years, as the scars from war wounds gradually faded, troubling new problems arose. Rapid industrialization began minting millionaires like Rockefeller and Carnegie, creating a "Gilded Age" that destroyed the profitability of the small-town family farms that had long served as America's middle-class economic backbone. People streamed into immigrant-packed cities to take work in dirty and dangerous factories, laboring fourteen-hour days in ghastly conditions. An angry populist movement broke out, particularly in rural areas and in the West, and an economic panic threw America into one of the most punishing economic depressions in its history. In 1896, a thirty-six-year-old former congressman named William Jennings Bryan delivered a barn-burning speech at the Democratic National Convention and came out the nominee. He threw out the old Democratic Party platform, pushed out the old party leadership, and replaced its creaking ideology with a populist platform. The Democratic Party now transformed into a populist party that claimed to represent farmers and working people crushed under the power of the elite. In response, the Republicans transformed into a good-government party of pro-business moral reformers. Their clashing visions of moral and social reform—populism and progressivism—launched a new great debate over how best to respond to the downsides of industrialization. A Fourth Party System began. Under this new party system, America implemented a flurry of dramatic reforms like banning child labor, imposing clean standards on food and medicine, imposing maximum work hours, creating public schools, banning the "demon rum" of alcohol, creating public parks, and extending the right to vote to women. By the 1920s, these reforms had alleviated many of the worst abuses of industrialization, while the religious revivals that drove many into the arms of progressive reform had cooled. America was a rich, powerful, prosperous nation on an upward boom. Then, in 1929, this confident and thriving America plunged into an economic catastrophe, the Great Depression.

By 1932, the end of President Herbert Hoover's first term in office, many once-middle-class Americans were now crowded into tented refugee camps relying on charity to eat. National unemployment reached about 25 percent. The Democratic nominee for president, New York governor Franklin Roosevelt, swept into the White House promising America a New Deal. In office, he assembled a team of experts to combat the crisis, pulling ideas from everywhere—from the Democratic Party's populist tradition but also from Republican progressives. These experiments coalesced into a novel governing ideology holding that America could harness expertise and rational planning to drive national progress that benefited working people and the least well off—New Deal liberalism. Roosevelt's opponents, both former Democrats and former Republicans, banded together to stop the New Deal's advance. Some of them believed the New Deal violated personal liberty, while others believed it undercut the virtues necessary for the republic's success. Taking over the remains of Hoover's now all-but-dead Republican Party, they blended their criticisms into a new Republican Party ideology—modern conservatism. A Fifth Party System began and it continues on today.

WHAT REALIGNMENTS ARE ABOUT

Realignments and party systems remain the dominant way we look at politics in America.[7] In recent decades, however, the theory has raised some discontent. Since every previous American party system lasted about four decades, give or take one or two election cycles, the original realignment theorists naturally presumed realignments must come about every thirty or forty years.[8] During the turbulent 1960s and 1970s, many political scholars and politicians therefore expected a realignment must be around the corner. Decades had passed since America's last realignment in 1932. Burnham suggested a realignment was surely on its way.[9] Richard Nixon even built his 1968 electoral strategy around the belief that he could spark such a realignment, as his aide Kevin Phillips hinted in his blockbuster 1969 book *The Emerging Republican Majority*.[10] Yet despite all the disruptive political change of the civil rights movement, the Great Society, the counterculture, the Vietnam War, the Goldwater campaign of 1964, the violence of the 1968 Democratic National Convention in Chicago, the rise of a New Left and a New Right, the election of Richard Nixon and his Silent Majority, Watergate, and the Reagan Revolution, the predicted realignment never came.

Some scholars theorized that America might have entered a period of "dealignment" in which its parties were simply decaying with no new party system forming in its place.[11] Others questioned whether the realignment theory was ever correct at all. They pointed out that no realignment had arrived in the middle of the twentieth century.[12] They noted that statistical analyses of voting behavior is often muddier then the sharp breaks that realignments in theory ought to produce.[13] They quibbled over the various indicia of realignments on which previous theorists relied, such as turmoil in nominating conventions or the rise of third parties.[14] These criticisms, however, ultimately came down to variations of the same complaint—"The theory has not been able to account for what has happened over the past generation of American politics, despite the often frustrating search by scholars to locate the electoral realignment that was due in 1964, 1968, or thereabout."[15] Political scientists have been "waiting for Godot," but "the political world stubbornly refuses to comply."[16]

Those who lost faith in realignments forgot what they're actually about. American politics isn't a natural system like physics. It's the messy way the American people negotiate their differences in an attempt to self-govern their republic. At any given time, we face great and terrifying questions about what we as a people ought to do and in which direction we ought to travel. Politics is how we navigate those debates to collectively work through our most difficult problems. Party systems aren't really about which of two arbitrary organizations the American people give control of government at any one time. Nor are they just about which party controls which offices, or the demographic coalitions, or even the agendas of issues that parties promote. Those are just the effects and indicia and results of realignments. As V. O. Key himself first observed, realignments are in reality stark breaks in what the parties stand for and what they represent. In other words, party systems are national debates carried out over decades through which the American people work through their most urgent problems over time. Realignments are the moments in which an old debate is resolved and a new national debate begins.

The reason America hasn't had a realignment since the 1930s is the conditions to create a realignment hadn't yet arrived. The New Deal debate that began in 1932 wasn't yet resolved. Now it is. A lot has happened since this Fifth Party System began. America waged and won a Second World War. The nation emerged an unrivaled world power, enjoying years of peace and prosperity from Eisenhower through Kennedy's Camelot. Lyndon Johnson's Great Society hoped to harness the New Deal's ideals to solve thorny social problems like poverty and racial injustice. In the late 1960s and 1970s, America's economy stagnated. There were bloody street protests, riots, political assassinations, and dissent over the Vietnam War. There was stagflation, an oil shock, Watergate, and a hostage crisis with Iran. The Reagan Revolution brought Morning in America. The Contract with America reformed welfare as we knew it. President Clinton fought impeachment. On September 11, 2001, the World Trade Center fell. President Bush launched a War on Terror and went to war in Iraq. In 2008, America hoped for change, and the age of Obama began. In 2016, Donald Trump won the White House, beginning his norm-breaking presidency.

America has also changed a lot since this party system began. The industrial age ended. We no longer live and work in an economic system designed to mass-produce good-enough products for everyone. We live in a fast, agile, postindustrial economic system designed to custom-meet needs through the use of masses of data. The economy went global and Americans found themselves competing for work with people across the world. The Cold War ended. America no longer stands as the head of one great-power alliance fighting an ideological battle against another great-power alliance. It stands as the greatest power in a multipolar world in which it attempts to shape global norms while others work actively or passively to see it decline. The family and cultural systems that support postindustrial life are fundamentally different from those of industrial America. Families look different, people live differently, and people value different things. An explosion of new technology is changing the basic rules of how we communicate with each other and fundamentally altering power relationships between people and institutions.

As the world we first designed our parties to debate has transformed, our parties have naturally started breaking down. Across America, there's a sense that we face an onslaught of disquieting new problems but no one knows what to do about them. Not only does America's political system appear unable to accomplish much of substance, but few policies of either party even seem relevant to addressing the new problems we face. People demand change, yet no one can agree what that change ought to be. No one in either party seems to have a solid theory of what's happening or why, much less a credible plan to address it. Neither party has developed an agenda of innovative policies. When confronting new problems, Democrats mostly apply the ideals of New Deal liberalism, which the party first pioneered during the early twentieth century and refined during the years of the Great Society. Republicans reach back to their instinctive opposition of such policies as "big government," applying the conservative ideals their party pioneered in the middle of the twentieth century and refined during the Reagan administration of the 1980s. Everyone seems to be waiting for the world to just go back to the way it was before, or for some magic to solve these scary new problems with a familiar solution. Yet no one honestly expects that to happen. Since no one is acting and nothing seems to be working, new people and disruptive ideas are creeping into the national debate. People are getting angry. Old norms are falling away. A real fear is spreading that these problems are in fact symptoms of a scary national decline. Perhaps the country really *is* starting to career out of control, and perhaps the vague foreboding so many sense is the feeling of an era ending, just as it once ended for the French Empire and the British Empire.

What everyone can sense, the reason everything seems to be careering out of control, is the conditions for a realignment have arrived and every indication says it's already on its way. Our parties are anachronisms, political coalitions and ideologies built to address another age's problems instead of those that now exist. We've lived our entire lives inside just one party system, thinking it's the natural way for things to be because it's the only system we've ever known. Yet our parties are still debating New Deal America, an America that no longer exists. Democrats continue to fight for the ideology of New Deal liberalism forged in Franklin Roosevelt's New Deal. Republicans fight against the "big government" the New Deal revolution wrought. The reason American politics seems so dangerous and uncontrolled is because the familiar party frameworks within which we organize everything have rapidly fallen away but we haven't yet replaced them with what comes next. The time has come.

Our parties are about to change. The only questions are when, how, and what happens next. Our decisions in the years ahead will determine not just how the remaking of our parties unfolds. We'll decide what sorts of parties emerge from the cycle of destruction and rebirth. Through it, we'll decide what sort of America will come to be.

WHAT THIS BOOK IS ABOUT

This book is about political parties and realignments, but most of all it's about the future of America. It's about how our parties got the way they are. What built them? Who built them? Of what are they really made? What ideas and philosophical principles sustain them, and what do those principles really hold? The book is also about the powerful forces tearing at our parties' hearts. How do realignments work? What causes them and what shapes them? Why was the utter and traumatic collapse of the Whigs so different from the launch of the Populist and Progressive Movements? How does the recurring eruption of awakenings, national spirits of moral reform that periodically spark powerful religious revivals and dramatic social movements, continually plunge America into crusades for moral and social reform? What forces are already quietly cutting the ties that bind America's political factions, and how are these forces combining in a potent mix, pushing America's parties toward collapse? Most of all, this book is about America's future. The choices we make as we navigate these disruptive changes will forge new ideologies for America's parties, affecting which problems we address and how, and ultimately redefining America as a nation.

To explain what drives realignments, the book delves into the history and stories of America's past party systems—Hamilton's Federalists and Jefferson's Democratic-Republicans, the Whigs and Jackson's Democrats, the Civil War parties of North and South, the Populist and Progressive

Era parties that reformed America out of the Gilded Age, and our New Deal era parties of today. Most important, it explores the great debates of history in which the American people sparred over how America should change, what it should become, and how it should address new problems and concerns. Through this telling of the story of America, the book proposes a better theory about what realignments are and why they occur. It demonstrates how, with each realignment, an old system is swept away in a moment of crisis. Americans, facing new problems, form new alliances better suited to address the new problems of a new age. A new party system forms, one designed to debate the most pressing problem of the era ahead. Those parties then wage that new great debate over years of elections and policy experiments, until ultimately the questions we created them to address are finally resolved. Then America changes again. Old problems fade, new technologies develop, and new troubles arise. Over time, parties perfectly designed to wage a critical debate from a long-gone era decay into anachronisms. No longer able to offer compelling solutions to problems, they become old and brittle until they break—clearing the way for new coalitions uniting different people, often former enemies who now have more in common than they once had, unleashing vibrant new eras of reform. The American political system is built around these periods of collapse and rebirth.

Perhaps most important, the book provides us with the tools we need to better see the seams and cracks now tearing our familiar New Deal party system down. The story of modern politics isn't just a story of liberals and conservatives hoping to push America "left" or "right." It's the story of a temporary debate launched amid the devastation of a depression and world war over how to adapt the American republic to the modern industrial economy. Understanding our own party system—how it came to be, the factions of which it consists, and the squabbling principles and idea it binds together into its dominant ideologies—is critical to understanding how and why it's coming apart and what's likely to emerge from its collapse. Realignments are always whirling eras of turmoil, breakdown, and uncertainty, as old patterns fall away and people have to find their way anew, but not every realignment is the same. Some are traumatic, like the one that followed the chaotic implosion of the Whigs. Others quickly channel the destructive energy into building something new, such as the realignment that birthed the Populist and Progressive Era. American realignments can be destructive. They can also become conduits for reform, clearing the way for fresh ideas and new approaches necessary for national renewal. If we understand how and why our own party system is breaking down, we can better guide the next realignment to ensure America's future is one we want.

We live at one of history's great turning points. Realignments always present America with a choice. We can choose to renew our parties before they inevitably collapse, ushering in a new political age with refreshed parties built around updated ideologies to ensure the national divisions that rule America's new era are ones that make America better, stronger, safer, and more prosperous. Or we can do nothing until a powerful storm beyond our control rips the system apart, hoping whatever emerges from the rubble doesn't lead the nation down dangerous towpaths into a darker era serving no one. Monumental change really is afoot. An old order really is falling away and a new one is emerging. We don't know what the future looks like, other than that it won't follow the rules of decades past. The anger, the bitterness, the dysfunction, the inability of our parties to grapple seriously with the difficult problems the nation faces—they're just tremors. They're symptoms of the beginning of the greatest shift in American politics in our lifetimes. Our parties haven't significantly changed since the days of Packard cars, the manufacturing economy, rotary telephones, and radio plays. Our era has stayed stable for so long—with "liberal" Democrats fighting the same war with "conservative" Republicans—that it started to feel permanent. That time is at an end. As our parties break and new ones emerge, our decisions will determine what sort of parties these will be. We should make this choice with open eyes and our shared interests as citizens fully in mind. If we're wise, we can renew our politics and our parties, launching a new age of national renewal that will restore what so many Americans in this troubled time now believe is lost—the promise of the American Dream.

CHAPTER 2

AMERICA'S FIRST AND SECOND PARTY SYSTEMS: THE EARLY REPUBLIC'S LOVE-HATE AFFAIR WITH TWO-PARTY POLITICS

Americans often dream of freeing themselves from the two-party system. Some find delight in the idea of a third party free of the dogmas of Republicans and Democrats, ideally one perfectly reflecting their own beliefs. Others imagine their preferred party vanquishing its rival for a generation, ushering in an era of unfettered one-party rule through a "permanent majority." Such dreams are utopian. America has always had two major political coalitions, each winning about half the vote. It will always have two major political coalitions, each winning about half the vote. America will never have a long-lasting third party of any significance. No party will ever win a permanent majority. That's because the American two-party system is more than an accident or tradition. It's part of the basic foundation of the American constitutional republic.

The story of America's First Party System, in which Alexander Hamilton's Federalists battled against Thomas Jefferson's Democratic-Republicans, is the story of how America's Founding generation discovered to their dismay the way American party systems work. You can forgive yourself if you despise two-party politics, since America's Founders didn't much care for political parties either. They never even mentioned parties in their Constitution because they never intended for them to exist. Yet almost as soon as their new republic opened its doors, two political parties formed and went on to dominate American government for decades. As America's Founders discovered to their dismay, political parties are an essential component of American democracy. We may not always like the two-party system, and for good reason, but party systems and the realignments that create and destroy them are fundamental components of the American republic and will always be.

THE FEDERALISTS AND DEMOCRATIC-REPUBLICANS ARISE

It was a generally accepted fact in both America and Britain during the eighteenth century that political parties were evils. The only question was whether they were necessary evils or ones that could be successfully suppressed and eradicated.[1] America's Founders agreed that political parties were dangers a rational republic would do well to avoid. As James Madison, the person most responsible for designing the America Constitution, wrote about them, parties are a "violence" that only inject "instability, injustice, and confusion . . . into the public councils." They cause "the public good [to be] disregarded in the conflicts of rival parties" and public decision to be made "not according to the rules of justice and the rights of the minor party, but by the superior force of an interested and overbearing majority," making them "mortal diseases under which popular governments have everywhere perished."[2] When America's Founders set out to create their new republic, not only did they never intend it to include political parties, or "factions" as they usually called them. They specifically crafted their Constitution to ensure political parties never arose.[3]

America's Founders wanted to create a republic of reason. They intended for citizens to elect the nation's wisest and most enlightened minds to reach decisions for the common good through rational argument and debate. They therefore designed a complex republic with three separate and independent branches of government, each with the power to check and balance the power of the others, further dividing authority between a national government and individual state governments— "Ambition must be made to counteract ambition."[4] Their Constitution gave the most power to a Congress in which elected representatives created the nation's laws through reasoned debate, and it further separated that Congress into two chambers, requiring mutual agreement to act. In light of this careful constitutional design, political parties look like corruption. Parties are private associations located entirely outside government seeking to coordinate action across every institution. They seek not to independently debate the common good issue by issue but to advance the party's already-decided agenda. They seek to overpower the independent thought of legislators in the name of party loyalty. They seek to overpower the independent thought of voters through partisanship and campaigning. Political parties are essentially conspiracies to overpower the Constitution's carefully designed mechanisms against any person or group ever gaining enough power to act alone. Their entire purpose is to circumvent the protections the Founders believed critical to rational government. Yet as soon as the Founders formed their first government, they quickly divided into two energetic political parties to their own bafflement and disgust.

We sometimes forget that when Washington and his administration set about charting a course for their young country, they had no idea what a democratic republic was supposed to look like, much less how one might actually work. We all carry a model about in our heads of how democratic politics functions because we've always lived in a world full of democratic republics. America's Founders, without our centuries of experience to draw upon, were inventing this form of government we take for granted from scratch. Most people at the time—living in an era in which everyone accepted the legitimate rule of kings—had grave doubts whether it was even possible to sustain a democratic republic at all without it tumbling into tyranny, turning itself over to the false promises of a cunning demagogue, or falling prey to the angry passions of the mob. America's Founders could look for guidance to ancient societies like Greece and Rome, republics built for a very different world over a thousand years in the past, which often functioned more like oligarchies and ultimately collapsed into tyranny or despotism. They could look to the British parliament, still awkwardly sharing power under an unwritten constitution with an honest-to-goodness king. They could look to the corrupt oligarchies of the Italian city states. Ultimately, however, they had to rely on their own intuitions and imaginations about what pitfalls might lie ahead for the democratic republic they would create.[5]

When George Washington assembled America's first presidential administration, its officials appeared to be likeminded and united. They all agreed with the American Revolution's ideals, supported the Constitution, and dared not challenge Washington. The chief political dispute at the time was between the Federalists, advocates of replacing the Articles of Confederation and Perpetual Union, America's first organizing document, with the Constitution, and the Anti-Federalists, who opposed the Constitution.[6] Washington's important officers were all Federalists, with the possible exception of Secretary of State Thomas Jefferson, who had flirted with Anti-Federalism before joining the Federalist cause.[7] As Washington's new government set to work, the Founding generation still considered the idea of an organized opposition to the government inherently disruptive, useless, and illegitimate.[8] Based on Britain's experience with factionalism in its own government, formal party opposition—as opposed to mere individuals independently opposing government—still had a somewhat unsavory reputation, tainted with a whiff of disloyalty and treason.[9] The members of Washington's cabinet, however, held very different ideas about how to safeguard the new republic.

As president, Washington relied greatly on his younger protégé and treasury secretary, Alexander Hamilton, a New York lawyer who had served alongside Washington as his aide-de-camp during the Revolutionary War.[10] Hamilton had a vision of America, the small colony at the world's edge, growing into a great commercial republic standing equal to the greatest powers of Europe.[11] As Washington's most trusted official, Hamilton quickly set about implementing policies and reforms to strengthen the national government, provide infrastructure to sustain a commercial economy, and remedy the failures of the Articles of Confederation. Hamilton wrote three reports detailing his plans, one proposing the national government assume state debts accumulated during the war, along with mechanisms to secure credit to pay those debts; a second creating a national bank like a Federal Reserve; and a third proposing tariffs and subsidies to encourage manufacturing and fund infrastructure like roads and canals.[12] Hamilton's plans—which incidentally benefitted the commercial economies of the Northern states that had failed to pay off their war debts while imposing costs on the Southern states that had already mostly repaid them—were meant to advance a vision of America as a growing nation of merchants and bankers, with taxes and officials and standing armies to compete in the squabbles of nations.[13] Secretary of State Thomas Jefferson and his protégé, James Madison, had a more romantic vision of what this republic was supposed to be. They believed those who worked in manufacturing or commerce, without the economic freedom afforded by owning their own land, were rendered by their dependency unfit citizens for a republic.[14] They yearned for a republic of independent yeoman farmers free of what they believed were the corrupting influences of state power and commerce, which they associated with aristocracy.[15] Of course, in practice this also served the interests of rich plantation aristocrats like Jefferson, whose wealth rested on the exploited labor of slavery and whose manners and lifestyle were far more elitist and privileged than a self-made lawyer like Hamilton, whom they accused of aristocratic pretensions.

As Hamilton marched forth with his bold ideas of reform to the cheers of New York and Boston, opposition gathered. What Hamilton and his administration faction saw as strengthening the young nation, Jefferson and his followers feared was a path toward corruption and aristocracy that would destroy their republican experiment. Jefferson's anti-administration faction waged a pitched battle to stop Hamilton's policies as violations of the American Revolution's ideals. Hamilton won most of the important battles, winning the implementation of his plan's critical cornerstones, but the powerful anti-administration resistance levied a toll. Hamilton and his supporters won the debt plan, in exchange for relocating the nation's capital to the Potomac River, and the national bank, but Jefferson and his faction thwarted the industrial proposals.[16] Both groups then worked to convince a reluctant Washington to stay on for a second term to keep the nation united, where they soon discovered new differences.[17]

When the French Revolution led France into war against monarchical Europe, Jefferson's followers, now calling themselves republicans, demanded America support France as its ally and revolutionary brother. Jefferson's republicans saw the French Revolution as a struggle against the same aristocracy and corruption toward which they feared Hamilton was leading America.[18] Washington, Hamilton, and the administration faction, still called Federalists, weren't interested in gambling the security of their new nation in a dangerous foreign war, much less one they feared might rip apart American society if the utopianism radicalism behind it ever spread at home.[19] Opponents of the administration began organizing into Democratic-Republican Societies, but their association with Jacobin radicalism and the Whiskey Rebellion tax revolt tarred them as dangerous and disloyal.[20] Washington denounced these "self-created societies" as inherently dangerous provocateurs of insurrection—seeming to claim any organized opposition to his government was tantamount to treason—helping to stomp them out.[21] As long as Washington remained president, however, this factionalism mostly roiled beneath a formally united government. Few dared to attack the hero of the American Revolution openly, instead criticizing ministers like Hamilton for misleading and deceiving him. Then, in 1796, Washington retired.

Alarmed at the warfare inside his government, Washington dedicated a Farewell Address to convey a grave warning to his successors—they were on course to rip apart the republic they had just laboriously created. His theme was more than just concern over the controversies pitting his administration's federalism against Jefferson's republicanism. It denounced in clear terms the idea of the political parties he saw forming in America:

> The common and continual mischiefs of the spirit of party are sufficient to make it the interest and duty of a wise people to discourage and restrain it.
>
> It serves always to distract the public councils and enfeeble the public administration. It agitates the community with ill-founded jealousies and false alarms, kindles the animosity of one part against another, foments occasionally riot and insurrection. It opens the door

to foreign influence and corruption, which finds a facilitated access to the government itself through the channels of party passions. Thus the policy and the will of one country are subjected to the policy and will of another.

There is an opinion that parties in free countries are useful checks upon the administration of the government and serve to keep alive the spirit of liberty. This within certain limits is probably true; and in governments of a monarchical cast, patriotism may look with indulgence, if not with favor, upon the spirit of party. But in those of the popular character, in governments purely elective, it is a spirit not to be encouraged. From their natural tendency, it is certain there will always be enough of that spirit for every salutary purpose. And there being constant danger of excess, the effort ought to be by force of public opinion, to mitigate and assuage it. A fire not to be quenched, it demands a uniform vigilance to prevent its bursting into a flame, lest, instead of warming, it should consume.[22]

Everyone ignored Washington's warnings.

In the election of 1796, all this factionalism broke loose. It was increasingly clear these two factions, federalists and republicans, weren't just two ad hoc groups sparring over an economic plan. Nor were they just the partisans of two ambitious personalities, Hamilton and Jefferson, scrapping over power. They were the start of two enduring political parties engaged in a philosophical debate about how a republic was supposed to work—not merely federalists and republicans but a Federalist Party and a Democratic-Republican Party.[23] Federalists, who mainly drew from New England and Northern elites, favored growth and commerce, a strong national government, national economic policies, preferred Britain over France in foreign affairs, and feared that the naive, utopian, and radical ideas of the Democratic-Republicans would bring bloody violence, destruction, and murder just as it had revolutionary France. Democratic-Republicans, who drew from the South and the growing middle class of merchants and artisans in the North, favored a decentralized nation of independent farmers, a weak federal government with states' rights, favored France over Britain, and believed Federalists were closet aristocrats, too friendly with England and supporting a corrupting economic and political program meant to choke off liberty in order to install a monarchy in America.[24] Their disagreements over policies and issues, they learned, actually represented rival visions of what the American republic was supposed to be. Could America really grow into a rich and powerful nation of commerce, standing armies, and national authority and retain its republican character? Did America need national institutions and taxes to grow and thrive, or were such things a path to aristocracy? Did a republic require the radical ideals of revolutionary France, or was that a path toward instability, bloodshed, and ruin? Each party had conflicting ideas about what a republic required, and each feared its rival's ideas were betrayals of the American Revolution that would inescapably lead to the destruction of the republic of liberty they won a war to create. These clashing ideas would echo across American politics for a generation.

In 1796, the Federalists rallied around Vice President John Adams as Washington's natural successor. The Democratic-Republicans promoted their leader, Jefferson.[25] Although the presidential electors were still supposed to be independent, both parties expected electors from the state legislatures they controlled to vote for their faction's candidate—subverting the original intent of the electoral college. Adams won the most electoral votes and the presidency. Some Federalist electors, however, cast their second vote for local favorites instead of the intended Federalist vice-presidential candidate, so Jefferson won the second-highest number of votes and, under the constitutional rules that existed at that time, the vice-presidency.[26] Adams personally loathed political parties, continuing to rail against them throughout his life, so he naturally hoped to govern above parties as Washington had sought to do.[27] He saw himself as bound to no party, attempted to move past the partisan battles of the Washington years, and even sidelined Hamilton out of a mixture of disagreement and jealously.[28] Jefferson and his faction, however, remained determined to fight Adams and his perceived Federalism.

After a series of political conflicts and diplomatic blunders between America and revolutionary France spread war fever and fear of French invasion across America, the clash between Adams and Jefferson's Democratic-Republicans really came to a head.[29] Fearing disloyalty from immigrants friendly to France, as well as angry political polarization from French partisans in America, Adams and his administration advanced a package of controversial laws called the Alien and Sedition Acts. These laws empowered the president to detain or expel foreign immigrants and to criminally prosecute anyone who opposed any "measures of the United States" or who spoke, wrote, or printed any statement bringing the president into "contempt or disrepute."[30] The Federalists—and Adams in particular—had long suffered great abuse by a more sophisticated and extensive Democratic-Republican press.[31] Not accepting or understanding the idea of legitimate party opposition, Adams viewed these Democratic-Republican attacks as corrosive assaults on the American government that threatened national stability and order. Neither party yet saw its rival as a legitimate opposition; both still believed the other an illegitimate band perverting the republic, a danger the nation needed to violently stamp out.[32] Believing he was fighting a disease eating away at the republic, Adams eagerly employed the Acts to prosecute Democratic-Republican newspaper editors, journalists, and political activists for speaking against the administration—enraging Democratic-Republicans who saw these prosecutions as unconstitutional partisan tyranny.[33] Backlash put the final coffin nail into the nonpartisan ideal.

The election of 1800, pitting Jefferson against Adams for a second time, was among America's ugliest. Both parties now waged nearly hysterical campaigns of mudslinging and hyperbole, claiming their opponent would destroy the republic if elected.[34] Democratic-Republicans denounced Adams as a fool, imbecile, tyrant, and closet monarchist plotting to overthrow the republic with a new aristocracy. Federalists accused the Democratic-Republicans of Jacobin radicalism that would plunge America into foreign wars, tear apart its society, and ultimately sink the nation into anarchy. Journalist James Callender, Jefferson's chief literary assassin, wrote on Jefferson's payroll that Adams prattled with "that strange compound of ignorance and ferocity, of deceit and weakness; without regard to that hideous hermaphroditical character, which has neither the force and firmness of a man, nor the gentleness and sensibility of a woman."[35] A Federalist newspaper, the *Connecticut Currant*, wrote that if Jefferson were ever elected president, "Murder, robbery, rape, adultery, and incest will all be openly taught, the air will be rent with the cries of the distressed, the soil will be soaked with blood, and the nation black with crimes."[36] Both parties worked diligently to elect partisan presidential electors, finalizing the transition of the electoral college from independent decision-makers to the party functionaries they remain today. Jefferson won the election in large part due to the outrage over the Alien and Sedition Acts, but since Democratic-Republican electors cast their two votes by party line, his vice-presidential pick, Aaron Burr, won the same number of electoral votes. (The Federalists arranged for one elector to throw his second vote to avoid this situation.) That tossed the election into the Federalist-controlled House of Representatives, which almost picked Burr until Hamilton convinced them Jefferson was the less-dangerous choice.[37] In response to the debacle, America scrapped the original system of independent elections for president and vice president in favor of party tickets—now tacitly recognizing political parties in the republic's election rules.

America's Founders, however, still hadn't accepted parties. Jefferson triumphantly proclaimed in his first inaugural address, "We are all republicans: we are all federalists."[38] That didn't mean he intended to respect his Federalist opposition. Jefferson believed his victory meant federalism, now defeated and discredited through his electoral triumph, would properly fade away as the entire nation, finally freed of the corrupting influence of the dastardly Federalist cabal, united as Democratic-Republicans.[39] To carry out his goal, Jefferson eagerly set out to undo all the horrors of Federalist policy he had spent the last decade denouncing. He pardoned those prosecuted under the Sedition Act.[40] He repealed Federalist taxes and cut national spending to rid America of the debt Hamilton had grown to create American credit.[41] He shrunk the national army dramatically.[42] As the Democratic-Republicans transitioned from an opposition railing against the decisions of others to leaders responsible for the republic's welfare, however, something interesting happened.

After investigating the Hamiltonian economic system, Jefferson declined to alter it at all. As his close adviser and Treasury Secretary Albert Gallatin counseled, after tearing into the details of Hamilton's economic policies to expose the corruptions and errors he presumed he would discover, "I have found the most perfect system ever formed. Any change that should be made in it would injure it. Hamilton made no blunders, committed no frauds. He did nothing wrong."[43] Presented with the opportunity to purchase the Louisiana Territory from France, Jefferson seized it to great applause—despite his party's strict view of constitutional powers that suggested the president lacked the authority to do any such thing and the debt the purchase required, which his party ideologically opposed.[44] Jefferson eventually bolstered the military he had previously cut so he could wage a foreign war against North African pirates and stave off possible European incursions.[45] Jefferson even proposed a Hamiltonian-sounding national infrastructure plan to strengthen the economy.[46] The Democratic-Republicans more than simply made peace with Hamilton's Federalist policies. They effectively adopted them.[47]

In public, Federalists and Democratic-Republicans continued waging the same wars over the same debates, denouncing each other as malevolent threats to the republic. In practice, however, there wasn't much left to dispute. After two decades, America had gone through three presidents from two rival parties. It established new institutions. It navigated foreign crises. It built banks, financial systems, and standing armies and found them not only useful but essential. The nation hadn't slid into tyranny. An Old World aristocracy hadn't risen to restore the monarchy. Jacobins hadn't plunged the nation into anarchy. The rational fears of the Founding generation in 1789—before anyone knew how their new system would work, or if it even would work at all—were no longer reasonable in 1808. After two decades of experience, the American people had tacitly reached a conclusion. The nation could have all of Hamilton's institutions without trampling on republicanism or courting aristocracy as Jefferson had feared. When Jefferson adopted Hamiltonianism under the name of Democratic-Republicanism, the First Party System debate was effectively over. All that really remained to hold these parties together was political tribalism, campaign ballyhoo, ambition, habit, and inertia.

THE INEVITABILITY OF AMERICAN PARTY SYSTEMS

As the Founding generation learned to their despair, the American system of government is designed to produce two major parties, each receiving about half the national vote. Powerful third-party movements will erupt from time to time. They may even temporarily capture the nation's attention before the existing parties coopt them or they simply fade away. Parties may briefly capture sweeping national majorities, like Roosevelt's New Deal Democrats, until America drifts back toward two-party parity. Yet unless and until we overhaul human nature, America's constitutional system, and the present election rules, America will always trend back toward two national coalitions just within striking distance of a national majority and no larger. America's Founders might not have intentionally designed a republic for two-party politics, but party systems with two fairly balanced parties is nonetheless implicit in their design.

The reason is obvious when you think about it. Under the current rules, you have to control over half the votes cast to influence the American government. If you control any less than half, you get nothing. In a society with three major factions, or four, or five, or more, none can win alone. If they instead share power in an alliance, they can collectively control enough votes to at least enact parts of everyone's agenda. A political coalition that controls any less than half the national vote will thus naturally add factions until it can reach a majority. What people often miss is that this same process also works in reverse. Every faction that supports a coalition expects to get some of its priorities enacted in exchange for its support. Each additional faction means satisfying more people, sharing more power, and everybody getting fewer of their priorities enacted. An alliance winning significantly more than half the vote can safely ignore or cast out the parts of its coalition that other members like the least so every remaining faction can get more of what it wants. An alliance has everything to gain by adding supporters up to fifty percent of the vote and everything to lose by adding supporters once it reaches the threshold. Given America's federal structure with overlapping institutions and multiple sovereigns that divide and separate power across institutions, jurisdictions, and levels of government, a party must do this nationally—coordinating the actions of senates, presidents, state legislatures, agencies, mayor's offices, state supreme courts, and more. While inevitably producing pockets in which one party dominates, the system overall produces two national parties capturing about half of the national vote.

Many Americans incorrectly blame this two-party tendency on America's "first past the post" or "winner take all" voting schemes of single-member voting districts, in which only the top vote-getter wins office. Such systems inevitably create two parties, a tendency political scientists call Duverger's Law.[48] To break the two-party monopoly, reformers often pine for proportional representative schemes in which parties receive legislative seats in proportion to the percentage of the vote won during the election, a system popular in many European-style parliamentary democracies. Since a party that wins 15 percent of the national vote still wins about 15 percent of the legislative seats under proportional representation, multiparty parliaments usually contain many smaller fluid parties, each of which exercise some power. American observers too often fail to appreciate, however, that once these smaller parties get to parliament, they still inevitably combine until a coalition controlling just about half the elected members form a government. Factions still have to share power in a majority coalition because the parliament still operates through majority rule, and the parties in opposition still have to cooperate to hold the ruling coalition accountable. Proportional representation still essentially breaks society into two broad political coalitions each receiving about half the vote, just pushing the process forward from the voting booth to parliament. Advantages and disadvantages exist in both systems, ones that strengthen or weaken certain sorts of factions, but under either system society ends up with two broad coalitions hovering around a majority. The only difference is at which stage the coalitions form and how stable they remain. The problem isn't single-member voting districts. The problem is the principle of majority rule on which the modern republic is based.

America's political system, moreover, isn't just designed to produce two roughly equal national parties but parties of a particular kind—deeply ideological ones. Political science has developed many methods to analyze parties and their coalitions. It was once common to view American parties as nonideological alliances driven by interest groups, issue activists, and discrete groups in society. Others chiefly focus on the measurable factions within each party, whether demographic identity groups such as "Catholics" or "soccer moms" or "Hispanics," issue advocates like "economic conservatives" or "feminists" or "labor voters," or self-identified factions like "religious conservatives." Others look at parties through their overarching ideologies like "liberalism" and "conservativism." Each method is valuable in context, with frameworks based around discrete and measurable identities particularly useful for people whose interest is in predicting and influencing individual elections in the middle of a working party system. It's obviously far easier to poll, measure, and study which candidates groups of people are likely to support in a specific campaign given a stable system of two well-defined parties than to delve into *why* people care about the things they do—something many people don't even understand about themselves. Party systems and realignments, however, are most powerfully driven by changes in ideology.

To explore whether American parties were mere coalitions of interest or something more, the political scientist John Gerring systematically analyzed the platforms and rhetoric of America's major parties across American history. He surveyed campaign stump speeches, party platforms, and campaign pronouncements to see what ideological principles parties invoked over time.[49] He found that American political parties promoted consistent ideological themes over eras roughly corresponding to America's five historical party systems.[50] In each era, America's major parties consistently relied upon the same collection of ideological principles and ideas. These same principles consistently echoed in the speeches, platforms, and policy agendas of the parties across the entire era. Out of these principles flowed the party's constantly changing agenda of specific policies and ideas. After each era, the principles each party relied upon changed. Gerring wasn't sure himself what accounted for the development of a party's ideology or what made ideologies suddenly change after long eras of stability, but he established the fact that American parties remain not just ideologically consistent but ideologically driven throughout each party system era.[51] The idea that American parties are nonideological coalitions bound by interest and not principles and ideas simply doesn't conform to either experience or evidence.[52]

That parties are inherently ideological and built out of powerful principles is obvious to most ordinary voters. Choosing a political party isn't a cold rational decision like choosing the right car insurance company. It's a powerful statement of personal identity and one of the most deeply emotional decisions people make. A party identity is a primal attachment that connects you to assumptions about the most fundamental aspects of your character. Your choice of party says more about you in the eyes of your neighbors than your profession, where you grew up, or the car you drive. It affects who you date, who you marry, what your employer thinks of you, and how family members treat you when you come home for Thanksgiving.[53] For many people it's an attachment that lasts for life.[54] People don't form lifetime attachments to something as deeply important as their party identity based on transient campaign issues that change radically from year to year—over recent decades, national campaigns have centered around everything from "Whipping Inflation Now," anti-missile treaties, a "nuclear freeze," crime control, tax reform packages, welfare reform, a "star wars" nuclear umbrella, term limits for members of Congress, a social security "lock box," adding a Medicare drug benefit, and eliminating corruption in Washington. People affiliate with a party not because of issue white papers or policy plans but because the principles in which the party believes resonate with their own. People attach themselves to a party because it confirms their identity and deepest values.

We all know this instinctively. Government policy touches on so many complicated topics—the energy industry, the history and policies of every foreign government, cutting-edge medicine, environmental science, the sociology of policing, the socioeconomic impact of immigration, the efficacy of various weapon systems for national defense, to name just a few—that it's unreasonable to expect ordinary voters who barely have time to keep their heads above water at work and at home to invest the time and attention necessary to understand it all. Ordinary voters have no way to judge whether the policy ideas political candidates propose are reasonable or likely to work, so most people have no choice but to use a proxy. The proxy is whether they think a candidate sees the world the same way they do. Does this candidate value the same things I care about? Is he or she someone I can trust to pursue the policies I would pursue if I understood the issues myself? Or is this someone who sees the world so differently they might seek to push America in a direction I won't like? Put simply, most people can only look at the principles a candidate and party represent through their ideology and compare them to their own principles. When we identify the factions of a party by issues or demographic groups—as pro-business voters, environmentalists, organized labor, working-class men, Catholics, women, African Americans, soccer moms, the South, rural voters, or suburban ones—we're talking about tips of icebergs poking out of the water, effects instead of causes. For most things, a party chooses to support an issue because it arises from one of the principles in which it believes, not the other way around. While parties tend to attract disproportionate support from certain demographic groups during an era, it's mainly because the life experiences of those groups at that moment in history disproportionately cause them to value similar things that align them with the party's ideology.

It could hardly work any other way. A party has to tell a story that taps into what people value, demonstrating they can trust the party to address problems as they might if they understood the details—a story that touches their values, their dreams, their nightmares, and their loves. The only way a party can conceivably do this, uniting half the voting population for decades at a time, is by identifying and answering a grand question that hovers over the age, a problem so large and meaningful that everyone in America frets about it for decades. Its answer to that question, which we usually call a party ideology, naturally combines several unrelated principles each appealing to different factions of people, to create a temporary political alliance. We all know this from experience because we all know that not everyone who identifies with a party and its ideology does so for the same reasons. We all know a professional business-minded "conservative" isn't coming from the same place as a rural religious "conservative," any more than a blue-collar labor union "liberal" is motivated by the same things as an urban progressive activist "liberal." What on the surface appears to be two great teams at war is in reality two big, messy coalitions binding millions of very different people around a collection of principles combined into two distinct party ideologies waging a national debate over the greatest issue of an age.

America's Founders during the early years of the republic unwittingly discovered this lesson about how and why their new government's design inevitably led to two broad and ideological parties. Then, upon Jefferson's retirement, James Madison assumed the presidency, and he and his party launched the disastrous War of 1812. America's Founders were about to learn a second lesson about American parties and party systems—one about how and why they also inevitably collapse.

THE COLLAPSE OF THE FIRST PARTY SYSTEM

Following the precedent George Washington set, Thomas Jefferson retired from the White House after two terms. He handed his office to his closest adviser and protégé, James Madison, who saw his duty as carrying forth Jefferson's Democratic-Republican vision. By now, the Federalist Party was floundering while Jefferson's Democratic-Republicans dominated politically.[55] What's more, after Madison allowed Hamilton's national bank to quietly expire, all that really remained to separate Federalists from Democratic-Republicans was lingering tribalism and a preference for Britain over France.[56] Then a war-hawk faction of the Democratic-Republicans under the leadership of House Speaker Henry Clay began agitating in Congress for what they believed would be a quick and easy war against Great Britain. America, they thought, could quickly seize British Canada, end British efforts to limit American expansion, aid France, and finally avenge America's honor in a second war for independence.[57] In 1812, these war hawks drove Congress to issue a declaration of war and Madison happily signed it. Their war was a disaster, one that brought the First Party System crashing down.

The War of 1812 was yet another outgrowth of the wars against Napoleon. Since the early days of the French Revolution, Great Britain and rev-olutionary France had been in a perpetual on-again, off-again state of war, leaving America—with its economy reliant on European trade—caught in the middle. France controlled the European continent by land with its powerful army, and Britain dominated the sea with the wooden wall of its grand navy, so for years these two powers—each unable to conquer the other—fought through the control of trade. The navies of both powers harassed American ships, although the British particularly seemed to relish humbling their former rebellious colony.[58] Britain even claimed the right to forcefully board American ships to impress into royal service sailors it suspected had been born subjects to its king. Off the coast of Vir-ginia in 1807, the British fired upon and boarded an American warship, the USS *Chesapeake*, killing several American sailors and hauling off four more into British service, leading the Jefferson administration to retal-iate with trade restrictions that mostly hurt America.[59] Britain had also embraced a policy of arming Native American tribes in the Midwest, in part to hinder American expansion toward what remained of its North American territory. With Britain distracted by Napoleon, the war hawks thought it was the perfect time to push back against British aggression with a quick American strike. A mixture of poor leadership, strategic mis-calculation, bad planning, and the unanticipated strength of the British response, turned Madison's triumph into an embarrassing quagmire.

The War of 1812 didn't go as the war hawks planned. The British repulsed an ill-advised American invasion of British Canada, landed troops in Washington, DC, chased the president out of town, burnt the White House, and blockaded American ports to shut down trade.[60] After the initial patriotic enthusiasm wore off, the war became unpopular everywhere, but Federalists especially loathed it.[61] Madison's government expected New England's militias to bear the brunt of the fighting on the Canadian front, while the powerful British Navy wrecked New England's trade-based economy, all while partisan Democratic-Republicans fiercely denounced as traitors everyone who questioned their ill-conceived war of choice. The Federalist-controlled states of New England naturally dragged their feet on providing resources and troops.[62] Before long, discontent

over the war was so strong Federalist newspapers began trumpeting that
the states of New England were considering outright secession from the
Union. In 1814, five Federalist-controlled New England states sent delegates to a convention in Hartford, Connecticut, to lodge demands. Madison's administration feared this challenge to national authority, even
making military preparations to quickly respond to a rebellion if the delegates dared to leave the Union.[63]

With the threat of secession lingering in the air, the Hartford delegates
drafted a strong report demanding policies and constitutional amendments to protect New England from further Democratic-Republican
folly. The delegates demanded fundamental constitutional changes such as
requiring a two-thirds congressional majority to declare war and changes
meant to weaken the lock the Democratic-Republican South seemed
to have on the presidency. Federalist delegates marched their petition
to Washington, expecting to make political hay of it in the middle of a
disaster of a war, but, unfortunately for them, their timing was horrible.[64]
The petition arrived just after General Andrew Jackson vanquished the
British at the Battle of New Orleans, a victory that took place just as a ship
with a signed peace treaty restoring the status quo was already on its way
from Europe. In the popular mind, Jackson's great victory transformed
the War of 1812 from a painful humiliation to a triumph—America had
once more stood up to a bullying superpower and held its own! Caught
in the unfortunate crosswinds of a sudden patriotic fervor, the Federalist
brand turned toxic and party support collapsed.[65] The Federalist Party
now looked like a party of traitors and secessionists. The label "Federalist"
would become the filthiest of political insults for decades to come.

Secretary of State James Monroe, Jefferson's other great protégé, swept
to an easy victory in 1816. Although the now nationally despised Federalist Party nominated a candidate, it hardly even contested the election.
The new president, who loathed the Federalist Party and genuinely held
the paranoid belief that it was intent on installing an American monarch,
saw an opportunity to stamp out partisanship and the Federalist Party for
good.[66] Monroe declared a policy of "de-Federalization" that welcomed
fleeing Federalists into his government but refused to recognize the Fed-

eralist Party or anyone still associated with it.[67] As Monroe explained in a letter to Andrew Jackson:

> My impressions is that the Administration should rest strongly on the republican party, indulging toward the other a spirit of moderation, and evincing a desire to discriminate between its members, and to bring the whole into the republican fold as quickly as possible. Many men very distinguished for their talents are of the opinion that the existence of the federal party is necessary to keep union and order in the republican ranks, that is that free government cannot exist without parties. This is not my opinion. That the ancient republics were always divided into parties; that the English government is maintained by an opposition, that is by the existence of a party in opposition to the Ministry, I well know. But I think that the cause of these divisions to be found in certain defects of those governments, rather than in human nature; and that we have happily avoided those defects in our system.[68]

Monroe even launched a good-will tour across America to rebuild the lost spirit of national unity, creating what one newspaper famously called an "Era of Good Feelings."[69] His policy was a smashing success. Eager to disassociate themselves from a now-fatal brand, most Federalists showily embraced the appeal to national unity. No real issues still remained to hold Federalists to their party outside old party loyalty and inertia, and with the party brand so damaged that was no longer enough. Although the Federalists formally lingered on in a few pockets for another decade, the Federalist Party was effectively dead within the year.[70] With no opponent left to fight, the Democratic-Republican Party lost purpose and soon withered away as well. America's First Party System effectively collapsed.

The next eight years of Monroe's Era of Good Feelings was perhaps the strangest period of American political history. Monroe hoped that America could once again function as the Founders intended, without parties or partisanship, and he modeled his presidency on Washington's. As long as Monroe remained in office, his plan even seemed to work. Under Monroe's leadership, the American government seemed to function as a rational republic with independent-minded leaders. In 1820, he even became the first president since Washington to run unopposed. Beneath this placid surface, however, the republic roiled with discontent. Without partisan pressure or common interest to bind them, Monroe's government was riven with factionalism, as ambitious rivals jockeyed for position.[71] Monroe's appointees and allies in Congress became more interested in petty wars against rivals over slights or personal interests. Without the tools to unite or motivate them, Monroe often even lacked the leverage to drive his agenda with his own subordinates, much less with Congress.[72] The Era of Good Feelings is rightly considered an era of national drift.[73] Without parties to unite and guide them, and without a common enemy to fight, ego and ambition ruled and the national government couldn't function. The failure of Monroe's Era of Good Feelings was a final coffin nail in the Founder's original vision of a nonpartisan republic. Without political parties to channel ambition and guide the government, the American republic simply didn't work.

When Monroe retired in 1824 after two terms, the illusion of national unity imploded. Four ambitious and powerful men wanted to replace Monroe in the White House—Secretary of State John Quincy Adams, House Speaker Henry Clay, Secretary of the Treasury William Crawford, and now senator Andrew Jackson. Since partisanship had been declared dead, the four candidates didn't compete over partisanship but through personality, regionalism, plus a little buried Federalist resentment against the son of John Adams. Splitting the votes four ways, no candidate won an outright majority. That meant the House of Representatives had to pick the president from among the top three vote-getters, making House Speaker Clay, who came in fourth, effectively kingmaker. Clay threw his support to Adams. Adams in return made Clay his secretary of state—an office people at the time saw as the presumptive president-in-waiting.[74] Jackson, who won the most electoral votes and thought that earned him the presidency, exploded in anger, claiming Clay and Adams had cheated him in a "corrupt bargain." America was once more dividing into two warring camps. Before long, America had two major parties fighting over government again. Jackson's supporters called themselves Democrats; the Adams-Clay faction, initially calling itself the National Republicans, took on the name Whigs. America hasn't looked away from party politics since.

WHY REALIGNMENTS?

The Founders' high-minded ideas about parties weren't wrong—party politics is often just as emotional, tribal, irrational, and corrupt as the Founders feared. The Era of Good Feelings, however, clarified their hidden but powerful virtues. Without parties to guide them, elected officials don't behave like beacons of Enlightenment reason. They squabble, indulge their ambition, elevate their own petty priorities, and fail to act. Parties serve as necessary vehicles to unite officials around common ideas and create the levers of reward and punishment leaders need to force self-interested associates to cooperate for the common good. Parties are distinctively worse than the ideal we imagined but far better than the reality of how real human beings behave without the direction they provide. Twice, America's Founding generation tried to fight against parties and partisanship. Twice, they failed. In a real world with real human flaws, the American republic would be a partisan republic.

America's Founding generation vigorously resisted the pull of political parties through Washington's final warnings, Adams's Alien and Sedition Acts, and Monroe's Era of Good Feelings, but nothing worked. Whether they wanted them or not, the natural influence of human nature and the structure of the American republic combined to create a system of two major parties fighting to control government. Although they didn't realize it—and would have hated it if they had—America's Founders designed a republic destined to create two national parties, each within striking distance of power. These two parties inevitably create rival ideologies built from a collection of principles that unite fractious coalitions, ones that disagree on many things but roughly agree on how to handle the great debate of their era. These parties conduct that grand national debate over decades until it's eventually either resolved or the world moves on and it becomes irrelevant. At which point, now lacking compelling ideologies capable of uniting their vast and querulous coalitions, those parties turn brittle. New issues about which their members disagree start to tear them apart. When a sufficient shock strikes, these decaying parties—no longer capable of holding their coalitions together—collapse. Upon their collapse, the factions and interests of the republic must once again find ways to unite half a nation into a coalition capable of winning a majority. Two new national coalitions emerge to debate the grand issue of the next age, and the process starts again.

Just like America's Founders, we might not always like the two-party system, but party systems and realignments are a natural cycle of rebirth and destruction built into the structure of the American republic. Party systems are how we channel our most important national debates, while the scary disruptions of realignments are how we clear away the cobwebs of the old and build something new. America is a two-party republic. America will always have two major parties that divide us for decades into two great coalitions engaged in a great national debate. America will always have realignments when the old coalitions falter and the time has come to build anew.

CHAPTER 3

AMERICA'S SECOND AND THIRD PARTY SYSTEMS: THE RISE OF JACKSON AND COLLAPSE OF THE WHIGS

When people warn of an epic political collapse, they often say a political party might "go the way of the Whigs." It's supposed to sound dramatic because the collapse of the Whig Party in 1852 was astonishing. Over a stunningly short period, one of America's two major parties just disintegrated. At the same time, it's also meant to sound a little overwrought because most people presume whatever blunders the ancient Whigs fell into must have nothing to do with modern politics. In fact, the Whigs—just like the Jacksonian Democrats they opposed—were just as stable and well-organized a party in their day as our modern Republicans and Democrats. That this political colossus collapsed suddenly into irrelevance, taking down the entire Jacksonian party system and plunging America into nearly a decade of national chaos, violence, and danger, is a chilling warning about how America's leaders can turn a realignment into a disaster.

America's First Party System was a debate about what sort of republic America was going to be. Its Second Party System was a debate over the future of that young America as it moved into the frontier. As a new generation of Americans, raised in a growing nation built around the American Revolution's ideals came of age, they had a different perspective about what America might become. Andrew Jackson and his Democrats offered an explosive vision of a popular democracy, demanding America directly empower ordinary people while sweeping away corrupt elites. Henry Clay and his Whigs proposed a counter-vision, one advancing a national vision of modernization, growth, and reform. Over the decades that these issues captured America's attention, these two parties built to debate them flourished. Then, as years passed, America slowly changed. Old issues faded. New issues rose. America's leaders failed to innovate or act. Eventually, America's parties decayed, the Whigs imploded, and the Second Party System came tumbling down, plunging America into years of chaotic turmoil before another stable party system rose to replace it. What happened to the Whigs will never repeat itself exactly—but if we're not careful, something very much like it could easily happen again. The story of the America's Second Party System is the story of how realignments can go wrong.

ANDREW JACKSON'S RISE

As it moved into the middle of the 1820s, America was no longer a scrappy patchwork of thirteen colonies at the far end of the world. It was a nation of twenty-four states spanning both banks of the Mississippi and claiming vast territories beyond. For decades, as the American government struggled to create the institutions of a new republic, hardy pioneers had packed their belongings into Conestoga wagons and set off into the wilderness to carve out new futures for themselves, their families, and their nation. Some were poor laborers with no prospects or property, some were immigrants looking for chances they could never have got at home, and some were young ambitious Americans looking for fresh starts in growing cities with seemingly unlimited opportunities to advance. As they settled in remote places like Kentucky, Tennessee, Ohio, Mississippi, Illinois, and Missouri, they built new homesteads, new towns, and then new cities. Those places boomed, eventually joining the Union as full states. Before long, a new generation of Americans had grown up, one whose worldview wasn't framed around colonies or Europe. They were the first generation of genuine Americans. Their nation was the America of the frontier.

American politics in 1824, however, was still stuck in the now-fading Founding era. President John Quincy Adams, the brilliant Harvard-educated son of President John Adams, was the last of the Founding generation's presidents. With a youth spent assisting his father on diplomatic missions in Europe, Adams had personally worked alongside the giants of the American Revolution. At only twenty-six, President Washington had appointed him an ambassador. Now president after a long career in the republic's service, Adams intended to extend Monroe's nonpartisan spirit of Good Feelings and usher in a good-government agenda of national improvement. Adams openly celebrated the end of partisan division in his inaugural address, and he appointed officials with varied ideologies and loyalties.[1] He proposed an agenda that would respect the interests of every American region—the commercial and industrializing East, the growing West, and the plantation South—through a united plan for national flourishing and growth.[2] To drive economic and intellectual progress, Adams proposed an ambitious and costly program of national improvement that included a national university, a naval academy, an astronomical observatory, and a new national road linking Washington with New Orleans.[3] He adopted Henry Clay's longstanding project, the American System, linking a high tariff to protect New England manufacturing to significant federal spending on public infrastructure and the credit of a national bank. Income from the protective tariffs would fund roads and bridges into the wilderness of new western states, while the bank regulated currency and provided the necessary credit to spur modernization and growth. Unfortunately for Adams, Andrew Jackson and his followers had little interest in allowing Adams to govern this way above the fray.

As soon as Adams settled into office, Jackson's supporters began marshalling forces to dislodge him.[4] Jackson and his partisans were still stewing over his loss in the four-way election of 1824. They insisted that Adams, Clay, and the establishment—by choosing Adams over Jackson, the top vote winner—hadn't merely cheated Jackson in what they denounced as a "corrupt bargain." They claimed this corrupt cabal had cheated the American people.[5] Jackson's partisans seethed that Adams's administration was corrupt and Federalist.[6] They accused Adams and his supporters of protecting unfair privilege and diverting national resources to enrich themselves and other elites. They denounced Adams's national improvement plans as waste and corruption. Resolved to disrupt what they believed to be an illegitimate Adams presidency, the Jacksonians labored diligently to attack, disrupt, and block anything Adams sought to achieve—hobbling his administration in what turned into a four-year-long election campaign.

Andrew Jackson was unlike the American aristocrats who mainly led America through its Founding era. Jackson's parents were poor Irish immigrants who settled in a remote part of the Carolinas. Although Jackson fought in the American Revolution, it wasn't as an officer. Only thirteen at the time, he served as a courier running messages for the militia. Jackson's father died before he was even born. His mother perished of an illness she caught nursing wounded soldiers during the revolution, making Jackson an orphan. With raw determination and ambition, the spottily educated Jackson managed to study law and then moved west to Tennessee, where he launched a successful career as a lawyer and politician. He became a wealthy planter and briefly served as a United States senator. At the outbreak of the War of 1812, Jackson was now the elected major general of the Tennessee militia, so he marched off to war. Jackson turned out to be a talented solider—his men called him Old Hickory due to his resolve—leading his men to the victory at New Orleans that made him a national hero. The tough, rowdy, commanding, uncontrollable, self-made Jackson was about as far from men like Jefferson, Madison, and Adams as you can imagine.[7]

What truly marked Jackson as different, however, wasn't his background—Hamilton after all was also a self-made orphan born in poverty. It was Jackson's perspective. The Founding generation never expected that ordinary people, without the public spiritedness and nobility they believed only an elite education and background afforded, would or should hold high public office.[8] Even Democratic-Republicans, who believed republican virtue rested with common farmers, saw themselves as a "natural aristocracy" forged by superior educations and merit and with a duty to represent the people.[9] As a self-made man from a frontier state with only a basic education, who rose by the force of his own will and ambition, Jackson believed everything that mattered could be handled with the common sense that common people possessed. He distrusted banks and commerce and people with fancy pedigrees. After years stewing at officials and elites milking the state in petty scandals during the corrupt Era of Good Feelings, Jackson had grown suspicious of complex plans for growth and reform and concluded the people needed protection from corrupt elites.[10] He suspected most great plans for national improvement were in reality convenient vehicles for self-dealing from the elites he despised. Jackson didn't believe in natural aristocracies. A product of the rough-and-tumble American frontier, Jackson was the people and the people loved him for it.[11]

When 1828 arrived, Jackson got his rematch against Adams, and it was beyond ugly. The public enthusiastically took part in an election that became a national spectacle. Each side reveled in untruths and personal attacks meant to portray their rival as morally corrupt and a threat to republican government. Jackson's supporters, taking the name Democrats, claimed Adams was squandering national treasure on gambling—he had installed a billiards table at the White House.[12] Adams's supporters, taking the name National Republicans, accused Jackson and his wife, Rachel, of engaging in adultery because she had divorced before marrying Jackson.[13] When Jackson won, and handily, thousands of ordinary working people crowded into Washington to celebrate. They paraded through town for his inauguration and then crushed into the White House, where they stomped with muddy boots across the grand floors, broke fancy china, and stood on the expensive furniture. The staff supplied pails of liquor on the lawn to draw them out, where the people drank and made merry.[14] The establishment was horrified.

As Jackson entered the presidency, he brought a new vision for America—a "Jacksonian Democracy" meant to take common people into the center of politics. Rejecting Founding-era notions of a natural elite governing for the people, Jackson wanted to overthrow corrupting elites so the people could rule themselves with himself as their sword. Jackson supported extending voting rights to all non-enslaved men, completing the elimination under way of property requirements that elites believed necessary to ensure voters were invested in the nation's success.[15] He opposed as wasteful corruption the national infrastructure spending Adams and Clay championed. He disliked and distrusted credit, banking, and banks. Believing there was nothing in any government job so difficult any ordinary person couldn't do it, Jackson made appointments not by qualification or merit but loyalty.[16] He developed a vast patronage network called the "spoils system" in which plum federal jobs went not to the pedigreed or connected, but as rewards to the common people who supported him. Jackson and his partisans considered this rotation in office not a corruption but a reform, breaking the elite hold on power, bringing the people into government, and stopping officials from becoming entrenched in office.[17] Jackson also supported aggressively expanding the nation west to provide cheap land for working people willing to build a fresh start in the wilderness—including "de-indianification" to clear more land for settlers. Jackson championed an Indian Removal Act to force Native Americans off their lands, which led to the infamous "Trail of Tears," to provide opportunity and social mobility to his supporters, but at the expense of the Native American pushed off ancestral lands.

Andrew Jackson's presidency alarmed a lot people. Jackson's headstrong temperament and quick anger struck the establishment as unpresidential and dangerous.[18] To them, Jackson's assaults on national elites sounded like ignorance that would sabotage their efforts to drive modernization and growth. Many feared Jackson was a demagogue or maybe even a would-be tyrant. With the now-unpopular Adams clearly outmatched, the anti-Jackson coalition turned to a new leader not so unlike Jackson himself—Adams's secretary of state, Henry Clay. On one hand, as a brilliant orator and strategist, Clay was long considered one of the greatest talents of American politics. First elected to the Senate before he turned thirty, Clay's colleagues, recognizing his ability, didn't even object he was too young to constitutionally serve. After two short Senate terms, Clay ran for the House of Representatives and his colleagues elected him Speaker as a freshman. Clay was a driving force in launching Madison's War of 1812 and was a powerful figure under Monroe. Clay was also, however, just like Jackson, a new American raised from the frontier. He too was self-made, growing up modestly in Virginia and then moving west to Kentucky to make his fortune. He was gregarious, a storyteller, a hard drinker, and a famous gambler.[19] Just like Jackson, he was a dueler (although unlike Jackson he hadn't actually killed anyone in a duel).[20] Clay was also a well-known charmer—when he spoke in Congress, Washington's women reportedly crowded into the gallery just to hear him.[21] Clay and Jackson were each frontier types, Jackson the bombastic brawler and Clay the silver-tongued rake.

As Clay organized opposition to Jackson, Jackson made two important decisions that would come to establish the Second Party System's battle lines. First, he launched a personal crusade to abolish the Second Bank of the United States. National banking was no longer a major political issue when Jackson's presidency began. After allowing the First Bank of the United States to expire, Madison created a Second Bank of the United States to stabilize the currency and economy after the War of 1812 and, since it proved useful, it had grown generally accepted. However, this Second Bank of the United States had grown wealthy and powerful, standing mostly outside government yet essentially regulating the entire American financial system because of its power over state banks.[22] Its leadership, moreover, had grown arrogant in the belief that, despite its incredible power as a national institution, the Bank, as an independent corporation, wasn't accountable in any way to the American people or the government beyond the narrowest limits of its charter.[23] The Bank was also becoming less popular as many Americans—not irrationally—blamed its inept handling of the Panic of 1819 for driving the country into a severe economic recession. Jackson, who thought banks and credit were inherently corrupt tools through which elites stole power and wealth from ordinary people, was determined to both wipe out the national debt and crack the power of banking.[24] He decided the Bank was his political enemy and he resolved to do everything in his considerable power to destroy what he viewed as an unaccountable bastion of inequality and privilege.

The Bank's charter was set to expire in 1836, during what would potentially be Jackson's second term. Seeing the political risk in Jackson's hostility, and taking the advice of Clay, who was looking for an election issue, the Bank asked Congress to reauthorize it early, sure Jackson wouldn't dare risk a veto before his 1932 reelection.[25] The Bank was wrong. Jackson issued a blistering veto message framing the issue as a great battle between plainspoken republican government and corrupt elites, stating, "Many of our rich men have not been content with equal protection and equal benefits, but have besought us to make them richer by act of Congress."[26]

> It is to be regretted that the rich and powerful too often bend the acts of government to their selfish purposes. Distinctions in society will always exist under every just government. Equality of talents, of education, or of wealth can not be produced by human institutions. In the full enjoyment of the gifts of Heaven and the fruits of superior industry, economy, and virtue, every man is equally entitled to protection by law; but when the laws undertake to add to these natural and just advantages artificial distinctions, to grant titles, gratuities, and exclusive privileges, to make the rich richer and the potent more powerful, the humble members of society—the farmers, mechanics, and laborers—who have neither the time nor the means of securing like favors to themselves, have a right to complain of the injustice of their Government. There are no necessary evils in government. Its evils exist only in its abuses. If it would confine itself to equal protection, and, as Heaven does its rains, shower its favors alike on the high and the low, the rich and the poor, it would be an unqualified blessing. In the act before me there seems to be a wide and unnecessary departure from these just principles.[27]

More alarming, Jackson explicitly rejected the right of Congress or the judiciary to control the president's power at all. According to Jackson:

> The opinion of the judges has no more authority over Congress than the opinion of Congress has over the judges, and on that point the President is independent of both. The authority of the Supreme Court must not, therefore, be permitted to control the Congress or the Executive when acting in their legislative capacities, but to have only such influence as the force of their reasoning may deserve.[28]

Jackson's attack on the Bank was completely different from the old Democratic-Republican opposition to the First Bank of the United States, which turned on the role of federal versus state power. The Jacksonians weren't enraged over abstract issues like the balance of constitutional power but over perceived slights by national elites against ordinary Americans.

Many across the American establishment naturally found Jackson's bank crusade worrying. Speaking as the voice of an angry common people, Jackson had launched what many saw as a bizarre and personal vendetta against a seemingly necessary national institution, simply because it was valuable to the elites he loathed. He further claimed no other institution or constitutional branch had any right to challenge anything he did. To many, Jackson sounded dangerously close to a would-be-dictator or populist demagogue. He would continue to carry this "Bank War" into his second term, eventually choking the institution off to its total annihilation.

In a second controversial decision, Jackson supported the "Tariff of Abominations," a high tax on imported foreign goods that alienated the South. Northern states in the nineteenth century pushed for high tariffs to protect their infant manufacturing economy from cheaper and superior European goods, causing higher prices across the agricultural South with no corresponding local benefit. Leading up to the 1828 election, Southern states in a high-stakes political move proposed a painfully high tariff rate that would also greatly raise the cost of industrial raw materials, believing the Adams faction would have no choice but to vote against it to protect New England manufacturing. They hoped to thereby avoid a higher tariff while pinning its failure on Adams, shielding Jackson from backlash in the North. To the South's horror, this "Tariff of Abominations" passed and President Adams signed it. After the election, most people naturally expected Jackson to support the tariff's repeal. He decided instead to keep it to help pay off his hated national debt. The tariff fight boiled throughout Jackson's presidency. Eventually, after Jackson's reelection in 1832, anti-tariff forces in South Carolina even managed to declare the federal tariff unconstitutional, null, and void in South Carolina. Jackson, hostile to the challenge to his authority, had Congress pass a Force Bill giving him the power to enforce the tariff by military force if necessary.[29] With the nation on the brink of war, cooler heads ultimately devised a compromise tariff at the last minute, defusing the crisis, but the controversy made Jackson powerful enemies among the plantation barons of the South.

As leader of the anti-Jackson National Republicans, Henry Clay worked to unite all these factions who feared or hated Jackson. His chief issue would be Jackson's crusade against the Bank, an institution Clay argued was not just economically necessary to drive economic growth and modernization. He denounced "King Andrew's"[30] war against the Bank as the act of a tyrant usurping the power of America's truly democratic branch, Congress. The issue would thereby unite business and political elites, who hated Jackson for his war on the Bank, and professionals and the middle classes, who feared his populist insurgency was dangerous demagoguery from an ignorant and violent rube. To this, Clay added Southern planters who believed in state's rights and chafed at Jackson's militant resistance to their idea of nullification in the tariff fight. Clay thus united a seemingly impossible alliance of merchants, professionals, old elites, and Southern plantation barons around the unlikely agenda of protecting a bank, a wonky economic program of tariffs and infrastructure, and the ideological principle of congressional supremacy.[31] Clay's new opposition party, which solidified after the Nullification Crisis during Jackson's second term, hardly even made sense except as an anti-Jackson party.

Clay ran against Jackson in 1832, but Jackson won reelection—it helped that a short-lived Anti-Masonic Party, organized around opposing Freemasons in government (Jackson and Clay were both Freemasons), siphoned off a fair share of the anti-Jackson vote.[32] Yet the arguments and alliances Clay assembled against Jackson would endure for decades. Unlike the Founding generation that hated political parties, this new generation of political leaders eagerly adopted them as useful and necessary means to protect liberty, organize people, and drive beneficial change.[33] Through the strategy of Jackson's close adviser Martin Van Buren, Jackson's Democrats built a ruthlessly effective party united around his rowdy populist Jacksonian Democracy that could organize, energize voters, and win. Clay's supporters, united around stopping Jackson in the name of modernization, growth, and opposition to a strong executive, soon embraced similar methods. Echoing the theme of fighting against a tyrannous King Andrew, Clay's opposition soon adopted a new name, one colonial-era patriots once used when fighting against the tyranny of King George—the Whigs.[34]

THE DEMOCRATS AND THE WHIGS

For decades, the Second Party System thrived. Politics during the early republic had been mainly an elite affair of dueling pamphlets. In the Second Party System, the American people threw themselves into democracy with enthusiasm.[35] The end of property requirements to vote, the Jacksonian celebration of popular democracy, and the promise of spoils, all combined to bring ordinary Americans directly into politics. Voting skyrocketed. Campaigns embraced the banners, rallies, parades, red-white-and-blue streamers, and brass bands we now associate with popular politics. Both parties eventually embraced Jackson's idea of the spoils systems, so ordinary citizens gleefully volunteered to campaign and argue for their party in hope of winning a plum patronage job in government.[36] Elections turned into a rowdy form of popular entertainment or sport.[37] Both parties were well-supported and well-organized, building local organizations, rallying their respective bases for elections, and employing partisan newspapers that wrote hyperbolic articles about how the other party threated the republic.[38] They were also pretty evenly balanced, essentially trading the White House back and forth every four years, although the Democrats usually controlled Congress. This great debate between the Whigs and Democrats over the future of young vibrant America turned the republic into more of a democracy.

Unlike the First Party System debate over national greatness and simple Republican yeoman farmers, the Whigs and the Democrats were parties clashing over this new America of covered wagons, homesteading settlers, and pioneers. As America pushed steadily west, Democrats saw a nation of unrivaled opportunity in which anyone from any background could remake themselves and rise. A rough laborer or immigrant with little education and no connections could pack up and move west, build a farm up from nothing, and become a landowner and businessperson. Democrats feared cities and banks and modernizing plans, which they believed had already choked off opportunity in the East. Whigs, on the other hand, saw a nation with unrivaled potential. They wanted civilization to spread across the wilderness, bringing education, growth, prosperity, and modernity.[39] Whigs feared Jackson's populism was in fact ignorance that would hold back economic and moral progress.[40] Democrats thought in terms of personal liberty and wanted a popular republic in which ordinary people could grow and thrive. Whigs thought more in terms of moral duty and believed in an active and meritocratic state that promoted the general welfare so the nation could grow and thrive.[41]

The policy fights between Whigs and Democrats reflected these clashing ideals. Both the Democrats and the Whigs commanded immense popular support nationally, both in the North and the South. The Democrats, celebrating the common man standing against the corrupt influence of the wealthy and the elite, championed a federal government with limited power but a stronger presidency. Whigs, promoting modernization, national progress, and American strength as "the champion of liberty, morals, and prosperity," believed in a strong federal government driving progress and growth, but a weak executive.[42] Democrats tended to do best with working people, farmers, and Catholic immigrants.[43] The more moralistic and modernizing Whigs tended to do best with professionals, the middle class, commercial elites, and Protestant reformers.[44] Democrats argued the nation needed to grow out into the West, where every man could, through his own hard work, make a fresh start on his own plot of land—despite the Native Americans who were pushed off their lands by that policy. Whigs were less enthusiastic about aggressively pushing west, fearing it would slow the nation's progress. Whigs preferred the nation to grow up rather than out, with denser cities, manufacturing, commerce, and citizens who developed skills rather than the manual labor of agriculture. Democrats supported a laissez-faire economy without the tariffs, banks, and what they considered wasted money going to the infrastructure boondoggles of Clay's American System.[45] Whigs supported high tariffs, investment in "internal improvements" like roads and canals, and more schools, education, and cultural institutions in order to build a wiser and more skilled citizenry. The Democrats boasted figures like Jackson, John Calhoun, Martin Van Buren, and Stephen Douglas. The Whigs had Clay, Daniel Webster, and a young Abraham Lincoln. Where free African Americans could participate in politics, they tended to be Whigs.[46]

This debate between Democrats and Whigs played out over decades. Jackson had two terms, followed by the administration of his protégé, Martin Van Buren. In 1840, the Whigs presented the wealthy Virginia-born former Ohio senator and popular general William Henry Harrison in the model of Jackson, a hard-cider-drinking general from a log cabin in the frontier.[47] Harrison, the hero of the battle of Tippecanoe, won the election but, in a bizarre turn of fortune, caught an illness after delivering a long inauguration address in the rain and died barely a month into his term. Harrison's vice president, the party-switching former Democrat John Tyler, assumed the presidency and then spent his term feuding with the Whig leadership and vetoing important parts of his new party's agenda.[48] Tyler became a man without a party, despised by both the Democrats he abandoned and the Whigs he betrayed.

As these parties fought, America slowly changed. A religious revival broke out and roared through the little homesteads and small towns dotting the American wilderness. As Americans came back into the church, the mostly practical nation of the early nineteenth century began thinking a lot more about morality and reform.[49] Itinerant preachers traveled from community to community, holding lively multiday tent revivals and spreading the idea that Americans could bring about Christ's return if they reformed America into God's Kingdom on Earth.[50] This revival flooded across America, bringing a nation that had lost interest in religion after the American Revolution into the grips of a religious enthusiasm that converted about 90 percent of American Protestants into evangelicals.[51] The preachers of this revival taught that the American republic had a holy mission to morally redeem the earth, but that it would suffer wrath if it failed in its special vocation.[52] Newly committed Christians threw themselves into charity and new crusades for reform, such as temperance from alcohol—a movement driven by a desire to morally reform working class men, particularly Catholic immigrants, while incidentally breaking up their political organizing in saloons.[53]

The greatest cause of these moral reformers and revivalists, however, was abolishing slavery. Powerful preachers like Charles Finney and Lyman Beecher built a passionate movement around the cause of abolition, while activists like William Lloyd Garrison, Susan B. Anthony, Frederick Douglas, and many more, energized followers through writings and abolition societies. For most of America's young life, the country sought to avoid the issue of slavery for fear it might tear the republic apart. Seeing no obvious way to politically resolve the matter, many hoped the wicked institution would gradually die out on its own. This new generation of passionate believers—many religious, others mainly secular but devoted to abolition—believed the destruction of slavery was an urgent necessity.[54] The abolition movement flourished everywhere, but it particularly bloomed within a Whig Party already more Protestant and moralistic than the Democrats.[55]

The issues that defined the Second Party System also gradually melted away. The polarizing Andrew Jackson retired, and then died in 1845. The Bank issue was settled and then disappeared from the national spotlight. As private enterprises began to build necessary internal improvements like canals and railroads, and state governments came to support such projects on a bipartisan basis, the American System economic platform was increasingly obsolete.[56] As American manufacturing grew, the need for tariffs faded. As the British started to invest heavily in America, high tariffs were also less necessary to stop American gold and silver flowing to Europe in an era of hard money—a trend that intensified near the decade's end when the California gold rush made gold more plentiful.[57] Most important, the old frontier was now blooming with cities like Cincinnati, Saint Louis, and New Orleans, and America was soon to reach the Pacific.

As the country moved into the middle of the 1840s, the Second Party System appeared, on the surface, as solid and stable as it ever had. Underneath that surface, change was undercutting its foundation. Then in 1844, America elected President James Polk, who promised to expand America to the Pacific and then conquered vast new territories from Mexico—setting into motion forces that made the Second Party System's disintegration inevitable.

THE COLLAPSE OF THE WHIGS

There was nothing in the election of 1844 that indicated the Second Party System was about to unravel. Heading into 1844, the Democrats and Whigs both looked like perfectly solid parties engaged in the same enduring debates over the issues of Jacksonian Democracy that they had fought for years. The Whigs were in particularly high spirits, since they expected Henry Clay, the Whig Party leader who had lusted after the presidency for decades, to face and defeat former president Martin Van Buren, the chief architect of Jackson's Democratic Party agenda—thereby vindicating the Whig agenda after the fiasco of Tyler's presidency.[58] In the run up to the election, however, Tyler topped his partisan treachery with a final parting gift. To secure an achievement as president and perhaps win favor from Democrats in a hopeless effort to win reelection, President Tyler agreed to annex the Republic of Texas.[59]

Texas had won its independence from Mexico in 1836 after a flood of American settlers changed the composition of its population, and it had sought to join the United States ever since. The American government, however, was wary of admitting Texas to the Union because adding what everyone presumed would be several new slave states would unbalance the issue in the Senate, not to mention potentially start a war with Mexico over the location of the new border. Tyler's unexpected political bomb disrupted the race. Van Buren, fearing splitting his party over slavery, opposed the annexation—committing political suicide and leading even his mentor Jackson to break with him.[60] The Democrats nominated instead former House Speaker James K. Polk, a man few people in America knew. At first, Whigs taunted the Democrats with the mocking battle cry "Who is James K. Polk?"[61] Polk, however, upset the race by aggressively campaigning on annexing Texas. In fact, he suggested it was America's destiny to occupy the continent all the way to the Pacific—what later became known as Manifest Destiny—proposing to secure a favorable border in the Pacific Northwest from Great Britain as well. Voters liked Polk's proposal so, when Clay couldn't walk back his now unpopular opposition to the Texas annexation, it turned out the answer to the Whigs' taunt was that James K. Polk was the next president of the United States.[62]

President Polk was good to his word, negotiating a treaty with Great Britain for what would become the states of Washington and Oregon, annexing Texas, and then asserting the Texas border extended into territory Mexico continued to claim. When Polk moved troops into the disputed territory under General Zachary Taylor, it meant war—exactly what Polk and the Democrats wanted. Outraged Whigs accused the Democrats of instigating a bloody war based on lies to make an immoral land grab against a weaker nation.[63] Although they took pains to express their support for soldiers in the field, and sometimes attempted to claim credit for military victories, the Whigs devoted Polk's presidency to opposing an unethical war.[64] Whig congressman Abraham Lincoln in fact made his name denouncing Polk's immoral warmongering from the House floor.[65] When America won a crushing victory against Mexico, Polk's administration negotiated a treaty annexing all the land between Texas and the Pacific Ocean: what is now Arizona, New Mexico, Oklahoma, Colorado, Utah, Nevada, and California, along with parts of Wyoming. Having achieved everything he sought to do in one presidential term, President Polk retired. With another election now looming, the Whigs decided, despite their previous opposition to the war, to support the popular peace deal in Congress. Over the next four years, the aftermath ripped America apart.

Adding so much new territory to the Union at once opened Pandora's Box. All the vast new territories Polk seized from Mexico would someday join the Union as new states. Southern slave states were obsessed with maintaining an equal balance of slave and free states in order to keep the issue deadlocked in the Senate. Newly energized abolitionists were unwilling to allow a moral evil to spread any farther than it already had. Each time a new state carved out of the new territory joined the Union, Congress would now have to decide whether to admit it as slave or free. Already during the war with Mexico, Democratic congressman David Wilmot had offered a rider to the war-funding bill to ban slavery in any territory America won in the peace. Wilmot's proviso failed, but antislavery politicians in the years that followed continued attempting to slip it into other bills again and again—it actually twice passed the House but was blocked both times in the Senate.[66] For antislavery forces, this "Wilmot Proviso" became a symbol representing not just whether the country ought to permit slavery, but of America's moral virtue. For slave states, it represented an existential threat. America would have to repeat this debate again and again every time a new state created from former-Mexican territory sought admission. Polk's war placed the spread of slavery at the very top of America's political agenda for years to come.

The Whigs in 1848, desperate for a win, nominated the hero of the war they just opposed, General Taylor. Taylor, a Louisiana slave owner, had no prior political experience or record as a Whig, and in fact both parties had courted him as a candidate.[67] As the Whig nominee, Taylor hedged on the slavery question, distanced himself from regular Whig politics, and promised to govern just as he had in the military—an independent man guided by pragmatism and his own judgment above any party.[68] The Democratic Party candidate, Michigan's Lewis Cass, who was friendly toward slavery, promoted the idea of allowing the people who settled in the new territories to decide slavery's status for themselves, named "popular sovereignty."[69] A group of antislavery Democrats led by former president Van Buren, upset at their party's refusal to oppose slavery's spread, walked out of the Democratic National Convention and joined with a group of antislavery Whigs to form a new antislavery party calling itself the Free Soil Party. Taylor won, although with less than fifty percent of the popular vote—the Free Soilers did surprisingly well.[70] American politics had begun tearing apart.

Spooked by the sudden divisiveness of the slavery question, old hands from both parties dedicated the next Congress to working out a great compromise to settle the issue. Whig titans Henry Clay and Daniel Webster, along with prominent Democrats like Stephen Douglas, brokered a package of related deals called the "Compromise of 1850" hoping to stuff the troublesome slavery issue back into Pandora's Box. America would admit all of California as one large free state, denying the spread of slavery to the Pacific, while also admitting Texas as one large slave state to balance it in the Senate. The southwestern territory, which would later become New Mexico and Arizona, would determine its position on slavery upon statehood through local popular vote. Perhaps most important to what was to follow, slave-state politicians—frustrated that Northern states had rendered the existing fugitive slave laws practically unenforceable—insisted on tougher laws to force Northern cooperation in recapturing the flood of slaves now reaching the North through networks like the Underground Railroad. A new Fugitive Slave Act obligated Northern law enforcement to help capture and return any accused slave upon nothing more than an affidavit from a slave owner. The accused couldn't obtain a jury trial, which many Northern states previously required, nor offer evidence that he or she wasn't property. Any Northerner sheltering or helping the accused slave faced punishment. President Taylor, who opposed the compromise, died while it was under negotiation.[71] The new president, Taylor's vice president Millard Fillmore, a doctrinaire Whig, was happy to sign it.

Upon passage of the Compromise of 1850, America let out a great sigh of relief at having skillfully avoided a terrible crisis. America's political establishment congratulated itself on putting the slavery controversy to bed so America could go back to arguing over the normal issues dividing Whigs and Democrats. It was soon apparent, however, that far from a final settlement, the Compromise was a disaster. Debate over the Compromise had bitterly divided the nation across sectional lines North and South, with each side believing parts of the settlement had either been too favorable to slavery or too conciliatory to abolition. The Fugitive Slave Act particularly outraged the North, which considered it an insulting and unjust concession to the Slave Power.[72] As America headed into the 1852 election, anger over the Compromise—particularly from Northerners deeply uncomfortable with slavery's spread—was now tearing politics apart. Major political figures even explored whether they needed to form a new Union Party centered around backing the Compromise to head off the growth of an antislavery party that might rip the nation in half.[73]

Since Fillmore was now toxic among Northern Whigs for his role in the Compromise, the Whigs in 1852 nominated General Winfield Scott, one of the most celebrated military officers in American history, a known opponent of slavery, and a terrible politician.[74] The Democrats backed Franklin Pierce, a proslavery Northerner with his own pedigree of military service in the Mexican-American War, nullifying Scott's military credentials. With no real policy disputes left between the parties, the campaign was mostly without substance, while the real issues—slavery and the Compromise—rumbled in the background.[75] Instead of Scott's distinguished military record gaining him support in the South as the Whigs had hoped, proslavery Whigs were now furious their party nominated such an outspokenly antislavery candidate. Northern Whigs, on the other hand, were still furious at their party for the Fugitive Slave Act. Abandoned by both groups, Scott won only four states. The Whig Party was reduced to only about one-third of the House and remained a weak minority in the Senate. It was an electoral disaster, one far worse than anyone anticipated.[76] Some feared the Whig Party might not even survive it.[77] As Whig congressman Lewis Campbell famously declared in the election's aftermath, "The party is dead—dead—dead!"[78]

At first, however, most Americans didn't fully appreciate what had just happened. Most Whig leaders believed the Democrats would eventually blunder, and when they did voters would have no choice but to go back to the Whigs.[79] The Democrats, on the other hand, believed the victory meant their party was now set to flourish.[80] Both Whigs and Democrats therefore continued to fumble forward as if nothing important had changed. In the next Congress, Illinois senator Stephen Douglas—wanting to make way for railroads connecting the rail hub of Chicago with the Pacific while also strengthening the Western bloc in Congress—carelessly pushed forward a bill to open Kansas and Nebraska for settlement and statehood.[81] His problem was the 1820 Missouri Compromise had already promised that territory would join the Union as free states, but Southern legislators weren't willing to vote for four more senators opposed to slavery. To pass his bill, Douglas and the Democrats therefore decided the citizens of these territories would choose for themselves whether to allow slavery in their new states under popular sovereignty.[82] Americans were outraged, particularly Northerners who saw the proposal as an aggressive attack perpetrated by the South. In passing this Kansas-Nebraska Act, the Democrats had just torn back open the very mess the Compromise was supposed to have closed. Worse, they had violated the trust upon which every compromise between free states and slave states relied. The national backlash against the Democrats was intense as an outraged North rallied against any further compromise with a ruthless Slave Power they felt they could no longer trust.[83]

In the midterm elections of 1854, disgusted voters reduced the Democrats to about a third of the seats in the House and imposed substantial losses in the Senate.[84] Yet voters didn't turn back to the Whigs. A shocking number of voters, now fed up with both the Democrats and the Whigs, looked for an alternative party to support, and many chose the political vehicle of an angry movement dedicated to fighting the mass immigration of German and Irish Catholics, the Know-Nothings.[85] The Know-Nothing movement began in the 1840s as a loose collection of conspiratorial secret societies, such as the Supreme Order of the Star Spangled Banner, that concocted complicated rituals and codes requiring members when questioned by outsiders to claim they "knew nothing."[86] Know-Nothings believed a great Catholic conspiracy or papal plot was afoot to use mass immigration of Catholics to steal control of America from its "native" Protestants, and that the existing major parties were complicit in their thirst to capture Catholic voters.[87] The movement saw itself as the defender of American liberty against national elites all too happy to sell out the republic, and it promoted a platform that was openly patriotic, stridently nationalistic, celebratory toward the Constitution, and hostile to immigrants and Catholicism.[88] It capitalized on a growing and rampant national hostility toward Catholic immigrants, particularly the Irish, based in religious bigotry and cultural complaints about their supposed abuse of alcohol, rowdyism, lack of social decorum, and proclivity toward crime.[89] The Know-Nothings had long dabbled in politics, but they were never major players before 1854. Now, frustrated voters flooded into their ranks under the banner of a "Native American Party" (meaning Anglo-Saxon and Protestant Americans), later shortened to just the American Party.[90]

The Congress elected in 1854 thus became perhaps the oddest in American history. The decimated Democrats were now in the minority, while the House fell into the control of a loose coalition of Know-Nothings, smaller parties, independents, and what remained of the Whigs. Many of these political newcomers, members of small antislavery parties formed in response to the Kansas-Nebraska outrage, quickly formed a second bloc. The most important of these Kansas-Nebraska parties proved to be one formed around Kansas-Nebraska activism in Wisconsin with only thirteen seats, calling itself the Republican Party. This strange alliance now controlling the House called itself the "Opposition," and it elected as speaker a Know-Nothing with Kansas-Nebraska loyalties.[91] Classifying the various cooperating blocs in this congressional alliance was messy, with members elected as Whigs or Know-Nothings or something else, often changing factions or even holding multiple affiliations at once.[92] Over time, the members of the Kansas-Nebraska bloc, including members from the more established Free Soil Party, gradually coalesced into one national movement using one convenient party banner—the Republican Party.[93]

American politics was now in chaos. With the old party coalitions broken, a vacuum had opened at the center of American political life— one that every faction, interest, and ambitious personality hoped to fill. Politicians and political activists, identifying as Democrats, Whigs, Know-Nothings, or Republicans, struggled to redefine America's agenda around their conflicting priorities and beliefs. At the same time, America's political situation just got worse. With the introduction of popular sovereignty in Kansas, passionate activists naturally flooded into the territory to influence the impending statehood vote. Freedom activists, many organized by abolitionist preachers in New England, poured in to ensure Kansas remained free. Militarized "Border Ruffians" crossed over from Missouri to defend the vote for the slavery side.[94] Each settled into fortified camps. Activists fought dirty to stack the new legislature, while President Pierce used his authority to put a thumb on the scale for slavery.[95] Open violence erupted. Rifles funded by abolitionists arrived, named "Beecher's Bibles" after abolitionist Preacher Henry Ward Beecher, who took up a collection in his New York church for two dozen rifles he sent to Kansas in boxes marked "Bibles."[96] Border Ruffians from Missouri attacked free state advocates in Lawrence, Kansas, setting fire to newspapers and a hotel.[97] Abolitionist John Brown and his followers retaliated, hunting down proslavery activists at home to hack them to death with broadswords.[98] After several antislavery attacks on proslavery settlements, a pitched battle was fought in Osawatomie in which proslavery forces employed a cannon.[99] The nation was horrified. This "Bleeding Kansas" tragedy dragged on for years as proslavery and antislavery activists attacked and murdered each other in an undeclared civil war.

Nor did the violence stay in Kansas. In 1856, a day after the Sack of Lawrence, Senator Charles Sumner gave an inflammatory speech denouncing the "Crime against Kansas." Sumner attacked the slavestate position using the sexual imagery of the rape of a slave girl, specifically calling out elderly South Carolina senator Andrew Butler as such a rapist of the "harlot, slavery." To avenge this insult, Butler's distant relative, South Carolina congressman and Democrat Preston Brooks, entered the Senate and beat Sumner just short of death with a heavy wooden cane, while a friend, Congressman Laurence Keitt, brandished a pistol to ensure no one intervened. Brooks struck Sumner on the head with a flurry of blows until the bloody senator fell into unconsciousness.[100] It was several years before Sumner recovered sufficiently to resume his Senate duties. Activists and editorialists in the North celebrated Sumner and attacked the proslavery forces as violent and intolerant of even basic freedom of speech. In the South, they celebrated Brooks as a chivalrous knight defending his honor against a scoundrel.[101] A few years later, abolitionist John Brown led a well-organized raid on a federal armory in Harpers Ferry, Virginia, to steal weapons with which he hoped to arm a slave revolt. Brown's capture and hanging seized the attention of the nation, with many in the North celebrating him as a martyr while the South responded in fury at Northern violence.[102]

In 1856, it was the American Party's turn to implode. The Democrats in 1856 abandoned Pierce, now tainted by the disaster of Bleeding Kansas. They nominated instead James Buchanan, a man whose chief appeal was that he was abroad as ambassador to Great Britain during the Kansas mess.[103] Given the solid support Democratic leaders had consistently offered slavery, the party now had a lock on the South. The important battle in 1856 would therefore be about which new party won over the North, emerging as America's other major party. The Know-Nothings nominated former Whig president Milliard Fillmore, hoping to win over former Whigs. The remains of the shattered Whig Party, seeing no better choice, endorsed him, finally extinguishing it as a political force. The Republicans nominated famed explorer and general John Fremont on a platform opposing the Kansas-Nebraska Act and the expansion of slavery into the territories—"Free Soil, Free Speech, Free Men, Fremont!"[104] Freemont came in a strong second and his Republicans became the second-strongest party in Congress. The humbled American Party, humiliated by the loss, quickly collapsed into irrelevance.[105] American politics was once again coalescing into two major parties, the Democrats and Republicans.

Over the next four years, the Republicans and Democrats clashed over slavery's expansion, particularly over which of two proposed constitutions for the new state of Kansas was legitimate, the one permitting slavery and the other free.[106] In 1858, the Republicans seized control of the House. In 1860, after a messy race in which the Democratic Party split in two and a new Constitutional Union party emerged on the platform of simply keeping the nation together, Abraham Lincoln won the White House.[107] South Carolina, horrified by the implication—an openly antislavery party captured the White House with almost exclusively Northern votes—seceded from the Union before Lincoln was even sworn into office. The Civil War began. In the North, pro-war Democrats joined the Republicans in a "Union Party," which became the postwar Republican Party. In the Confederacy, the Democrats ruled an effectively one-party state.

When the blood and smoke of the Civil War cleared, the Republicans had become the party of the North, professionals, and business, representing an ideology linking social and economic progress, the Yankee work ethic, and the old Whig vision of economic improvement and moral progress. The Democrats had become the party of the South and urban immigrants united around fighting the Republicans, particularly the scalawags and carpetbaggers governing Southern states under martial law. Over the following decades, these parties feuded over tariffs, political corruption and patronage, immigration, Catholicism, and temperance. Republicans "waved the bloody shirt," while Democrats served as the party of "Rum, Romanism, and Rebellion."[108] After years of turmoil, political violence, and a civil war, a Third American Party System had begun.

WHAT DESTROYED THE WHIGS AND WHY IT MATTERS

The collapse of the Whig Party and the destruction of the Second Party System stands as the starkest example of how a realignment can go horribly wrong. America's leaders in the 1840s and 1850s made almost every possible mistake necessary to turn a realignment into a disaster. Replacing the now irrelevant Jacksonian parties was both necessary and inevitable. The party implosion, years of political chaos, horrific decade of violence and disorder, and the rise of a nasty movement like the conspiratorial and anti-Catholic Know-Nothings, were unnecessary man-made disasters. There's a case to be made it all worked out to the good—slavery might not have ended as quickly without an implosion and civil war. Even so, few would choose this model for future party realignments when anything less than mass enslavement was at stake. The reason the Second Party system crumbled in the way it did, forcing America to endure a difficult decade of disorder, violence, and chaos, is because, in the face of realigning pressures, America's political leaders chose to hide from reality. Failing to act first, the river's current swept them away, dashing them and America against the rocks as they went.

By the early 1850s, the old Jacksonian arguments over banks, tariffs, and internal improvements were no longer pressing or relevant. Northern industry had matured. Private investment was building the necessary internal improvements. America was clearly now the popular democracy Jackson represented. Property restrictions on voting had long been removed. Campaigns were no longer elite affairs but a popular sport with parades and bands and bunting of red, white, and blue. The spoils system had turned government service from an elite occupation for the educated and connected into a reward available to everyone. American politicians now competed to demonstrate how ordinary they were, with office seekers from comfortable backgrounds like William Henry Harrison pretending to have grown up in log cabins. The nation had expanded all the way to the Pacific Ocean, so there was more than enough land for settlers to keep moving west. Economic development had turned settlements into towns, and then into cities with roads and canals and then railways. The young nation of pioneers pushing west to build homesteads and little towns had grown into a rising power and a vast nation of thirty-four states spanning a continent.

At the same time, while an influx of new states required a constant rebalancing of Senate power, a religious revival and a national spirit of moral reform had washed over the nation, radicalizing Americans on both sides of the slavery divide. That revival spread apocalyptic notions, a belief that the nation's fate turned on a great confrontation between good and evil, and that America could either live up to its destiny as God's Kingdom or else collapse as a republic. For many Americans, the idea of civil war was no longer a national horror to avoid at all costs—it was an opportunity to win a final victory against evil in the service of moral righteousness.[109] The most important divisions in America in 1850 were no longer between Jacksonians and Whigs. They were between North and South, between an economic system based on plantation slavery and its national eradication.

The Jacksonian debate was over. It was a debate suited to solving the problems of young frontier America, not the America of the mid-nineteenth century. America had debated Jacksonian Democracy for decades and, after much time and experience, the American people had resolved it. They decided the Jacksonians were right. America could and would be a popular democracy in which the people, not elites, would rule. They also decided the Whigs were right. America could and would also be a meritocratic republic that would continue to build, modernize, and reform. America would be a nation of individual opportunity in which laborers, new immigrants, and the driven and ambitious could, whatever their background, remake themselves and rise. It would also expand manufacturing and erect great cities, canals, and rail lines across the continent. America would usher the people into politics, listen to their desires, and still pursue modernity, progress, and reform. It turned out there was no conflict after all. America could, and would, do both.

With the Jacksonian debate now resolved, America in the 1850s naturally fell into political decline. Unwilling or unable to talk about the issues that now mattered to people, politics turned empty. Political debate turned toward slogans and campaign hoopla in place of ideas because there was no real substance on the table. Both parties resorted to clever campaign tactics, nominating popular military heroes with no political experience or agenda, and offering pragmatic government inoffensive to all but without a compelling sense of vision. Short-sighted leaders ran campaigns without big ideas founded on personality and politicking, massaging short-term interests of important constituencies instead of offering a unifying vision. The Whigs and the Democrats were mainly walking-dead parties operating by habit and inertia bound no longer by pressing national interests but the mere formalities of politics. All it took was one bad election night to shatter the inertia propping up the dying system, and the entire party system tumbled.

It's no surprise that America's parties came apart in the 1850s—they were anachronisms that no longer served a purpose. The only question is why the Second Party System imploded so suddenly, driving the nation into years of chaos, violence, and disorder? It's commonly said the Whigs collapsed because disagreements over slavery drove the party apart, as if that alone were a persuasive answer. Slavery had divided America since its Founding. The Democrats and the Whigs were, from their beginnings, national parties with strong Northern and Southern wings divided over slavery. Saying slavery killed the Whigs is like saying a bullet caused a murder—technically true but evading the real question. The reason the transition between the Second Party System and the Third was so tragic and difficult was because America's leaders, when faced with a changed nation, sought to ignore it. In the face of a changing country, America's leaders looked for quick settlements that might push what they saw as annoying distractions away to get back to arguing about "normal" politics—meaning the outdated arguments of the Jacksonian era. What they failed to realize was the issues over which they obsessed—the Jacksonian backbone of their party ideologies—were in reality the irrelevant ones. The "distractions" they hoped to ignore were the new normal. In attempting to prop up a dying system that could no longer hold, America's leaders doomed their country to nearly a decade of disorder, chaos, and violence.

Instead of responding to the change and reforming their parties, America's political leaders essentially waited for their parties to collapse and then waded through the calamity their inaction had created. Neither party was prepared for the undoing of the old political order, nor was the country. The sudden crash in stability unleashed the worst voices and instincts. Ugly movements like the Know-Nothings captured the nation's attention. Political violence broke out in Kansas. Instability and violence even reached into the halls of Congress. Once the parties had crumbled, there was no way to easily put them back together again. The only way forward now was through. Every faction and interest in America had to grope about in the dark to find new allies. The process took years, during which factions jostled and new parties rose and fell, none of them strong enough yet to become a foundation for the next party system—not to mention the outbreak of a bloody civil war that killed over half a million Americans. Instead of a quick transition from one era to the next, America had to fight its way through years of anger, instability, and violence before a new order emerged.

If an individual or group had come along to renew America's parties with new ideas, and the American people had embraced the changes, the nation might have transitioned to its Third Party System quickly and cleanly. In refusing to acknowledge this reality and act, America's leaders instead ceded control to events. American politics after the collapse of the Whig Party was disruptive and chaotic because it was sudden and unplanned. The collapse of the Second Party System is a warning of what not to do when a realignment looms.

CHAPTER 4

AMERICA'S THIRD AND FOURTH PARTY SYSTEMS: THE INCREDIBLE STORY OF WILLIAM JENNINGS BRYAN

William Jennings Bryan's story is so dramatic and improbable that if Hollywood ever made an epic movie about it, critics would complain the plot was preposterously unrealistic. A thirty-six-year-old from Nebraska, a failed Senate candidate with only two terms in the House of Representatives behind him, decides to run for president. He walks into the 1896 Democratic National Convention as the darkest of dark-horse candidates. He hardly has the resume or the political stature of a president. He has only four years of national office to his name, in the House at that, and he lost his last election. At the convention, this young man gives probably the best political speech of all time. He rails against the elites. He all but compares himself to Jesus Christ, ending his speech with his arms outstretched as if in crucifixion. The speech so electrifies the crowd that he walks out as the youngest person in history to ever be nominated for president by a major party. As if that weren't enough, he drives out his party's longstanding leadership, radically remakes its agenda, and all but adopts the ideology and message of a third party then sweeping over the American plains. Before long, Bryan's total transformation of the Democratic Party sparks a similar transformation in its Republican rival, and America launches a new party system eager to take on the new problems of a rapidly industrializing America.

Realignments don't always have to be frightening eras of political violence, constitutional crises, ugly movements, and national disorder. They can also be quick rocket rides to national reform—like William Jennings Bryan and his 1896 campaign that launched America's Fourth Party System. Few today can more than vaguely recall the name William Jennings Bryan, and fewer might recognize his photo, but not so long ago every American knew the story of the dazzling speaker who captured his party's nomination for the presidency, completely replaced its message and agenda over one remarkable election campaign, and then marched America into a transformational political realignment. It's a fascinating story of one man's run for the presidency. It's also a story about how realignments can go right.

RECONSTRUCTION'S END, CORRUPTION, AND THE GILDED AGE

The 1890s were the heart of America's Gilded Age, an era famous for political corruption, patronage, and a dangerous mix of wealth and struggle. At the outset of the Civil War in 1860, America's economic and social life revolved around small towns dotting the landscape, each supporting a cluster of family farms, each with a general store, a bank, a doctor, a lawyer, and a tiny one-room schoolhouse.[1] Then industrialization rapidly swept over the nation and America surged with new wealth and marvels.[2] Thomas Edison invented the electric light bulb. Carnegie built an empire in steel.[3] Rockefeller built an empire bringing heating oil to every corner of America. Business monopolies were growing to enormous sizes, and those savvy enough to seize the right new opportunities were becoming millionaires. New cities erupted out of what just a few decades before had been wilderness[4]—Chicago in 1833 was a village of two hundred people, yet by 1890 it was a city of a million and the sixth largest in the world. New factories appeared. Railroads sprang up across the country connecting small towns with big cities. As opportunities appeared, immigrants flooded in to fill the new jobs.[5] By the 1890s, America looked like a completely different country.

Yet the Gilded Age wasn't all glittering opportunity and vast new wealth. The same economic revolution that had created so much opportunity for some, making them inconceivably rich, had disrupted the traditional livelihoods of others. As people flooded into the growing cities, the small towns of agricultural America began to empty.[6] Crop prices fell as the economy changed. Corn that sold for seventy cents a bushel in 1870 was selling for only about forty cents by the 1880s; wheat had fallen from a dollar a bushel to about seventy cents.[7] The increasing importance of rail to transport agricultural goods to market gave railroad companies a new stranglehold on farmers.[8] Farmers in debt to eastern banks fell into a downward spiral in which every year their crops lost value, making it even harder to pay off the banks.[9] In plains states like Kansas and Nebraska, most farmers likely would have had a neighbor who lost their farm to foreclosure.[10] Many Americans who had spent their entire lives playing by the rules as they understood them—take over the family farm, raise a family there, run the business prudently, and thrive—suddenly found those rules no longer worked, and they suspected someone was cheating them.[11] Life was no easier for urban workers, living in the harsh world of early industrialization with brutal working hours and dangerous conditions.[12] Immigrants, children, and others crowding into the cities were too often abused by a harsh new economy with no rules.

As industrialization was completely remaking America, America's two major parties, the Third Party System Republicans and Democrats, remained stuck in the world of the Civil War and its aftermath. The Republican Party that emerged from the Civil War was Lincoln's party of the Union, a pro-business party of moralistic reformers that had saved the nation, abolished slavery, and struggled to drag America into its postwar future. The Republicans were divided between two factions, the pro-business Yankees drawing on the party's Whiggish legacy and moral reformers descended from the crusaders who abolished slavery.[13] They united around an ideology based on the sanctity and dignity of labor, one that simultaneously explained why slavery was an evil system, because it stole a person's sacred labor, and supported the industriousness and pro-business Yankee work ethic.[14]

The Democratic Party that emerged from the war was a pro-business party of the South bound in an arranged marriage to other groups resentful toward Republicans. The party was mainly under the control of a faction often called the Bourbons, mostly the remnant of the old Southern plantation class eager to restore the Southern social system and economy in the wake of the war.[15] The Southern Bourbons, along with some Northerners sharing their sentiments, celebrated Thomas Jefferson's vision of a decentralized republic with limited interference from the national government. They were strongly pro-business, although they favored the agricultural business of the South. At the grass roots, the party attracted many rural working people in the South, who blamed Northern Republicans for the wartime devastation and sudden uprooting of the slave-plantation economy that turned the South from among America's richest regions to its poorest.[16] It also attracted Northern immigrants, many Irish Catholics, who organized in powerful urban political machines like New York's Tammany Hall to combat local Republican elites who looked down on them.[17] The Democratic Party united these factions around their shared opposition to the Republicans, a party they considered an agent of privilege and centralization.[18]

In the years after the Civil War, these Third Party System Republicans and Democrats mainly continued to fight over the issues of the war that created them, most powerfully through the difficult, traumatic, and sometimes violent era of postwar Reconstruction. For a time, while the battle over Reconstruction thundered, America's Third Party System parties were energetic and engaged as North and South fought over how to rebuild and reform America's institutions as America gradually shepherded the Confederacy back into the Union. During the decade of Reconstruction, the Republicans, victorious in war, fought to force reform on a defeated South while the Democrats, the South's political voice, sought to resist them. The Republicans ensured America passed the Constitution's Civil Rights Amendments that ended slavery and promised equal citizenship before the law.[19] America created a national Freedman's Bureau to integrate the former slaves into freedom and citizenship.[20] "Radical Republicans" sought a harsher reconstruction policy to ensure the total eradication of slavery's legacy, while "moderates" wanted to achieve that end more gently to pursue national reconciliation.[21] A president, Andrew Johnson, was impeached.[22]

After the war, much of the South was initially under military occupation and the administration of provisional governments, supervised by federal Reconstruction policy in Washington. Northern Republican "carpetbaggers" set up new Republican governments, alongside some locals whom their neighbors vilified as turncoat "scalawags," and they elected many African American former slaves into Southern legislatures.[23] One by one, however, federal military governments packed their bags and former Confederate states rejoined the Union. Militants like the Ku Klux Klan, working in league with local Democratic Party leaders, used violence to resist Republican governments claiming to resist tyranny.[24] They employed terror tactics, including murder, to chase Republicans of both races out of politics to restore local control under the Democratic Party banner. Over time, Republican regimes across the South were systematically rendered ineffective, leading to their collapse. Southern "redeemers" seized back power in one after another Southern state, chasing out the carpetbaggers, destroying local Republican organizations, and removing the newly freed slaves from public participation through harassment, schemes, and violence. Then America descended into a horrific economic depression, the Panic of 1873, bringing Reconstruction to its end and ushering in the politics of the Gilded Age.

When the economic depression of the Panic plunged America into national pain and crisis, the popularity of the ruling Republicans plummeted.[25] A battered nation, fatigued at enforcing Reconstruction on an intransigent South, was ready to turn its attention back inward toward bread-and-butter issues. After a closely contested presidential election in 1876 marred by disputed votes and accusations of fraud, the Democrats agreed to accept Republican Rutherford Hayes as president in implicit exchange for local—inevitably Democratic—rule and the withdrawal of the federal troops meant to supervise and safeguard Southern politics.[26] After almost two decades of conflict—five years of a horrific war and then more than a decade of often-violent occupation—a weary America declared Reconstruction over, even though the work of making the former slaves equal citizens was still undone.

As America crumbled into exhaustion after Reconstruction, politics fell into a deep decline. Officially, the parties continued to debate important issues like tariffs, with Northern Republican still favoring high tariffs to protect Northern manufacturing and Southern Democrats opposing tariffs as unfair burdens.[27] The parties sometimes fought over moral issues, like temperance, which, while it cut across both parties, the moralistic and Protestant Republicans tended to favor and Catholic Democrats opposed.[28] As the turbulent economy seesawed between boom and bust, political leaders tried to manage the depressions and economic crises. Reformist candidates ran campaigns against the corruption and graft pervading both parties.[29] In reality, these issues mostly served as proxies for the era's true great debate— resentments left over from the war. At election time, although America was changing profoundly and difficult new challenges were popping up everywhere, powerful veteran's societies like the Grand Army of the Republic influenced elections, lingering war resentments hung in the air, and many Americans continued "voting as they shot."[30]

With America now too tired to engage politically, politics in this post-Reconstruction Gilded Age became probably the most corrupt and empty of any era across the entire history of America. As Henry Adams wrote of it, "One might search the whole list of Congress, Judiciary, and Executive during the twenty-five years 1870–1895, and find little but damaged reputation. The period was poor in purpose and barren in results."[31] Politics tragically descended into cynical office-chasing, sloganeering, listlessness, and graft.[32] Both parties had by now refined the spoils system into political machines with bosses and corruption. The worst of them, like New York's Tammany Hall, bought support from constituents with money siphoned from government contracts, while filling the pockets of the bosses. Politicians from both parties got cozy with railroad corporations and business interests in ways that shock us today, receiving large retainers, positions to supplement their income, and gifts like free railroad passes, in implicit exchange for favors.[33] With politics exhausted and little to debate, there was no longer much at stake except spoils. Political disputes often broke out not between the parties but within them as reformers sought to clean up the corruption in their own ranks. The Republicans fought a decades-long cold war between the party's moral reformers, who demanded civil service reform to abolish the corrupt spoils system, and its regulars, who wanted to sustain the political order that supported them.[34] The reformers bolted the party with regularity, as "Liberal Republicans" when they defected against Grant in 1872, "Half-Breeds" when they warred against their party's "Stalwarts" to break the patronage machine with civil service reforms, and "Mugwumps" when, in 1884, they refused to support nominee James G. Blaine due to his perceived corruption, making Grover Cleveland the first Democrat to win the White House since the Civil War.[35] All the while, some were getting rich, America's traditional middle class struggled, and the economy continually lurched between expansion and bust.

Then another horrible depression, the Panic of 1893, rocked the nation. After decades of corruption and national drift, as America's Civil War parties continued nursing war resentments while mainly ignoring the new problems of the staggering economic revolution fundamentally remaking America, everything finally flew apart.

FREE SILVER, THE POPULIST INSURGENCY, AND THE STORY OF WILLIAM JENNINGS BRYAN

Before 1896, William Jennings Bryan's career had been notable but hardly extraordinary. He grew up in Illinois, the son of a local politician.[36] His was an evangelical family at a time of Christian revival, and Bryan was raised to believe the devout had a duty to help others and improve society, and that the heart mattered more than the mind.[37] Like his father, Bryan was also a strong Jeffersonian who distrusted cities and federal power and believed in the republican purity of the simple farmer.[38] After practicing law for a few years in Illinois without much distinction, Bryan moved west to Nebraska to find his fortune. A Union state, Nebraska was at the time of Bryan's arrival solidly Republican. In 1890, Bryan ran a long-shot campaign for Congress, even though he had only lived in the state a few years. With the help of a vote-splitting independent candidate, he became only the second Democrat to win a Nebraska congressional seat since the Civil War and won reelection two years later.[39]

As Bryan was building his political career in Nebraska, the state was at the heart of a growing populist revolt. A "populist movement" of angry small farmers was sweeping across America, and it was strongest in Great Plains states like Nebraska and across the agricultural South. The movement represented an intense anger at the gradual destruction of the small-farm economy, long America's backbone. For its entire history to this point, America had been a nation of small independent farmers—many Americans even saw family farming as a sacred way of life, and the rural communities those farms supported as the lifeblood of democracy.[40] Now the family farmers who made up America's great middle class, who then, as now, mostly ran on credit, fell deeper in debt to eastern banks while their crops sold for less and less. They increasingly depended on railroad corporations to get crops to market, which set their rates outside the farmers' control and took a big cut of any profit.[41] At the same time, newly bursting cities were slowly draining small farming towns of their populations. For all the wonders and progress it delivered, industrialization was choking the great network of farms and small towns that sustained generations of Americans. Farmers who had held land for generations wondered how their farms would survive. People naturally became enraged at these forces destroying their livelihoods and way of life. Believing Republicans and Democrats were both in the pockets of corrupt Gilded Age interests, they formed an independent political party called the People's Party, often called the Populists. By 1892, the party had elected a significant number of governors, senators, and members of congress on its populist platform. It won over 8 percent of the popular vote and several states in the 1892 presidential election.

The People's Party had roots in prior farmer-laborer movements like the Greenback Party, the Grange, and the Farmers' Alliance, and it built on many of the policies these movements first advanced.[42] The Populists built a platform of far-reaching reforms meant to break up what they saw as the corrupt links between government and elites—banks, railroads, and the politicians in their pockets. They wanted an income tax. They wanted nationalization and public control of railroads, telephones, and telegraphs. They wanted to abolish national banks. They wanted an eight-hour work day. They wanted civil service reform. They wanted the direct election of senators by the people instead of through state legislatures. They wanted pensions for Union soldiers. They wanted a single term for presidents and vice presidents.[43] Taken together, the Populists wanted to stamp out elite power, to regain control of their lives, and as best they could restore the world to the way it had existed before industrialization had so profoundly disrupted their lives.[44] As the Populist platform of 1892 proclaimed, "corruption dominates the ballot-box, the Legislatures, the Congress, and touches even the ermine of the bench" as "the fruits of the toil of millions are boldly stolen to build up colossal fortunes for a few," which would "endanger liberty" and threaten "the establishment of an absolute despotism."[45]

Among the populist movement's most important issues, however, was its great passion around the unlikely issue of bimetallic monetary policy or, as it was then known, "free silver." Free-silver advocates wanted the government to move from a gold standard—a national currency the government promises to exchange on demand for gold—to a bimetallic standard—a currency the bearer can exchange on demand for either gold or silver. The idea was to vastly increase the national supply of money and thus cause inflation. America's middle class of suffering farmers, struggling under enormous debt from Eastern banks, believed the inflation free silver would produce could relieve them of economic pressure while loosening the credit they needed to survive. While inflation is bad for people with money, it's quite good for people whose wealth is tied up in assets and struggling with debt—like farmers with huge mortgages. Free silver was also an attractive idea for people who mined silver, like the silver-mining boom towns that supported a lot of people across the American West.

The silver issue wasn't new in the 1890s. It had been roiling underneath American politics since the last time the national economy melted down, during the Panic of 1873. Farmers and debtors during the 1873 depression wanted cheaper money to lighten their burden and loosen credit. America's economic elites, however, believed cheap money had helped to cause the disaster and wanted the opposite. America's currency had long been bimetallic—Alexander Hamilton's economic system was based on a bimetallic dollar—and while the system sometimes caused some problems when the prices of gold and silver fluctuated, bimetallism was well established.[46] America's economic elites, however, influenced the government during the Panic of 1873 to move America to a strict gold-only standard.[47] Not only did they convince the government to demonetize silver, the federal government also eliminated the "greenback" dollars it had issued out of desperation during the Civil War—currency backed not with precious metal at all, but simply the government's credit—converting them into notes redeemable only for gold.[48] Free-silver advocates called it the "Crime of 1873." They saw it as an act of treason in which the government deprived ordinary people of the capital they needed to prosper for the benefit of the rich. In light of the criticism, a few years later Congress, in compensation for demonetizing silver, agreed to purchase a small amount of silver each year to make silver coins.[49] In 1890, it foolishly agreed through the Sherman Silver Act to increase that amount to almost the entire national supply.[50] Worse, it agreed people could exchange that silver for certificates redeemable either for silver or gold priced at a fixed rate between metals of 16–1. Then, when the Panic of 1893 arrived, the free-silver issue really took off.

The Panic of 1893 was the worst economic depression up to that point in America's history. With the invention of the miraculous railroad, entrepreneurs and speculators seeking glory and profit borrowed absurd sums of money from banks and investors to build railroads into every corner of America. Their exuberance naturally led to the creation of many profitless railroad spurs to areas with too little demand. That led to a crash, followed by the bankruptcy of investors and bank runs.[51] Businesses failed, banks closed, stocks crashed, and unemployment skyrocketed. Unemployment reached as high as 20 percent, and in some areas even higher.[52] It was a national disaster. The Panic destroyed the livelihoods of many ordinary Americans living in small towns who had never invested in a railroad, or even purchased a railroad ticket. Many Americans were angry, their anger directed at Eastern fat-cat bankers and railroad executives whom they believed had corrupted the system and destroyed the economy.

Just as during the Panic of 1873, bankers and elite opinion blamed the Panic of 1893 on silver.[53] The price of silver was already depreciating against gold before the depression, so investors started buying up all the silver they could find to exchange it for the government's gold under the Sherman Silver Act at 16–1, giving them a risk-free profit. When the Panic struck, people then started converting more money to gold to protect their assets. Before long, the nation's gold reserves were almost depleted and America risked national insolvency.[54] A frantic President Cleveland, desperate to prop up the economy, called an emergency session of Congress to repeal the Sherman Silver Act.[55] To shore up the nation's credit, he also accepted an embarrassing bailout of gold from Wall Street investor J. P. Morgan in exchange for government bonds that Morgan and his friends sold at a nice profit.[56] Farmers who hated bankers and needed cheap money were outraged at the debacle. The western states, whose economies depended on silver mines, were outraged. Many ordinary people, seeing corruption and collusion with rich bankers and elites, were outraged. In light of these events, the free-silver issue came to represent for many ordinary Americans the ultimate symbol pitting what was good for them against what was good for bankers, railroad barons, and Gilded Age elites.[57]

As a fierce agrarian with a Jacksonian worldview based around notions of championing the people against the elite, William Jennings Bryan was naturally sympathetic to the Populist cause.[58] Over his brief congressional career, Bryan forged close relationships with the Populists, whose crossover support he need to stay in office as a Democrat in a Republican state.[59] In Congress, he became an advocate for free silver, and, given his political skills and powerful oratory, quickly became a champion of the issue.[60] For the same reasons, Bryan frequently clashed with his party's leadership, particularly with President Cleveland, given Bryan's populist sentiments and views on silver.[61] Bryan gave up his seat in Congress in 1894 in hope of winning a seat in the Senate, but when the Panic turned that year into a Republican landslide, he lost. Once out of office, Bryan began editing the *Omaha World-Herald* and giving paid speeches on political topics to raise his profile and promote his views— something of the 1890s version of a political talk-radio host.[62] With only this political experience, Bryan with great confidence decided in 1896 he could ride the forces of populism to the presidency. The idea was so ambitious it was almost absurd.

When Bryan arrived at the Democratic National Convention in Chicago in 1896, few took his presidential bid seriously—polls placed him last among the possible candidates.[63] It's a prevalent myth that Bryan was nationally unknown before the 1896 convention. Still, as a thirty-six-year-old former congressman from a Republican state at odds with his party's leadership, he was far from what most considered presidential timber.[64] The convention, however, was destined to be about silver, and it was an opportunity Bryan was well-prepared to seize. A large contingent of "Silver Democrats" had arrived at the convention committed to launching a war over silver, viewing it as a proxy for the party's soul—were Democrats truly on the side of the little people, or were they on the side of the moneyed elite? President Cleveland, now unpopular due to the Panic, had chosen not to run for reelection. The Democratic Party's Bourbon establishment, however, were, like Cleveland, mainly Gold Democrats convinced that the "sound money" gold provided was essential to a healthy economy. In the months before the convention, Bryan diligently worked the pro-silver delegates to win their favor.[65] Knowing his only hope lay in the power of his oratory, he convinced them to let him have the prime speaking slot at the close of debate on the party platform to champion silver.[66] Then he delivered what is almost without dispute the most significant convention speech in all of presidential politics, transforming a minor politician into the youngest presidential candidate in American history, and transforming a fading Democratic Party into the vehicle for a popular revolt.

On its face, the speech Bryan delivered at the 1896 convention was about silver. In reality, it was a barn burner about an America in which common people suffered under the yoke of the wealthy and powerful. It put the silver issue at the heart of a great struggle between the inherently good people of rural and working America and the greed and corruption of urban and wealthy America. It celebrated the common working man, particularly those in small towns and farms. It villainized Eastern bankers and railroads executives and spit loathing at cities and those who lived in them. It radiated hatred toward the wealthy. This passage from the speech gives an idea of what it was like:

> Mr. Carlisle said in 1878 that this was a struggle between the idle holders of idle capital and the struggling masses who produce the wealth and pay the taxes of the country; and my friends, it is simply a question that we shall decide upon which side shall the Democratic Party fight. Upon the side of the idle holders of idle capital, or upon the side of the struggling masses? That is the question that the party must answer first; and then it must be answered by each individual hereafter. The sympathies of the Democratic Party, as described by the platform, are on the side of the struggling masses, who have ever been the foundation of the Democratic Party.
>
> There are two ideas of government. There are those who believe that if you just legislate to make the well-to-do prosperous, that their prosperity will leak through on those below. The Democratic idea has been that if you legislate to make the masses prosperous their prosperity will find its way up and through every class that rests upon it.
>
> You come to us and tell us that the great cities are in favor of the gold standard. I tell you that the great cities rest upon these broad and fertile prairies. Burn down your cities and leave our farms, and your cities will spring up again as if by magic. But destroy our farms and the grass will grow in the streets of every city in the country.[67]

As he ended, Bryan cast himself not as just a presidential candidate but as a redemptive savior:

> Having behind us the commercial interests and the laboring interests and all the toiling masses, we shall answer their demands for a gold standard by saying to them, you shall not press down upon the brow of labor this crown of thorns. You shall not crucify mankind upon a cross of gold.[68]

Then Bryan slowly stretched out his arms in the pose of the crucified Christ. He held the position in silence for several seconds before dropping his arms to his side as the crowd stayed still.[69] He left the stage in silence. Then bedlam broke out in the hall, the quiet replaced with loud cheers and wild applause, as hats and coats were thrown into the air like caps at a graduation ceremony.[70] The next day, the Democratic Party nominated Bryan for the presidency.

In the general election campaign, Bryan faced Ohio governor William McKinley, a leading member of the Republican Party's Yankee business wing. Bryan traveled up and down America by train giving speeches to take advantage of his oratory skills. American presidential candidates traditionally viewed such grubby politicking as unseemly, preferring a "front porch campaign" in which crowds of supporters came to the candidate's house until he came out and delivered a speech—maintaining the illusion of a candidate just talking to friends rather than actively promoting himself. Bryan's gifts as a speaker and his common-man message, however, captured America's attention, and his whistle-stop tour attracted enraptured crowds. In towns across America, masses of cheering Americans came out to hear Bryan speak, meeting him with elaborate pageantry such as a presentation of maidens dressed in white, a procession of dead "goldbugs" carried by pallbearers, wagonloads of huge boxes labeled as Republican campaign money, a parade of twenty thousand horsemen, a lighted trail, and a little girl in a silver dress presenting him with a rose.[71] Bryan's central campaign issue was the free coinage of silver, but his message was for the little people. He villainized the railroads and the banks. He accused greedy Eastern elites of causing the suffering of farmers and workers. An evangelical Protestant, Bryan loudly trumpeted the Christian basis of his politics in the spirit of the religious revival then coursing through the nation.

Bryan, and his rapturous reception across America, stunned and frightened the American establishment—not only Republicans, but Bourbon Democrats as well. A group of Bourbons from the Democrats' leadership, furious at what Bryan was doing to their party—they dismissed Bryanism as the "Popocratic Party" or the "Bryanarchy"[72]—splintered into a third party of their own called the "National Democratic Party," although it ultimately only drew about one percent of the national vote.[73] Bryan's enemies believed he was the republic's nightmare, a poorly educated bumpkin with dangerous ideas preying on the ignorant during a terrible economic crisis. As Bryan moved around America demonizing bankers and railroad presidents, the business community saw a terrifying demagogue stirring up hate among the working classes.[74] They distrusted his fiery speeches and religious fervor. They found his policies naive. They thought his enthusiastic crowds were nothing more than a stirred-up mob. Money flowed freely from the America establishment to promote McKinley, including some dirty tricks and incidences of outright corruption.[75] Legendary political strategist and wealthy industrialist Mark Hanna, who largely engineered McKinley's nomination, methodically collected a historic campaign war chest from terrified banks, business leaders, and the wealthy desperate to stop Bryan.[76] Hanna's professional campaign operation also outworked and out organized a Bryan campaign the Bourbon-controlled regular Democratic organization mainly abandoned, flooding the nation with over 120,000,000 copies of various pamphlets and speeches, compared to Bryan's mere 10,000,000.[77]

Bryan's campaign placed the People's Party in a bind. Populist leaders saw no choice but to also nominate Bryan as their party's candidate so Populist voters could vote Bryan without destroying the movement. Bryan therefore became a fusion candidate running under the Democratic banner but heading both parties simultaneously.[78] The Populists nominated a prominent Populist leader as their ticket's vice-presidential candidate in the hope that Bryan would do the same, but Bryan refused to abandon his conservative Democrat running mate.[79] By the end of the campaign, most Populists had followed Bryan into the Democratic Party and the People's Party soon faded away as a separate political entity. It's therefore often said that the Democrats absorbed the People's Party during the 1896 campaign, but the truth is the opposite. The Democratic Party brand survived, but it did so with the message, agenda, and ideas of the People's Party. The Democratic Party didn't swallow the People's Party in 1896. It was the other way around.

The 1896 election was close. At first, Bryan had momentum. America was mesmerized at the crowds and energy Bryan's whistle-stop tour attracted as it moved from town to town making as many as thirty-six speeches a day.[80] Bryan appeared to be making great inroads into the traditionally Republican Midwest and West, as his agrarian populist message resonated among struggling Midwestern farmers, and the silver issue resonated in the West. As the race wore on, however, some of the passion for Bryan cooled, and McKinley's money chipped away at Bryan's popularity. McKinley's campaign was well-funded, efficient, and organized. It trumpeted a vision of shared prosperity in a stable economy based on "sound money"—the gold standard—creating jobs and wealth for everyone. It attacked Bryan as a dangerous radical and crusading religious fanatic who was launching a revolution with unhinged ideas that would destroy the economy. Bryan's losses among Democratic Bourbons worried about Bryan's antibusiness rhetoric and Catholic Democrats uncomfortable with his Protestant zeal offset his gains in Republican middle America. Ultimately, McKinley pulled out the victory.

That hardly, however, brought an end to Bryan's populist revolt. Bryan might have lost the presidency, but he won control of the Democratic Party for a generation. American politics would never be the same. The Third Party System was over. With Bryan's remarkable 1896 campaign, a Fourth Party System had dawned.

THE POPULIST AND PROGRESSIVE ERA

After the 1896 campaign, not only did Bryanism become the new model for the Democratic Party, but Bryan himself personally maintained control of the party for decades to come. He won the Democratic nomination a second time in 1900, losing a rematch against McKinley. He declined to run in 1904 against the nearly invincible Teddy Roosevelt but, when Bryan couldn't prevent the nomination going to a Bourbon Democrat, Alton Parker, he gave a weak and half-hearted endorsement and then pledged to take back the party for populism.[81] In 1908, Bryan won the Democratic nomination again, this time losing to William Howard Taft. In 1912, he finally stepped aside, selecting Woodrow Wilson as his preferred Democratic nominee and later becoming secretary of state in Wilson's administration.[82]

In addition to Bryan's political career, he made himself into a millionaire political media celebrity. He earned large sums on the chautauqua lecture circuit, giving fiery sermons on politics and religion to great crowds across America. When he took a tour around the world after the 1904 election, the media followed him with fascination.[83] He launched a popular and very profitable weekly newspaper called the *Commoner*, which trumpeted his populist political beliefs; its name was taken from the name Bryan's fans and followers had given him, "The Great Commoner."[84] Even after Bryan resigned from the Wilson administration and active politics, his influence remained. In 1924, the Democrats nominated his brother Charles Bryan for vice president, in order to appease Bryan and his followers, losing that election to Republican Calvin Coolidge.

The Democratic Party under Bryan picked up some support in formerly solid Republican areas in the Midwest and West, and its appeal weakened a little among Catholics alarmed by Bryan's evangelical Protestantism. Bryan's Democrats, however, still attracted a similar constituency—the South and Northern cities with large immigrant populations. In his later campaigns, Bryan's agenda also evolved. When an improved economy and new gold discoveries in Alaska cooled the silver issue, Bryan moved on to other ground.[85] In 1900, he focused on anti-imperialism—McKinley had taken the Philippines and Puerto Rico as colonies in the Spanish-American War, and Bryan believed colonialism was inconsistent with republican democracy. Bryan ran his third campaign, in 1908, on the slogan "Shall the People Rule?" proposing reforms to bring the people closer to government.[86] What changed was less demographics or even policies than ideology. Over the course of his many years of influence, Bryan turned the Democrats from a party based on lingering resentment over the Civil War into a party of full-throated populism proposing a new debate over the problem that now worried most of America—how to manage the severe economic and social disruptions of industrialization.

Bryan's political revolution didn't end with its transformation of the Democrats. Not long after Bryan transformed the Democratic

Party, the Republican Party updated and reformed its party too. Since the Civil War, the Republican Party consisted of two strong and often-squabbling factions, the "pro-business" Yankees and the moral reformers. The upstanding Yankees were interested in national stability and economic growth. The moral reformers were interested in good-government, morality, and social reform. They united around a Republican agenda celebrating the sacred right for people to control their own labor, which meant to them both the advancement of civil rights and also the right for citizens to control their own business arrangements without state interference. In response to the new problems of industrialization, these factions now updated that ideology to provide an answer to the problems of industrialization, one different from Bryan's Democrats. They became the pro-business, crusading, reformist, energetic party of Teddy Roosevelt's progressivism.

While the People's Party and Bryan were developing a populist agenda to address the disruption of industrialization, another movement had risen with a different solution to the problem, the Progressive Movement. In the years since the Civil War, a new confidence in rationalism and expertise had spread across America, and Americans increasingly believed social scourges that had long bedeviled human societies might be managed and tamed.[87] Around the same time, another religious revival had burst forth. Unlike the revivalists and reformers before the Civil War who helped end slavery, this new generation of Christian reformers embraced a new theology, the "Social Gospel." They believed that, instead of seeking to morally redeem individual citizens, they could instead implement national social reforms that could uplift and improve all of America, bringing about God's Kingdom on Earth and the Second Coming.[88] The mix of this confidence in expertise, the ideas of the Social Gospel, and the demand for national reform, combined into a movement seeking to address the same industrial-era disruptions that drove populism. This Progressive Movement, which blossomed at the end of the nineteenth century, was intent on deploying planning and social science to improve society and address the downsides and abuses of an industrializing economy.

Progressivism was a new crusading spirit that bound an interrelated network of activists, journalists, charity workers, preachers, and politicians. It inspired a network of overlapping endeavors from settlement houses built to serve and uplift poor and working people in the cities; to the muckraking journalists who exposed corruptions and outrages in magazines like *McClure's*; to thinkers like Herbert Croly who wrote books and founded intellectual magazines like *The New Republic*; to the social reformers who fought for new laws to help workers; to preachers like Walter Rauschenbusch who proclaimed the need of a Social Gospel to reform America.[89] Progressives took up a staggering array of causes and reforms, seeking to fundamentally remake America to tame the power of growing industrial business, eliminate abuses against workers, break up corruption in business and politics, bring rational efficiency and planning to the economy, ensure the purity of food and medicine, and protect the natural environment. They sought to improve the social condition of America among the poor and disadvantaged through personal charity and education. They fought against political corruption and political machines. They fought to prohibit child labor, enact maximum work-hour laws, treat the mentally ill, regulate worker safety, eliminate impure food and quack medicine, build parks, and conserve the natural environment. They sought to break up large monopoly businesses through antitrust laws.

Progressivism mainly attracted the rising generation that grew up after the trauma of the Civil War, one no longer interested in waging old battles or rebuilding stability like their elders, but instead wanting to shake up society to create justice and reform. It flourished among the comfortable and educated and was overwhelming middle class, professional, and Protestant.[90] Much like similar reform campaigns before the Civil War, progressivism particularly flourished among educated middle-class and wealthy women for whom it provided an important outlet to participate in the public square. Women associated with the movement flooded into charitable projects to assist the working poor, such as the thriving settlement houses springing up across America, like Jane Addams's Hull House. They became influential muckrakers, like Ida Tarbell whose articles in *McClure's* took down the Standard Oil monopoly. They took up social activism and lobbied for new laws, like Frances Perkins who, after the infamous tragedy of the Triangle Shirtwaist Factory Fire, rose to prominence winning important new labor regulations in New York City. They joined and became leaders in powerful temperance societies fighting for alcohol prohibition like the Women's Christian Temperance Union and Anti-Saloon League. Most famously, they became the suffragettes who fought and won the right to vote.

This new spirit of moral and social reform naturally flourished inside a moralistic, Protestant, and reformist Republican Party, where it became the motivating spirit turning the party's moral reformers into its most powerful faction.[91] Progressivism became a powerful force in Republican politics, creating a new generation of leaders like Bob LaFollette, Charles Evans Hughes, and Herbert Hoover. The champion and greatest leader of the movement, however, was Theodore Roosevelt, who ascended to the presidency after McKinley's death in 1901.[92] Over the seven years of his dynamic presidency, Roosevelt captivated America as he plunged the country into a new era of energetic reform. Under a philosophy he called the New Nationalism, which regarded "the executive power as the steward of the public welfare," Roosevelt offered America a "Square Deal," one he proclaimed would "equalize opportunity, destroy privilege, and give to the life and citizenship of every individual the highest possible value both to himself and to the commonwealth."[93] As Roosevelt said in one of his campaign speeches, "I mean not merely that I stand for fair play under the present rules of the game, but that I stand for having those rules changed so as to work for a more substantial equality of opportunity and of reward for equally good service."[94] As president, Roosevelt advocated a progressive program to restore what he saw as fairness and fair play to the industrial economy, including regulating large business conglomerates called trusts through "antitrust" laws, a graduated income tax, breaking the political power of wealthy "special interests," establishing national parks to conserve natural resources, creating workman's compensation laws, imposing maximum work hours, and ending child labor.[95]

Members of the Republican progressive faction, such as Teddy Roosevelt, and members of its pro-business Yankee faction, such as Calvin

Coolidge, mostly cooperated around an active modernizing agenda. These factions naturally sparred for influence within the party, sometimes fiercely, such as when Roosevelt and the progressive Republicans challenged Roosevelt's successor, William Howard Taft, for reelection, believing he had drifted too far toward the Yankees and away from progressivism as president.[96] The Yankees also sometimes chaffed at progressive ideas, usually when they infringed on the right to enter into contracts without interference. As proponents of a muscular government that strengthened business and modernized America, the Yankees mainly accepted national spending and government intervention to regulate the immoral business practices of shady low-class operators that they, as upstanding pillars of business, equally detested.

The Progressive Era Republicans sought to address many of the same problems as Bryan's populist Democrats, and sometimes even supported similar policies, although their approach was completely different. Bryan's populists were struggling farmers and workers raging during an economic depression. Progressives were middle class and well-to-do and flourished as the economy moved back toward easy prosperity.[97] Bryan's Democrats wanted to overthrow elites in the people's name. Progressives sought to empower those elites to harness their skill, judgment, and character to improve life for the people. Where Bryan sought to empower poor and working people across America, progressives wanted to assist, uplift, and reform them. The progressive perspective more naturally identified with a turn-of-the-century Republican Party of modernization, Protestantism, wealth, commerce, business, the Yankee work ethic, and the middle class, than a rural and populist Democratic Party of angry farmers, struggling workers, poor Catholic immigrants, and a South distrustful of Northern manufacturing and commerce.

No longer simply waving the "bloody shirt" of the Union, the Fourth Party System Republicans broke with their Civil War past just as Bryan's Democrats had done. The Republicans continued to be a moralistic pro-business party of modernizers based in the North, attracting middle-class professionals, shopkeepers, bankers, and America's industrial elite. They still favored a vigorous federal government to turn America into a great industrial nation and global power. They continued to support civil rights for African Americans and still connected their economic beliefs to the fight against slavery under the ideal of the sanctity of labor. They were still friendly to commerce and industrialization and advanced protectionist economics for most of the era, before shifting toward free markets in the 1920s. The party still hosted a faction of moralistic reformers and a pro-business faction that believed in the values of the steely old Yankee aristocracy—the Protestant work ethic, moral forthrightness, and national greatness. Yet Republicans now wrapped these tendencies in a wholly new ideology.

Republican progressivism was also, moreover, quite different from the "progressivism" that briefly prospered inside the Democratic Party under Woodrow Wilson. At the height of progressive popularity in 1912, Woodrow Wilson—who spent most of his career as a conservative Bourbon Democrat and strong critic of Bryan—ran for president reinventing himself as a progressive.[98] Other Democrats, of course, had previously worked with progressive activists, particularly urban leaders like New York's Al Smith, since cities were often the focus of progressive activism. When Wilson ran for the presidency in 1912, he faced not only Roosevelt's handpicked successor, President William Howard Taft, but also Roosevelt himself running as a third-party candidate under the "Bull Moose" Progressive Party banner.[99] Roosevelt and Wilson, and even sometimes Taft, all had claims to progressivism, and they sparred throughout the campaign over their rival interpretations of what progressivism meant. Wilson's campaign centered around attacking Roosevelt's progressive "New Nationalism" ideology, promoting an alternative Wilson called the "New Freedom" that would pursue progressive policy goals without infringing too much on states' rights.[100]

Roosevelt's New Nationalism, what we normally call historical progressivism, was an ideology seeking to wield strong federal power to reform society. Wilson's New Freedom was built instead around a Jeffersonian philosophy of states' rights and small government.[101] Wilson opposed vigorous federal intervention and supervision to combat economic inefficiencies and abuses, promising instead that by simply restoring fair competition with antitrust laws, national progress and freedom would bubble up from the market.[102] As the progressive leader and journalist Herbert Croly wrote of it, "The New Nationalism of the Progressives, with its emphasis upon purposive social and political reconstruction, was opposed by the New Freedom—a doctrine which proclaimed substantially that if the system of letting things alone was properly regulated and its abuses eliminated, a permanent peace would be restored to the distracted American Nation."[103] Arguably, Wilson's New Freedom was philosophically at its core a dressed-up version of Democratic Bourbonism, one accepting the necessity and popularity of specific progressive reforms in light of a changing America, but wrapping them in classic Democratic Party ideology.

As president, Wilson worked with progressives and gained the support of many progressive leaders.[104] He also, however, dragged his feet on implementing many progressive priorities, to the great frustration of progressive activists, and often only came out in support when he politically had no choice.[105] Many important progressive achievements took place under his watch, and it's fair to call his administration progressive in its policy accomplishments. Wilson's record, however, also includes many markedly "unprogressive" elements, from racially segregating the federal civil service for the first time since the Civil War, pushing African Americans out of federal jobs to which Republicans had appointed them, jailing political opponents who criticized his entry into the First World War on the ground of national security, fighting against the labor movement, and prosecuting for sedition prominent labor leader and Socialist Party presidential candidate Eugene Debs.[106] While Wilson adopted many of the most popular Progressive Movement ideas, he did so much in the same way that Bill Clinton "triangulated" around free-market conservativism almost a century later. Wilson's "progressive" ideology embraced many progressive policies and issues, but for completely different ideological reasons than the progressivism of the Progressive Movement.

Between Bryan's populism and Roosevelt's progressivism, the Fourth Party System launched a new national debate over what to do about the abuses and disruptions of industrialization. Bryan's renewed Democrats threw off their Civil War resentments to make populist arguments directly expressing the needs, anger, and resentments of struggling rural and working Democrats. The renewed Republicans gave up their "bloody shirt" campaigns to propose progressive reforms to bring efficiency and modernization, and to alleviate abuses of the poor, immigrants, and children. Between these two dueling visions, populism and progressivism, America entered the most significant era of national reform in its history. By its end, America had emerged a prosperous great power ready to play a major role on the world's stage. Bryan's campaign launched the most remarkable realignment in American history. With remarkably little disruption, it renewed not just America's parties, but also America itself.

WHY 1896 IS THE MODEL REALIGNMENT

America in the 1890s desperately needed a realignment. Its Civil War parties had nothing important to say about industrialization, urbanization, or the collapse of the family-farm economy. They had nothing important to say about the disruption the new industrial economy had brought to dying small towns, the abuses it brought in the new factories, or the anxieties many felt about the booming cities attracting a stream of new immigrants to fill new jobs.[107] A lot of Americans felt angry and cheated, and neither the Democrats nor the Republicans, bickering over tariffs and old Civil War wounds, offered anything relevant to their lives. Both Gilded Age parties had stagnated into empty institutions engaged in office-seeking and graft, fighting the same tired battles over increasingly irrelevant issues. All the necessary conditions existed in 1896 for a tragic party collapse and years of national turmoil—corrupt and decrepit parties trapped in dead debates, new and scary problems in need of solutions, political anger and national discontent, and a new crusading spirit washing over America demanding major change. It's surprising America didn't burst.

Defying the usual course, Bryan seized his party, embraced the change that was coming, and jumped directly into the chaos. Before long, the Republicans, forced to address the same problems for which Democrats proposed solutions, underwent a similar renewal. The 1896 realignment transformed two Civil War–era relics into the Populist-and-Progressive-Era parties that ushered America into the modern age without the usual danger realignments bring. There was upheaval and national anger, and there were new movements. The populist revolt and Bryan's campaigns involved a lot of hot language and rough politics. Yet there was also no party collapse, constitutional crisis, outbreak of political violence, or years of painful national instability that realignments often create. The realignment of 1896 therefore offers a lesson in how to avoid the years of uncertainty, breakdown, and danger that normally accompany realignments. Instead of descending into a decade-long unruly scrum where the worst factions in society are given a chance to grasp for power, a national party renewal can create an orderly process that quickly channels passions to useful ends.

Bryan's new Democratic Party was hardly a model for winning elections. Bryan ran three races for the presidency and he lost three times. His strident personality and unforgiving style made him a hero to his fervent fans but hardly endeared him to less-committed parts of the electorate. His perceived radicalism scared off moderate voters, as did his opponents' pillorying him as an ignorant demagogue. His Protestant-based biblical moralism pushed away Catholics, a traditional Democratic party base. Bryan's antibusiness rhetoric made Bourbon Democrats uncomfortable. The sense that he had turned the Democratic Party into something of a cult of personality made anyone who cared about democracy wary. Only one Democrat won the White House during the entire Fourth Party System—Woodrow Wilson, who only won because Teddy Roosevelt splintered the Republican vote. Democrats under Bryan's leadership did worse than the Democrats of the post-Reconstruction era. There's a lot of reasons a campaign consultant wouldn't want to copy the polarizing style and tactics of William Jennings Bryan. Yet despite these faults as a party strategist, Bryan succeeded in sparking fundamental transformation of American politics, leading the smoothest party system transition in American history.

The realignment of 1896 is a model for how everything during a realignment can go right. Instead of sitting back and letting a realignment happen, America can rush into one on its own terms. Instead of waiting for a party collapse, America can instead choose a renewal that quickly rights the national ship and points it back toward stability. The result is not only a fast transition to a new party system built around the next era's great debate, but also a debate we choose instead of one that unpredictable events force upon us. A national party renewal rescues the American people from the fear and pain of living through decades of turbulent, difficult, and scary times. At worst, it involves a few spirited political campaigns. Instead of hiding from inevitable change, America can reshape its parties by choice.

Realignments don't have to be disasters. They can be opportunities.

CHAPTER 5

AMERICA'S FIFTH PARTY SYSTEM: HOW THE NEW DEAL FORGED THE PARTIES WE KNOW

In 1928, America was a confident and prosperous nation of flappers and speakeasies reveling in exciting new technologies like aeroplanes and telephones. Amid such easy prosperity, America's political parties mainly fretted over cultural issues like re-litigating the national ban on "demon rum." By 1932, the prosperous flappers and gin-drinkers of the Roaring Twenties were living in the squalor of shantytowns, relying on breadlines and soup kitchens just to eat. People's minds no longer focused on cultural battles but on putting food on their tables and clothes on their backs. No longer a haughty new world power, America now flinched in fear as totalitarian dictatorships spread across Europe. It's hard to fathom what that was like—so rich and comfortable and confident in one moment, and so poor and desperate and scared the next. This national disaster called the Great Depression created America's modern political parties.

Before the Great Depression, America had two political parties, the Democrats and the Republicans. Yet those parties consisted of completely different coalitions of people, who believed a completely different mix of ideas, wrapped into two completely different ideologies, than the Democrats and Republicans of today. When the world fell apart during the Depression, those parties fell apart with it. When America finally made its way through to the other side of the economic catastrophe and a global war, it had two different parties still called Republicans and Democrats but now representing a different mix of people and standing for very different things. The story of our modern Republican and Democratic Parties begins with the destruction of the old ones during the Great Depression and their rebirth during the administration of Franklin Roosevelt.

HOW THE DEPRESSION DESTROYED AMERICA'S PARTIES

When the stock market crashed in 1929, Republican Herbert Hoover had only been president for eight months. He won the White House in a landslide in 1928 over New York governor Al Smith in a campaign fought largely over Prohibition, even though Prohibition was already the law. Although you would never guess it from his reputation today, Hoover actually had one of the most distinguished backgrounds of any American president ever. He was an efficiency whiz kid from his party's progressive wing—he supported Teddy Roosevelt's Progressive Party campaign in 1912—who rose to national acclaim as one of the most successful commerce secretaries in American history under Presidents Harding and Coolidge. He was a Stanford-educated mining engineer whose work earned him an international reputation and personal fortune, had lived in various places around the world, spoke Mandarin Chinese, and wrote an academic mining treatise still in use today.[1] He was something of a military hero, having stepped up as a civilian to play a key role in the defense of the American embassy in China when trapped there under siege during the Boxer Rebellion. He was also a renowned humanitarian, having organized, on his own initiative, a massive humanitarian relief mission during the First World War that both helped stranded Americans escape home to the United States and fed and clothed European civilians. At every stage of life, Hoover displayed unusual competence, expertise, and a noble heart. He seemed the perfect president to have at the helm during a national economic meltdown—educated, a self-made businessman, knowledgeable about economics, popular, compassionate, and a wonkish efficiency expert.

Hoover was a perfect president for the Roaring Twenties, elected amid broad prosperity after America's populist and progressive reforms had tamed the excesses of industrialization. With the First World War behind it, America settled fat and happy into its new role as a strong, modern, rich world power. The progressive movement had mostly burned out after putting its great reforms into place. The Fourth Party System's debates over the abuses and downsides of industrialization now over, a new modern economy emerged like a butterfly out of the pain of late nineteenth-century economic disruption. Politics turned trivial in the careless way of a nation enjoying its well-earned respite from worries or consequence because there was little left to debate. Between the flood of petty scandals from the charming but incompetent Harding, and the boring steady hand of Silent Cal, American government was coasting by and things were going well. Then the stock market crashed and the economy fell apart, beginning the most devastating economic crisis in American history.

When the Depression struck, Hoover saw the task for government as cushioning the blow of the downturn the best it could as the nation waited the crisis out. It's a popular presumption that Hoover failed to more aggressively address the destruction of the Depression because, as a pro-business Republican, he wasn't ideologically inclined to wield federal power to combat economic suffering. Except Hoover wasn't a modern free-market libertarian but a progressive who quietly modeled his presidency around Teddy Roosevelt's ideals.[2] Hoover's failure to do more was less a failure of ideology than one of judgment and degree.[3] America had endured an almost constant cycle of major economic crises before the 1920s—the Panic of 1837, the Panic of 1857, the Panic of 1873, and the Panic of 1893. Each time before, the American economy crashed for a few years and ultimately recovered, leading to another boom. Hoover, like many people, expected the Great Depression would follow the same progression.[4] He initially viewed his role as a moral leader who would cheerlead America through the crisis and encourage voluntary measures to address the social ills of the collapse.[5] As the Depression progressed, Hoover reached for various policy tools he thought might help cushion the downturn until it inevitably turned. He launched a flurry of new regulations and programs to right the economy. He founded the Reconstruction Finance Corporation to get banks making loans. He worked with unions and industry to keep wages high, and he signed the Davis-Bacon Act to make governments pay union wages. He hiked tariffs in the protectionist Smoot-Hawley Tariff Act in an attempt to protect American jobs. He steeply raised taxes on the wealthy and corporations to pay for these programs to cover declining national tax revenue.[6] After each action, Hoover professed to America that the worst was over. Each time, the Depression got more terrible. Only after the crisis had worsened, and then came to seem never-ending, did it become apparent substantial intervention or even structural reform might be necessary. By then it was too late.

By the end of Hoover's term, unemployment was just shy of 25 percent.[7] Shantytowns—which people mockingly called "Hoover-villes"—were springing up across America to shelter more and more unemployed Americans. Over the course of just one presidential term, America had tumbled from the golden prosperity of the Roaring Twenties into the abject misery of the 1930s.[8] As one would expect, the election of 1932 was an epic disaster for Hoover and his party. The economy was horrible, people were in pain, and no one trusted that things would ever get better. America had come to hate Hoover for presiding over the disintegration of America, and it loathed his party by extension. The Democrats nominated New York governor Franklin Roosevelt for president, the party's failed vice-presidential candidate of 1920. Ironically given what followed, Roosevelt ran a traditional campaign for a Fourth Party System Democrat, vigorously attacking Hoover's spending and deficits and pledging if elected to cut government and bureaucracy.[9] Democrats, after all, traditionally distrusted the federal government, thought federal authority should be limited, and sincerely believed in balanced budgets. Yet Roosevelt also promised that, if elected, he would bring about an end to the Depression, giving Americans a "New Deal." Voters abandoned the Republicans in droves, with even some of the most loyal Republican constituencies bolting for the Democrats. Roosevelt won forty-two of forty-eight states, leaving Hoover with only Pennsylvania and a few holdouts in Republican New England. The Republicans lost 12 seats in the Senate. They lost 101 seats in the House. Roosevelt even won about 30 percent of the African American vote, a historic break given that Republicans had consistently won well over 90 percent of the African American vote since the Civil War. Hoover received a famous telegraph during the campaign asking him to "vote for Roosevelt and make it unanimous."[10] People weren't just voting for Roosevelt. They were voting out the Republicans.

What many people didn't yet realize was that this wasn't a short-term reversal. The election of 1932 permanently destroyed the Republican Party. Many of those traditional Republican voters were never coming back.

FRANKLIN ROOSEVELT CREATES THE NEW DEAL

Franklin Roosevelt wasn't a conviction politician, a political philosopher, or a policy wonk. He wasn't one of those politicians who spend decades defining their beliefs, seeking national office to implement a well-considered plan of change.[11] Roosevelt had always been an ordinary office seeker representing the established Democratic Party and its platform with a dose of pragmatism and executive competence. When he promised to bring "a new deal for the American people," it wasn't an ideological promise to change the direction of American government but rather a stray phrasing in a speech that captured the attention of the press.[12] Roosevelt's policy pronouncements during his campaign had been jumbled, often contradictory, and included few of the policies that would come to define his New Deal later.[13] Winning the White House, however, made Roosevelt directly responsible for doing what he had attacked Hoover for failing to do—devising a program to end the most devastating economic disaster in American history. Desperate for results and mindful of Hoover's fate, Roosevelt decided to throw every idea he could find at the crisis to see if any might stick.

During the campaign, Roosevelt had already collected a group of intellectuals and academics to help with policy.[14] Once in office, with this group as a nucleus, Roosevelt assembled the best public-policy minds he could find to address the crisis. The group, which added and lost members over time, originally centered around a group of professors from Columbia University like law professors Raymond Morley and Adolf Berle and economist Rex Tugwell, and later revolved around Harvard lawyers like Ben Cohen and Felix Frankfurter, alongside the brightest lights of Roosevelt's cabinet such as Interior Secretary Harold Ickes and Labor Secretary Frances Perkins. Roosevelt wasn't partisan in these appointments, stocking his intellectual team and his administration with a fair number of progressives with Republican backgrounds, including some of its most influential members, like Berle, Ickes, Perkins, and Frankfurter.[15] As the New Deal progressed, it also wasn't at all unusual for the New Dealers to appoint progressive Republicans instead of Democratic regulars to local New Deal positions, to the irritation of local Democratic politicians expecting opportunities for patronage.[16] This wasn't without intent. Roosevelt admired the progressivism of his relative Theodore, and he sincerely hoped progressive Republicans might join the Democrats in a future "realignment of parties."[17] Roosevelt empowered these experts with extraordinary authority to devise aggressive new ideas to bring the Depression to an end. This group of academic policy advisers came to be known as Roosevelt's "brains trust," popularizing the term. This brain trust created the substance of the New Deal.

Contrary to popular belief, the brain trust's New Deal plan wasn't to spend a great deal of money in a massive burst of Keynesian stimulus.[18] That was one result, but it was hardly the motivation at the time. Most of the early New Dealers distrusted spending as a policy mechanism, either out of fiscal conservatism or the belief that spending was a temporary patch that covered up the need for more fundamental reform.[19] Roosevelt himself not only ran his campaign on balanced budgets, but like most politicians of his era he genuinely believed in them. Deficit spending to Roosevelt was a necessary evil to endure in order to finance emergency programs, not a goal to enthusiastically pursue. To prove himself a fiscal conservative, Roosevelt even made significant cuts to balance the "regular" federal budget, as distinct from the increase in spending in the "emergency" budget of measures to fight the Depression. The central ideal behind Franklin Roosevelt's first term New Deal agenda wasn't to spend money but—counterintuitively to us today—to raise prices.

The New Dealers, mainly adherents of the New Nationalism progressivism of Teddy Roosevelt, thought the competitive free market was outdated and that a modern society required a cooperatively managed economy of government, industry, and labor.[20] They believed "competition in most of its forms is wasteful and costly" and that "unrestricted individual competition is the death, not the life, of trade."[21] They therefore believed the solution to the Depression was to accept concentrations of power and "bigness," but to control and harness it to impose rational planning on the economy's natural chaos. They further believed too much competition in an economic depression was harmful because it drove down prices, which then drove down wages as businesses lost revenue. Higher prices, they believed, would create healthier firms by increasing their revenue. Those healthier firms could in turn hire more workers and raise wages, increasing employment and the welfare of workers. To this way of thinking, kick-starting the economy would require eliminating so-called "ruinous price competition" between firms. Instead of competing against each other through market competition, firms needed to cooperate to boost their profits. Then government could help coordinate those healthier firms to collectively raise wages and improve working conditions.[22] Roosevelt's brain trust began boldly experimenting with every activist policy proposal they thought might increase economic coordination, raise prices, and thereby increase employment.

Some of what the New Dealers tried were simply more aggressive versions of things Hoover had already cautiously tried. Hoover spearheaded unprecedented federal spending in public works to create jobs, totaling billions of dollars, and poured federal money into subsidizing home mortgage loans to save people's homes. Roosevelt's team expanded these initiatives and sent even more federal money to states and localities to create jobs through the building of public works. Roosevelt's team launched an overhaul of the nation's securities and banking laws modeled on prior work of the Hoover administration, creating the modern securities laws and the Securities and Exchange Commission. Roosevelt's team put Americans directly to work on public infrastructure projects financed under the new Public Works Administration and put many unemployed young men to work in environmental conservation on public land under the Civil Conservation Corps.[23] They bailed out cash-strapped state and local governments and provided matching funds for them to provide direct relief to citizens. Roosevelt's team also targeted hard-hit rural areas with a rural electrification program and rural poverty programs. The centerpiece of the New Deal, however, which many Americans came to see as the New Deal itself, was its twin economic recovery administrations—the Agricultural Adjustment Administration, regulating the farm economy, and the National Recovery Administration, regulating the industrial economy.[24] Both programs had the goal of eliminating competition to drive up prices.

The agricultural program was the simpler of the two programs. The Agricultural Adjustment Administration, or AAA, created a powerful agency with immense discretion to raise farm prices by limiting the production of food, along with some ancillary measures like regulating marketing.[25] In practice, the government effectively paid farmers to slaughter a portion of their animals, burn a certain portion of their crops, and leave some of their productive farmland fallow, in order to reduce the overall national supply of food and agricultural products such as cotton.[26] The more daring effort of the New Dealers, however, was the National Industrial Recovery Act, which created a National Recovery Administration, or NRA, with a mandate to coordinate the industrial economy. The NRA empowered leaders in each industry to design comprehensive "competition codes" for all firms to follow. The codes were technically voluntary, but only firms that agreed to join their industry's NRA regime could display the Blue Eagle placard in their business or on their product—and the government had, with much success, vigorously encouraged citizens to boycott any business unpatriotic enough not to do its part under the NRA, making the codes practically mandatory.[27] The government even launched a national campaign to ensure compliance, which included the largest parade in New York City's history, with a quarter million Americans marching for the Blue Eagle.[28] NRA codes governed in detail how each business could create products, how they could sell them, and the minimum prices they could charge. The NRA ultimately approved thousands of rules affecting the specific conduct of every conceivable industry, totaling millions of pages. It also created various boards and authorities, both national and local, to promulgate rules and interpret them, and in some circumstances these were enforced by the courts. Hugh Johnson, former general, businessman, and Roosevelt brain trust member, headed the powerful new agency.[29]

The NRA intended to coordinate business, labor, and government under a united national industrial policy. It effectively sought to organize American industry into managed industrial cartels run by the heads of the most powerful firms and unions to create a more "rational" industrial policy that was less competitive but more predictable and stable.[30] The NRA seems strange today, as the very small-business entrepreneurial energy that many Americans now see as key to a healthy economy—challenging major firms with new innovations and nimble ways—was the threat the NRA sought to stamp out. Novel practices or new methods that make one firm more competitive put downward price pressure on all firms, even forcing some out of business. Forcing every firm to follow the same practices ensures every firm can comfortably compete. The New Dealers hoped this more planned economy would eliminate "ruinous competition" between firms, which they believed was holding down prices and thus wages.

Roosevelt's First New Deal agenda marked a radical departure for the Democrats. The Democratic Party had always taken pride in its Jeffersonian legacy as the party of strong states and small national government. Since the very beginning of the party, Democrats resisted expensive plans for national infrastructure projects and modernization schemes. Traditionally, Democrats didn't like big business, or, really, big anything.[31] The First New Deal's expansive projects to centrally manage the economy, build national infrastructure, and provide employment to hordes of unemployed young men ran directly counter to everything for which Democrats had always stood. It had always been Federalists, Whigs, and Republicans who promoted the national industrial policies, internal improvements, and American Systems that Democrats fought fiercely against. Roosevelt's New Deal was progressivism, and not Wilsonian small-government "progressivism" but the progressivism of Teddy

Roosevelt's New Nationalism.[32] The Democrats under the First New Deal weren't simply expanding the size of the federal government. They had thrown in their lot with bigness—big business, big labor, and experts engaged in national planning in a powerful federal government.[33]

As Roosevelt reached the end of his first term, this First New Deal agenda ran into resistance. Roosevelt remained popular, as did his New Deal in general, yet the crown jewels of his agenda, the NRA and the AAA, had raised hackles. The AAA wasn't wildly popular for the obvious reason that, at a time when many Americans were literally going hungry, the government was paying farmers to slaughter pigs, spike fruit with kerosene to turn it inedible, and burn bushels of corn—all to drive up the price of food that many Americans already couldn't afford.[34] What's more, while the program benefited larger farmers, it devastated small farmers and sharecroppers. When the government ordered landowners to leave land fallow, many landowners pushed sharecroppers off their land while continuing to farm the remainder themselves.[35] The program drove up agriculture prices as intended, making larger agricultural businesses more profitable, but at the expense of poorer farmers and sharecroppers who now could no longer make a living at all. Yet problems with the NRA dwarfed those of the AAA.

The NRA effectively granted code-making power to the leaders of the most powerful firms in each industry. Allowing the largest and most politically connected businesses to dictate the daily minutia of how their smaller and less powerful competitors had to conduct business led to the inevitable abuses of rule-making power to hinder rivals.[36] Many also feared businesses were using their code-making power to raise prices without also increasing production or wages, taking the extra profit for themselves.[37] As complaints mounted, the Senate created an independent review board to assess the NRA codes, appointing the highly respected lawyer Clarence Darrow to lead it. Given Darrow's political views, Roosevelt expected him to be friendly to his New Deal centerpiece. Darrow instead issued three blistering reports that charged business leaders with abusing NRA codes to eliminate low-cost competitors they didn't like, insulating themselves into cartels and monopolies, and creating rules that were ultimately bad for consumers.[38] Embarrassed, the administration attempted to sideline Darrow's review board until, after the third report, Darrow resigned in frustration. Roosevelt abolished the review board by executive order.

High-handed enforcement of the NRA codes also led to stark injustices. Journalist John Flynn, once a populist Democrat and early Roosevelt supporter who later became a harsh Roosevelt critic, authored the famous 1948 *Roosevelt Myth*, in which he wrote about the enforcement regime:

> Only the most violent police methods could procure enforcement [of the NRA codes]. In Sidney Hillman's garment industry the code authority employed enforcement police. They roamed through the garment district like storm troopers. They could enter a man's factory, send him out, line up his employees, subject them to minute interrogation, take over his books on the instant. Night work was forbidden. Flying squadrons of these private coat-and-suit police went through the district at night, battering down doors with axes looking for men who were committing the crime of sewing together a pair of pants at night.[39]

Another famous incident that garnered national attention involved a New Jersey tailor named Jacob Maged. A New Jersey Court sentenced Maged, a Polish immigrant, to serve thirty days in prison and pay a hundred-dollar fine for pressing a suit for 35 cents when the New Jersey state NRA had set the price at 40 cents.[40] After a public outcry at the injustice, the judge released him after serving only three days of the sentence, but not without giving him a public lecture from the bench about the importance of the NRA, the government's war on "price cutters," and the value of community. According to the *New York Times*, the judge "gave him a little lecture on the importance of cooperation as opposed to individualism" and told him he "should uphold the president and his plan."[41]

By 1934, many former Roosevelt allies from the old populist Democratic Party base had reached a breaking point with the First New Deal. Since Jefferson and Jackson, the Democratic Party was proudly suspicious of federal power. It was the Democrats who long opposed national authority, championing the power of states. Democrats fought against the crusading moral reforms of Whig and Republican elites. Democrats distrusted national economic and industrial policy as sops to bankers, speculators, and industrialists living in far-off places like New York City, prizing instead the common sense of ordinary people who labored on farms and worked with their hands. Democrats opposed national efforts to modernize the economy with national industrial policies like Henry Clay's American System. The elite-driven NRA schemes and public works projects of the First New Deal looked to these populist-minded Democrats like a betrayal of everything for which the Democratic Party had always stood.[42] Some Democrats blamed the deviation on Roosevelt welcoming so many Republican progressives to infiltrate his administration.[43] These critics weren't just a party fringe, but included many of the most important Democrats of the preceding era including its most recent presidential nominees, John W. Davis and Al Smith, both of whom viewed Roosevelt's New Deal with disgust as a repudiation of Democratic Party principles.[44]

The populist base of the Democratic Party found its champion in Senator Huey Long, the rabble-rousing Democratic boss of Louisiana. Long rose to national attention as Louisiana's governor during the late 1920s by turning the state's poor and working class against its former ruling elites. Long was brash, unconstrained by democratic tradition, and sometimes thuggish. As governor, he converted the Louisiana government into a powerful and often vindictive political machine loyal only to him, hounding enemies out of jobs, harassing journalists, and collecting funds through corruption to reward allies. Armed state policemen constantly followed Long around as personal guards in a show of force.[45] Yet Long actively used his vast power to shower tangible benefits on the poor and working Louisianans who enthusiastically supported him. He used the money taken from wealthy elites and corporations to build hospitals, erect public works, and provide free schoolbooks to children.[46] While maintaining his complete control over Louisiana from the Senate, in 1934 Long brought his populist revolt national. Attacking Roosevelt as a rich man in bed with bankers and businessmen, and his New Deal as a useless program that left the rich man rich without relieving the masses,[47] Long proposed a plan he called "Share Our Wealth" that promised to make "every man a king." Long's plan would cap personal fortunes and limit top incomes by confiscating all income over one million dollars and personal fortunes over five million to guarantee every American a minimum income, free college education, old-age pensions, veteran's benefits, a free month's vacation, and a maximum thirty-hour work week.[48] The plan became a movement that spread over America, with struggling Americans forming their own "Share our Wealth Clubs," which reached eight million members.[49]

Long was not alone. Long and his "Share Our Wealth" plan had vocal support from another former Roosevelt supporter, the famous radio priest Father Charles Coughlin.[50] Coughlin, whose talk radio show reached millions of Americans, was now attacking Roosevelt as a tool of big business and the banks.[51] In fact, Coughlin was attacking all of modern capitalism, and he announced his own movement, the National Union for Social Justice, backing policies like income guarantees, high taxes on the rich, labor protections, and public control of industry for the public good.[52] Around the same time, a California medical doctor, Francis Townsend, began attracting national attention for his "Townsend Plan," which would provide publicly funded old-age pensions for every American.[53] In a nation in which the Depression had forced older Americans to helplessly scrounge for food on the streets, the popularity of Townsend's plan boomed, so he began organizing across America for its adoption—and attacking Roosevelt for refusing to endorse him and his plan.[54] Roosevelt and his New Deal were under assault from legions of populist Democrats who believed his administration had sold out poor and working people to benefit big business and the rich. Long was clearly gearing up to challenge Roosevelt for the White House in 1936.[55] Roosevelt, who believed Long was a dangerous threat to the republic, feared he might win.[56]

In response to these populist attacks, Roosevelt's brain trust pivoted in 1935 to create a "Second New Deal."[57] Around this time, the influence in Roosevelt's brain trust was shifting away from the Teddy Roosevelt–style New Nationalism progressives, who disliked spending and liked bigness, toward acolytes of Wilson's New Freedom like Louis Brandeis and Felix Frankfurter, who didn't mind spending and distrusted big business—and this new agenda reflected it.[58] While the First New Deal was a progressive program to rationally plan the economy through expertise, the Second New Deal would be a populist attempt to steal Huey Long's thunder. The crown jewel of this Second New Deal agenda was a new old-age pension program modeled on the Townsend plan called Social Security, which provided federal social insurance payments in the case of old age or disability. In answer to Long's Share Our Wealth plan, Roosevelt pushed through a tax hike on the richest Americans with the Wealth Tax Act, which came to be called the "Soak the Rich Tax." Roosevelt's tax plan included a new top marginal tax rate of 79 percent specifically tailored to target one man, John Rockefeller. It also imposed a new tax on the undistributed income of corporations to force them to pay out wages and dividends. In addition to all that, the Roosevelt administration created programs explicitly meant to benefit organized labor, workers, the poor, and even African Americans, such as a new Works Progress Administration. The WPA employed millions of unemployed Americans to create federal projects in nearly every community in America, including parks, roads, public buildings, and bridges, and also funded the works of writers and artists. The Wagner Act created the modern labor union law regime of recognition and collective bargaining. The Fair Labor Standards Act created a minimum wage and maximum work hours—although the terms were far less generous than the ones Long proposed.[59] Roosevelt, around this time, even began to identify with Andrew Jackson.[60] Roosevelt's stark shift from the progressive First New Deal to the populist Second New Deal shored up his exposed flank. Long didn't challenge Roosevelt in 1936—in fact, an assassin shot and killed him at the end of 1935—and although the supporters of Long, Coughlin, and Townsend attempted to join forces in a third-party challenge in 1936, it was a failure.[61]

The synthesis of the radically different First and Second New Deals, however, birthed a new American political ideology. The First New Deal was progressive in its confidence in business and its comfort with further empowering corporate leaders, highly educated professionals, and others with great social and economic power. The NRA and the AAA worked with the powerful, deferring to their wisdom and increasing their influence while disregarding the interests of—and at times even victimizing—small-business owners, immigrant shopkeepers, and sharecropper farmers. These programs valued the rational and utilitarian management and stability of the greater system over the interests of the weak, establishing rules that made the rich and powerful more rich and powerful, sent struggling tailors to prison, and pushed penniless sharecroppers off their land as an unfortunate but fair cost to advance the greater good of a larger plan. The Second New Deal did the opposite. Minimum wage laws, Social Security, boastfully punitive taxes on the rich, and vigorous protection of labor unions were about using government to redistribute power and wealth from the rich and powerful to ordinary citizens. In the Second New Deal, progressives put their ideas about planning, modernization, and social science in the service of the populism of Long and Coughlin. What emerged was a new hybrid ideology merging progressivism into traditional Democratic populism. It was progressive in its confidence that neutral experts can use knowledge and planning to continually push the nation toward progress. It was populist in defining progress as moving toward a society that sided with the people against the elite, particularly in empowering the least well off. At the time, it was a surprising synergy. Populists and progressives came from different parts of society, and up to that point in history were mainly on opposite sides of the political debate. Their unlikely combination, something that could only have happened in the heat of the Great Depression, created a new political ideology unlike anything existing in America before. We call that ideology New Deal liberalism.

Roosevelt's New Deal liberalism embodied a new idea about the role of government—that it both could and should plan and coordinate an increasingly complicated industrial society to benefit workers and the least well off. Planners could regulate markets and banks to avoid booms and busts. They could provide work to eliminate economic hardship. They could ensure capital, labor, and government worked together in harmony to plan business processes. They could use taxes and regulations to engineer fairness and allocate wealth. They could leverage resources to provide public works and modernize rural areas across America. Using the modern tools of social science, experts could coordinate and supervise the countless moving parts of the industrial economy to impose rational planning and stability, eliminating chaos and ensuring things never again got so out of hand. Traditional progressivism was moralistic, hoping to improve the lower classes to remake them into mirrors of their upstanding betters. Roosevelt's ideology wasn't about improving the working class and the poor but putting progressivism to work in their service. Traditional populism was suspicious of reformer elites wielding federal power. Roosevelt's ideology trusted it could enlist these reformers as allies. This new ideology, unlike anything that had existed before, has been the heart of the Democratic Party ever since.

THE REACTION AGAINST THE NEW DEAL

Franklin Roosevelt and his New Deal were overwhelmingly popular, but not with everyone. Some people didn't just oppose the New Deal. They feared it and despised the man who implemented it as a tyrant and traitor. From where we stand today, this terrified opposition seems overwrought if not unhinged. Most Americans now consider Roosevelt and his New Deal to be national high points. Roosevelt is mainly remembered as a kindly man in a wheelchair who led America through the Depression with folksy fireside chats and then navigated it through a world war with steely determination. His New Deal not only doesn't seem radical, it now seems traditional and even a bit archaic—a quaint collection of boring government agencies like the FCC and SEC, public-works spending at the time of high unemployment, and some of the most popular government programs ever created, like Social Security. It's easy to forget that, for Americans living through the 1930s, the New Deal was a radical and terrifying revolution imposed at a deeply unstable time in which it was reasonable to fear that the republic might even crumble.

The Great Depression inflicted unthinkable economic pain on ordinary Americans at a scale almost difficult for us to fathom. Overnight, a rich and confident nation had plunged into a desperate and insecure one. In the Depression's first years, American industrial production fell by almost half.[62] The stock market dropped by almost 90 percent. At least a quarter of the nation's working population was unemployed. People who thought of themselves as middle class were now living like desperate refugees in their own country. When looking at old photos of Americans suffering through this national devastation the way we look at photos of starving people in war zones, it's sometimes hard to remember that these miserable people hadn't always lived like this. Just a few years before, they were ordinary Americans enjoying comfortable lives in the easy prosperity of the Roaring Twenties. Somebody had suddenly taken all that away, and now they were struggling to survive. As one would expect, the catastrophe caused a widespread collapse in faith in America's government, but also in the republic itself. In 1932, over twenty thousand First World War veterans, many unemployed and homeless, marched on Washington demanding early payment of the "bonus" they had been promised they would receive in 1945. This "Bonus Army" built elaborate camps outside the Capitol, where they organized and even held drills. Some in government feared they might attempt a coup, so they sent in the army. General Douglas MacArthur flooded the camps with tear gas and then charged the veterans with cavalry backed by six tanks under the command of George Patton.[63] America was on the brink of collapse.

That people might rise up to demand radical change that might topple the republic was hardly impossible. Just as the nation transformed into a true industrial power, its economy had melted down, leaving ordinary people in misery. People began to wonder whether the American system, designed for a preindustrial agrarian economy, might be inadequate to govern a complex industrial economy. Perhaps liberal democracy and decentralized market capitalism weren't up to the task of administering a vastly larger nation of millions with automobiles, telephones, and factories. Maybe the problem was democracy, capitalism, and the American constitutional system itself?[64] It became fashionable in many circles to believe that the Depression had proved America's political and economic system, built ages ago to govern a colonial outpost of independent farmers, was outdated.[65] Nor was this wholly irrational. While we often talk about the Great Depression as a global phenomenon, it was really a crisis of Western democratic capitalism. Other systems of government, with strong centralized states, didn't experience the Depression in the same way as liberal-democratic nations with laissez-faire capitalism. Germany as a parliamentary democracy suffered perhaps the worst depression of any Western nation, with employment falling from 20 million Germans to only 11.4 million, while the registered unemployed rose from 1.25 million to 6 million.[66] When Hitler and the Nazis came to power, unemployment fell until Germany reached nearly full employment.[67] The Soviet Union, a state-directed communist economy with state-directed employment, wasn't directly affected by the global depression in the same way as the world's capitalist economies.[68] The Soviet economy was rapidly industrializing, driven by demanding national plans.[69] The planning and agricultural collectivization policies the Soviet regime employed to achieve such growth was of course in reality often inefficient, produced substandard products, induced shortages, and spread misery across large portions of the Soviet population, including a brutal famine in Ukraine— facts mostly hidden at the time to the West.[70] To Americans, the Soviet Union looked to be thriving as their own country struggled.[71]

Maybe, people wondered, prosperity in the modern era required a more planned and centralized state like the ones that fascist or communist regimes provided. Maybe America even needed a strong dictator to set things right. Today, people often wonder why so many Americans during the 1930s openly flirted with communism or fascism. While the ranks of communist and fascist parties never swelled to directly threaten an overthrow of the government, many ordinary Americans did attend Communist Party meetings in the 1930s—to their detriment in the congressional hearings of the 1950s—while others who would have never dared to consider actually joining a fascist movement nonetheless openly admired European fascists like Mussolini and looked eagerly through their successes for lessons and models they might bring back to America.[72] Others wonder why so many Americans flocked to thuggish and authoritarian figures like Huey Long. Because the Depression was so horrible, many Americans lost faith in the republic and wondered whether the time had come to replace it with a more "modern" system built for the modern world—meaning a strong leader freely wielding public power as a benevolent dictator to manage the new economy.[73] In 1934, Congress held extensive hearings on a "Business Plot" in which a group of wealthy businessmen had allegedly sought to entice a popular Marine Corps general to lead a coup against the president with their financial backing.[74] In 1935, Sinclair Lewis wrote a popular novel, later adapted for the stage, called *It Can't Happen Here*, in which a demagogic US Senator modeled on Long transforms the country into a dictatorship after getting elected president—and people took the work seriously as a warning.[75] After becoming president, Roosevelt's adviser Adolf Berle reportedly warned him with all seriousness that his presidency would either end with an economic recovery or a revolution—and that the chance was about fifty-fifty which one it would be.[76]

Roosevelt's New Deal might have saved the republic because it assured Americans their government not only understood the gravity of the crisis but was aggressively pursuing solutions. The very fact that the New Deal was so immense, visibly radical, and a total divorce from traditional government was exactly what gave so many struggling people who had lost faith the hope it might work.[77] Had Roosevelt not restored people's hope in the republic, it's impossible to say what might have happened. America's parties would certainly have collapsed—the Republican Party under Hoover effectively already had. That collapse, however, could have unleashed unimaginable forces with unthinkable ideas. Desperate Americans might eventually have become willing to listen to something more radical, whether from a demagogue like Long, a Bonus Army–like revolt, a more competently executed Business Plot, or something worse. Had Roosevelt at the brink of disaster not pursued a course so radical it restored desperate people's faith, a catastrophic realignment could have followed, perhaps one so ugly it brought the entire republic down. Yet the same reason the New Deal restored trust to those who lost it was the reason others feared it. Confidence in the American republic had collapsed, people were desperate, many appeared open to authoritarianism, and a new president backed by an unquestioning congressional majority was pushing through radical and controversial programs, ones significantly strengthening the power of the state and the president in ways unlike anything in the history of America. Not only was the New Deal both radical and controversial, but some of its many aggressive and untried policies turned out to be unwise, poorly implemented, and constitutionally questionable. It was inevitable opposition would rise against Roosevelt and his New Deal.

In the first years of Roosevelt's administration, both the president and his New Deal enjoyed vast popular support as most Americans tacitly agreed to allow the new president as much room as he needed to tackle the Great Depression. Congress was overwhelmingly Democratic, while the progressive faction of what was left of the Republican Party tended to vote for Roosevelt's policies, so the president was free to experiment with overwhelming congressional majorities at his back. As the New Deal dragged on, however, opposition grew, much of it inside Roosevelt's dominant Democratic Party. New three-letter agencies with uncertain new powers were springing up constantly, making people uneasy. Rich farmers were profiting by destroying desperately needed food, while poor farmers were driven from their land. The government had granted leaders of the most powerful businesses the authority to make rules, resulting in millions of pages of competing mandates, directives, and interpretations from various local and national boards designed sometimes to harass competitors. Deficit spending continued, and the emergency looked like it might never end.

Most important, over time many Democrats grew wary of how starkly the New Deal had increased the president's power and the power of his government in an era in which dictatorship was spreading across the world. It was alarming when the government was employing vast armies of young men, complete with military camps and drills and uniforms, often reporting to officials appointed through political patronage for loyalty to the Democratic Party. It was alarming when businesses were asked to place government-issued Blue Eagle placards in their windows to demonstrate loyalty to the president's programs, and when the government encouraged citizens to boycott those who refused. It was alarming when the president wielded his powers to punish one specific person, as with the "Soak the Rich Tax." Above all, it was alarming when Roosevelt proposed his disastrous Court-Packing Plan.

It was inevitable that people would challenge the New Deal's programs in court, and those challenges finally reached the Supreme Court around the middle of Roosevelt's first term.[78] To little surprise, the Court held many New Deal programs unconstitutional—because according to the conventional reading of pre–New Deal Supreme Court constitutional precedent they *were* mostly unconstitutional. When drafting the New Deal in the mindset of addressing an emergency, the members of the Roosevelt administration put very little thought into how to justify their radical new ideas under existing constitutional law. Yet the New Deal was a radical innovation granting the federal government expansive powers to plan the entire agricultural and industrial economy, things the federal government had never done before, in part because no one thought it could. One Monday in May of 1935, the Court handed down three separate unanimous decisions holding that parts of Roosevelt's New Deal and actions he had taken in implementing it violated the Constitution. New Dealers called it "Black Monday."

The most important of those three cases was *Schechter Poultry Corp. v. United States*, striking down as unconstitutional the First New Deal's centerpiece, the National Recovery Administration.[79] The government had charged four Jewish immigrants, the Schechter brothers, with violating their industry's NRA code in their kosher poultry business in Brooklyn for failing to follow rules for slaughtering chickens that clashed with Jewish dietary laws. When the Schechters refused to alter their slaughtering practices, the government sent them to prison. The Court held the conviction unconstitutional because Congress couldn't constitutionally delegate its lawmaking power to the code-making authorities under the NRA, and because, under the Constitution's Commerce Clause, it couldn't regulate activity that didn't actually cross a state line. The government couldn't just claim, as it had, that the entire national poultry industry was one great interstate market.[80] The Court's reasoning threatened the entire New Deal.

The sole constitutional justification for much of the New Deal program was Congress's power to regulate interstate commerce. If the federal government could only regulate actual commerce crossing state lines, much of the New Deal would collapse. It's said the decision drove Roosevelt into a rage, convincing him that the Supreme Court had become his enemy and the chief obstacle to his presidency.[81]

Modern commentary tends to describe the clash between the Court and the Roosevelt administration in terms of "conservative" and "liberal" politics, noting a majority of the justices had been Republican appointees—although at a time when Republicans were progressives. The disagreement was less partisan or policy-driven than philosophical.[82] A bloc of the Court dubbed the "Four Horsemen" (which included two Republicans and two Democrats, one appointed by a Republican) believed in a "formalist" view of the Constitution, construing it strictly according to traditional meanings—thus striking down New Deal innovations.[83] The "Three Musketeers," on the other hand, were Roosevelt's appointees (including a Republican) who believed in what Oliver Wendell Holmes once claimed was a Constitution that acts like a live organism, a living Constitution the interpretation of which judges pragmatically adjust over time—thus wanting to evolve constitutional understandings to uphold what they saw as needed New Deal programs.[84] Two swing votes drifted toward the Horsemen.[85]

Roosevelt first attempted to rally the public against the Court, attacking its "horse-and-buggy definition of interstate commerce" on the radio, which to his surprise earned him significant backlash from the public.[86] As he weathered several more adverse rulings, including one striking down the AAA,[87] Roosevelt looked for another strategy. In 1937, he settled on a bill giving him authority to immediately appoint a new justice for every justice over the age of seventy, claiming it necessary to reduce the workload on older justices. The Constitution doesn't specifically set out the number of Supreme Court justices, leaving the court's size to Congress. As the republic grew in its early years, Congress had added justices over time, settling on nine in 1869. Nonetheless, everyone immediately saw through Roosevelt's weak justifications about the age and workload of the justices to understand the implications of what he proposed.[88] Roosevelt's plan allowed him to instantly appoint six new justices, giving him nine safe votes and a friendly majority. Justice Louis Brandeis, the oldest justice and a strong Roosevelt ally on the Court, was personally insulted.[89] Opponents called it an attempted coup of a coequal branch of government to bring the entire federal machine under Roosevelt's control.

Debate over the Court-Packing bill in Congress was intense, and opposition among congressional Democrats made it doubtful it would pass. John Nance Garner, Roosevelt's formerly loyal vice president, left Washington to publicly distance himself from the president he served.[90] In the middle of contentious Senate hearings, the Supreme Court handed down a collection of opinions upholding New Deal programs. Justice Owen Roberts, a swing vote, switched his allegiance to the Musketeers. Soon after, Justice Willis Van Devanter, one of the Horsemen, announced his retirement. The Court had sent Roosevelt a message—it would give him what he wanted to save the court's integrity as an institution.[91] Roberts's vote is called the "switch in time that saved nine" because, by making the controversial bill unnecessary, Roberts gave Congress the rationale and leverage it needed to force Roosevelt to drop his unwise crusade against the Court.[92] After the Roberts switch, the Court now became a consistent New Deal ally, working to justify instead of strike down New Deal programs. A few years later, it even overturned *Schechter Poultry*, holding that Congress could, under its commerce power, regulate anything that affected interstate commerce in some way—turning the Commerce Clause into the de facto general legislative power it still serves as today, since just about everything theoretically affects commerce in some way. Roosevelt got his constitutional revolution, but at a steep price.

For many Democrats, a direct attack on the American constitutional system of checks and balances was a step too far. When added to the already-controversial First New Deal, the Second New Deal controversies—the "socialism" of Social Security, the openly punitive "Soak the Rich Tax," and the new armies of young men in federal work programs—had hardened congressional resistance to any radical new programs or government innovations.[93] Then the economy crashed again in late 1937, erasing most of the New Deal economic recovery and beginning what many called "Roosevelt's Depression." After that, Roosevelt, during the 1938 midterm elections, ordered a ruthless "purge" in party primaries of disloyal Democrats whom he felt had insufficiently backed his New Deal.[94] When most of the targets of Roosevelt's purge were reelected despite the intervention, a new Congress returned quite unhappy with the president. For the first time, a significant portion of Roosevelt's own party broke with him. Traditional Democrats, particularly in the South, now agreed that Roosevelt was driving too much change too fast, and that not all of it was consistent with the American system they knew.[95]

A group of Democrats reached across the aisle in Congress to form a coalition with disaffected Republicans to stop any further expansion of the New Deal. This informal alliance took on a name, the "conservative coalition."[96] The ideology of the members of this coalition wasn't exactly "conservative" in the ideological sense in which we use that word now. Many Republicans in Congress at the time, first elected in a prior era, held strongly progressive views. Many Democrats in this coalition believed they were also progressive, although of the Wilsonian New Freedom variety that was their party's heritage. They were conservatives in the sense by which people used the word then, to mean anyone opposing the New Deal. Enough anti–New Deal Democrats now joined this ad hoc alliance with congressional Republicans that Roosevelt would never expand his New Deal further. The Democrats continued to control the federal government for years more. New Deal programs already enacted would not be repealed. The New Deal would remain America's dominant national frame for government for generations. For now, however, this was as far as it would go.

CREATING THE MODERN REPUBLICAN PARTY

While Franklin Roosevelt held office, the Republican Party remained weak and disorganized. Republicans not only struggled to win elections, but the party struggled to define exactly what it believed in Roosevelt's new political era. For a time, many progressive Republicans insisted their party's best path forward was to re-embrace its progressive heritage, including those parts of the New Deal founded in progressive principles.[97] That, however, was never a realistic strategy. The old political party of Teddy Roosevelt and Herbert Hoover was clearly dead. In fact, in 1936 many of the most important progressive politicians, like Robert La Follette Jr. and Fiorello La Guardia, advocated for Roosevelt's reelection.[98] The only thing Republicans knew in this strange age was that the Republican Party was the political opposition to the Democrats. The arguments people used against Roosevelt and his New Deal, therefore, soon became the arguments this emerging new Republican Party would embrace.

Opponents of Roosevelt's agenda principally leveled two charges against him. First, people feared the president was seizing too much power and his government encroaching too much on traditional American liberty.[99] Whether it was all the new regulatory agencies with considerable new powers, the abuses of the National Recovery Administration, the punitive Soak the Rich tax, the Court-Packing scheme, or the overwhelming majorities of the "rubber-stamp" Congress, opponents argued the president's administration was trampling on liberty. Second, people feared Roosevelt's policies were moving the country too far and too fast, violating American traditions and potentially changing the nation's character and culture.[100] That Roosevelt's revolution in government was essentially "un-American." Whether new social welfare programs like Social Security, government centralization, cooperation between governments and unions and large corporations, armies of young men in uniforms laboring under government programs, or boycotts and Blue-Eagle placards, a lot of people saw in the New Deal something that didn't look like traditional America. They worried that people who grew up in this new society wouldn't be the same rowdy and industrious and innovative people who had streamed into the frontier, built railroad empires, or invented motor cars and airplanes. Their concern was that the New Dead would change unwritten rules intertwined in the culture of America, and that America would decline if citizens failed to accept these cultural norms and rules. It was a concern centered around what America's Founders called republican virtue—that a republic needs citizen with specific traits of character because in a republic the people choose the government. These two ideals—defending liberty against growing federal power and protecting the character of the republic—summed up the uneasy sense among the New Deal's opponents that Roosevelt's program was dangerous. These ideals thus became the arguments of the conservative coalition in Congress, and thereby the core principles identified with "conservatism." Over the years, they would develop into the core of a new Republican Party.

It's no surprise that the first organized opposition to Roosevelt and his New Deal was therefore called the American Liberty League. The league presented itself as a nonpartisan group of Republicans and Democrats organized to defend the Constitution and traditional American liberties against the New Deal. Far from a fringe group of unhappy Republicans, the League's leadership included many prominent Democrats including Al Smith, the 1928 Democrat nominee for president; John Davis, the 1924 Democratic nominee for president; and Dean Acheson, a former chair of the Democratic National Committee.[101] Heading into the 1936 election, the Roosevelt administration dismissed the League as a stalking horse for the Republican Party, and for good reason. Yet the principle around which it rallied wasn't opposition to taxes, spending, social welfare programs, or regulation. It was the cause of liberty and fidelity to the American Constitution.

The first Republican campaign of the New Deal era, that of Kansas governor Alf Landon, also centered around the theme of liberty. Landon had been a progressive Republican and was generally supportive of parts of the New Deal.[102] Yet under the influence of his party, the theme of his 1936 campaign became the defense of liberty and the Constitution. By the end of his campaign, Landon and his party charged Roosevelt with usurping the power of Congress, creating armies of bureaucrats to supervise the American people, and imposing on Americans' economic liberties:

The President spoke truly when he boasted . . . "We have built up new
instruments of public power." He spoke truly when he said these instruments could provide "shackles for the liberties of the people . . . and
. . . enslavement for the public." These powers were granted with the
understanding that they were only temporary. But after the powers had
been obtained, and after the emergency was clearly over, we were told
that another emergency would be created if the power was given up.
In other words, the concentration of power in the hands of the President was not a question of temporary emergency. It was a question of
permanent national policy. In my opinion the emergency of 1933 was
a mere excuse. . . . National economic planning—the term used by this
Administration to describe its policy—violates the basic ideals of the
American system. . . . The price of economic planning is the loss of economic freedom. And economic freedom and personal liberty go hand
in hand.[103]

Given the historical moment, the radical disruption of the New Deal
agenda, the degree of new power it invested in the president, and the over-
reaches of programs like the AAA and NRA, it was natural that opponents of Franklin Roosevelt and his New Deal agenda, whether Democratic or Republican, found common cause under the principle that the
president's policies were eroding liberty in the republic.

The second idea intertwined with these invocations of liberty was that
Roosevelt's New Deal was damaging the American system of government
and altering its national character. Attacks on the New Deal as "socialism"
that would destroy "free enterprise" and sap away "rugged individualism"
are so familiar to us now they hardly resonate. These weren't, however,
simply claims about preferred economic policies or articulations of a
reactionary fear of change. They were claims that Roosevelt's New Deal
was too radical, too fast, and that it was effectively changing the character
of America by destroying the traditions and values that had caused the
nation to thrive and prosper. As Landon's notes for his campaign's whistle-
stop speeches claimed, "We have a choice to make between the American
system of government and one that is alien to everything this country
before has known."[104] When grasping to put these feelings into words, the

New Deal's opponents often labeled it as fascist or socialist or sometimes simply un-American. They publicly worried that new programs like Social Security would sap the rugged individualism that had made America thrive. These were all ways of saying they feared Roosevelt's policies were unwittingly destroying the hidden things that had made America special and that they would ultimately break the republic. In the campaigns that followed, the union of these principles—liberty and virtue—coalesced into a new party ideology, one we now call conservatism.

In responding to the crisis of the Depression, Franklin Roosevelt ultimately played a role not unlike that of Andrew Jackson. In the wake of the Depression, Americans worried about how to adapt their institutions to the realities of a new modern industrial world of dense cities, factories, and cars. Roosevelt gave them a program drawing on both populism and progressivism, creating the foundation of the new ideology of New Deal liberalism. In reaction, an opposition coalition formed of those opposed to Roosevelt's plans, which became the nucleus for a new Republican Party. Much like Clay's Whigs, these opponents combined their various and often unrelated concerns and causes into a new ideology taking all their objections into account. It was the start of a new great national debate. On one side Roosevelt and his Democrats proposed New Deal liberalism, holding that America could design and plan a more efficient and prosperous nation that better served working people and the least well off. On the other side, Roosevelt's opponents joined together inside the shattered shell of the Republican Party, objecting to this Democratic solution as "big government" that would trample liberty and damage the culture of the republic. A new Fifth Party System was born.

Franklin Roosevelt presided over the second most dangerous time for the American republic, second only to the Civil War that literally split the nation apart. In such dark times, it's easy to imagine a different history, one in which violent riots, a coup, or the emergence of a dangerous totalitarian leader led to the death of American constitutional government. Roosevelt ushered America through this minefield in one piece and birthed institutions that became staples of American government. Yet in preserving the republic during these hard times, Roosevelt also radically transformed what America was and how it worked. Roosevelt ran for president four times and remained in office until he died. George Washington—who could have become king had he wanted it—famously relinquished the presidency after eight years to return to his farm, keeping in mind the tradition of the Roman dictator Cincinnatus who saved his country and then handed absolute power back to the Roman Senate. Every president after Washington followed his example, stepping down after two consecutive terms even when they didn't want to, and even though the Constitution didn't yet require it. To Democrats, Roosevelt's longevity in office signified the greatness of his agenda. To Republicans, it symbolized exactly why that agenda troubled them.

When Roosevelt finally left the national stage, he hadn't just transformed his party. He had guided America into a great realignment, sparking a new national debate between New Deal liberalism and modern conservatism. Ever since, these two ideologies have dominated America's national discourse. The way America has talked about, debated, and even thought about every national issue since 1932 has always come down to this same ideological fight. On one side stands the principles of populism and progressivism. On the other side stands the principles of liberty and virtue. That's what the Fifth Party System, forged in the Great Depression and then fought across decades of elections through to today, has really been about. For the better part of a century, often without realizing it, America's parties—and all of America—have battled over Franklin Roosevelt and his New Deal.

CHAPTER 6

THE LIBERAL AND CONSERVATIVE MYTH

The left-right political spectrum is a myth. No great divide slashes across the electorate, cleanly separating humanity into two political tribes. Neither the "left" and "right," nor "liberals" and "conservatives," represent naturally occurring divisions in humanity. Human history isn't a tale of two eternal forces, the armies of the left and the right, clashing from age to age through issues and empires. There were no liberals or conservatives, as we currently define those terms, in the court of Henry IV or the councils of the Chinese Emperors or among the electors of the Holy Roman Empire. The political battles in the ancient Rome Senate weren't the same as the battles we now wage in the modern American Senate, with business suits in place of togas. These two great political identities we frequently portray as though they're natural features of humanity are, in reality, little more than temporary alliances that unite inconsistent principles, holding squabbling groups together around ideologies built to address the questions of a specific time and place. Democracies naturally divide society into two roughly equal coalitions. For convenience, we label one of them the left and the other one the right.

There's no spectrum of policies and positions running left to right in a neat line. In fact, it's impossible to define what makes something "more" left or right other than it's the sort of thing the people we've labeled left or right prefer. Nor is there a "center" between them because no one line exists connecting them as poles. "Left" and "right" are just the arbitrary labels we plaster onto whatever the two coalitions in a democracy at a specific moment happen to say and do. As the values and beliefs of those coalitions change across time and societies, the specific beliefs we label left and right change too. Our New Deal parties, like every system of parties, doesn't represent two great and permanent forces of humanity. They represent an ad hoc collection of principles and issues tossed together to address a specific collection of problems—specifically to debate the industrial-era problems of Depression-era America.

HOW THE FRENCH REVOLUTION CREATED THE LEFT AND THE RIGHT

We all agree that the Democrats are the party of the "left." The Republicans are the party of the "right." We all seem to have an innate sense of what these labels mean, since we use them for parties and movements of all kinds across the world. When describing any electoral system, we inevitably describe one party as representing the left—the British Labour Party, the German Social Democrats, the Canadian Liberal Party— and the other as representing the right—the British Conservatives, the German Christian Democrats, or the Canadian Conservatives. We use the same terms to identify political movements and even nondemocratic and authoritarian regimes, attaching to a multitude of groups with varied ideologies labels like "left wing," "center left," or "far right." To this way of thinking, our Fifth Party System Republicans and Democrats—and indeed the parties within every party system—must be merely vehicles for waging this recurring and permanent war between humanity's liberals on its "left" and conservatives on its "right," with a smattering of "centrists" stuck in the "middle" between them. Except the left and the right aren't ancient concepts of human politics rooted in nature and history. They're a reasonably recent invention that arose by accident to describe an argument that's been irrelevant for a century.

We only talk about a political left and right because King Louis XVI of France ran out of money in the 1780s. France ran up substantial debts helping America beat Great Britain in the Revolutionary War, and the king needed more money to keep the French state functioning—not to mention keep himself in finery and palaces. The king called a traditional French advisory legislature, known as the Estates-General, looking for new taxes.[1] Unfortunately for the king, the old feudal order was breaking down, and many commoners elected to the Estates-General arrived in Paris believing it an excellent opportunity to seize additional power from the nobility and the crown to befit their rising status. The Enlightenment was also then at its height in France, and many representatives elected to the Estates-General dreamed of a constitutional monarchy, if not a republic like the new one in America. As the proceedings began, a group of commoners sought to increase their representation at the meeting, but the king rebuffed them.[2] The commoners declared themselves a National Constituent Assembly and, when the king sought to lock them out of the meeting hall, commandeered a tennis court where they took an oath to bring about a new French constitution. After armed uprisings in Paris and an attack on the royal Bastille prison demonstrated the king was powerless, their legislature became the new French government.[3] As it began debating a new constitution for France, those who supported the king and wanted a constitutional monarchy sat together, for no particular reason, on the right side of the meeting room. Those who wanted to overthrow the king and impose a republic sat on the left. People started calling the monarchists "the right" and the republicans "the left."[4]

As the revolution raged through France, moving the country from an ineffective constitutional monarchy to a republican tyranny to the Napoleonic dictatorship, "right" and "left" became shorthand terms for one's position on the revolution. The Jacobins of the "left" wanted to shatter the old regime to build a new republic, and their cause attracted intellectuals, revolutionaries, rabble-rousing populists, and the poor and working-class "sans culottes," who believed overthrowing kings would make their lives better. The "right" wanted to preserve the stability of an ordered monarchy and it mainly attracted aristocrats, the clergy, sober upper-middle-class professionals, pragmatists, and the military, who had a lot to lose in the uncertainty of revolution.[5] People came to associate the "left" with radicalism, the elevation of Enlightenment rationalism over authority and tradition, and deference to the popular will. They associated the "right" with traditionalism, religion, social order, incrementalism, and pragmatism.[6]

The terms "liberal" and "conservative" originally grew out of related events. The label "liberal" rose to popularity during the Enlightenment to describe the philosophers and statesmen wanting to replace traditional authority with institutions based in reason—"liberal" having the same root as the word "liberty."[7] "Liberals" were Enlightenment heroes like John Locke, Jean-Jacques Rousseau, Adam Smith, John Stuart Mill, Thomas Paine, and nearly every leading light of the American Revolution who wanted reason to replace traditional authority as the basis for government, wanted republics to replace monarchies, wanted citizens to replace subjects, and wanted markets to replace state monopolies. The original "liberals" and "the left" therefore mainly overlapped. During the troubled reign of King Louis XVIII, who had reclaimed the French throne from Napoleon, the royalist Vicomte de Chateaubriand is said to have coined the term "conservative" for those who, like him, defended the monarchy against republicanism.[8] These "conservatives" hoped to "conserve" the traditional social order—monarchy, aristocracy, and traditional church authority against what they saw as republican radicalism. The concept of "conservatives" thus grew out of and overlapped with the original idea of the right.

As Enlightenment ideas spread during the nineteenth century, this clash between republicanism and aristocracy dominated politics in the West. France flip-flopped between monarchy and republicanism several times. The British parliament continued fighting over the supremacy of parliament or the king. Most important, Europe rose up in mass revolts in 1848 in support of more democracy—revolts the monarchs ultimately put down. During those revolts, while educated liberals in the cities demanded liberal concessions to the monarchs' absolute rule, like freedom of speech and representative parliaments, the struggling and discontented peasants and workers in the provinces who eagerly joined in made different demands, like the end of peasant abuse from landlords, economic security, and better working conditions. In the popular mind, the interests of workers and labor naturally blended into the interests of these liberals of the left.[9]

As republicanism and monarchy fought it out over the years, the people kept agitating for democracy, and the monarchs ultimately made concessions to the idea of constitutional restraints on their rule.[10] The people gradually chipped away at absolutism, and parliaments with parties and real power became the norm. The new democratic political systems that emerged tended to divide society into two broad coalitions, as majority-rule systems are naturally inclined to do. The most powerful issue dividing those coalitions was the fight between monarchy and republicanism.[11] Since the two political coalitions of society were divided over the same issues as the coalitions first formed in the French assembly hall, the same labels designed to describe one's position on republicanism during the French Revolution—the "left" and "right"—got repurposed into labels for the naturally occurring coalitions of democratic politics.

That's why democracies talk about the left and right. The birth of democratic politics coincided with the left-right debate over aristocracy and republicanism. Since the sorts of people who we thought of as "the right" during the revolutionary era tended to work together in early democratic politics, we continued to think of them as "the right." Since the sorts of people we thought of as "the left" during the revolutionary era tended to work together in early democratic politics, we continued to think of them as "the left." The idea of "left" and "right" as positions on the dispute over republics or kings bled into the overlapping idea of "left" and "right" as convenient labels for the two grand coalitions that inevitably emerged under democratic political systems. What began as a matter of convenience became one of custom.

It's absolutely bizarre, however, that modern democracies continue to talk about the left and right at all. By the early twentieth century, the idea of the traditional left and right declined into irrelevance. In the aftermath of the First World War, the kings, emperors, and czars of Europe got swept away or else were rendered figureheads. Around the same time, new models for organizing society arose. Socialism took off as a new idea for government. A revolution in Russia led to the Bolsheviks seizing power, committing a powerful state to worldwide Marxist revolution. The Germans elected Hitler their nation's chancellor, and he transformed the German state into a fascist dictatorship, joining the dictatorships of Italy and Spain. The western world broke into three competing spheres

advancing three philosophies of government—liberal-democratic capitalism, state communism, and fascism. The world's dominant political
question had moved away from the now archaic question of republics
and kings to one of communists and fascists and democracies. Yet people
accustomed to thinking of politics in terms of the political left and right
found the notion impossible to let go. In democracies, people continued
to think about politics in terms of two coalitions of the left and the right.
People therefore puzzled over how best to fit these three ideas into the
still prevailing left-right spectrum.

Since the days of the 1848 revolutions, people had associated the
cause of workers and labor—peasants, workers, and the common people,
resentful of their lords and masters and demanding status, wealth, and
better conditions in the harsh world of early industrialization—with the
"left." Demands for labor reforms, social welfare laws, and worker protections blended into liberal demands for parliaments and free speech.
Communist support, moreover, tended to come from intellectuals,
workers, utopian reformers, and populists—the sorts of people who traditionally made up the "left."[12] In fascist nations, the dictators drew much
support from those pining for the stability of a monarch after the chaos
and economic devastation of democracy during the Depression—mainly
the sorts of people we were in the habit of calling the "right."[13] As fascists
sparred with communists, the communists—who considered themselves
the "left"—also made great efforts to distinguish these philosophical and
political opponents as part of the hated "right."[14] In the popular mind,
communists became a modern interpretation of the "left," while fascists
became a modern take on the "right," with liberal-democratic capitalists
placed somewhere in the "middle" between them.

It was true, of course, that socialists and communists, forced to pick
between the two parties in a democracy, tended to prefer the party we generally labeled as the left. Fascists preferred to pick the party of the right.
Except the fascist and communist regimes had more in common with
each other than with any of the major parties of any liberal-democratic
state.[15] Both favored heavily militarized totalitarian states with no real
democratic participation. They involved mostly state-directed eco-

nomic systems and they gave very little personal freedom to their citizens, employing the apparatus of a police state. Fascists and communists even historically competed for the same space in the public square—angry people, mostly poor and working class, seeking to topple their governments. Most importantly, both fascism and communism rejected liberal-capitalist democracy and the entire Enlightenment value system on which it's based. The Nazi and Soviet regimes both had far more in common with each other than they did with Republicans or Democrats. Democrats and Republicans, on the other hand, as liberal parties in a democratic republic, have, then and now, far more in common with each other than either have with Nazis or Soviets. They both favor a completely different political system, completely different economic system, and completely different social system—liberal democracy—which both communists and fascists reject.

Calling fascism an ideology of the right and communism an ideology of the left was superficially appealing but logically incoherent. What "far right" fascists believe isn't a more "extreme" version of what modern Republicans believe, nor are the things "far left" communists believe a more "extreme" version of what modern Democrats believe. Communists might bear a shallow similarity with liberals in their rhetoric about workers and their wariness of the excesses of wealth, but otherwise reject liberal values. Studies of fascism almost inevitably note that fascist ideology bears little relationship with historical or philosophical conservatism or the historic political right, while the fascists themselves considered themselves neither left nor right but something completely new and different.[16] Neither ideology has any relationship to any mainstream political belief in liberal capitalist republics. At best, when communists and fascists have to fit themselves into one of two unsatisfying choices in a liberal democracy, they pick the party they hate least—while advocating for the abolishment of the entire liberal system in favor of something radically different. Despite our insistence on continuing to use the labels left and right, the left-right spectrum no longer made much sense in the context of twentieth-century politics. Nor is it coherent to suggest the left-right spectrum is actually a "circle" in which, if you go too far in one direction, you wind up at the other end. Either something is a stark division of ideas or it's not.

It has now been over a century since the political labels left and right had any real meaning. They're labels meant to describe the two sides in the fight over republics and kings, yet we continue to apply them to increasingly unrelated ideological battles long after their original purpose has passed into the obscurity of history, even when the labels obviously no longer fit. Few serious people still favor a hereditary monarch. It simply became a matter of habit and convenience. Democratic political systems always trend toward two big political coalitions. We arbitrarily stick the best name we can on each, labeling their whole agenda as right or left. As we move into new eras, with new issues, we keep the same old boxes out of habit, whether or not it still makes sense to do so at all. The "left" and the "right" aren't descriptions of where political parties fall on a spectrum of ideas. Unlike in that French assembly hall, it's hard to even know what we mean when we classify something as left or right, other than that it's something the sorts of people we're accustomed to labeling the left or right tend to think. They're just names we stick on after the fact to whatever ideas our parties come up with in building winning electoral coalitions.

LIBERALS AND CONSERVATIVES ARE
TEMPORARY AND ARBITRARY COALITIONS

Many smart people have worked diligently to identify how the left and right might represent not just arbitrary ad hoc coalitions but rival basic dispositions of humanity.[17] It's our common intuition that certain personality traits usually correspond to certain political views. It's said that liberals on the left are creative, open to experience, and eager to improve things—but also sometimes imprudent and blind to risk. Conservatives on the right are said to be more practical, reliable, and stable—but sometimes hidebound and resistant to necessary change. This roughly corresponds to how we use the words "liberal" and "conservative" in ordinary speech. If we ask a colleague to be conservative in estimating figures for us, we mean a cautious forecast. If we ask a friend to spoon out a "liberal" portion of ice cream, we mean a heaping scoop overflowing the dish. These stereotypes of liberal and conservative personalities seem to support the incorrect notion that our political coalitions must be driven by our nature.

Scholars have indeed found that one's political beliefs often correspond to certain personality traits, with conscientiousness linked to conservative beliefs and openness linked to liberal ones.[18] Psychologist Jonathan Haidt, for example, suggests five distinct foundations of moral reasoning in which political liberals chiefly care about two, care for others and fairness, while political conservatives also highly value authority, loyalty, and sanctity.[19] Theorists like Haidt raise important insights about why different people looking at the two major political parties on offer in a democracy ultimately choose the party they do. They explain why certain people might choose to become liberals or conservatives as we presently define those terms. They describe how the two parties that presently exist fit into the moral universe. They might even provide reasons for how, when presented with two parties, we choose to label one as right or left. What these theories don't do—nor are they meant to do—is explain why the left or right party in a society stakes out the specific mix of ideas and policies they do. If you had to construct the agendas of America's two major political parties from scratch using just these differences, you wouldn't arrive at the agendas of the modern Republican and Democratic Parties.

Political conservatives are cautious about some change—they oppose "liberal" policy proposals requiring new regulations or increased spending, as well as those that encourage the culture to move in a more "liberal" direction. They also happily support experimental economic policies, new government intervention into cultural matters, constitutional amendments, and more, which would together not only unwind some of the most significant parts of the modern American state but also implement new programs untested anywhere before. Political liberals favor some changes, such as new programs that further advance their policy priorities, while instinctively resisting any effort to reform or adjust any of the half-century-old programs of the New Deal or Lyndon Johnson's Great Society. They also favor caution when political conservatives propose reforms in public schooling, such as charter schools and testing regimes; they resist liberalizing national labor practices, wanting to keep in place the conservative workplace regimes encoded in labor union agreements; and they generally oppose experimenting with vouchers to overhaul the Medicare and Social Security programs.

Conservatives and liberals take a more "conservative" or "liberal" position depending on whether a proposal moves the country toward their policy preferences. Why don't conservatives, said to value authority and loyalty, favor a stronger government with a highly regulatory state? Shouldn't conservatives dislike the chaos of free and unregulated markets and the disruptive changes of capitalism? Shouldn't they like the order labor unions create? Shouldn't the value they place on loyalty lead to more support for generous Social Security and Medicare programs, even if it means higher taxes—sacrificing some fairness for loyalty to and respect for elders? Why do liberals, said not to value highly the morality of the sacred, embrace an environmental politics rooted in a sacred value, the purity of nature? Whatever created the distinct mixture of issues and ideas that we group together as "liberal" and "conservative," differences in personality or moral intuition don't account for them.

No one has ever adequately explained with any neutral principle why "liberals" support the specific mix of positions they do or why "conservatives" support the issues they do.[20] In an alternative political alignment, it's perfectly plausible that people who believe in tax cuts could be on the same side of public debate as people who believe in free immigration and restricted off-shore drilling. It's plausible that, in that universe, people who believe in stronger environmental regulation might find themselves on the same side of public debate as people believing in charter schools and banning stem-cell research. A belief in free trade might not go with opposition to same-sex marriage. Support for labor unions might not go with support for affirmative action policies. In fact, there's no reason the issues we group together as "liberal" or "conservative" have to go together at all. Few people in the real world even agree with everything their political "team" is supposed to believe. People believe some of it, and not all of them agree with the same parts as others. The country is full of people who describe themselves in political terms that demonstrate only partial adherence to their "team"—they're libertarians, or "economically conservative and socially liberal," or Blue Dog Democrats, or "sort of progressive," or some other common formulation that communicates only partial agreement with what we call "conservatism" or "liberalism."

While most liberal-democratic governments facing most of the same problems as America have parties we identify as "left" and "right," they don't perfectly mirror the American left and right. The British Tories, on the "right" in the UK, adore a government-run healthcare system that would terrorize the American right as dangerous socialism. Many worldwide parties of the "left" are honest-to-goodness socialists advancing unabashedly socialist agendas that make America's Democrats look like conservatives. The German Christian Democrats, the mainstream party of the "right" in Germany, support a highly regulated economy that the American right would detest on principle. Outside Western liberal democracies, the labels break down further. Who's truly on the "right" and the "left" in China, an officially communist state with limited political freedom, carrying out a market-oriented economic program? How do you classify elected authoritarians like Russia's Vladimir Putin or Turkey's Tayyip Erdoğan, who in practice reject the entire premise of liberal-democratic capitalism itself?

Looking back at history, you don't find people in societies beyond the last few centuries debating the same issues and value choices conservatives and liberals debate today. None of what triggered passionate debate in these societies, not to mention political assassinations, armed rebellions, and wars, had anything to do with our debates between Democrats and Republicans. If you analyze old conflicts, you can always find the side that people of modern democracies would consider more enlightened and then label them the "liberals" of the situation. You can also always find people demanding change and people favoring stability and order. What you can't find in the places humans came together to debate politics—the ancient Roman Senate, the councils of medieval European kings, or the halls of the Doge of the Venetian Republic—are debates over the same issues over which modern democratic societies obsess. The kings of medieval Europe weren't debating how best to create jobs. The Maharajahs of India weren't considering how best to implement a social welfare state. Members of the pre-modern English parliament weren't chosen based on pledges to fight unfair racial discrimination. People then fought over different issues that don't easily break down as left or right, such as which family would rule, the balance of power between nobles and the king, the dictates of the church, and other disputes over inheritance, family, religion, and power. Indeed, for most of the world's history, the principles and agendas of both "liberal" Democrats and "conservative" Republicans would be seen as indistinguishable radicalism.

Free markets and free trade? In a world of peasants, or one controlled by guilds, the very notion is absurd. Environmental protection? In a pre-industrial world, protection from what? Education? Why do we want peasants to read? Labor unions? Workers do what they're told or they lose their heads. Voting rights? Kings are divinely ordained to rule. Gender politics? Women were essentially property. Everyone who matters in politics in every modern democracy would back then be a radical outside all bounds of political debate. Modern conservatives and liberals all want to live in a dynamic society of growth, innovation, and commerce—not a static world of stable landed hereditary estates. Modern liberals and conservatives all agree citizens should rule through representative democracy. They all agree we should form policy through rational debate based on evidence, not deference to ancient authority earned by birthright or bestowed by divine power. Unless you abstract the complex ideologies we call liberal and conservative down to some simplistic notion like who you think is most fair, which ruler is less tyrannous, or which historical figure you find the least cruel, then nobody in the world before the modern era is a conservative or a liberal.

Put plainly, no one has ever succeeded in identifying a value or universal principle we can take as a starting point, plug it into our political situation, and reliably spit out the two actual political parties that now exist. Since we can't even agree on what it means for something to be left or right in the first place, we certainly have no coherent way to decide whether something is "more" or "further" to the left or right than something else. That means we have no coherent way to line up every issue in politics into some spectrum moving left to right, much less to call anything a "middle" or "center" between them. The only method by which we know to reliably identify whether something is left or right is to observe what the people labeling themselves as liberals or conservatives currently support. The left-right spectrum is nothing more than a byproduct of a metaphor run amok. We talk about political factions using directions like "left" and "right" and then start actually thinking the world has ordered politics into some neat line. The metaphor wasn't even originally about ideology. It's was about seating arrangements.

THE TRUE IDEOLOGICAL COALITIONS OF AMERICA

Liberalism and conservatism, and the left and right identities we associate with them, are just labels for the current agendas of the Democratic and Republican Parties. At different times and places, these agendas can and do change. When they do, whatever we consider the liberal or conservative position changes too. It's unfair to call them completely arbitrary because some issues naturally "go together," in the sense that they flow from the same basic principles and premises. The people who tend to share a common value naturally tend to support a cluster of related issues springing from that value. One coalition will always attract more of certain groups in society, whether intellectuals, artists, the poor, professionals, or business leaders. One party will always want more change and another will inevitable want to preserve more of the status quo. We can use those and similar markers to label one coalition more to the "left" or "right" based on our prior associations. Yet in critical ways every coalition we label left or right is always going to look somewhat different. They will all support a seemingly strange mixture of issues and contain somewhat different alliances. Changing the axis of evaluation from one policy to another, like economics and labor to social culture, the party that looks more liberal or conservative can even flip.

Previous American party systems don't neatly conform to our current definitions of liberalism and conservatism. Conservatives often claim Alexander Hamilton and the Federalists, but the Federalists supported a powerful federal government driving economic progress at the expense of state authority—seemingly liberal. Liberals claim Jefferson and the Democratic-Republicans, but Jefferson was a slave-owning rich aristocrat who thought the elite should rule, distrusted strong federal power, and wanted strong states that could defend themselves against the federal government. Each was liberal in some ways under our present definition but conservative in others. Andrew Jackson was a populist who hated banks and corporations and wanted to break the power of elites for the benefit of ordinary working people—seemingly liberal—who also was militarily aggressive and despised fancy cultural elites in a way that sounded like a Tea Party conservative. Most people call the Civil War Republicans the liberal party—they ended slavery, sought to expand national civil rights, were aggressive in the use of federal power for reform, and favored investing in national projects—unless you're talking about business policies and keeping state power out of commercial matters, in which case the Democrats suddenly seem to be taking liberal positions. William Jennings Bryan, the most important Democrat at the turn of the twentieth century, was a strong populist fighting for the interests of poor farmers and laborers, promoting economic policies benefiting these groups against the "big money" of the East. His politics centered around his evangelical Christianity and belief in personal morality. He was a strong anti-elitist, raging against the Eastern elites he despised and terrifying the establishment of both major parties; he wanted to ban alcohol for religious reasons; and he fought to allow schools to fire teachers who taught evolution. Was he a conservative or a liberal? Theodore Roosevelt, the most important Republican around the same time, was strongly pro-business and the nation's leading progressive championing regulatory reforms to stop bad business actors, civil service reforms to stop patronage, and antitrust laws to break up monopoly corporations. He was agreeable to unions, created agencies like the FDA, and, as an avid hunter and outdoorsman, became the first great environmentalist creating the national park system. Was he a conservative or a liberal?

Just like the party ideologies of previous American party systems, the two major party ideologies we now call liberalism and conservatism are in fact big messy coalitions binding millions of very different people around two big visions addressing the problems of their age. They don't represent places on an everlasting political spectrum. They represent temporary coalitions of people united around party ideologies built out of some-times clashing principles to engage in a specific debate about a unique time and place in history, the mid-twentieth-century industrial world. We constructed these ideologies we too often wrongly take for granted as eternal—New Deal liberalism and modern conservatism—fairly recently to debate Franklin Roosevelt's New Deal.

The Democratic Party's New Deal liberalism, which holds we should enlist expertise to design a better society that serves working people and the least well off, is not one universal principle. Its ideology combines two broad principles, populism and progressivism, to unite very different groups of people. Progressivism believes careful study, elite knowledge, and the application of social science can design rules to improve America to create a more just, fair, and prosperous society. It's the principle behind Democratic activism for environmental protection, financial reform, education reform, social justice activism, and social programs that help at-need children. Populism seeks to empower people who feel locked out by the elite. It's what's behind Democratic talk of working for the "little guy," or "working Americans," or "the common man" against "the rich" or "the corporations," and it's why Democrats champion the inter-ests of the struggling and the poor, support progressive taxation, support labor unions that empower workers at the expense of corporate brass, and support regulatory schemes that seek to hold corporations to account. Since the 1930s, nearly everything the Democratic Party has said and done it has justified on one of these two principles, defending the people versus the powerful (defending entitlements, supporting labor unions, regulating powerful industries, progressive taxation) or promoting justice and progress (women's issues, pro-choice policies, support for same-sex marriage, gun control, environmental protection, and green energy). When Democrats rage that Republicans are in the pocket of the rich, that's an argument based in populism. When they complain that Republicans are selfish individualists standing in the way of social progress, that's an argument based in progressivism.

The Republican conservative ideology, which opposes New Deal liberalism as dangerous "big government," also merges two broad principles, liberty and virtue. It's rare to listen to a Republican politician for any length of time without hearing either an invocation of liberty (or freedom) or virtue (or values, morality, or family). Liberty is the belief that democratic majorities should be wary about wielding democratic power carelessly over weaker political minorities to avoid a tyranny of the majority. Republicans thus advocate small government, reducing regulation, reducing taxes, and free-market solutions, so people can make choices without state interference. Virtue is the worry that a republic like America, in which citizens choose and control the government, must foster a specific culture in its people for the nation to survive and thrive. Republicans thus seek to promote cultural traits to encourage virtues like national community, family, tradition, faith, the value of work, and love of country. Since the 1930s, the Republican Party has justified nearly every major issue either as the defense of political liberty (lower taxes, reduced regulation, "smaller government," school choice, a strong Second Amendment, a more active foreign policy) or national virtue (pro-life policies, per-child tax credits, opposition to same-sex marriage, flag-burning amendments, keeping "In God We Trust" on currency). When Republicans thunder that Democrats champion a "big government" "nanny state" agenda, that's an argument based in liberty. When they accuse Democrats of social radicalism, "Hollywood values," or failing to love and support America, those are attacks based around virtue.

To understand the present party system, we have to unlearn much of what we all think we know about what our parties represent. The Democratic Party isn't just a party of liberals on the left. Nor is the Democratic coalition simply an ad hoc alliance of various demographic or identity groups—a mere "coalition of the ascendant" uniting African Americans, Hispanics, women, gays and lesbians, millennials, labor unions, environmental activists, and more. The Republicans aren't just a party of conservatives on the right. The party is more than just a "three-legged stool" of economic conservatives, social conservatives, and foreign policy conservatives lobbying for their specific favored policy priorities. These common descriptions all have it backward, mistaking the result of a coalition—which groups it attracts and what issues it favors—for the cause that unites it. The Democrats are an alliance of populists and progressives united around the ideology of the New Deal. The Republicans are an alliance of liberty conservatives and virtue conservatives united around fighting the New Deal as harmful big government. Populism and progressivism are different things. Liberty and virtue are different things. There's no logical reason these principles have to be paired together inside the same political coalition. Sometimes they find themselves at odds. A populist sometimes demands power and spoils at the cost of meritocratic good government, while expert-led technocratic reforms sometimes harm the interests of ordinary people or demand change they won't like. A virtue conservative might sometimes believe it's necessary to wield government authority to bolster the nation's virtue in a way that alarms a liberty conservative, while a liberty conservative might advocate allowing society to freely take a course a virtue conservative might fear will undercut the virtue necessary for the republic to survive.

Liberty, virtue, populism, and progressivism all have deep roots across American history, from liberty's role in America's Founding, to virtue's role in American revivals, to the populist revolts that have shaken the system, to the Progressive Movement that transformed the nation around the turn of the twentieth century. Deep and forgotten fissures lie between each party's principles, ones we too frequently gloss over or ignore in our careless grouping of people as mere conservatives or liberals. When our parties eventually break, our party coalitions will be undone in the spaces between these principles, and these spaces are where the next era's coalitions will most likely emerge. To understand how this party system is breaking, and what's likely to happen next, we must first unpack the constituent parts of these cobbled-together ideologies that we have taken for granted since the days of Franklin Roosevelt.

CHAPTER 7

THE AMERICAN IDEAL OF LIBERTY

Imagine you've been invited to join a group of friends at a vacation house. The rules for the weekend are majority rule. When you arrive at the lovely little beach house, your friends let you know they've already had a vote and you'll be spending the weekend in the tiniest room—the one with only a couch next to a ventilator that hums and rattles all night. You trudge off to put your bags in the closet of a room, when your friends inform you that they're also heading out to a well-reviewed restaurant. Except you'll have to house-sit one of their dogs. Majority rule and all. When they get back, they'd really appreciate finding the pool muck skimmed out. Someone has to do it. They had a vote and you lost. Majority rule. You'll also be paying twice as much in rent for the weekend. You got a great bonus this year, right? They all voted on it, and it's only fair. Majority rule.

That nightmare weekend is the key to understanding liberty conservatism. It's an insight about democratic government central of the ideas of the American Founding: the tyranny of the majority.

LIBERTY, AMERICA, AND THE ENLIGHTENMENT

Liberty is at the heart of the American story. When colonial patriots organized to fight for their rights against the British crown, they called their organization the "Sons of Liberty." They launched a revolution to promote, as they wrote in the Declaration of Independence, "life, liberty, and the pursuit of happiness." As they fought to free their nation from what they believed to be a tyrant king, they waved a flag reading "don't tread on me." Patrick Henry cried out "give me liberty or give me death." The American republic these revolutionaries created now stamps the word "Liberty" prominently on its coins. Its pledges allegiance to its flag "with liberty and justice for all." Among its most potent national symbols is the Statute of Liberty standing in New York harbor, depicting a national symbol we call Lady Liberty. Liberty is America's sacred national value.

Nearly everyone in mainstream American politics, whether out of sincere reverence or mere political necessity, has always sought to connect their beliefs to principled American liberty. Throughout American history, the words "liberty" and "freedom" have peppered political speeches. Every major American party has claimed to stand for liberty. Every successful American political leader of real significance, from Washington to Jefferson to Lincoln to Roosevelt, has proclaimed their reverence for liberty. A genuine commitment to political liberty is a baseline precondition to legitimacy in American politics. Which is why, whenever anyone has sought to implement major and controversial change in America, their opponents have frequently accused them of acting like a demagogue or a tyrant. Because liberty is America's national value, every powerful figure, energetic movement, and political party seeking radical change first has to prove it isn't flirting with tyranny, demagoguery, or mob rule.

When the Federalists proposed national reforms during the early republic to strengthen the national government, Democratic-Republicans attacked them as monarchists and aspiring tyrants. In return, the Federalists painted Democratic-Republicans as Jacobin demagogues harnessing the mob. A few decades later, National Republicans didn't just call the strong executive Andrew Jackson "King Andrew," they renamed their party the Whigs, after the revolutionaries who defeated King George.[1] In the middle of the nineteenth century, the enemies of Know-Nothingism attacked the followers of the American Party as a dangerous and ignorant mob. Abraham Lincoln's enemies called him a tyrant so often it might as well have become part of his name—when John Wilkes Booth shot Lincoln he yelled out "death to tyrants" in Latin. After the Civil War, Democrats howled about federal tyranny over the defeated states of the

Confederacy. William Jennings Bryan's enemies called him a terrifying demagogue. Elites from both parties dismissed the Gilded Age Populists as a stirred-up mob. Huey Long they (quite correctly) called a demagogic would-be dictator. When Franklin Roosevelt's opponents called him a tyrant and his controversial New Deal an attack on liberty, it was hardly an innovation. When politicians and parties win an election, their supporters naturally see opportunities to push through their most cherished ideas. The election's losers naturally seek to remind them of their obligations to the republic.

What frequently makes these attacks invoking liberty contentious in American politics is not everyone agrees on what liberty means or what it requires. Countless definitions of liberty exist, from those of John Stuart Mill to Robespierre to Ayn Rand to Milton Friedman. To some people, liberty means freedom to live life as you wish without judgment or interference from neighbors. For others, it means the freedom to speak and write and organize against the government. For others, it means the freedom to compete on fair terms against the friends and children of the powerful. For others, it means freedom to conduct the affairs of your business without interference from government authorities. For others, it means freedom from want. For many, liberty has come to mean a government that leaves as much as possible to the individual with as little state interference as possible, leading to policies like low taxes, minimal regulation, and market-based rules rather than those of command and control. For others, liberty has become just a word to describe a nation with free elections and representative government. The liberty revered in American politics that grew out of the American Revolution, however, has always meant just one thing—the Enlightenment idea of a rational government wary of majority tyranny.

The American Revolution was a product of the intellectual whirlwind that swept over Western Europe during the seventeenth and eighteenth centuries that we call the Enlightenment. From the days of the Roman Empire, through the Dark Ages, the Middle Ages, and the Renaissance, authority and tradition—not reason—governed Western culture. Everything from government to science to culture was dominated by the dogma of kings and bishops. Ideas were true or not true, and actions taken or not taken, because people born or raised into authority said so. Those figures of traditional authority naturally supported what had always been done and what kept them securely in power over the common men and women of the world. Then a generation of new thinkers arose to question this consensus, unleashing an intellectual and philosophical tsunami that crashed into the foundational rocks of Europe. That storm, proposing that reason replace tradition and dogma as the foundation of Western culture, was the Enlightenment.

We widely consider the start of the Enlightenment to be Isaac Newton's publication of his *Principia Mathematica* in 1687, which popularized a radical new idea—the scientific method.[2] Throughout human history, philosophers had mainly guessed at the laws of the universe through conjecture and a dose of mysticism, constructing stories to explain forces they didn't yet understand. Newton observed the workings of the world, recorded them, crunched the numbers, and from there established truths, revealing with mathematics how the fundamental laws of the universe actually worked.[3] Newton's discoveries awed people, but, just as importantly, his method inspired them. Over the next century, a parade of thinkers such as Voltaire, Rousseau, John Locke, David Hume, and Immanuel Kant applied similar methods to one new realm after another. Like Newton, these philosophers examined beliefs that had ruled Western society for centuries and subjected them to rigorous testing, study, and logic.[4] Embracing the radical idea that reason could replace tradition and dogma as the basis for society, they collectively challenged almost every bedrock assumption of European society.

The Enlightenment they sparked led to countless new ways of thinking across every human endeavor, from government to economics to religion to science and even to the nature of the good life. As the idea of reason seeped into one field after another, it triggered a vast flowering of scientific and social change. It spread the scientific method—that we should understand the world around us by conducting experiments and recording our results. It led to classical liberal economics—that economies should be governed not by guild rules and royal decrees but by individuals freely exchanging items of value. It led to religious tolerance—that people should be free to choose their religious traditions. Perhaps most importantly, it led to new ideals of republican democracy—that the people should choose their rulers instead of accepting those born into authority as their betters.[5] Each of these revolutions grew out of the same big idea, that reasoning, experimenting, and discovering truth can guide us toward a better society. Traditional authority crumbled.

Among the most important ideas to grow out of this Enlightenment was republican democracy. Enlightenment thinkers naturally rejected traditional and nonrational sources of political legitimacy, such as the divine right of hereditary kings or brute power. They sought instead a rational basis for some people to rule over others, and the only reasonable basis they could discover was consent. Enlightenment thinkers thus mainly agreed the most legitimate social order was a republic in which the people elected leaders to represent them. They disagreed, however, on how those elected representatives ought to govern in the people's interest. The philosopher Jean-Jacques Rousseau—who believed people were inherently good and it was society that turned them toward evil—believed such a republic had a duty to rule according to the people's general will.[6] To Rousseau, inherently good people, freed by republican government of the wicked pressures of social oppression, would never choose to oppress themselves. A just government, he therefore believed, should follow the majority's general will wherever it led, as if it were a sacred trust. Rousseau became an idol of the leaders of the French Revolution, and they put his ideas of liberty at the center of their republic. The French revolutionaries were eager to sweep aside anyone who dared oppose the general will of the people—naturally defined as the policies that French leaders had developed in the people's name—even in a bloody Reign of Terror against the Revolution's perceived enemies. Rousseau's conception of republican liberty continues to hold a powerful influence in many democracies around the world, particularly European ones that connect their legacies to the French Revolution.

America's Founders, relying on a second strain of thinking based in the works of philosophers like Locke, Hobbes, Hume, and Montesquieu, had very different ideas about what liberty required in a republic.[7] They didn't believe people were inherently good, like Rousseau did. In fact, they believed imperfect people often tended to abuse power and authority. Some people, when given power, take advantage of others. Some people are careless, selfish, greedy, or cruel. Sometimes irrational passions run through segments of society. Sometimes groups bear such hate toward others they would eagerly use any power available to them to torment perceived enemies. A majority of citizens, the Founders recognized, if left unconstrained, might band together into a ruling class to abuse the losers of elections—subject them to indignities, seize their property, and render them slaves with the legitimacy of a majority vote. To prevent this, America's Founders believed liberty required strong antidemocratic protections for minorities so a republic didn't become a different sort of irrational tyranny. It wouldn't do much good, after all, to replace a king with a majority of citizens who acted like one toward electoral minorities. In *Democracy in America*, the essays he wrote about his journeys through the young American republic, French writer Alexis de Tocqueville popularized a phrase for this concern—the "tyranny of the majority."[8]

America's Founders struggled with how to create a republic of the people that didn't turn into a horrific rule of the mob. Just because people consented to an election, they thought, didn't mean people had consented to everything the election's winner might decide to do. Some actions fall outside any consent—things people would never agree be done to them, no matter who wins. The Founders therefore intentionally designed their republic to frustrate momentary passions stirring through society, making sure leaders were only able to act when broad national agreement existed.[9] They created a complicated republic loosely modeled on a proposed design by the political philosopher Montesquieu, with three federal branches, a two-chambered legislature, substantial power preserved in coequal state governments, and an extensive Bill of Rights placing limits on these institutions. It's a system intentionally designed to be so clumsy that it's nearly impossible to ever "get anything done" apart from things that already have broad support across every significant faction of America. America's Founders hoped this untested and often frustrating republic would ensure government would always rule by reason.[10] As James Madison said in a speech to the Virginia ratifying convention about the Constitution he designed:

> On a candid examination of history, we shall find that turbulence, violence, and abuse of power, by the majority trampling on the rights of the minority have produced factions and commotions, which, in republics, have more frequently than any other cause, produced despotism. . . . This danger ought to be wisely guarded against. Perhaps, in the progress of this discussion, it will appear, that the only possible remedy for those evils and means of preserving and protecting the principles of republicanism, will be found in that very system [the Constitution] which is now exclaimed against as the parent of oppression.[11]

This insight about liberty—that democracies need strong counter-majoritarian protections to shield minorities from majority abuse—is one of the reasons America's Founders are considered among the greatest philosophers of the Enlightenment, and their works—the Declaration of Independence, the Constitution, and *The Federalist*—are seen as core Enlightenment achievements. This didn't mean, however, that the Founders thought their Constitution was just some interesting system for majorities to game. They intended these constitutional protections only as last-ditch safeguards against the worst actors. The Founders certainly didn't believe it would be acceptable or moral for a majority strong or savvy enough to get around the protections of their Constitution—controlling enough offices and levers of the republic to impose its will on the election's losers—to do everything the Constitution gave them the power to do. The Founders presumed liberty's primary and most important safeguard would always have to be the American people vigilantly protecting it. In most cases, they expected the American people to guard against encroachments on their liberty, and to stop would-be-tyrants from trampling on the liberty of others, long before the Constitution's safeguards were necessary to kick in as a last resort. This constant political pushback against political majorities seeking to impose their will on minorities is what American political liberty is about.

Where the French Revolution's conception of liberty, following Rousseau ideas, believed liberty meant a society following the majority will, the American Revolution's conception held almost the opposite. According to the American conception of liberty, a republic is free only when political minorities are protected from majority abuse. The American idea of liberty doesn't believe human beings are inherently good and that it's only the external influences of society that pushes them to act badly. It believes people are inherently flawed and that those in power must be constantly restrained, checked, and balanced to ensure those under their power are not unfairly abused. Societies obviously need laws and governments to survive. In a democratic republic, the majority is empowered to make those laws and govern under them. That doesn't mean, however, that majorities can morally use those vast powers however they please. Throughout American history, we have always separated the issue of the legal exercise of a democratic government's power from its just and moral use. We draw a careful line between legitimate democratic self-government and what's essentially majority bullying. That's what political liberty has always meant in America since its Founding—protecting minorities from the tyranny of the majority.

THEORIES OF LIBERTY DURING THE FIFTH PARTY SYSTEM

For most of American history, liberty was a universal American ideal any party might invoke when its opponents overstepped. It wasn't partisan. That changed during the New Deal debate, which was essentially a fight over the size and power of government. In practice, one party during the Fifth Party System found itself adopting liberty as its own, while its rival constantly had to fend off charges of tyranny and demagoguery. Over time, many Americans started to associate liberty with the agenda of the Fifth Party System Republicans. For decades, Republicans—applying the principle to the specific issues of the New Deal political debate—invoked liberty when advocating for their agenda of tax cuts, reducing regulations, empowering markets, and limiting the scope and role of government. They got comfortable seeing themselves as the defenders of liberty. Liberty conservatism became an identifiable ideological faction within the party. Democrats, on the other hand, grew suspicious of a word often used to attack their plans. In the course of this debate, two alternative theories of liberty rose to prominence, each a partial application of principled liberty to the specific issues of the Fifth Party System era.

The first of these theories proposes that liberty is fundamentally about limiting the power of government so individuals can live with the least possible interference from the state. It holds as its model what some philosophers call a "night watchman state,"[12] an idea with roots going back to Enlightenment philosopher John Stuart Mill's "harm principle." According to Mill:

> That principle is, that the sole end for which mankind are warranted, individually or collectively, in interfering with the liberty of action of any of their number, is self-protection. That the only purpose for which power can be rightfully exercised over any member of a civilized community, against his will, is to prevent harm to others. His own good, either physical or moral, is not sufficient warrant. He cannot rightfully be compelled to do or forbear because it will be better for him to do so, because it will make him happier, because, in the opinion of others, to do so would be wise, or even right.[13]

According to the harm principle, the only legitimate reason for the state to coerce people is to protect others from harm. Thinkers have reached conflicting conclusions about what constitutes such harm. Some believe government should only step in to prevent direct acts of harm, such as physical violence or theft. To others, including Mill, a failure to do something—such as watching a child drown—was also harm, meaning government sometimes has an obligation to affirmatively intervene to prevent bad things from happening. Philosopher Robert Nozick, among the most celebrated libertarian thinkers, believed liberty meant government that treated people like means instead of ends, leading to the most minimal government possible, one responsible only for preventing assaults, thefts, and fraud.[14] Ayn Rand believed that, since humans had reason and free will to choose, the highest moral value people could pursue was following their reason and perception toward their own well-being—meaning it was immoral to demand anyone betray their self to act for the benefit of others.[15] The specifics of these various theories differ, but under most versions the state is to act solely as a policeman stopping individuals from using guile or violence to hurt or dominate one another.

The night watchman state, which advocates a starkly limited state without extensive government intervention, was politically attractive in an era in which many associated liberty with opposing "big government." The problem is no major party in American history—including the current Republican Party—has ever seriously advocated for a night watchman state. A night watchman state makes no place for national infrastructure like the roads and bridges and airports that power the nation's commerce, presuming the private sector will provide them and private owners will coordinate them without creating so-called "tragedies of the commons." It leaves no room for economic regulation or regulation of the natural environment, simply presuming that negative effects on others—what economists call externalities—won't cripple the nation. It has no place for social welfare programs like Social Security and Medicare, or for any assistance to even the temporarily poor or unemployed. Despite the rhetoric sometimes employed, only the most utopian activist actually advocates abolishing all government—no public roads or infrastructure to backbone our economy, no army to protect us, no public schools to educate the next generation, no one to enforce contracts, and no one to stop cheats and swindles. It's possible a society built around the night watchman state might work, but it would be a completely untested society requiring a radical restructuring of America. It certainly isn't what America's Founders meant when they employed the term liberty. Sharply limiting the power of government and empowering individuals are concepts the modern conservative movement developed as applications of principled liberty to the specific problems of the New Deal era, but the core philosophical basis for the liberty that America's Founders proclaimed is clearly something else.

A second popular theory holds liberty is about using market incentives in place of central planning to decentralize government power. This idea too developed out of the specific battles of our Fifth Party System. The New Deal involved a stark expansion in the role of government regulation. The Great Depression convinced many Americans that a rational human hand was necessary to supervise all the tentacles of the complex industrial economy to ensure they cooperated with orderly precision—or else the country risked careless and selfish humans accidentally plunging it into another depression, if not something worse. Franklin Roosevelt's New Deal agreed, seeking to employ central planning and state regulation to centralize economic authority. Republicans, protesting this increase in government power, championing the vigor of "free enterprise" as a superior alternative. By the middle of the twentieth century, as the New Deal consensus grew to dominate American politics, few in America's establishment even took seriously the idea that decentralized markets could possibly outperform comprehensive regulatory regimes designed after intense study and planning, whether in government or in great business conglomerates spanning industries.

Over time, however, a number of respected voices rose to question the consensus in favor of planning. Many were scholars with backgrounds in economics, such as Friedrich Hayek, Milton Friedman, or other academics clustered around economics departments in places like the University of Chicago.[16] These "free-market economists" believed human knowledge is inherently limited, and that even the most dedicated and wise experts are unable to know everything. Any system relying on central planning, they believed, would be inefficient and flawed because imperfect human planners, no matter how well-intentioned, couldn't actually know every fact necessary to design a wise or efficient plan—where everything is, what everybody is doing, what they all need, or what they all want. As individuals, however, we each possess pieces of knowledge, meaning that as a group we collectively know almost everything. These free-market economists argued that centralized government regulatory schemes accomplished goals less successfully than decentralized ones in which individual choice and the mechanisms of price powered markets.

In a market, price acts as a signal to weigh the wants and needs of every individual and organization in society to instantly determine an efficient allocation of scarce resources. Adam Smith, the author of *The Wealth of Nations* and considered the world's first economist, described the price mechanism as an "invisible hand" shaping the world. As Friedrich Hayek famously explained using the example of allocating tin from a mine in his essay "The Use of Knowledge in Society":

> Assume that somewhere in the world a new opportunity for the use of some raw material, say, tin, has arisen, or that one of the sources of supply of tin has been eliminated. It does not matter for our purpose— and it is very significant that it does not matter—which of these two causes has made tin more scarce. All that the users of tin need to know is that some of the tin they used to consume is now more profitably employed elsewhere and that, in consequence, they must economize tin. There is no need for the great majority of them even to know where the more urgent need has arisen, or in favor of what other needs they ought to husband the supply. If only some of them know directly of the new demand, and switch resources over to it, and if the people who are aware of the new gap thus created in turn fill it from still other sources, the effect will rapidly spread throughout the whole economic system and influence not only all the uses of tin but also those of its substitutes and the substitutes of these substitutes, the supply of all the things made of tin, and their substitutes, and so on; and all this without the great majority of those instrumental in bringing about these substitutions knowing anything at all about the original cause of these changes. The whole acts as one market, not because any of its members survey the whole field, but because their limited individual fields of vision sufficiently overlap so that through many intermediaries the relevant information is communicated to all. The mere fact that there is one price for any commodity—or rather that local prices are connected in a manner determined by the cost of transport, etc.—brings about the solution which (it is just conceptually possible) might have been arrived at by one single mind possessing all the information which is in fact dispersed among all the people involved in the process.[17]

Nobody has the knowledge or expertise to plan even a small part of the complex economy of the entire world. In theory, by simply allowing people to trade goods and services in a market, everything in the world gets delivered in an efficient way that keeps the entire system functioning without anyone having to understand what's going where or why.

By the later part of the twentieth century, however, central planning gradually lost luster across the West.[18] Western policy makers couldn't help but notice the experiences of nations like the Soviet Union and China, which, when attempting to rush mainly agricultural economies into the industrial age using rigid central plans, floundered.[19] Plans that made sense in national capitals, supported by data and sophisticated analysis, too often failed to anticipate the real-world consequences of their ambitious policies. The Soviets forced independent farmers into large-scale collective farms with the most modern equipment, believing they could jump-start industrial food production—and national agricultural output fell.[20] Mao imposed national quotas for metal production in China to quickly industrialize the country, but national bureaucrats passed down unrealistic production orders to peasants living in areas with little metal, who then melted down household implements and tools in backyard forges to meet the aggressive quotas—not only inflicting great hardship, but also producing a product that cost three times more, only a third of which was even usable.[21] Conservative political leaders like Ronald Reagan and Margaret Thatcher, who believed that central planning implanted over previous decades was now choking the vibrancy and innovation of their own economies, became popular by promising to replace planned regimes with systems based on markets.[22] Even large conglomerates in the private sector began to unwind into more nimble and competitive entities. With the causes of political liberty, free markets, and conservative politics increasingly overlapping and intertwined, people started to think of liberty and "free markets" as aspects of the same thing.

As support for market-based regulation grew, however, something interesting happened. By the 1990s, Democrats started to jump on the market bandwagon. A rising group of "New" Democrats suggested liberalism could also harness insights about markets to better meet their own policy goals.[23] They embraced ideas like tax cuts, "reinventing government" to reduce regulatory burdens on industries, and welfare reform plans that engineered the incentives of recipients. They embraced carbon trading as an alternative to hard limits on carbon emissions. They embraced regulated insurance exchanges as an alternative to a single-payer government health-insurance plan. They embraced sin taxes on less healthy foods, congestion pricing to reduce traffic, and even, in some quarters, privately run charter schools that competed with public school systems. Instead of commanding outcomes, regulators could enlist markets by engineering incentives so citizens mainly chose the preferred government outcome on their own. Professor and former Obama adviser Cass Sunstein popularized this sort of thinking as market-based regulatory "nudges."[24] As Democrats increasingly injected market mechanisms into public regulation, something even more interesting happened—Republicans opposed them. What's more, Republicans frequently cited principled liberty as the reason for their objections. Suspecting hypocrisy and crass political calculation, Democrats became indignant that Republicans would reject market-based regulatory schemes, many the party had once endorsed.

The reason Republicans rejected these Democratic plans was because markets and decentralization were never the real principle at stake. As a practical matter, since the New Deal was at its heart a program of industrial planning, when liberty conservatives argued against the New Deal during the Fifth Party System, they often found themselves arguing about economics and markets. They frequently found it easier to convince people who didn't agree with their principles by discussing tangible policies and their intended effects—things like markets, decentralization, lower taxes, jobs, and prosperity—than by discussing abstract and theoretical things like liberty or encroachments on dignity. Yet markets were always simply the means to pursue liberty given the specific political battles at the time, never the principle at stake. Liberty conservatives made pragmatic arguments about free markets, devolving power to local authority, efficiency, and the wisdom of crowds because market regulatory schemes that achieve goals with a lighter hand are less likely to leave minorities feeling abused. While a liberty conservative might prefer a "nudge" by which government sets up penalties and incentives over a system requiring more centralized control, that liberty conservative would probably prefer no government scheme at all. In practice, Republican arguments about liberty and policies based around markets were frequently intertwined during the Fifth Party System. That doesn't mean markets are what liberty is philosophically about.

The policies and programs since Franklin Roosevelt's New Deal over which Democrats and Republicans have argued while citing principled liberty were always mere applications of liberty to specific problems of middle-of-the-twentieth-century America. The principle of liberty, however, is and always was something far greater. It was never just a practical philosophy about the limits of state power. It's a moral philosophy about separating what's legal for a democratic majority to do from what's moral for it to do—what's wrong for the people who win elections to do to those who lose.

DEMOCRACY VERSUS BULLYING BY THE MAJORITY

The freest society with the broadest form of market capitalism can't function without a government that establishes and enforces the rule of law so citizens are protected from random violence, confident their agreements will be enforced, and sure frauds against them will be punished. Where there's no rule of law or public order, warlords carve out turf and terrorize people. Violence becomes a daily threat. The strong prey on the weak. The powerful wall themselves off from the people. A society with no government wouldn't be one of freedom but of chaos, as the violent and cunning dominated and subjugated the kind and the meek—as the philosopher Thomas Hobbes said of this state of nature, mankind would live in "continual fear and danger of violent death, and the life of man [would be] solitary, poor, nasty, brutish, and short."[25] As James Madison wrote in *The Federalist*, "If men were angels, no government would be necessary."[26] But men are not angels. It's not a question of whether government is good or bad; some government is necessary.

That "government," moreover, is merely an abstraction. It's just the name we give the collective decisions of the people currently empowered to make and enforce the laws. While those officials theoretically represent everybody in a republic, in reality we know they owe their positions to the factions that voted them into power. Government is also the one social institution to which we give what political philosophers call the "monopoly on violence"—the legitimate power to force everyone else to obey.[27] Corporations, criminals, gangs, and individuals may grow powerful. They can dominate people or even influence government. Yet government can, if it wants, always break the power of any other group in society because only government has the lawful power to maintain armed police forces and armies and judicial courts with which to impose its decisions on everyone else. That's what makes something a law—if you refuse to obey its command, an official with a gun strapped to his belt will eventually find you and force you to comply, or drag you in front of a tribunal to punish you if you won't. When we say "the government" has done something in the American republic, we therefore mean the people who won the last election ordered something to be done. The question, therefore, isn't really what an abstract "government" should or shouldn't do. The question is when is it okay for a group of human beings to band together through politics to impose their will by force over weaker or less organized groups?

What, then, separates legitimate democratic governing from majority bullying? Where is the line separating Rousseau's general will from the Founders' counter-majoritarian concerns? It's easy to see that line when a law or plan isn't actually intended for everyone's collective benefit. It's never legitimate or moral in the American system for a faction to use its control of government to loot the state for itself or its friends, or to punish others in society it doesn't like. Majorities aren't supposed to use their greater numbers to take advantage of minorities. They're not supposed to use their power to reward their friends. They're not supposed to act indifferently toward those who didn't vote for them. When officials take office, they're supposed to represent all Americans equally, not act as the sword of the dominant group. Americans have always recognized it's immoral for the winners of the election to use their power to benefit themselves or to hurt their enemies, as opposed to governing in the best interest of everyone without regard to faction or identity. That's why

FDR's "Soak the Rich" tax—a bill meant to punish one specific man—was so controversial. It's why the South's Jim Crow laws outrage us. It's why Americans have always loathed politicians who waste public money on pet constituencies. A republic can't long survive if losing an election becomes a tragedy because those who won refuse to treat us with respect when they exercise power over us—much less intentionally set out to hurt us. Americans shouldn't gloat that "elections have consequences" because that's essentially bragging that we have our neighbors at our mercy and intend to make it hurt. It's corrosive to democracy. This sort of factional politics, governing not for the benefit of all Americans, is always immoral majority tyranny violating principled liberty.

The more complicated case exists when a majority believes its plans are best for everybody, but the election's losers deeply disagree. It's important to never forget that overpowering someone's will, using power over them, is an assault on their autonomy and thus their human dignity. When someone with power forces you to do something against your will, it makes you feel small, angry, and horribly injured. The indignity of feeling weak and powerless and at the mercy of the strong is embedded in human nature. When people use power to dominate us—to force us to do things they want us to do, or to not do things we want to do—it hurts our autonomy and injures us. Since every government policy essentially involves the political majority wielding its collective power to subdue the desires of political minorities—the winners of the election overriding the interests and desires of the losers—every time the government acts, some people are going to feel weak and powerless. That inflicts a real harm, one that often matters to people just as much as any physical harm. Even when the government makes things better in some way. Sometimes, especially when it does.

Majorities in America are supposed to respect the dignity of minorities by sometimes refraining from pushing through policies they like, respecting the fears and strong views of the minority with whom they disagree. Since overriding somebody's will by force does them an injury in itself, we must always take that cost into account. Even if you're sure your plan really will benefit everybody equally and not just yourself, it still matters that the minority disagrees. It's never enough to simply ask whether the expected benefits of a plan outweigh its surface-level costs. A government committed to political liberty always places onto the scale the additional moral cost of overriding the will of the minority—even when we think they're wrong or will come to love our ideas once we implement them. Sometimes the moral thing to do is to not use power, even when you're right, even when your plan is better, and even when a majority of your fellow citizens agree with you.

Separating a democratic result from majority bullying is therefore a weighing process dependent on context, one that places on one side the benefit of the plan and on the other the cost to the dignity of the minority compelled to go along by force. The more broadly accepted the plan, the more likely it's moral to bind everyone to its implementation. The more a minority group opposes a plan, the more likely the majority cramming it through over the minority's objections is wrong. If a proposal is urgent and essential to the nation's survival, it's almost always fair to enact it. If a proposal isn't urgent and is highly controversial—something the majority really wants but that other Americans don't—it's probably wrong to override the will of the minority, even if the majority is correct and the minority mistaken. If the proposal is the result of careful negotiation with minority factions to build a national consensus, the cost in forcing compliance is usually small. The more the plan benefits everybody in society equally, the more acceptable it is to force those who disagree to obey it nonetheless.

In American politics, liberty isn't about defining clear bright lines dividing what's acceptable for government to do. Nor is it a philosophy of small government, low taxes, market regulation, or leaving people alone—those are just applications of liberty to the issues of a specific place and time. Liberty in America is a philosophy of individual dignity. It holds that great care is owed before public officials can morally wield power to force others to obey them because their commands inflict an additional and hidden human cost—damage to the dignity of those whose will they override with force. No one in mainstream American politics wants to become a tyrant, yet every other political faction is organized around forcing agendas on political minorities. People get involved in politics because they have agendas of changes they hope to implement through government. To accomplish that, they have to defeat their political enemies at the ballot box and use the power they've won to impose change on everybody else. They accept that their political enemies would do the same to them given the chance. Liberty arguments in America are about telling everybody else in politics "no." That right and popular aren't good enough reasons to force something on other people—people who disagree or who may be harmed by your plans, or who may simply not want the changes you seek to impose on their lives. They essentially tell the victors of elections they're acting immorally by turning their victories into power.

This American conception of liberty leaves plenty of room for citizens to work together through government. There's nothing in principled liberty that says citizens can't agree to pool their resources through government or enforce the broadly shared norms of society, so long as those efforts aren't hidden methods for election winners to abuse election losers. Making everyone chip in to build roads and airports that make us collectively richer doesn't violate anyone's liberty, so long as it's truly a consensual joint decision. There's nothing wrong with citizens enforcing a broadly shared consensus that careless or sloppy people shouldn't pollute the air and water we share, that predators can't freely cheat their neighbors, or that institutions can't comprehensively lock certain groups out of public necessities. If a society believes it's better off with interstate highways, health regulations, retirement programs, and public education systems, nothing in principled liberty prevents it. In the right political context, it's possible to imagine liberty conservatives heartily approving all those programs and policies. What matters is what the majority seeks to achieve, why the minority objects, and whether a compelling reason exists for the majority to overpower those objections with its collective power.

Liberty is a principle deeply embedded into America's institutions, its culture, and its values. American liberty separates what's legal from what's right, and it separates joint decision-making from majority bullying. It ensures the awesome power of the state is only brought to bear when there's broad consensus across every segment of society. It prevents government of the people, by the people, and for the people from becoming the rule of the mob. It ensures the winner's idea of utopia doesn't become the loser's prison. It's about ensuring republican government means citizens cooperating together to solve problems in a way that's fair to all. Whenever a winning majority has sought to impose significant national change, those who disagreed have demanded their liberty be respected. They weren't claiming their political leaders had become cruel despots. Neither were they claiming their opponents weren't legally entitled to impose their will under the existing constitutional regime. They were making a claim about how American democracy is supposed to work. Majorities in America aren't supposed to do as they like. That's what America's Founders thought Enlightenment reason demanded, and it remains just as true today. During the Fifth Party System, liberty was a core Republican ideal given the New Deal debate. As we tackle new problems in the next party system, liberty will continue to play a critical role— the only question is how.

CHAPTER 8

THE PROGRESSIVE PLAN

O ver the last two decades, Democrats have increasingly labeled themselves "progressives," repurposing an old word long fallen out of use. Before the 1990s, you rarely heard anyone call themselves or anyone else a "progressive" outside of historical accounts of turn-of-the-century politics. The Progressive Movement flourished back when suffragettes wore elaborate hats, bicycles were a craze, and Teddy Roosevelt hunted big game. Liberalism was the political philosophy of the New Deal Democratic Party. Over the 1970s and 1980s, however, associations with student radicals, utopian ideals, and urban dysfunction had tarnished the word "liberal" in the minds of too many voters, and Republicans learned they could win a lot of campaigns by simply pinning the word "liberal" to their opponent's lapel. Republican political consultant Arthur Finkelstein rose to national fame with this strategy, airing devastating attack ads in countless campaigns that simply repeated "liberal" again and again as if it were the filthiest of words.[1] The label "progressive" rode to the rescue.

When adopting the name of this old historical force, many modern Democrats presume the historical progressives believed much the same things they believe. Conservatives, on the other hand, attack the policies and sins of the historical Progressive Movement, presuming that discrediting the historical progressives discredits modern liberalism by extension. Neither seems to understand a basic historical fact—progressivism isn't the same thing as New Deal liberalism. Not all modern Democrats are progressives. Nor do progressive ideals inevitably lead to all facets of modern liberalism. The modern Democratic Party contains substantial progressive impulses, but a lot of what people now call progressivism isn't.

THE IMPULSE FOR MORAL REFORM

Every human society that has ever existed has been flawed. Human beings, after all, are flawed. From the smallest ancient tribes to the greatest modern civilizations, every human community has in different ways tolerated gross inefficiency, rank injustice, and the perpetuation of unspeakable evils by some people against others. Time and again, in every corner of the earth, accidents of birth like race, tribe, or social class have arbitrarily placed the boots of some people on the necks of others. Time and again, ignorance has defeated knowledge and the ignorant have punished the wise. Time and again, the cruel and the dull witted have risen to power to destroy the lives and families of the meek and the just. Everywhere in the world, during every era in history, cruelty, injustice, and ignorance have prevailed despite our best hopes. No one has yet devised the perfect society. Depravity lurks inside too many human hearts. The world is imperfect. Life is not fair.

At the same time, human societies aren't just cruel and irrational Hobbesian struggles of man against man. For every cruel dimwit on a throne, a near-saint rises to protect citizens against misrule. For every unjust proclamation, someone else imposes a just one at personal cost because it's the right thing to do. For every unkindness, someone else offers self-sacrificing kindness. There are always people pushing to make things better. Along with cruelty, murder, and war, humanity has created prosperity, joy, art, and culture. The struggle between these two sides of humanity creates civilization, which, while never perfect, protects us from the countless wicked depravities we would suffer if we were ever cast back into the savage wasteland. Despite all our flaws, humans have done a reasonable job of creating fair and workable social orders because some people have always sacrificed to improve the human condition, creating societies more just, fair, and prosperous than before.

The root of modern progressivism thus stretches back to the very beginnings of civilization, with all those who looked at flawed societies, saw imperfections, and had the impulse to work toward improving them to make them a little better, richer, more moral, or more just. For most of world history, that mostly meant advancing the moral codes of religion. That's because, until recently, nearly every society was under a near-absolute ruler backed by a small and powerful ruling class. Whether that ruler was a king, a queen, a prince, a warlord, a chief, a sultan, a high priest, or a khan, the bottom line was always the same—while culture and custom imposed some limits on dealing with other members of the ruling class, rulers and those around them could essentially do to peasants what they liked. For millennia, the politics of improving society was therefore the politics of improving kings. If you wanted your society to be ruled better—not just for the king but for the people at large—you needed to convince the king and nobles to be judicious in the exercise of power over others. You needed to convince them not to hoard the nation's bounty and to govern fairly under laws and not by whim. You needed to convince them not to rape, murder, and steal when the law, as it existed, allowed them to do all that and worse for no reason other than that they felt like it. The citizens in societies with just kings and relatively benevolent ruling classes enjoyed more fairness, justice, and prosperity than citizens in societies with ruthless kings and unscrupulous ruling classes. The only way to impose limits on an absolute ruler is with the help of someone stronger. The only person stronger than a king is God, or in some circumstances the gods.

A king and his courtiers are unlikely to restrain their appetites just because it's the right thing to do. The threat of eternal damnation is more likely to seize their attention. When reformers sought to reform kings, they naturally tended not toward abstract arguments about the benefits of a just society but arguments of personal morality based on religious teachings. A king could easily understand that it was in his personal interest to obey the will of the only being stronger than he was. It was therefore in the interest of reformers to connect their arguments not to abstract public policy or grand theories of society but to the tenets of the king's religious beliefs. Whether it be hell and Satan, reincarnation as a lowly earthworm, the possibility of shaming one's ancestors, or having one's heart weighed too heavy before Osiris, the powerful would suffer if they behaved too unjustly. For kings and nobles, fear of the divine instilled good reason not to behave like monsters. For most of human history, social justice and religious morality were therefore essentially intertwined. While philosophers sometimes thought and argued over systems of rules or abstract fairness, and while some eastern systems of morality had both secular and spiritual elements, the core of most social reform was grounded in codes of personal morality backed by the tenets of belief. Even an eastern philosophy like Confucianism that didn't directly call on the will of a god was invoked and obeyed like religion. From antiquity to the Renaissance, the practical work of reforming society was mostly about ensuring the personal morality of individual lords and kings, encoded and enforced by the authorities of a religious establishment. A society where justice depended on whether the ruler was personally receptive to arguments about religious morality, however, was perilous. While a pious king and ruling class meant society would most likely be more fair, a king and ruling class who didn't much fear God often meant nightmares. Worse, even pious rulers sometimes interpreted religious morality to justify cruel or unjust actions. World history is chock full of wars, jihads, human sacrifices, crusades, tribal raids, and inquisitions justified on the basis of moral belief.

During the eighteenth century, the Western world embraced the Enlightenment and Western societies began to believe that people ought to order their affairs according to reason instead of according to the whims of authority or the habits of tradition. Among the many earth-shaking results of this simple premise was the spread of republican governments responsible to the will of the people and not to absolute rulers or powerful nobles. How society treated its citizens no longer turned on whether the current cabal of rulers happened to be good people. If officials proved cruel, selfish, evil, or indifferent to the needs of any class, the people could replace them. How a democratic republic treated its citizens turned on the morality not of kings but of voters. If you wanted to reform society in a democratic republic, you needed to reach its people. The most powerful tool available for reforming people, however, remained the same—morality and religion. From attempting to instill morality into a few powerful rulers, moral reformers turned their attention to saving the souls of the great mass of ordinary citizens. The first of these new republics was the United States of America.

In the first half of the nineteenth century, these forces—democracy, religion, and reform—intermingled in America through the religious revivals of the Second Great Awakening, helping to bring America's Second Party System to its end by the middle of the century. Reformers launched movements for the better treatment of prisoners and the mentally ill.[2] They threw themselves into poverty aid work. Most important, they began a crusade to abolish slavery from America's shores. Their methods, however, still mainly involved teaching personal religious morality as a tool to improve the individual characters and behaviors of Americans.[3] Where prior generations of reformers would have achieved their goals by making arguments of religious morality to a king, the reformers of young America quoted scripture at the American people. Reformers reasoned that, since the people of the republic controlled the government, the only way to improve and perfect society was to improve and perfect its citizens.[4] For all the Enlightenment and democracy had changed about politics, social reform was still a battle to save souls.[5] The only thing that changed was whose souls must be saved—the king's or everybody's. The desire for social justice we associate with progressivism and the desire to protect and advance virtue were, for most of human history, for all intents and purposes the same thing. Then we invented social science.

SOCIAL SCIENCE AND THE PROGRESSIVE MOVEMENT

The birth of social science finally severed the cause of social reform from religious morality. For most of human history, what we call the social sciences—economics, sociology, anthropology, psychology, political science, and their cousin disciplines—weren't considered sciences but fields of philosophy. Human behavior wasn't something we could study and catalogue or describe with the rigidity of theorems, statistics, and axioms. It was a mystery to contemplate. Those who attempted to understand humanity were "moral philosophers," while those who studied the natural world of what we now call the hard sciences were "natural philosophers."[6] Then Isaac Newton popularized the scientific method as the most rational means to solve problems. Before long, people in the West began to wonder whether the same method Newton used to examine, understand, and manipulate the natural forces of physics might also help examine, understand, and manipulate the patterns of human societies. That idea transformed the contemplations of moral philosophy into the empirical systems of social science.[7]

The moral philosopher Adam Smith invented the first social science—economics—in 1776, with his now famous work *The Wealth of Nations*. Smith, who had previously written on philosophical ethics, now dismantled prior mercantilist understandings and set the stage for the modern view of capitalism by setting out theories on how labor and capital actually interrelate in practice. As the nineteenth century progressed, political philosophy transformed into the new field of political science. Anthropology emerged out of the philosophical field of natural history. Emile Durkheim invented sociology. Psychology was recognized as a valid field of study. By the late nineteenth century, looking at human problems through the lens of scientific vigor had gone from a pathbreaking concept to an established academic discipline to a booming and trendy field.[8] In each discipline, thinkers adopted Newton's scientific method to move past philosophical theories about how human societies might behave to real experimental explorations into how they actually do behave. The scientific exploration of social questions promised to transform the world—if poverty, war, and prosperity could be studied, measured, and understood, perhaps that meant they could be tamed.[9]

This new tool of social science arrived just as novel technological marvels were driving astonishing economic progress. New technologies like railroads, photography, and electric current were changing the country. Factories transformed cities. Telegraphs allowed long distance communication. America was booming with new innovation and inventions and opportunities. It stood to reason that the innovation of social science might just bring social progress that rivaled the economic progress these technical marvels had delivered. At the same time, with peace and stability restored after a brutal civil war, America's appetite for social reform resumed once more. A new generation had grown up without scarring memories from the conflict. Free of Civil War era obsessions, they looked at a changing Gilded Age America and saw a host of troubling new problems without solutions.[10] America was no longer an agricultural secondary power building farms in the wilderness but a budding industrial powerhouse and rising global power, with its young people fleeing farms for new opportunities in cities. It was a nation with new immigrants crowding into dangerous tenement houses, exploitative and dangerous sweatshop labor, and women and children working grueling fourteen-hour days. Social reformers faced social ills for which no solutions yet existed.

At about the same time, a new religious revival swept across the land. American religion had grown quiet after the Civil War as the nation focused on rebuilding, but now evangelical activists, seized by the belief that they might bring about God's Kingdom on Earth by reforming away society's ills, rushed forth again eager to reform America into a more just and moral nation. This new generation of reformers, however, discovered they had a new tool to address the problems of their era that previous reformers hadn't had—social science. Instead of improving every individual one by one, reformers could use social science to design and implement institutions that redirected human impulses toward moral outcomes. Despite the inevitability of individual moral weakness, wise and moral experts could employ social planning as a tool to transform a nation.[11] Not only could they build a society that yielded just, fair, and moral results, but they could even use these tools on malleable humans to reshape them using education and public policy.[12] This marriage of reformist moral fervor and social science created the Progressive Movement,[13] whose crusade to remake and reform America shone across America's Fourth Party System.[14]

The Progressive Movement was an interrelated network of movements, activists, journalists, social scientists, and professionals who shared a common perspective and philosophy. Believing change didn't bubble up from below but rather came from moral and just leadership above, progressives wanted to empower strong, wise, educated, and rational leaders to impose beneficial change on society.[15] Progressives, therefore, wanted to employ modern knowledge and expertise to socially plan a more fair, moral, and efficient America, eliminating the novel ills the new economy had brought as well as older ones that had long plagued human societies. Progressivism was a phenomenon of the educated middle and upper classes.[16] It flourished most with the generation that grew up amid new stability after the carnage of the Civil War.[17] It mixed scientific rationalism with evangelical revival, as many progressives held millennialist beliefs about the importance of reforming America into God's Kingdom through a new "Social Gospel."[18] It was both business friendly and pro-regulation, drawing lines between good and moral wealth (like that of its frequently wealthy followers) and bad immoral wealth (like that of the "trusts").[19] It prized efficiency, order, and professionalism as keys to advancing human progress over irrational human impulses.[20] It was a movement "middle class in its outlook, moralistic in its temper, moderate and resourceful in its approach to problems of policy"[21] that united social reformers, poverty workers, good-government advocates, evangelical preachers, business leaders, efficiency experts, and energetic social scientists into one single political group.

Since progressivism was more a common spirit and philosophy than a united political organization, it linked a multitude of interrelated efforts to reform America. There were the settlement houses that sprung up in major cities, such as Hull House in Chicago, in which people like Jane Addams, mainly young middle-class women with a Christian outlook, sought to assist, educate, and reform the urban poor.[22] There were the social workers like Frances Perkins, who advocated for new laws that would stop factory abuses such as the ones that had caused the infamous Triangle Shirtwaist Fire, and lobbied for maximum work hours laws and the end of child labor.[23] There were the Muckrakers who exposed abuses and outrages in muckraking magazines like *McClure's*, such as Ida Tarbell and her famous expose on Standard Oil.[24] There were the suffragettes who organized and battled to finally win the vote for women. There were the temperance crusades and prohibitionists who, through the Women's Christian's Temperance Union and Anti-Saloon League, convinced America that alcohol was immoral, leading working-class men (especially Catholic immigrants from places like Ireland) to squander money their families needed desperately and to become violent toward their wives and children.[25] There were the middle-class reformers who campaigned for good government against political machines such as Tammany Hall. There were the journalists and writers like Herbert Croly, who created an intellectual framework for progressive reform, and the professionals and social scientists who offered up their expertise to solve public problems.[26] There were the preachers of the Social Gospel, such as Walter Rauschenbusch, who taught that it was every Christian's duty to throw themselves into national projects for social reform to remake America into a truly godly society.[27]

For the first two decades of the twentieth century, progressivism reigned as the most powerful political and social movement in America. Progressives cooperated to stamp out abuses, impose rational planning, and morally reform America. Their accomplishments were astounding.[28] Progressives targeted the new social problems industrialization had brought at a time when abuses ran rampant—dark practices like child labor, wage slavery, and hard fourteen-hour working days; huge new factories with inhumane conditions; cities newly bursting with poor and struggling immigrants from every corner of the world; massive new transportation networks bringing processed food and untested medicines from unknown sources; behemoth trust corporations run by wealthy and powerful men who dominated entire industries; and organized political corruption keeping it all in place.

Progressives won laws that eliminated child labor, eradicated abusive sweatshops preying on working women and children, imposed maximum work hours, and implemented minimum wages.[29] They created public assistance regimes to help the struggling working class and poor.[30] They created the Food and Drug Administration to ensure contaminants didn't enter the industrial food supply and to eliminate quack remedies from medicine in an era in which new national markets empowered unscrupulous fly-by-night schemers to harm masses of people with scam products. Progressives created antitrust laws to stop anticompetitive behavior like price-fixing that unfairly drove competitors out of business at a time in which powerful national businesses had emerged that could leverage their size to drive smaller competitors from the market.[31] They fought for good government providing competent service to everyone, without the graft most Americans had come to take for granted in an era in which patronage and machine-boss politics dominated. They pushed parties to pick candidates through primary elections and fought to replace city bosses with nonelected expert city managers to degrade the power of the political bosses who had previously handpicked machine candidates they controlled.[32] They won a constitutional amendment to allow citizens to directly elect their senators (whom state legislatures had elected previously). They built parks in cities so children had healthy green places to play.[33] They promoted the conservation of nature and created the National Parks.[34] They promoted an "efficiency movement" in the public and private arena, inventing a new science of business management that taught that expert managers could create optimally efficient systems to produce more for the benefit of all.[35] They finally won the vote for women and cleared the way for national alcohol prohibition to eliminate the corrupt influence of intoxicating drink.

The historical Progressive Movement, however, wasn't the same thing we call modern "progressivism." At its heart, the Progressive Movement wasn't a movement to empower poor and working people. It was a national movement with a moral and religious backing seeking to use rationalism and science to purify America. Progressives wanted to help the poor and destitute, but they didn't want to empower the downtrodden. They wanted to reform and uplift the lower classes to instill the habits of their betters.[36] Progressives didn't want more representation for the poor in government or to break the power of elites—in fact they actively worked to break up the very urban political machines built to do so in the belief that they were inefficient and corrupt.[37] Progressives didn't want the people to rule, as William Jennings Bryan demanded, but to empower a brilliant, strong, independent, and morally good elite group of experts who would drive progress for everyone.[38] Progressives had an uneasy relationship with labor unionism.[39] Progressive charity was often explicitly predicated on the recipient's moral character because it wasn't motivated by solidarity with the poor but their improvement. Progressives seized upon the new science of eugenics—holding that experts could even improve the quality of the human race by rationally intervening into the human gene pool—seeing a scientific method to permanently eliminate social ills by breeding out undesirable human traits (leading to abominable discrimination against the disabled, compulsory sterilizations and abortions, racial classifications, and interventions into the family life of the poor).[40] Progressives wanted to regulate low behavior in business not because they distrusted capitalism— they often came from wealthy business-owning families themselves—but to drive immoral people of low character from the marketplace. Many progressive reforms also had secondary motives that would trouble modern progressives, such as the good-government reforms meant to break up the power of Democratic-voting immigrant political machines, alcohol prohibition meant to break up the saloons where Catholic immigrants politically organized, education meant to Americanize Catholic immigrants and instill moral righteousness, and women's suffrage that would dilute the votes of immigrant Catholic men who wouldn't let their wives or sisters vote.[41] The poor and immigrant targets of progressive reform usually held progressive causes in contempt, such as temperance, women's suffrage, and good government initiatives.[42] The religious Republican progressives weren't modern liberal Democrats.

During the Great Depression, when Franklin Roosevelt invited so many progressives into his party, he created a new ideology that drew in part on this progressive tradition. Progressivism is the part of the Democratic Party that believes experts using knowledge, science, and planning, can design more fair, just, efficient, and prosperous systems for everybody. A progressive believes human society is imperfect but perfectible—or at least greatly improvable. Progressives have confidence in the ability to study and plan away human ills, working around the human condition to design more fair, efficient, and prosperous societies. Progressives believe in good government, meritocracy, and ambitious plans. They're the "cause Democrats" who see the party as a base for their activism. They're the environmentalists who think we can enjoy prosperity while also leaving a wholesome and undamaged earth. They're the civil rights activists who believe we can eradicate prejudices and intolerance. They're the social reformers who think we can stamp out poverty. They're the advocates for smart regulation that smooths out the jagged edges of private enterprise. A working-class Democrat who believes in the party's economic agenda but who is also religiously conservative, uncomfortable with homosexuality, suspicious of claims about what must be done to protect the environment, unsure about the truth of evolution, and deeply worried that social and economic change is shattering the America he knew and leaving him and his family behind, is not a progressive. His political beliefs come from a completely different place than the politics of an upper-middle-class university professor concerned about gay rights, climate change, whether women can break into the corporate suite, and the advance of social justice.

Progressivism remains a powerful idea in American politics. It's a political expression of the can-do American spirit that believes any problem, no matter how seemingly impossible, can be solved if only good men and women roll up their sleeves and fully apply themselves to the task. Progressivism is about planning, good government, expertise, efficiency, and making systems more fair and just. It's about belief in the perfectibility of human societies and the promise of a better future if we just find the right institutions, interventions, and plans. It's only one part of New Deal liberalism, but it's also bigger than New Deal liberalism. Societies will always have social and moral reformers looking to make things better. In America, the progressive impulse to engineer a better society with knowledge and expertise remains a strong expression of that impulse, one that's likely to remain an influential driver of our politics as far into our future as we can now foresee.

CHAPTER 9

THE VIRTUE OF A REPUBLIC

Highway speed limits must be one of the most comprehensively policed laws in all America. We've established dedicated law enforcement agencies in every state to enforce this one infraction. Speeding takes place on predesignated narrow strips of land with limited obstructions, easily monitored from the side of the road or by air. We often line entire highways with cameras and speed traps just to catch speeders. It hardly makes a difference. It's not just criminals and shady operators who openly flout the speed limits without a second thought. On every highway in America, you find little old ladies who would never dream of breaking "real" laws still buzzing by at eighty miles per hour without a care in the world. Completely law-abiding people who file their taxes on time, always use their turn signal, and cluck loudly at jaywalkers, happily break the speed limits as if they were mere suggestions. Despite all the effort we put into stopping it, it's impossible to get people not to speed.

Why do nice people who normally respect the criminal code regularly break these laws without a moment's embarrassment, and often with a bit of pride? Because most of what we all actually do, or won't do, isn't governed by our desire to comply with the legal code. It's governed by a completely different set of rules, social norms and our cultural and moral beliefs. People speed because, while everyone knows speeding is illegal, most people don't think it's wrong. That truth is at the heart of the philosophy of virtue conservatism.

WHAT IN THE WORLD IS NATIONAL VIRTUE?

As Ben Franklin walked out of the Constitutional Convention, a woman reportedly approached him and asked, "What do we have Doctor, a republic or a monarchy?" "A republic," Franklin replied, "if you can keep it."[1] Franklin's famous reply expressed one of the Founding generation's greatest concerns about their creation. Constitutional rules and legal protections that look great on paper only yield a free society in practice if citizens honor them. Rules, separations of powers, and Bills of Rights, have to be constantly interpreted, administered, and applied by people. If citizens in an expedient rush to pursue other goals—whether personal selfishness, factional interests, utopian projects, or partisan power-chasing—fail to put the preservation of the republic first, republican government will eventually collapse.

It was an item of faith at the time of America's Founding that monarchies and dictatorships had a significant advantage over republics because a republic's strength is also its greatest vulnerability—the people are the government. A monarchy can flourish so long as the small circle around its king has the necessary wisdom and foresight to rule. For a democratic republic to flourish, its people must demonstrate the wisdom and foresight to continually place the nation's collective interest before their own. A republic populated by wise and capable citizens will make good decisions, and therefore succeed and thrive. A republic populated by ignorant and selfish citizens will perish. Formal institutions that separate power between competing factions, that protect rights, or that call for all citizens to be treated with justice, are a good start. Yet if citizens then ignore these restrictions when they find them inconvenient, or chip away at rights with a flurry of exceptions that allow them more freedom to act, or wield rights not as shields but weapons to bash others in society who they don't like, the republic will decay regardless of what its laws and constitution say on paper.

Among the most important influences on the American Constitution's design was the French philosopher and lawyer Charles-Louis de Secondat, popularly known as Montesquieu. America's Founders adopted almost wholesale Montesquieu's suggestion—set out in his 1748 work,

The Spirit of the Laws—that a republic should separate power between an executive, a judiciary, and a two-chambered legislature.[2] Montesquieu also believed, however, that separating power through a clever constitutional design was hardly sufficient to preserve a republic's liberty. He also believed a republic needed a certain character in its citizens to survive and prosper. Montesquieu believed three forms of government had existed throughout human history—the republic, the monarchy, and despotism—each of which required a different character to succeed. The citizens of a democratic republic, he believed, needed what he called virtue.[3] By virtue, Montesquieu didn't mean sexual purity, a harsh and upstanding persona, or rules of social manners. He meant the virtue of good citizenship. As he put it:

> One can define this virtue as love of the laws and the homeland. This love, requiring a continuous preference of the public interest over one's own, proceeds all the individual virtues; they are only that preference.
>
> This love is singularly connected with democracies. In them alone, government is entrusted to each citizen. Now government is like all things in the world; in order to preserve it, one must love it.[4]

Montesquieu, like America's Founders, was keenly aware that republics across history inevitably descended into oligarchy or dictatorship when their people failed to put the interests of the republic before their own. Plato famously held aristocracy, by which he essentially meant rule by meritocratic philosophers, a higher form of government than democracy for just this reason.[5] An enlightened monarch with his people's best interest in his heart, Plato thought, would back his decisions with more wisdom and ability than the unruly mob of democracy.[6] On the other hand, democracies, Plato believed, inevitably degenerate into tyrannies because people crave order in hard times, and a powerful demagogue will always arise to promise it.[7] Much evidence across human history supports Plato's view. The democracy of Athens had its periodic tyrants and an oligarchic coup. The republic of Florence devolved into a hereditary duchy. Most troubling, even the Romans who believed that their republican traditions—their Senate, their Consuls, and their complicated ladder of public offices—were the key to their nation's extraordinary success gave up on republican government for the authority of an emperor under the charismatic Julius Caesar, followed by Augustus. The fact that even Rome cast off its cherished republican institutions, the system that brought the Roman people unrivaled power, wealth, and dignity within the ancient world, is outright distressing.

America's Founders agreed with Montesquieu that a lasting republic required something beyond just well-crafted institutions to succeed; it also needed a republican virtue in its people.[8] We too often forget that the Founders considered the formal institutional safeguards of their Constitution, like dividing power across branches of government and creating a sturdy Bill of Rights, as mere last-ditch defenses against a demagogue, factional corruption, or the tyranny of the mob. Clever constitutional safeguards, well-crafted institutions, and wise systems of checks and balances setting ambition against ambition, are only as good as the people who administer and interpret them. The Founders also believed the citizens of their republic had to honor certain values, hold specific traits of character, and put the republic's welfare first if their republic was to survive.[9] Citizens had to be public-spirited enough to root out corruption. They needed to be wise enough about the substance of issues to choose representatives willing and able to do the public's business. They couldn't exercise their power like an uneducated mob. They couldn't use their power over government to loot the public till at others' expense, nor could they put their own factional interests before the interests of the state. If citizens used their democratic power to pursue their own short-term desires at the nation's long-term expense, abuse groups they disliked, or seek power for the sake of it without regard to prudent governing, their republic would ultimately fail. The experience of other republican experiments across the world suggest this was no fanciful concern. The world is littered with nations that copied, almost to the letter, the institutions set out in America's Constitution, expecting them to transform autocratic societies into democracies as if by magic. When the people in societies importing America's institutions by rote refused to honor their formal safeguards, they failed to keep them.

What the Founders called republican virtue is ultimately just another way to say culture or norms. As we all know, much of our day-to-day behavior isn't shaped by the fear we might get punished for violating legal rules, but by the complex code of traditions and cultural beliefs and social cues we carry about in our heads. We operate in a social world in which social expectation governs much of our behavior. We don't want to seem rude. We don't want to disappoint people. We don't want to feel embarrassed. We don't want to threaten our status in the community. We don't want to look ignorant. We don't want to say the wrong thing, or make people uncomfortable, or use the wrong fork. Sometimes it's something small, like whether you always politely line up into a queue or whether you push yourself to the front of the line. Sometimes it's something big, like whether you agree to marry a stranger your parents picked for you, one you don't even like, even though there's absolutely no legal requirement saying you have to do it. People expect certain behavior from us—that we honor agreements, care for our families, and behave honestly in certain situations. We come to expect those things from ourselves. These countless invisible rules we unthinkingly obey about what we're supposed to do, how we're supposed to live, and how we're supposed to behave in particular circumstances, are of more consequence to how a society actually operates than all the visible rules written into law books. No police need to catch us breaking these "laws" because we catch and punish ourselves.

Imagine yourself in a convenience store. You grab a Snickers bar and take it to the cashier. The man behind the counter is transfixed by a little television set behind him. In this moment, you realize you could easily slip the candy into your jacket pocket without anyone the wiser. Instead you get the cashier's attention and pay full price for your chocolate. Why did you do something contrary to your self-interest? It's not because you were afraid of getting caught; you could have easily escaped without anyone knowing. It's not because you were afraid of hurting the convenience store; it's part of a big corporation for which you have no real affection. If you were somehow caught shoplifting such a small item, the legal consequences wouldn't be all that great. You paid because you believe stealing is wrong. What you would dread if you got caught wouldn't be the legal slap on the wrist you would likely receive. It would be telling your mother what you had done. Or potentially losing out on a job someday when a potential employer found out you had a record for shoplifting. Or not getting a second date when someone you liked discovered your criminal record.

The idea that virtue is important to maintaining a republic—that a republic's citizens must embrace and live by certain cultural beliefs and norms if the republic is to survive—suffused the thinking of America's Founders, and indeed of most intellectuals during the eighteenth century.[10] The Founders understood the traits of character they sought were rare and extraordinary in people, which is why, they believed, monarchy and despotism had ruled so much of human history.[11] They nonetheless hoped America's unique foundation, its legacy without the feudalism and monarchy of Europe, and the structure of its society based around small independent farms, might foster the necessary republican virtue to succeed.[12] As James Madison, the Constitution's principal author, said in a speech seeking to win approval of his Constitution at the Virginia ratifying convention:

> I go on this great republican principle, that the people will have virtue and intelligence to select men of virtue and wisdom. Is there no virtue among us? If there be not, we are in a wretched situation. No theoretical checks—no form of government, can render us secure. To suppose that any form of government will secure liberty or happiness without any virtue in the people, is a chimerical idea.[13]

As Madison wrote of his Constitution in the *Federalist*, "A dependence on the people is, no doubt, the primary control on the government; but experience has taught mankind the necessity of auxiliary precautions."[14]

The traits of character the Founders prized, moreover, are important to more than simply maintaining a republic. After over two centuries of success, we've come to take for granted that the American republican experiment can and ought to work. These traits are also important to ensuring it thrives. We worry now just as much about whether the republic will continue to prosper, or whether it will fall into decline. We worry about whether citizens through the democratic process will choose wise leaders, or whether they will select short-sighted, corrupt, or incompetent ones. We worry about whether the democratic process will result in smart policies guiding the nation toward long-term success, or whether it will implement short-term kludges, backroom deals selling out the nation to some constituency, or simply fail to respond to looming crises at all. We worry about whether citizens will create innovations and infrastructure, or whether they will seek to profit at the nation's collective expense. What the Founders thought of as republican virtue is really something greater, national virtue—the cultural habits that lead to national success.

Two strong traditions exist in America about what this national virtue is and what we ought to do to safeguard it. One tradition is grounded in the belief that America's traditions reflect hard-won knowledge that have endured the test of time. The other is grounded in a zeal for moral reform, a fear of corruption and decline, and the belief that America represents an opportunity to build a more pure and perfect society. In some ways these traditions are quite similar. But the differences between them matter too.

WHO WAS EDMUND BURKE?

Edmund Burke is widely recognized as one of the world's most important political philosophers. No cloistered academic toiling away on abstract theories far away from the public scrum, Burke was a working politician—in fact, one of the most successful and famous politicians of his day. As the principal writer and idea-man of his faction of the British Whig party in Parliament, as well as a top aide to the prime minister, Burke was something of an eighteenth-century equivalent of chief party strategist. Burke's rise to the top of British politics and English society was extraordinary because his background wasn't illustrious, nor was he even English. Burke was born in Ireland at a time when the English considered the Irish something like backward foreigners.[15] After graduating from Trinity College in Dublin, Burke emigrated to London where he became the protégé and private secretary of the powerful Marquess of Rockingham, who controlled the strongest faction in Parliament.[16] Rockingham arranged for Burke to stand for an English parliamentary seat, where he quickly rose to influence through his talent as a writer, thinker, and orator. As Burke's influence grew, so did his national fame. He became a staple of the most select intellectual circles in London. By the outbreak of the American Revolution, Burke was one of the most powerful and renown men of ideas in Britain.

Burke involved himself in all the great questions of his day—the British treatment of his native Ireland and the immoralities involved in maintaining the empire in India among them—but the issue that came to define him most was his views on his era's republican revolutions. The British Whigs were what we would now consider a party of the left, championing innovation, progress, and change.[17] Whigs tended toward Enlightenment values and classical liberal economic views, favored commercial interests over the landed aristocrats, championed rationalism and commerce against the feudal remnants of the British aristocracy, and prized the ideal of liberty over traditional authority. The party's defining issue, however, was defending Parliament's power and the traditional rights of citizens against royal authority.[18] At the outbreak of the American Revolution, Burke, like most Whigs, jumped to the colonists' defense. To Whigs like Burke, Americans were fellow British citizens defending their traditional liberties against a monarch trampling upon them.[19] Burke spoke out in Parliament that Britain ought to honor the American colonists' reasonable grievances and make peace with them.[20] While he hoped America would remain within the British fold, he also believed the British government was principally at fault for the division.[21] Burke treated the American struggle against the king as another part of the Whiggish cause—defending the traditional rights of free English citizens against usurpation from the monarch. If Whigs allowed such injustice to stand in the colonies, it would only encourage the Crown to stomp on more liberties at home. Had history ended there, Burke would now be remembered as simply another great Enlightenment philosopher—a British counterpart to Madison and Jefferson.[22]

A few years after the end of the American Revolution, the French sought to install in France a republic much like the new republic in America.

Most British Whigs saw the French Revolution and the American Revolution as part of the same cause—the same embrace of liberty, rejection of monarchical authority, and support for Enlightenment reason over arbitrary authority—and they rushed to the defense of the French revolutionaries. Edmund Burke, however, loathed the French Revolution. He didn't see it as a noble people defending their traditional liberties against a dangerous monarch. Rather, he saw radicalism and utopianism. At first, Burke kept his opposition somewhat quiet, speaking against the French revolutionaries but not making too much noise. In 1790, however, he published a political pamphlet, *Reflections on the Revolution in France*, fully setting forth his views.[23] Many fellow Whigs recoiled, viewing Burke's opposition to the French Revolution as a betrayal of Whig principles. *Reflections* sparked a pamphlet war, with luminaries like Thomas Paine and Mary Wollstonecraft penning high-profile responses.[24] Burke became a controversial figure among Enlightenment liberals, and many openly broke with him.[25] Burke's popularity swiftly declined and people whispered he must be going mad. The Whigs even split into two opposing parties, with Burke leading an "Old Whig" faction against a "New Whig" faction led by party leader Charles James Fox.[26] Within a few short years, Burke lost many lifelong friendships, resigned his seat in Parliament, and then died.

Why did Edmund Burke, a man with a pristine liberal record for his era, a leader of the liberal party, and a champion of the American Revolution, come out so publicly against the revolution in France? As he explained in his writings, Burke loved liberty but believed it could only be protected as a part of a stable and ordered society.[27] As a Whig, Burke believed change was unavoidable, necessary, and often good.[28] He also believed society must pursue that change slowly and carefully, keeping consistent with tradition, to avoid breaking what it had already achieved. Real human beings, he believed, weren't creatures of reason ruled by neat abstractions and a nation, as he saw it, was a vast clockwork of complicated mechanisms that no one truly understands:

> It is the result of the thoughts of many minds, in many ages. It is no simple, no superficial thing, nor to be estimated by superficial under-

standings. An ignorant man, who is not fool enough to meddle with his clock, is however sufficiently confident to think he can safely take to pieces, and put together at his pleasure, a moral machine of another guise, importance, and complexity, composed of far other wheels, and springs, and balances, and counteracting and co-operating powers. Men little think how immorally they act in rashly meddling with what they do not understand. Their delusive good intention is no sort of excuse for their presumption.[29]

Societies to Burke were complex machines with too many moving parts for any one person to really understand. Underneath all of a society's formal laws and institutions are deeper cultural rules encoded in tradition.[30] Burke thought these traditions encode carefully negotiated methods by which complex societies work through difficult issues. This second set of rules developed over centuries of trial and error. Although nobody can really see these rules, or completely understand their workings, they exert a powerful force on everything. To just charge forward into radical change without taking these cultural rules into account risks accidentally breaking them, thereby breaking invisible but powerful forces responsible for the nation's success.

But none, except those who are profoundly studied, can comprehend the elaborate contrivance of a fabric fitted to unite private and public liberty with public force, with order, with peace, with justice, and above all, with the institutions formed for bestowing permanence and stability, through ages, upon this invaluable whole.[31]

Burke, therefore, believed destroying a system that took centuries to build only to replace it in a moment with a well-intentioned but abstract scheme was doomed to fail.[32] If you plunge a nation into disorder, looking to root up its foundations to make it anew, the chaos you create will more than likely lead not to the utopia you dreamed of but something worse. As he wrote, "To innovate is not to reform."[33]

Burke saw the American Revolution as a noble cause because it sought to preserve well-established traditional liberties against the radical actions of the king. The French Revolution, on the other hand, was to Burke the foolish casting off of tradition in the name of an unknown plan that was unlikely to function in practice the same way it did in books. Burke feared the French were throwing out centuries of carefully negotiated tradition they didn't understand in the name of abstractions. The disorder they would create wouldn't lead to liberty. It would create violence and chaos.[34] Burke's predictions proved more or less correct. Throwing off the old regime so abruptly to implement nice-sounding and rational yet untested new institutions in reality led to blood pouring onto Paris streets in a Reign of Terror, years of brutal war, the collapse of republican government, and the rise of a new monarch in Napoleon Bonaparte. When the French Revolution turned to bloody squares and guillotines, Burke had told them so. Burke's critique of the French Revolution transformed him in history's memory from an Enlightenment liberal to the first modern conservative.

Under the Burkean conception of national virtue, when we charge into reforms, even when they seem to make sense on paper, we risk breaking important safeguards we often don't even know exist. Burke has come to represent the idea that while change is necessary and even good, it should be enacted slowly, gradually, when there's no other alternative, and in accordance with a society's deep traditions. To a Burkean, the complex relationship between culture and institutions is often mysterious. While constitutions, laws, and institutions are important to a society's success, so are the invisible rules embedded in its culture—notions like ensuring fairness, prizing freedom, rewarding entrepreneurialism, celebrating the pioneer spirit, or cherishing democracy. Under the exact same laws, a society prizing merit operates differently than one with a strong sense of family and tribe. Hiring your cousin over a more qualified candidate is shameful in the first society; hiring a stranger over family is shameful in the second. These strands of law and culture are like tree roots grown together, each taking its shape because of the presence of the other. The formal laws and institutions we see are simply the visible tips of powerful social rules and culture entwined with them underneath the soil.

To a Burkean, romantic notions of imposing progress too often ignore complexity, choices, tradeoffs, and the impossibility of creating a perfect world by simply willing it to exist. Achieving our current state of progress was no easy task, and simply maintaining that progress is difficult work requiring constant vigilance. At their worst, these reforms can lead to idealistic but unrealistic actions that permanently damage society. The formal legal rules written in books only police the margins, reining in the minority of people who refuse to live up to the social bargains the rest of us take for granted. Which is why law breaks down when people don't believe the behavior the law targets is actually wrong—such as the vast number of law-abiding Americans who regularly break speeding laws. If one acts incautiously, well-meaning reforms can break unwritten rules and accidentally break the very system that should provide peace, freedom, and prosperity.

Burkeans are often labeled traditionalists, but Burkean virtue isn't about tradition for the sake of tradition or knee-jerk resistance to change. Burkean virtue is based in doubt. Burkeans defend tradition not because they know the traditional way is right—in fact, they know some tradition is certainly wrong—they defend it because they believe sudden change might break a critical piece of culture that can never be repaired. Burkeans support measured and careful change that organically arcs toward progress, but avoid sudden moves that might unwittingly throw society backward instead of forward. Burke was aware that, in addition to things getting better, things can also get worse. Violently discarding a tyrannous and out-of-touch king for a regime founded in democracy and liberty might, if you go about it too quickly and in the wrong way, lead to a mass-murdering dictator like Robespierre, followed by a warmongering out-of-touch monarch like Napoleon Bonaparte. Burke's philosophy, balancing a desire for progress with respect for tradition, echoes through much conservative thought in modern democracies. Many believe Burke's defense of tradition and ordered change is the very heart of conservatism.

Edmund Burke's ideas are not, however, the only American tradition concerning national virtue. A second tradition also holds that culture is important to national success and prosperity, but this tradition isn't based in doubt. It's based in confidence. This is the virtue of national improvement, and over the last few decades it's been ascendant.

THE VIRTUE OF NATIONAL IMPROVEMENT

There's a second strain of virtue politics in America, one based not in Burke's doubt and humility but rather in assurance and zeal. This virtue not only holds out confidence that we already know how and why culture is important, but also demands we take bold action to improve it now. It sees the culture as already degraded and declined. It sees corruption setting in to eat away at the republic's foundation. It wants to urgently restore the virtue it believes is already lost—perhaps even morally improve America to become better than before. This virtue doesn't just want to stave off foolish utopian proposals. It isn't looking to dig defensive trenches against dangerous ideas. It wants to blow the trumpets of a crusade.

Throughout American history, movements, groups, and factions have repeatedly pushed into the public arena on urgent missions to improve the character of the republic and its people. These movements also believe culture and norms are important. They fear, however, that these cultural protections are breaking, if not already broken. Sometimes they fear the proper virtues were never there at all, that a more perfect society lies tantalizingly ahead if only the republic's citizens might be improved and morally uplifted. Some feared the republic was overrun with corrupt forces threatening to erode its republican character. That was the crux of Andrew Jackson's populist rebellion, which believed it was taking back the republic from corruption threatening republican government.[35] A similar fear drove the late-nineteenth-century populist revolt, which wanted to rid the nation of the Gilded Age industrial titans, bankers, and railroad barons who they believed were corrupting America's institutions. More darkly, the Know-Nothing rebellion believed they too were defending America's republican character—in this unfortunate case from the Roman Catholicism of new immigrants they believed were threatening America's republican traditions with a degraded morality and the potential for papal tyranny.[36]

Other movements have grown out of America's continual bursts of moral revival. These movements have believed republican democracy is the most moral form of government, but one requiring an equally moral citizenry to flourish.[37] Fearing the moral decline of its people, reformers have embarked on missions to improve and uplift America's citizens in order to save the republic. One such revival swept through America in the years before the Civil War, undertaking to morally improve the nation to turn America into God's Kingdom on Earth and thereby trigger Christ's thousand-year reign.[38] They believed God specifically sanctioned republican government, meaning Christians had a special duty to defend the American republic and its virtue as a part of God's divine plan.[39] They sought to turn Americans toward personal morality and charity, and they advanced programs of personal improvement such as abstaining from intoxicating drink. They decried the moral corruption of public officials, and often the immoral grasping for offices of party politics itself.[40] Most importantly, they built an enthusiastic movement to abolish slavery and limit its spread, believing slavery not just immoral but also a corrupting influence on republic government.[41] To preserve the republic, they sought to uplift and reform the character of America's institutions and that of its citizens.

A similar revival broke out near the end of the eighteenth century, one also committed to creating God's Kingdom on Earth, this time through the Social Gospel. Working with secular reformers, Social Gospel reformers joined the Progressive Movement's great national crusade to enact fair and just policies across America to purify and improve the republic. Progressives fought against industrial-era abuses, seeking to ban child labor, to limit the length of the workday, and to impose a minimum wage. They fought for good government reforms to combat corruption and political machines, for health and safety measures to ensure clean food and medicine, for public schools to educate the young, and for public parks to provide a clean natural environment. They won constitutional amendments to allow the ban of immoral "demon rum," which they believed destroyed families, and also to grant women suffrage, in part in the belief that women would exercise their public power more morally than men. They also sought to uplift the poor, offering them charity and public assistance but also education, which they presumed would transform the destitute into better people. Their agenda was to comprehensively reform an America they feared was falling into injustice and decline.

This second strain of national virtue, the virtue of national improvement, agrees with Burke that hidden laws and rules are critical to the nation's success. It agrees that the character of citizens and the morality of institutions exercise tremendous influence on the republic's survival and success. Unlike Burke's virtue, however, the virtue of national improvement doesn't believe it's sufficient to simply defend culture and traditions. It believes the nation's culture and norms are already broken, or at least at risk of breaking. That institutions are damaged. That corrupt forces are hijacking the republic. That citizens have become too selfish, short-sighted, greedy, lazy, or immoral to serve as proper guardians of the American experiment. It believes it's urgent to actively intervene to re-instill necessary virtue where it no longer exists—that to stave off the risk of failure or collapse, the virtuous must embark on great projects of national improvement to perfect and improve the American republic and its people, so the nation will properly thrive.

The virtue of national improvement agrees with the Founders and Edmund Burke that culture and norms are critical to the republic's success. It rejects, however, the Burkean notion that tradition already encodes the necessary virtues to succeed. Reformers embracing the virtue of national improvement believe those virtues are already under assault, if not lost. They see their duty not as merely defending tradition, but instilling new virtue. They want to remake and perfect institutions and the American people, thereby saving the republic from its impending decline and doom. Burke's virtue is one of tradition, stability, and careful progress. The virtue of national improvement is one of radical reform and revival. It's a crusading sprit that, when it pours into politics, can lead to amazing reforms. It can also radicalize and alarm as it seeks to remake not only America, but also its people, in order to save and uplift the republic.

BURKE, NATIONAL IMPROVEMENT, AND VIRTUE

American virtue politics isn't really about blocking change, protecting the privileged, entrenching the status quo, or imposing social order. It's about protecting and strengthening the fragile machinery of a republic. When the people become the government, the nation's success turns on the habits and culture of citizens. Virtue conservatism is about ensuring that citizens embody the necessary habits and culture for the nation to thrive. The content of this virtue has meant different things to different people at different times—the virtue of the well-read Enlightenment gentlemen, the virtue of ordinary people running farms in small towns, the virtue of upstanding Christian citizens, the virtue embodied in ideals like faith, patriotism, merit, work, and family. What's constant is that in every era of American history voices have always warned about the importance of preserving, if not actively instilling, virtue in citizens as a key to the republic's success.

The virtue of Burke and the virtue of national improvement express in different ways the same basic idea—that culture and norms are important and the success of a democratic republic turns on getting them right. These two virtues often agree on the traits that lead to national success— in our modern age, traits like hard work, patriotism, faith, merit, the pioneer spirit, and family. Yet where Burke's virtue is about defending the culture, the virtue of national improvement is about changing it. Burke's virtue clings to tradition, while the virtue of national improvement trumpets crusades to reform corrupt or immoral institutions and policies. Burke's virtue believes great projects of national reform are doomed to fail, risking national catastrophe, where the virtue of national improvement believes great projects of national reform are necessary to the nation's success. Where Burke's virtue champions stability and caution, the virtue of national improvement leads to great crusades to remake America. Burke wants to keep the nation moving steadily forward, while the virtue of national improvement hopes to turn America into the promised shining city on a hill. Burke stands athwart history yelling stop; the virtue of improvement stands athwart history yelling we must do better.

The idea of national virtue has served as an important component of Republican thinking since the New Deal. In the early decades of our Fifth Party System, that mostly meant the virtue of Burke. Republicans during the New Deal worried that the optimistic plans of the Democrats to transform America into something better, stronger, and richer might, in reality, destroy its foundation. They thought the radical innovations of the New Deal could destroy the republican institutions that served America well and undercut bulwarks of the American cultural disposition like entrepreneurialism, independence, and the pioneer spirit. They feared the central planning of the New Deal might even produce citizens who, by ceding power to experts, would lose the will and ability to govern themselves. In 1953, academic and writer Russell Kirk published one of the definitive books of American conservatism, *The Conservative Mind*, arguing that Burke's ideas were among the foundations of American conservatism.[42] When Kirk became one of the principal intellectual architects of the early conservative movement, and his book a leading authority of the new conservative movement's philosophy, the eighteenth-century British politician Burke became the intellectual patron saint of modern American conservatism.[43]

In the 1970s, however, an evangelical revival emerged within Protestant America alarmed about issues like a secularizing nation, the sexual revolution, the coarsening of culture, the decline of traditional Christian morality, legalized abortion, and the end of prayer in schools. As this movement surged into the political arena, it brought an agenda of social and moral reforms it believed essential to restoring the morality of America's people and institutions. At the same time, the tumult of the 1960s and 1970s saw the culture of America changing in a turbulent era of social and political disruption. Some inside the Republican Party feared these changes were signs of national decline, signs the American people were shedding the traits of character required for national success. As the Democratic Party adopted the young radicals of the New Left and the party took on a new Great Society agenda, others feared the Democratic Party was pushing forward in the name of progress changes that they saw as decay. These new virtue conservatives were less interested in Burkean caution. They were moral crusaders on a mission of national improvement. As the New Deal debate fades with time, the differences between America's two conceptions of virtue—the one cautious and the other one crusading—have put the Republican Party increasingly under strain because they're increasingly at odds.

Virtue politics has always played an important role in the politics of America, and it's almost certain it always will. The Founders weren't wrong. The greatest strength of a republic truly is its greatest vulnerability—its people are the government. A republic cannot, and will not, survive, much less thrive, if its citizens don't embrace norms and values that put the republic first. If a republic's citizens don't cherish their republican traditions, or if they won't exercise their democratic power to govern wisely and for the benefit of all, they will not keep their republic. The debate is merely over what virtue means at each specific point in history, and what we must do to ensure it flourishes. Must we defend our traditions and norms as guardians of the nation's virtue, as Edmund Burke believed? Or must we bang the drums of revival to throw off corruption, restore America from decline, and instill the virtue necessary to truly perfect America?

CHAPTER 10

THE FURY OF POPULISM

Since the Democratic Party emerged under Andrew Jackson, Democrats have run campaigns on the theme of the people versus the powerful. This was, more or less, the campaign theme of Andrew Jackson, William Jennings Bryan, Al Smith, Franklin Roosevelt, and most of the Democratic Party ticket up and down the ballot for every decade in between them. At times, the "people" have meant rural farmers and at other times urban workers. The "powerful" once meant railroads and Eastern money, and at another time it meant big box stores and multinational brands. Although the details change from year to year, if you want to identify one great unifying ideal running throughout every historical incarnation of the Democratic Party, it would be that Democrats have always identified as a party of little people fighting against the interests of a powerful elite.

Except haven't both major parties always attracted legions of the powerful, all happily bundling millions of dollars for candidates and getting Lincoln bedroom sleepovers and attending White House dinners? Doesn't each party just attract different kinds of powerful people, whether corporate executives, energy tycoons, Wall Street titans, Silicon Valley billionaires, Hollywood moguls, popular media personalities, and so on? And don't a lot of struggling Americans, like the rural working class, viscerally hate the party that's supposed to represent them? Don't Republicans regularly maintain that they're the party representing the authentic America and that the Democrats are actually the party of out-of-touch elites—college professors, wealthy tech titans, and opinionated actors?

People sense that the Democrats are, and have always been, the party of populism—it's just that populism isn't what most people think it is.

THE IDEOLOGICAL FOUNDATIONS OF POPULISM

Populism is probably the oldest and most persistent idea across the entire history of human politics. Although the specifics of the arrangement change across time and societies, every human social group ultimately forms some hierarchical scheme consisting of rulers and the people over whom they rule. Sometimes that has meant a hereditary king. Sometimes that has meant a warlord. Sometimes that has meant a powerful tribe and tributary tribes. Sometimes that has meant a caste of priests. Sometimes that has meant nobles and slaves. Wherever there have been groups of people living together, some have had more wealth and power and some have had less. The people who had more generally fought to keep it, first for themselves, then for their families, and then for people like themselves, whether their caste, their tribe, their class, or their culture.

History books tend to focus on the politics of the ruling class. Claimants struggle over thrones. Barons fight with kings over rights and powers. Priests, warriors, and nobles maneuver to determine who has power over whom. Leaders of one tribe promote their own and destroy rivals in other clans. Yet most times these political battles were always a mere sideshow to the real political story, the simmering tension between rulers and those under their rule. Underneath most political struggles of nobles fighting over thrones was an unspoken fear lurking across the entire civilization that one day the peasants and slaves might rise up, storm the castle, and put every noble head they found upon a spear. Every once in a while, they did. In ancient Greece, sometimes the mob would rise up to overthrow the tyrant. Rome had periodic slave revolts that expanded into full-scale wars, with entire armies clashing in battles. In Medieval Europe, mobs of peasants stormed the capital and murdered the Lord Chancellor and Archbishop of Canterbury in the Tower of London. In China, the great peasant revolt of the Yellow Turban Rebellion tore China apart for years and terminally weakened the Han Dynasty. Long before we had elections and democratic politics in which "the people" were consulted about their government, this smoldering tension between "the people" and "the powerful" was the single most important issue motivating human politics.

Despite its importance throughout human history, however, populism traditionally has had a bad reputation among academics. For a long time, most scholars widely dismissed it as angry, emotional, and violent, a force that, when unleashed, destroys good government, damages democracy, and disrupts societies. Many scholars classically disdained populism as an empty, irrational, angry, and destructive ideology of no real value to civilization. In fact, many contested whether populism was even an ideology at all, as opposed to a method of political performance or a democratic pathology.[1] This glib view of populism, while understandable, is a mistake. Populism is a primal force in human politics. When it erupts, time and again across history, it rocks societies, knocks down institutions, forces change, and often threatens national stability as it chases off national elites without a thoughtful plan for what comes next. Yet populism is also a lot like fire. It's an immensely dangerous force of nature when allowed to burn out of control, yet it's also valuable when it's understood and beneficially harnessed.

One of the reasons populism has historically received so much scholarly disdain is it's an ideological force nearly impossible to describe or define using the traditional tools of political analysis. As Ernesto Laclau, one of the preeminent scholars of populism, wrote of it:

> A persistent feature of the literature on populism is its reluctance—or difficulty—in giving the concept any precise meaning. Notational clarity—let alone definition—is conspicuously absent from this domain. Most of the time, conceptional apprehension is replaced by appeals to a non-verbalized intuition, or by descriptive enumerations of a variety of "relevant features"—a relevance which is undermined, in the very gesture that asserts it, by reference to a proliferation of exceptions.[2]

Nearly every other popular political ideology—from liberalism to conservatism to socialism to progressivism to communism to fascism to democratic republicanism—promotes a discrete political framework setting forth how people ought to organize society and how they ought to govern it. Populism doesn't offer such an easily identifiable agenda, program of ideas, or vision for society. In fact, it's frequently observed that populism is on its face contentless and empty. It's considered what's called a "thin ideology," meaning that, while it offers a coherent approach to politics consistent with calling it an ideology, it lacks the expected ideological answers to political questions like "who gets what and how."[3] Populism tells you who should get to rule, but it doesn't tell you what they ought to do with the power they acquire. That's why populist movements have almost inevitably attached themselves to other ideologies like socialism or nationalism to give content to their program.[4] History thus yields up a cacophony of rival populisms, from right-wing populism to left-wing populism to populist socialists to populist nationalists, all of whom agree on little yet whom we all recognize as populist.

It turns out what every form of populism has in common isn't a political program but a common claim. Populism is an ideology about power, control, justice, and ultimately redemption that separates society into two rival groups, the people and the elite. Populists claim to speak for "the people" fighting to replace a corrupt "elite."[5] Society, the populist believes, is under control of the elite—corrupt outsiders who neither understand nor care about the people. The populist claims to speak for the people—the humiliated, disrespected, and alienated majority of society unfairly subjected to elite power. The people, in whatever way the populist defines them, are the rightful heirs of the community. Not only because they're the actual majority, giving them a democratic right to rule, but because their specific life experience, perspective, demographic roots, and cultural beliefs make them the most authentic and virtuous part of the society. While the people, to the populist, are thus the most legitimate representation of the people's will and thus entitled to rule the elites in power, who don't share a common interest or identity with the people, can't possibly represent the society. These elite outsiders have no legitimacy to exercise power over a virtuous people they neither care about nor understand. These elites are therefore both illegitimate and corrupt, as they're siphoning from the people power and resources to which they have no right. Thus, what populists want is to overthrow the corrupt elites, replacing them with the people—meaning people more like them.

Dividing society between a virtuous people and a corrupt elite is the heart of every populist movement in history. It's the essence of "left-wing" populist revolutionaries, "right-wing" authoritarians, South American caudillos, Latin American Chavistas, and European populist-nationalists. Populists make an almost Rousseauian moral claim that the people—meaning people like them—have a legitimate right to rule because only they embody the general will of the society.[6] As one scholar of populism wrote, "Those who are excluded and stigmatized with administrative categories such as 'the poor,' 'the informal,' and 'the marginal' become 'the people' conceived as the incarnation of all virtue. And the elites, who constantly humiliate them, become moral reprobates."[7] The elite—outsiders exercising power where they have no right—are thus essentially stealing wealth and honors they have no right to take from a people they denigrate and disrespect: "[Populism] transforms the humiliations that the rabble, the uncultured, the unseen, and those who have no voice have to endure in their daily life into sources of dignity and even redemption."[8]

Populist claims aren't subject to negotiation or compromise, because populism isn't about specific policies or programs or even seizing resources. Populist claims are moral claims about who is a legitimate and authentic representative of society and who is entitled to rule. Populism seeks not spoils but dignity, representation, and justice to remedy what they see as corruption, disrespect, and humiliation. Populism is moreover both representative and antidemocratic at the same time. Populists generally believe in representative government, but also believe the only legitimate representatives of the people are themselves. Any outcome other than one in which the hated elite is vanquished and the "people" are allowed to rule is itself evidence of corruption and illegitimacy.[9] Populism therefore demands one thing, to remove the elite from power, replacing them with the people—in practice, with populist leaders claiming to speak in the people's name.

Populist politics is one of the fundamental drivers of human civilization. As a species, we inevitably anoint leaders, or leaders seize power over others. The people shut out of the top of the new hierarchy become resentful at the unfairness of their situation. They want to topple a system they believe is unjust. There's no way to avoid this cycle of populist resentment and revolt because every society will always have a people and an elite. When one group has power, it means some other group doesn't. If some people are better off, others are worse by comparison. No matter how kind those who rule are to those under them, no matter how equally those rulers share the resources they control with others, no matter how fair rulers seek to make their orders, they can't change the glaring fact that they have power when others don't, and those who don't are keenly aware of their relative powerlessness. In the real world of fallible human beings, moreover, those with power have never been perfectly kind to those they rule over, have never sought to equally share resources in a way everyone in society believed fair, and have never only issued orders that are angelically just.

This tension between the people and the elite exists everywhere humans gather. It's in the relationship between line employees and the bosses in the C Suite. It's the relationship between students and principals. It's the relationship between the "cool kids" and the not-so-cool kids. And it's in the relationship between ordinary working people struggling to get by and the glamorous people on their televisions drinking champagne, driving Bentleys, and using phrases like "the help." Sometimes this resentment lies lurking underneath a seemingly stable system. Sometimes a Che Guevara comes along to organize the resentful to do something about it. Populism is everywhere. It's powerful. It's disruptive. It is, and has always been, a major driver of human politics. Including in America.

THE DEMOCRATS AND POPULISM

One might think a democratic republic in which the people choose the government would have no use for populist politics. Yet populism has thrived in America since the republic's earliest days. The American Revolution was itself a great populist revolt. To the British, Americans were rubes whom they thought of in the same way as refined people today dismiss "rednecks" from "fly-over country."[10] The colonists' rebellion was motivated as much by resentment at blueblood Englishmen who looked down on their unrefined colonial cousins and refused to grant them seats in their parliament as a hatred of unfair taxes. Once they established their new republic, America's Founders—wealthy and educated intellectuals living lives far different from the struggling common working American—continued to flirt with populism. Thomas Jefferson was a rich plantation-owning wine connoisseur with European tastes and a philosopher's pen, yet he and his Democratic-Republicans won countless elections by attacking Federalists as aristocrats and elitists. Then Andrew Jackson rode to the forefront of American politics, and American populism really took off.

Old Hickory saw himself as a common man of the people. His party, the Democrats, built an ideology around celebrating the wisdom of the common American and fighting against corrupt elites.[11] Jackson and his party decried the corruption and "special privileges" of the American "aristocracy," which profited the few off the backs of the people.[12] It hated elite institutions like banks. Democrats wanted to elect judges, instead of obeying judges appointed by their alleged betters. They wanted to appoint ordinary people to high office in the belief that any man could do the job. They wanted to expand westward, where any hardworking settler could build a better life with his own hands without having to obey those who already had wealth and power. Jackson's Democrats were a classic populist movement pitting the people against corrupt elites, and its elite resentment and glorification of the common American became the backbone of every iteration of the Democratic Party since.

After the Civil War, the Democrats became a mostly Southern party representing the grievances of the Reconstruction South married to the anger of mostly Catholic immigrant workers who were locked out of the Protestant establishment in Northern cities. Although controlled by wealthy and powerful Bourbons, the Democratic Party voiced the resentment of people who felt trapped under the boots of outsiders—under the rule of military governors and "carpetbagger" Northern Republicans as the South transformed from a wealthy region into a mostly impoverished one left out of the Northern commercial boom. Again, Democrats claimed to represent the people against corrupt elites. With the rise of William Jennings Bryan, who proclaimed as his campaign slogan "let the people rule," the Democrats stood up for agrarian Americans against Gilded Age elites—faraway Eastern bankers, industrial titans, corrupt politicians, and railroad presidents who they saw as treading upon the farmers and workers of America. Once more, Democrats claimed to represent the people against corrupt elites. In the wake of the Great Depression, Democrats repainted themselves as the party of the blue-collar and working-class average Joes who resented the rich, waspy, cocktail-sipping aristocrats hanging out in country clubs after crashing the national economy into depression and throwing working people into poverty. During the civil rights era, the party later extended its populist appeals to other groups it considered disenfranchised, such as African Americans, Hispanics, and women. Democrats again claimed to represent the people against corrupt elites.

Through every era and through every realignment, the Democratic Party has remained a party claiming to represent common working Americans against the interests of the elite. The Democratic message has always been that the party represents "the people," and that its enemies are "the powerful." The Federalists, the Whigs, and now the Republicans, until quite recently, have through every era always represented the elites against whom populists raged. Over the years, Democrats married their populist politics to other movements, ideas, and principles, as populists inevitably do and must. The substance of the party's agenda shifted and changed over time, as did its model picture of who exactly constituted the "people" and who was the "corrupt elite." What never changed is that Democrats embraced populism's logic, that politics is a great battle between the people and the powerful—and that Democrats represented the authentic American people, the true source of political legitimacy.

Of late, however, working people with seemingly the most to gain from Democratic programs, and who until recently overwhelmingly supported Democrats, have increasingly come to embrace the Republicans. Americans living in small towns in Middle America, in bleak industrial towns in the Rust Belt, or in rural areas across the South, until quite recently were the "people" Democrats claimed to represent—the real

Americans and ordinary working people who feared they were beset by corrupt outsiders carelessly ruling their destiny. The Democratic Party still presents itself as the party looking out for the interests of common Americans against the power of wealthy elites on Wall Street and in corporations. It favors policies and programs like national health insurance, social insurance, and regulatory controls intended to redistribute income and power toward ordinary people and those struggling. It defends labor unions and supports raising the minimum wage. Yet many of the working people the Democratic Party sees itself as championing viscerally hate it.[13] Democrats sometimes see something untoward in this, believing that Republicans have unfairly stolen away a core Democratic constituency by tricking them to vote against their interests.

What many modern Democrats fail to appreciate about their party is that populism has nothing to do with money or programs. Providing programs to help people and improve America isn't populism—that's progressivism, an ideology more associated with Republicans than Democrats for much of the era in which Democratic populism reigned. Populism isn't about, and has never been about, which party offers the most to "the people." Populism isn't about what government provides at all. Or what government is going to do. Or even whether government treats certain groups right. Nor is it about segments of society seeking to leverage their numbers to get more resources from their rulers. Populism is about the indignity people feel when they have to ask in the first place. It's about righting the injustice humans inherently feel when they believe others control their destiny. It's not about material things but power and dignity. Populists don't want gifts from their betters. They want to overthrow and replace them with people like themselves, seizing back the dignity and control that goes to members of the ruling class. It's about the people—meaning people like "us"—taking back power and control from the elites in power—people like "them."

Democratic populists through most of America's history weren't elites offering to shower gifts and programs on workers and laborers. From Jackson's patronage programs to Tammany Hall's political machines, Democrats offered real power to people the system locked out. Destroying the Bank of the United States, opening up more settlement in the West, breaking the power of railroads, and "free silver" were more than ways to help working people in America. They were about sticking it to elites, breaking elite power, and freeing working people from their control. William Jennings Bryan wasn't a Bourbon offering gifts to struggling farmers and laborers; he promised to overthrow the elites in bed with bankers and railroad presidents, replacing them with people more like them. In the early part of this party system, New Deal Democrats strengthened labor unions, organizations run by ordinary workers who rose to union leadership. They worked through political machines, which built vast patronage networks that provided public jobs and opportunities to immigrants and other working people who might not have otherwise qualified in a purely merit-based system. New Deal Democrats celebrated the virtues of ordinary working people as the backbone of America and proclaimed the people for whom they worked, to whom their farms were mortgaged, and whom they served as undeserving elites. Most of all, they elevated politicians who came from among them—people from humble backgrounds without elite educations, who had worked on farms or lived in urban slums. Voting for Democrats meant voting for people with unpolished exteriors and rural or working-class backgrounds, politicians like Lyndon Johnson or Richard J. Daley. The Democratic Party offered populists more than beneficial policies, they also offered them dignity, respect, and a full seat at the banquet of power. Voting for Democrats didn't just mean more benefits for you. It meant electing more people like you.

During the 1960s and 1970s, however, the way the Democratic Party related to working-class populists changed.[14] Around the time the baby boomers came of age, American politics shifted attention from economics to moral issues. A counterculture of young activists known as the "New Left" rose to prominence within the party, young radicals interested in rowdy protest movements and moralistic politics. These "New Left" Democrats began to clash with the traditional working-class populist Democrats, whom many in the New Left viewed not as allies but enemies and impediments to progress. The New Left progressives saw the Old Left populists—with their conventionality, their pragmatism, and their traditional social beliefs—as at best antiquated relics, and at worst backward bigots holding the nation back. The Old Left populists saw the young New Left progressives—with their noisy protests, their transgressive appearance and dress, and their shocking-for-the-time social beliefs—as disruptive radicals. For decades, these two rival groups struggled for power inside the Democratic Party while spitting contempt at each other. Over time, as young New Left activists aged into party leaders and officials, the New Left perspective strengthened its hand within Democratic Party councils as the once-formidable Old Left machines lost relevance. Where Democrats once lionized rural America and the working class as the nation's backbone, more and more prominent Democrats became openly dismissive of rural and working-class America as backward places without enlightened values. While the Democratic Party still wanted to speak for the working-class populists of the party's traditional base, key elements of rising party constituencies no longer seemed to like them.

That shift from economic to moral issues within the Democratic Party created a profound shift among its traditional working-class populist base. The party didn't change ideologically. Democrats still believed in New Deal liberalism and offered America the same New Deal programs. Democrats still promised to empower institutions like unions. They even promised to extend new programs that helped working people and the middle class against the elite. Just as in the days of Jackson, the Democratic Party was still formally a populist political party. At the same time, party leaders also changed the way they prioritized and interpreted their party's ideology. Democratic leaders began to worry less about labor and lunch-pail issues and more about issues like social justice, racial equality, and environmental purity. Democrats also began extending their populist appeals to new groups as America changed and new communities joined the party's coalition, offering the benefits of populism to African Americans, women, Hispanics, and gay and lesbian people—respect, seats at the table, and shared resentment. Most important, Democrats stopped providing the same power, respect, and opportunities to its old working-class populist base. Archie Bunker was no longer the party's base but the problem.

Populism and progressivism are hardly natural allies. Progressives may want to help "the people" but they're also by definition elites. The progressive desire for rational management and good government is in natural tension with actually empowering ordinary people, who progressives may believe don't fully appreciate their complex plans. In a prior era, progressives and populists grappled fiercely over issues like civil service reform, as progressives worked to dismantle the very patronage networks that supported populists. Progressives saw themselves as molding the lower classes into reflections of their betters, while populists resented the expert-loving scientific-minded progressives as representatives of elite condescension.[15] Lumping these two very different principles under the ideology "liberalism" too often causes Democrats to mistake progressive policies intended to help the working class as a kind of populism—which they are not—and outbursts of resentment-driven populism as cries for progressive solutions—which they are not.[16] It's possible to champion a form of progressivism that hopes to improve the lives of the powerless without actually ceding them power and control, much as the pro-business, moralistic, and elitist turn-of-the-century progressives once did. It's also possible to champion an angry populism of resentment with no interest in the expert-driven good government that progressives prize.

When working-class populists first attached themselves to the Democratic Party in the 1930s, the alliance made sense. Populism, as a thin ideology, had to attach itself to another ideology to provide direction. Economic progressivism, which championed an agenda specifically meant to elevate and benefit people like them, made a reasonable partner. The moral progressivism that grew out of the 1960s and 1970s, on the other hand, specifically sought to remove people like them from influence as obstacles to progress. The Democratic Party wanted to continue to represent working-class populists; it considered them key members of the Democratic voting coalition, and it thought it could buy their continued loyalty with policies and programs that benefited them. Yet an alliance between working-class populism and moral progressivism never made much sense. This evolving Democratic Party now no longer offered working-class populists what populists actually crave—the respect and power that comes from replacing elites with people like them. The Democrats no longer offered parts of its populist base the same route to respect and power in exchange for votes as it once did. Electing Democrats no longer meant replacing elites with people like them. It was a deeply desta-bilizing shift both within the Democratic coalition and our current party system, unmooring many working-class populists from America's for-mally populist party and encouraging them to seek what they as populists actually desired—respect and dignity and representation and power—somewhere else.

Ideologically, the Democrats have remained a populist party offering a populist program under the banner of New Deal liberalism. For some populists—women, African Americans, Hispanics, and other tradition-ally disenfranchised groups—voting Democratic remains a reasonable way to replace elites with people like them. For traditional working-class Democratic populists, however, the Democratic Party in practice no longer really offers what populism demands—power, dignity, and redemption. The Democrats no longer offer working-class populists a full seat at the table of power. Electing Democrats no longer means throwing out the hated elites to restore power to the authentic American people—meaning people like them.

THE POWER OF THE POPULIST TRADITION

America has always had, and will likely always have, a populist political party. Wherever there are human societies and power there will also be populism. While populism has waxed and waned in intensity throughout American history, at different times attaching itself to new ideas and allies, it has always played a role and never truly disappeared. People who feel locked out of power and disrespected by others will always find a political outlet. Nor would we want populism to disappear. Despite its unfortunate unsavory reputation, populism isn't actually inherently bad. In fact, it's almost certainly essential to maintain the integrity of repub-lican democracy. As various scholars of populism have justly noted, populism is indeed an angry, reactive, and resentful ideology. It's not a philosophy about building or improving things. It places little value on good-government policy ideas and much onto identity, resentment, and raw power. It's a political ideology that must always find an ideological partner because it lacks any ideas, agenda, or political program of its own. Populists aren't organized around what they want to do with power, they simply want to take it away from the outsiders who have it and get it to people like themselves. Yet populism is also the natural counterweight to stagnation and corruption in a democracy.

While populism may lack a ruling agenda of its own, it's also the primary force holding national elites accountable. Ruling factions naturally tend to entrench and reward themselves at the expense of others with less political power. Worse, they too often justify that control and privilege as the well-earned reward for what they consider their superior educations, values, and backgrounds. What limits this inevitable pull toward elite corruption is the fear of angry populist backlash. Populism may not have ideas about what to do with power, but it's a potent force for stopping national elites from leveraging their power and advantages to reward and entrench themselves at the rest of the society's expense. Populist pressure has time and again stopped America from drifting too far into corruption and unaccountable privilege. Jackson's revolt helped correct the drift toward elite privilege during the Era of Good Feelings, bringing ordinary Americans into the democracy. Bryan shocked the corrupt Gilded Age elite into cleaning up the graft for good government and reform. The constant pressure of populism is what discourages national elites from indulging in too much corruption, and periodic populist eruptions are what cleans up such corruption when it goes too far. Were populism ever to disappear completely from our politics, disaster would likely follow.

When attached to the right ideology, moreover, populism is a valuable vehicle for reform. Since populism inevitably attaches itself to other ideas for direction, when it's attached to the right movement its anger and resentment can become energy driving necessary change. Jackson's, Bryans, and FDR's Democrats all harnessed the might of populism to drive their agendas of innovation and reforms. They brought people who felt like outsiders back into the political system and used their enthusiasm to force through change. They didn't just seek to replace elites with the people they claimed to represent, they then put those people to work building a better America than before.

As the most ancient and primal force in all human politics, populism can be harnessed either for good causes or destructive ones. Populism is by itself nihilistic, which is why populists attach themselves to other powerful ideas with firm agendas for concrete change like agrarianism, nationalism, communism, or progressivism. While populism can be horrifically damaging to rational government when directionless or attached to the wrong ideology, when attached to a better one it can drive important change by providing energy, emotion, and urgency. If channeled poorly, it can rip apart a nation's politics in favor of primal irrational politics of power and resentment. If channeled well, populism can become a beneficial force keeping the powerful in check and driving necessary reforms. You can't destroy populism. You can only let some air out of populists pressure from time to time to reduce its strength, while watching which allies populists choose. As we navigate the next political realignment, populism can become a key driver of political renewal, but it can also become an angry whirlwind of disruptive emotions, rough politics, violence, and political chaos. It can be a force around which we rebuild the next party system, or the one that tears the old one down—or both.

CHAPTER 11

THE CHOICE: COLLAPSE OR RENEWAL

O ur world has always been one of Republicans and Democrats standing for the same things Republicans and Democrats have always represented. Almost everyone alive today has lived their entire lives inside this single party system, established back in 1932. Since it's been this way as far as we remember, it's difficult to even comprehend this familiar and seemingly solid framework that has governed our entire lives suddenly and with little warning coming to its end, much less soon. Yet there was no great break in history in 1932 making our present party system immune from realigning pressures. The four realignments and five party systems of American history are therefore more than just history. They're also important lessons. The stories and points of data we can lift from them can help us understand, in our own political era, how and why our own parties will come apart and what challenges and choices we might face as they do. As Mark Twain reportedly warned, "History does not repeat itself, but it does rhyme."[1] Based on what we know from the history of America's prior party systems and realignments, our familiar old Fifth Party System is coming to its end. What sort of realignment, however, will our next one be?

Every realignment is, of course, unique. Nothing in history is set in stone before it happens, and human events are always unpredictable because people aren't automatons. Each realignment takes place at a particular moment in history with a particular collection of challenges and a unique cast of characters having different talents and personalities. Past realignments therefore have all been very different stories ending in very different ways. The 1896 realignment that ushered America into the Populist and Progressive Era was optimistic and constructive. America went through an exciting presidential campaign that unleashed new ideas, which then launched an eager new era of national reform that turned America into a prospering great power. The collapse of the Second Party System, on the other hand, was a horror. It unleashed almost a decade of political uncertainty, violence, ugly movements, and national trauma that ended in a bloody civil war. In between those two completely different stories was America's bungling through the Era of Good Feelings and the sad disintegration of the progressive Republicans during the Depression leading to the New Deal. Looking at these very different stories, however, we can see that American realignments seem to follow two distinct patterns. One is a collapse in which America tumbles into years of uncertainty and turmoil before new parties eventually rise from the rubble of the fall. The other is a swift and hopeful party renewal, as America rapidly reforms its parties for the problems of a new age. The difference between them, moreover, lies not in external factors. It lies in our choices.

America is heading toward a realignment no matter what we do. The important question is what we intend to do about it. It's our decisions as America transitions from its Fifth Party System to its Sixth that will decide not only what sort of realignment this will be, but also what sort of new parties rule our future. If we heed the lessons of our past, we can influence the next realignment to ensure America's future is a hopeful one we want—and not a dangerous one we don't.

HOW WE KNOW A REALIGNMENT IS COMING

Three familiar signs have always appeared when an American party system is coming to its end. What's more, these signs make sense because they're essentially indications that the bonds holding America's political coalitions together are weakening while powerful forces pulling at their seams are gaining strength. When all three signals appear, they're heralds that the political ideologies holding together America's existing party coalitions are losing the power to unite half of America around compelling agendas promising a better future. All three of these signs, moreover, have already appeared.

First, parties always crumble when the great debate that defines a party system fades away because party factions no longer share a common purpose worth putting aside other disagreements to work as a united front. Whenever the great debate of an era turned stale, America's parties have always begun to stagnate, corruption flourished, and the next realignment arrived soon after. When America resolved its debate over the early republic, American politics turned empty and its parties fell into empty mudslinging campaigns and personal attacks, until the aimless Federalist Party discredited itself and imploded. When America resolved the Jacksonian debate in the middle of the nineteen century, the Whigs and Democrats—now nominating military heroes with no interest in policy to run empty campaigns of sloganeering and election hoopla—floundered until, after an electoral battering in 1852, the Whig party collapsed. When America resolved the Civil War debate after Reconstruction, America's parties stumbled through years of ineffectiveness and corruption until a populist explosion and William Jennings Bryan rose to demand reform. When America moved past the Populist and Progressive Era debates over the abuses of industrialization, it got the feel-good parties of the 1920s running campaigns on prohibition even though it was already the law, parties that finally disintegrated in the catastrophe of the Depression.

When a great debate fades away or gets resolved, America's parties no longer share a common purpose worth putting aside other disagreements to work as a united front. They no longer share a common vision for the future, a common enemy to fight, or a common fear to root out. They're no longer capable, or even interested in, solving the problems Americans want and need resolved. Their existing agendas and policy toolkits lack the tools to address new problems. Their aging ideologies even lack the language or framework to think about them. American politics naturally stagnates. Parties become mere vehicles for status-seeking and career advancement. Corruption and graft flourishes. There's nothing left to hold vast, fractious, and often conflicting factions together other than tribal loyalty, habit, careerism, and inertia. When a great debate is resolved or dies, parties built around it become weak and empty shells vulnerable to collapse.

The second sign of an impending realignment is the rise of new problems. America creates parties and party systems to solve its most pressing and difficult challenges at a certain moment in history. Only something that compelling and powerful could possibly hold half the nation together in a political coalition at all. Whether these issues concern new technologies, economic transformations, cultural change, new patterns of living, religious revivals, or the spread of new ideas, parties have to transform to address a changed world or die so others can. It's rare, however, that coalitions built to solve one set of problems are capable of devising solutions to the very different problems of the next age. Coalitions united around one era's concerns rarely share a common interest or perspective around the next. Nor are officials and partisans who built careers inside old frameworks inclined to throw away ways of thinking and orthodoxies that brought them past success. When the world changes and new issues arise, parties either adapt or outsiders come along offering the solutions people demand.

Whenever significant new problems have arisen outside an existing era's great debate, America's parties began to stumble, outsiders willing to address the new issues emerged, and a realignment inevitably followed. As the ideals of the American republic settled in, a new generation of Americans demanded full participation in its politics. Andrew Jackson provided what the people demanded. When the spread of slavery and the rise of a powerful abolition movement brought the issue of slavery to the fore, people demanded a party that would commit to ending slavery's travesty. A new Republican Party emerged to provide what they demanded. When industrialization disrupted the lives of America's working and middle classes, people demanded policies that would protect them from this peril. William Jennings Bryan provided what the people demanded. When the Great Depression shattered people's faith in America's institutions serving in a modern world, people demanded radical policies that would end the Depression and restore their faith in the republic. Franklin Roosevelt provided what the people demanded. As new problems emerge that our parties can't or won't address, it's just a matter of time before someone or something comes along to spur the necessary innovations.

The third sign of a coming realignment is a disruption striking the system hard enough to finally knock the old system down. Parties sometimes stumble on for a surprisingly long time with a fading agenda, weak coalition, and no answers to the problems to which people demand solutions. So long as nothing strikes the decaying system hard enough, stagnant parties can coast for quite some time through inertia. The parties of the early republic plodded along for years until the Federalists collapsed, and then the Era of Good Feelings reigned for years more until Jackson finally emerged. The Whigs and Democrats faded for almost a decade before the Whig implosion, and then almost another decade passed until the Third Party System settled in. The Third Party System parties spent almost twenty years locked in corruption and inaction until Bryan emerged. The Populist and Progressive Era parties lost focus after the First World War and lingered until the Depression. Even when nobody would think to create them anew, and even when it would be impossible to rebuild them given how much the world has changed, weak and ineffective parties can stumble along powered by habit so long as it remains in everybody's self-interest to cooperatively prop up the ineffective and widely disliked status quo.

During the stable decades of a party system, every major player in politics—party leaders, potential candidates, activists, donors, and voters—unwittingly coordinate to defend the ideologies and coalitions that provide them a well-known path to power. The savvy thing for everyone who wants to build a career in politics or who has an agenda of policies they want enacted to do, whatever they personally think about the two existing major parties, is to pick the party closest to their views, work within it as best they can, and conform their public persona to its agenda, beliefs, and orthodoxies. It's also in their self-interest to attack as threats anything challenging their party's orthodoxies—the fragile compromises and agreements that hold the party's existing coalition together—even if in secret they might prefer them over the status quo. Since everyone is quietly cooperating to maintain, and even defend, the existing party system's coalitions and ideologies, those parties appear sound and unas-sailable. Decaying and aimless parties can therefore stumble on for quite some time, propped up by self-interest and careerism, creating the illu-sion of party strength and inevitability. Yet this invisible bulwark has one obvious vulnerability—if anything pops the illusion, there's a run on a political party just like a run on a failing bank. When an illusion is the only thing holding a party system together—not a compelling agenda of exciting ideas about the future—lifting that illusion brings it tumbling down. Which is exactly what makes weakened political parties vulnerable to sudden collapse.

Disruptions that inject danger and chaos into American politics happen all the time. Some build up slowly in the background for years, like the religious revivals that intensified abolition and inspired the Pro-gressive Movement. Others fester, like the economic changes that ate away the prosperity of America's family farms. Some shock the world suddenly, like economic panics and depressions. Some are disruptive policy choices, like the Nullification Crisis, the launching of the Mexican-American War, the Fugitive Slave Act, the Kansas-Nebraska Act, or the Sherman Silver Purchase Act. Some are disorderly and zealous political movements, like Jacksonian populism, the abolition movement, the Know-Nothings, or the Populist Movement. Some come with outsized and headstrong per-sonalities smashing against the system, like Andrew Jackson or William Jennings Bryan. The specific reasons each American party system failed after so many years drifting at sea are all unique. There were one-time per-sonalities, social movements, policy failures, religious revivals, events, and more that combined into a distinct and combustive mix that, when suddenly ignited, burned the old system down. Something or someone, however, always arrived to light the match, and when it happened these walking-dead parties quickly incinerated.

Eventually, something, or some combination of somethings, always arrives to make the major stakeholders inside the party question whether it truly remains their most useful vehicle for winning elections and enacting agendas. They question whether they still need the party to advance, or whether the party is still a useful path toward power, or whether they really want to bond politically to factions they never liked, or whether a better alternative reflecting their true beliefs and desires might actually be possible. When such disruption strikes at the right moment, making a party look factional, weak, disgraced, or discredited, stakeholders realize there's no longer much to gain by remaining married to allies they don't like, trapped in orthodoxies in which they don't believe, and working for stale agendas unrelated to the things they care most about. Like waking from a stultifying dream, everyone suddenly sees the world with fresh eyes, free to consider new ideas, new issues, and new alliances that actually excite them. The bubble pops and the entire stale older comes crashing down. Like Humpty Dumpty, it's impossible to put the system back together in the same way.

When all three of these factors—the end of the last great debate, the rise of new problems, and disruption—emerge at the same time, we know from experience a realignment is soon to come. The only question is how America chooses to respond. The decisions we make when the time for a realignment arrives determines which of two distinct types of realignments occur. Here, we have a choice, one with real consequences for our future.

COLLAPSE OR RENEWAL

Some realignments are quick and purposeful, as America quickly transforms and enters a new era of forward-looking reform. This happens when, in a moment of stagnating parties and realigning pressures, America's leaders leap into the fray to drag America's parties into a new age. For example, as America headed into the 1890s, it looked as if the nation was on the verge of a national breakdown. The Gilded Age offered wild opportunities for those positioned to take them, but decimated the middle-class family-farm economy that was America's backbone. Old parties still squabbling over the Civil War were wholly incapable of thinking about, much less addressing, the sweeping changes of industrialization. People got angry. They lost trust in America and what seemed to them its ineffective institutions. A populist revolt demanded radical reforms. You would normally expect this story to end with years of social turmoil, the out-break of radicalism, possibly violence, and perhaps much worse, as angry Americans tore down a decaying system and then fumbled through the task of building something new. Had nothing intervened, something or someone would have inevitably ripped those useless old parties down. Then somebody intervened.

Instead of dawdling until America's political coalitions eventually disintegrated, William Jennings Bryan captured the Democratic Party's nomination with a disruptive new agenda creating a new party ideology that addressed the problems of the future instead of the past. Bryan's campaign not only remade his own Democratic Party, it spurred a similar transformation of the Republicans. This 1896 realignment became the quickest and least disruptive realignment in American history. Because there was no party collapse, there was no vacuum for malignant forces to fill. Because the process happened deliberately and intentionally, Americans got to choose their new party ideologies carefully instead of accepting whatever emerged from the chaos of a collapse. The result was an era of reform and national prosperity. Bryan's realignment shortcut the regular process of collapse, chaos, and rebirth in favor of a drastic and swift renewal.

The New Deal realignment followed a similar path. The Fourth Party System parties were already floundering, meandering through the Jazz Age without compelling agendas. Then the Great Depression knocked America onto its back, creating dramatic demands for solutions neither party had the tools to provide. With America's parties unable to address the desperation sweeping the nation, many Americans lost hope in the very concept of democracy and liberal democratic capitalism. No one would have been surprised if the story ended not only with a party collapse, but even a populist revolt or the rise of a radical demagogue, as occurred in many European nations. Instead, Roosevelt's radical New Deal experiments created a new agenda and ideology for his party that restored trust in the republic and ushered in a new party system. Roosevelt's realignment was more unstable and scary than Bryan's, with its constitutional crises, Court-Packing Schemes, and Business Plots, but it nevertheless staved off the worst—the usual years of chaos, the rise of radical movements, and who knows what other dangers had the parties actually crumbled—to create two new parties prepared for a useful debate about America's future.

What's distinguishes this first model of political realignments from its alternative is it's intentional. In both the Bryan realignment in 1896 and the Roosevelt realignment in 1932, America's parties were clearly heading toward collapse. America's parties no longer had the ability to solve the problems they needed to address, or to hold together coalitions that no longer made much sense. It was only a matter of time until something or someone shattered those fragile coalitions and America's parties came apart. Yet instead of waiting until America's political coalitions collapsed, Americans came together to rebuild their parties around new ideologies and ideas before events forced change upon them. They renewed their parties first and ushered America into a new age. They created America's next party system through an intentional choice.

A second path realignments can take, however, is a sudden, uncontrolled, and disruptive collapse. Under this second model, when America's parties stagnate and realigning pressures loom, no one steps forward with an agenda of reform, so eventually those parties crash. In the rubble of the collapse, Americans then must muddle through the darkness, often for years, until eventually someone picks up the pieces to rebuild anew. The classic example of this second sort of realignment is the Whig Party collapse that caused America's Second Party System to disintegrate. For years, the stagnating Second Party System was ready to break. Instead of looking for ways to renew their parties around new issues, like slavery, America's leaders hunkered down into their familiar ideologies, hoping the crisis might pass on its own. Eventually, the Whigs collapsed and the entire party system tumbled with it. Nearly a decade of national turmoil followed as a result. Marginal and radical interests jumped into the vacuum to bid for center stage. The once-marginal Know-Nothings captured America's attention. Politics became violent. National disorder endured for a full eight years, until the Republican Party finally emerged as a new national party, at which point the nation plunged into a civil war. With no framework to channel the disputes and debates of democracy, the nation went mad.

The First Party System's collapse was a somewhat less catastrophic version of this second model. After the debate over how to organize the early republic that divided Federalists and Democratic-Republicans was all but settled, and then the Federalists discredited themselves with the Hartford folly, the Federalist Party crumbled. America wandered for years through the corrupt and ineffectual Era of Good Feelings until, eventually, Jackson and Adams went to battle for the presidency and the nation's mood got hot. Politics got vicious. Political debate got apocalyptic. A conspiratorial third party formed—the Anti-Masonic Party, which sought to break what they believed to be a Masonic conspiracy corrupting the republic—that competed seriously to become America's second major party. America remained in turmoil for years before Jackson's new party system settled in. The First Party System's collapse was milder than the Second's, but was similarly uncontrolled.

The difference separating the first and the second models of political realignments is in how America's leaders respond to looming change. When parties become old and decayed, no longer offering forward-looking messages, it's merely a matter of time before they come tumbling down. America's leaders can decide to seize the moment, renew their parties, and usher in a new age of national reform. Or they can do nothing until some event, some crisis, some new idea, some movement, or some ambitious figure shatters America's political coalitions, and then struggle to pick up the pieces after the inevitable collapse. Put simply, we can either take charge of a coming realignment, sparking a party renewal by choice, or we can do nothing and wait for our parties to collapse before we begin the work of rebuilding amid the disorder our inaction caused. The difference between these two paths lies mainly in our choices—whether we rush into a party renewal to shape the future we want, or instead plunge our heads into the sand and wait for the inevitable collapse to arrive.

Every realignment is disruptive and sometimes scary. No realignment is easy or without risk. A realignment under the first model, however, is far more gentle than its alternative. It avoids the years of turmoil and chaos. There's no vacuum for scary movements to fill. There's no opportunity for demagogues or radicals to seize control by promising people things the dying parties can't provide. There's none of the uncertainty and struggle that makes politics so angry and hot that violence might erupt. There are no constitutional crises, and the republic is safe as we choose to move from one era to the next on our own well-considered terms. Most important, in a renewal under the first model, we pick the coalitions and ideologies that will divide us for decades to come by choice. We can ensure our next party system launches a useful debate about our future, rather than setting us against each other in ugly ways that lead to years of strife.

A collapse under the second model, on the other hand, is dangerous because it means years of chaos before the next realignment comes. In the interim, people and factions and movements can rush out of the dark to seize opportunity. A demagogue can rise. A horrible movement can seize power. Incompetents or the corrupt can win high office and squander the nation's treasure, good name, and legacy. Disastrous decisions can slip through the turmoil. Constitutional crises can erupt. Violence can take root amid the fire of chaotic debates. Radicals can jump into the fray. National disorder can overwhelm everything. Even under the best of cases, it can take years before stability is restored. Most importantly, it's mainly up to luck as to which movements and issues spur new parties to form, what ideologies they bring, and how they will divide us in the years to come.

There's no way to avoid a realignment when the time for one arrives. Our choices in navigating such a realignment, however, shape what sort of transformation it will be. If we move purposefully into change, refreshing the ideologies and agendas of our parties to make them relevant for the coming era, we can choose new parties we want while avoiding the usual cycle of collapse and turmoil that realignments too often bring. If we don't, before things get better they get worse. Possibly, much worse.

THE RISE AND FALL OF THE FIFTH PARTY SYSTEM

If we examine the story of our own party system, we can see the Fifth Party System is at the brink. The New Deal debate was a debate about how to reform modern industrial capitalism after a cataclysmic depression and world war. That debate is over and has been for some time. We face new problems. We now live in a postindustrial information-age global economy that increasingly looks nothing like the mass-production world around which we built our parties. The Cold War ended and a new multipolar world emerged to take its place. American culture has changed, looking very different from the postwar world we take for granted as "normal." A host of new issues and concerns have risen, which our New Deal parties simply can't or won't address. At the same time, disruptive forces course through American politics. If we evaluate our own New Deal party system in light of everything we know about the history of party systems and realignments, we can see every condition for a realignment is now in place. The only question that remains is what sort of realignment it will be.

Will our next realignment be slow and difficult, or quick and purposeful? Will the parties that emerge from it be ones we have reason to dread, or ones that help us to debate a better future? Will the years ahead be ones of turmoil and instability, or the beginning of a hopeful era of reform? Will our next realignment be a collapse or a renewal? That's still up to us. If we understand the course of our own New Deal debate from its inception to today, we can better see why and how our Fifth Party System is about to break—so, when the time comes, we can ensure we choose a future we want and avoid one we don't.

CHAPTER 12

THE LAST HURRAH OF THE FIFTH PARTY SYSTEM

Two presidencies tower over the Fifth Party System—Franklin Roosevelt's and Ronald Reagan's. It's easy to understand why Roosevelt's administration is historically important. Roosevelt's administration launched the New Deal debate that defined an era of history. Reagan's administration is significant for the mirror of that same reason. Reagan, by bringing the conservative movement to power and starting to unwind the institutions of the New Deal, put the Fifth Party System debate on the path to its conclusion. The story of twentieth-century American politics isn't, as often presented, the story of a static battle between the forces of conservatism and liberalism. It's the story of a debate that runs from its inception, to its battles with the conservative countervision of government, to its ultimate resolution and decline. Reagan's presidency and Roosevelt's stand as bookends. Roosevelt and his New Deal philosophy created and defined the Fifth Party System debate. Reagan conservative counterrevolution began that debate's resolution.

Franklin Roosevelt created and defined the debate that dominated twentieth-century politics. Ronald Reagan unleashed the movement through which America would resolve the limits to what Roosevelt had proposed. In the decades in between their two contrasting presidencies, Democrats and Republicans presented America with two opposing visions about how to adjust America's preindustrial institutions for the modern industrial world. The American people watched and listened as those parties argued and conducted their policy experiments, agreeing with some of their ideas and beliefs while rejecting others. Over time they finally reached their verdict. The difficult questions America first asked in the hard days of the Great Depression are now resolved. The New Deal debate is over.

THE FIFTH PARTY SYSTEM

The way we usually view modern politics is as a great seesaw between liberalism and conservatism. With each election, momentum rocks to and fro across a largely static debate. When liberals win, they push the liberal agenda forward. When conservatives win, they push back. According to this worldview, the story of modern American politics is the story of push and counter-push, as liberal victories are met by conservative ones and conversely. This story is so popular that it's the way most of us are conditioned to see and think about politics. Unfortunately, it's wrong. The grand argument between conservativism and liberalism isn't static. It doesn't simply rock back and forth over the midpoint of a spectrum of opinion. Nor is it the story of a progression of liberal victories and conservative ones. It's the story of a debate. Since 1932, American politics has been one grand discussion conducted by its political parties before the American people. Liberals proposed one set of ideas, while conservatives proposed another. The American people listened and, over the decades, sought not to crown one side with total victory but to determine who was right about what and with what limits—in order to reach a consensus taking from both.

In its early days in the 1930s, the New Deal was contentious. Roosevelt offered a radical new vision for American government, one he actively implemented with large majorities at his back. He pushed forward his bold agenda with its new agencies and stunning initiatives like the National Recovery Act, Works Progress Administration, and Social Security program. Critics across both parties pushed back, and when Roosevelt responded with his Court-Packing Scheme and attempted party purge, a majority in Congress united against advancing the New Deal further. Then war broke out in Europe, and America's attention shifted to winning the greatest industrial military conflict in world history. By the war's end, after Roosevelt's four terms as president and the administration of his successor Harry Truman, New Deal liberalism—not just the list of individual New Deal programs, but the ideology that supported them—had been in place so long it was no longer merely uncontroversial. It was the unquestioned basis for American government.

During the New Deal revolution, the Republican Party cried out in outrage against Roosevelt's sweeping transformation of government. The New Deal's opponents, united in the Republican Party, committed to undoing everything "that man"[1] in the White House had done. In the 1930s and early 1940s, Republicans attacked the New Deal's "alphabet soup" of new programs and agencies. They attacked Roosevelt's interventions into the economy. They attacked Social Security. They were heartfelt, passionate, livid, and honestly committed to reversing what they believed was a harrowing wrong turn before it was too late. Many of the Republican Party's candidates—its candidate in 1936, Alf Landon, who is widely considered a progressive, or its candidate in 1940, Wendell Willkie, who went on to become a Roosevelt adviser—we now consider "moderates." The party's message in those years, however, wasn't moderate at all. Republicans didn't just oppose Roosevelt's innovations as a collection of bad ideas and mistakes. They denounced them as a comprehensive program to shred the American Constitution, destroy national tradition, and undermine the very foundations of the American republic. In national election after election, Republican candidates railed against the New Deal and promised to reverse it. Every time, the American people rejected them unequivocally.

In 1948, the Republican establishment had enough. After a decade and a half of sustained attacks, Republicans had clearly failed to convince America the New Deal was evil or dangerous. In fact, it remained broadly popular. In the 1948 election, the Republican Party saw its first real chance in years to reclaim its status as a competitive national party. Franklin Roosevelt wouldn't be on the ballot for the first time since 1932. His successor, President Harry Truman, was unpopular and widely dismissed as a lightweight who had only ascended to the presidency because Roosevelt, sadly, had died in office. The Depression was history, the Second World War over, and America was eager to move on to stability and prosperity. The Republicans had even retaken Congress. Republicans both saw an opportunity to finally restore their fortune and feared that, if they failed yet again, the weight of the disillusionment might even push their party toward collapse.[2] After defeating rivals like Harold Stassen, New York governor Thomas Dewey emerged as the clear candidate of a Republican Party establishment ready to declare a truce in the war against the New Deal.

Dewey was a former prosecutor famous for fighting the mob. As New York governor, he had been comfortable with social welfare spending and eager to build state infrastructure. He also believed strongly in efficiency and budget solvency and was a powerful friend to business. He supported what he called "pay-as-you-go liberalism," supporting progressive government while insisting it be run efficiently and that money be available to pay for it.[3] As the party's nominee in 1944, Dewey had managed to win twelve states and ninety-nine electoral votes—the best a Republican had done in years.[4] At the convention, however, Dewey faced a challenge from Ohio senator Robert Taft, the most important Republican in the Senate, known as "Mr. Republican." Taft built his career as a tireless warrior against Roosevelt and his innovations, and he continued to believe the New Deal was an abomination—one he still hoped to reverse. The nomination battle between Dewey and Taft thus presented the Republican Party with a choice. Dewey meant accepting the New Deal as a permanent feature of America. Taft meant continuing to fight. With the widespread feeling that Taft was unelectable, Dewey and his establishment wing won.[5] Dewey went on to run a sunny campaign about the future, one quite unlike his 1944 campaign denouncing the New Deal. He even endorsed the expansion of New Deal programs like Social Security. Given two Democratic splinter campaigns against the unpopular Truman, one from progressive former vice president Henry Wallace and the other from "States' Rights Democrat" Governor Strom Thurmond, Dewey was widely predicted to win—the *Chicago Tribune* famously printed the premature headline "Dewey Defeats Truman" in anticipation.[6] In the end, Dewey still lost, but the close race convinced the Republican establishment it was on the right track.

Dewey's establishment now believed acquiescence to the New Deal essential to winning back the White House. The Taftites, supported by a small but growing group of intellectuals organizing against the New Deal consensus, were convinced the party failed in 1948 because it hadn't aggressively presented a clear alternative to the Democrats.[7] The Taft and Dewey factions, each clinging to their clashing visions for the party's future, began organizing fiercely for 1952. Taft's conservative followers rallied once again around Taft. Dewey and his establishment wing recruited General Dwight Eisenhower, the victor of the Second World War, a popular figure with similar views and no political record fighting the New Deal at all.[8] Viewing Eisenhower as a mere front for the hated Dewey, Taft and his conservatives fiercely contested the nomination.[9] Once again, the Republicans faced an ideological turning point. Taft and his followers represented a resumption of the Republican Party's uncompromising fight against the New Deal. Eisenhower and the establishment represented acceptance. After a close nomination battle, the party once again picked the establishment.[10] Eisenhower campaigned for the presidency in 1952 without attacking the New Deal at all, focusing instead on foreign policy, communism, and anti-corruption. For the first time in decades, the American people allowed a Republican to move into the White House.

As president, Eisenhower implemented the establishment's vision of a more compromising Republican Party. Eisenhower remained philosophically opposed to the regulatory and welfare state of the New Deal, but in practice his administration made no real effort to undo it. Eisenhower's Republicans treated the New Deal as an unpleasant fact of life with which Republicans would simply have to coexist. Mostly focusing his presidency on the Cold War, Eisenhower expanded Social Security, built the interstate highway system, refused to lower taxes, and otherwise pretty much left the entire New Deal in place. He appointed an attorney general, Herbert Brownell, who was dedicated to fighting for civil rights, sent in federal troops to enforce the *Brown v. Board of Education*[11] decision, and proposed the most ambitious civil rights legislation since Reconstruction, the landmark 1957 Civil Rights Act[12] that segregationist Democrats in Congress tragically defanged. People liked Ike.

Eisenhower's popular presidency confirmed for many Republicans that the establishment wing had been correct. Although it never disappeared, and some supporters continued fighting in the grass roots, Taft's conservative wing slowly dwindled into near irrelevance.

By the early 1950s, the New Deal consensus now firmly set in place, polite society no longer tolerated questioning the New Deal's foundations. As liberal writer Lionel Trilling famously wrote at the time, "In the United States at this time Liberalism is not only the dominant but even the sole intellectual tradition. For it is the plain fact that nowadays there are no conservative or reactionary ideas in general circulation."[13] For the next quarter century, Republicans would focus on better managing the New Deal state. They would call for limiting its further expansion. They would promise efficiency, management, and a more pro-business perspective. They would, however, no longer campaign to actually reverse what had already been done, presenting themselves instead as merely a check against Democratic excess. Through the middle of the 1960s, this mid-twentieth century New Deal consensus ruled. When Democrats won elections, they pushed forward New Deal liberalism. When Republicans won, they played defense, recognizing they were playing on the other party's ideological turf. To suggest the New Deal might ever actually be unwound was now widely viewed as reactionary, if not a crackpot notion. America had given the Democratic Party carte blanche to implement and refine its ideas, with Republicans mainly serving as critics to ensure they stayed honest.

In the shadow of this overwhelming national consensus, however, a small band of young reformers gathered who believed the New Deal could and should still actually be undone. They didn't just want to win political victories against Democrats, they believed they could change the assumptions that had come to support the entire American political system. They dismissed Eisenhower's Republicanism as "measured socialism," with its "easy and whole-hearted acceptance" of "the great statist legacy of the New Deal."[14] Led by a brash young man named William F. Buckley Jr., this odd collection of New Deal opponents intended to not only reignite the New Deal battle but to win it, actually taking apart what Democrats had done. Or as Buckley wrote in the first issue of the magazine he founded, *National Review*, they would "stand athwart history yelling Stop."[15] This was the conservative movement.

THE CONSERVATIVE MOVEMENT'S RISE

William F. Buckley Jr. is among the most consequential figures in twentieth-century political history. This may be surprising, since Buckley is mainly remembered today, when at all, as a popular television pundit and author who spoke with patrician speech and threatened on national television to punch out Gore Vidal. He's placed into a category with influential writers and pundits like Will Rogers, Horace Greeley, or Rush Limbaugh when in reality he was more like Henry Clay—a man who built the ideology of a major party from scratch and thereby reshaped his era's political debate. Buckley was the architect of the conservative movement. There's so much overlap today between the conservative movement and the Republican Party that people often speak of them interchangeably. Yet the conservative movement is no mere figure of speech to describe the Republican Party's most enthusiastic base. It is—and always was—a legitimate independent social movement seeking to overturn a broad societal consensus. Not only did the conservative movement arise separately from regular Republican Party politics, it was in fact a direct rebellion against it that Buckley created and then led.

Buckley first burst onto the national scene in 1951 as the author of the breakout book *God and Man at Yale*, which attacked the philosophical liberalism Buckley believed was overtaking the university from which he had just graduated—an argument that was shocking at the time.[16] The book made him a star.[17] Buckley cut a compelling figure—Ivy League educated, brilliant, witty, pugnacious, and wealthy. He was a writer, a novelist, musician, sailor, and public intellectual who carried himself with aristocratic manners as if he were an old money Episcopal, although he came from an Irish Catholic background.[18] He was completely unlike what people thought a conservative looked like, and his entrepreneurial spirit, showmanship, and intellectual heft embodied all the qualities the establishment respected, making him difficult to dismiss as a crazy on the fringe. In 1955 Buckley co-founded a new conservative magazine, *National Review*, and before long assumed sole control.[19]

Buckley's *National Review* was less a publication than a think tank, leadership development institute, and nucleus for a popular movement. He attracted around his magazine the most brilliant anti–New Deal writers and thinkers of his age, assembling a strange collection of powerful voices.[20] Some were former communists, who, when the romance had worn off in the face of Stalin, became fierce opponents of their former beliefs—the most famous was Whittaker Chambers, a writer nationally famous for his role in the Alger Hiss affair.[21] Others were conservative traditional- ists, people like academic Russell Kirk, author of the influential *Conserva- tive Mind*. Others were libertarians attracted to Ayn Rand and Friedrich Hayek. Others were devout Catholics, like Buckley's brother-in-law Brent Bozell. It was a bizarre collection of writers to find under one banner. At the time, many of these thinkers saw each other as ideological enemies.[22] Lib- ertarians like Rand despised what she thought were authoritarian impulses among the moralists and traditionalists, leading her followers to openly reject the label conservative. The moralists and traditionalists dismissed Rand's libertarianism, particularly its aggressive atheism, as immoral and selfish, and they sought to cast her Objectivism out of the movement.[23] Chambers famously wrote a scathing book review in *National Review* of Rand's central work: "From almost any page of *Atlas Shrugged*, a voice can be heard, from painful necessity, commanding: 'To a gas chamber—go!'"[24] The only thing uniting this great philosophical Noah's Ark was a shared hatred of Franklin Roosevelt and the centralization of power these writers all feared in his New Deal. As Buckley wrote in the founding statement of the magazine, "It seems altogether possible that did *National Review* not exist, no one would have invented it."[25]

Buckley and his team hoped to forge this squabbling group of mar- ginalized thinkers into a united movement.[26] Most of the yeoman's work fell to another former communist at *National Review*, Frank Meyer. Meyer was a rumpled intellectual who rarely made it into the office—

he kept nocturnal habits, sleeping during the day and scribbling through the dark night at his kitchen table.[27] He distilled the arguments of these anti–New Deal writers into the two great principles of liberty and virtue, combining them into one philosophy he called "fusionism" or "fusion conservatism," as it "fused" both principles together. Fusionism held that every New Deal critique ultimately sprang from the same two ideas, liberty and virtue, which were in reality the same idea because one grew out of the other.[28] Liberty requires virtue because only a virtuous society can support political liberty. Virtue requires liberty because freedom from tyranny is a prerequisite to leading a moral life.[29] As Meyer put it:

> What I have been attempting to do is to help articulate in theoretical and practical terms the instinctive consensus of the contemporary American conservative movement. . . . That consensus simultaneously accepts the existence of an objective moral and spiritual order, which places as man's end the pursuit of virtue and the freedom of the individual as a decisive necessary force for a good political order.[30]

In other words, the New Deal's opponents weren't squabbling factions in a temporary alliance, but acolytes of the same philosophy, conservatism. Meyer proposed that all the New Deal's opponents were adherents of the same political philosophy that neatly incorporated every New Deal critique—the jilted communists worried about the Cold War, the Randians worried about creeping socialism, the social traditionalists worried about undercutting the traditional American social order, the religious thinkers worried about the rise of secularism, and the men and women of business worried about the New Deal's restrictions on their work. No longer a group of squabbling cranks unwilling to accept the New Deal, they were in Buckley's magazine now one great movement backed with one well-developed and consistent philosophy.

Before Buckley, the Republican coalition was a loose collection of people who opposed the specific collection of regulations and programs we call the New Deal. Taft represented this in its most uncompromising form, desiring to abolish those programs and regulations, and Dewey and Eisenhower represented a more accommodating form, wanting to limit their expansion. They all, however, saw their role as stopping a collection of policies. Buckley proposed that Republicans were united around stopping not a collection of programs but an idea—New Deal liberalism. His conservatives recognized the New Deal not as just a grab bag of policies but a comprehensive philosophy of government that had become so embedded into the culture most Americans no longer even noticed it was there.[31] Like Henry Clay, Buckley took an ad hoc coalition of interests objecting to a disruptive presidency and crafted from them a coherent ideology that didn't just smooth away factional conflicts but philosophically eliminated them. In doing so, he put not just his rivals' policies but also their ideas into play. After Buckley, Republicans no longer simply face a choice between accommodating the New Deal or going back to 1925. They now offered their own countervision of government, one that accepted some of what the New Deal had wrought, rejected other parts, and presented limits on the rest. Buckley had provided the basis for Republicans to no longer just oppose the Democratic Party's ideas, but to also offer a positive agenda of their own built around an alternative ideology of what government should and shouldn't do.

Also like Clay, Buckley didn't just content himself with this ideological work. He then became a field general for his ideas, launching that movement into the public through the hurly-burly of electoral politics.

THE GOLDWATER REVOLT

After the 1960 election, a group of activists around *National Review* decided the time had come to nominate a candidate of their own. Although Buckley's band had gradually gained influence among Republicans over the 1950s and 1960s, the party establishment had carefully kept these "New Right" forces at arm's length out of a mixture of personal distaste and fear of getting tarred as radicals by association. A small group led by conservative political operative Clif White and *National Review*'s publisher Bill Rusher chose Senator Barry Goldwater as their candidate.[32] Goldwater was already a conservative darling after his impassioned speech at the 1960 Republican convention calling for conservatives to "take this party back." Buckley's brother-in-law Brent Bozell even ghostwrote Goldwater's 1960 book, *The Conscience of a Conservative*, which naturally echoed the ideas of *National Review*.[33] Goldwater was reluctant to run, so the Buckleyites formed a Draft Goldwater Committee.[34] They organized at the grassroots level to take control of local Republican Party organizations, building an impressive network of local activists and multitudes of young people in strong Young Republican organizations, all of whom were for Goldwater. Simultaneously, the Buckleyites promoted Goldwater aggressively as their champion in the pages of *National Review*. With the nomination now within his reach, Goldwater finally agreed to join the race. Buckley and the leadership of his *National Review* thus created the Barry Goldwater bubble, energized the grassroots support behind it, and then supplied its message—the fusion conservative message of *National Review*.[35]

The Republican establishment was deeply alarmed at this uprising for a candidate they believed wildly unelectable. Even Goldwater's professional campaign team, out of fear this New Right "boarding party" was too radical, marginalized Buckley's band from the campaign's inner circle.[36] To take down Goldwater, the establishment rallied around New York governor Nelson Rockefeller, launching a nominating contest both sides correctly saw as a war for the party's soul. Rockefeller had governed New York in the tradition of Dewey, aggressively expanding programs for poor New Yorkers and supporting arts funding, environmental and parks programs, and state infrastructure, with the belief that Republicans could administer such programs more efficiently and with less cronyism than Democrats.[37] Rockefeller initially had the advantage, but Goldwater picked up popular momentum as the excited grass roots of the New Right organized across America on his behalf. Then Rockefeller's campaign imploded in scandal when Rockefeller's wife, his former staffer Margareta "Happy" Murphy, gave birth right before the California primary, reigniting popular anger that Rockefeller had broken up Murphy's first marriage and stole her away from her small children.[38] By the time of the Republican National Convention, Goldwater had all but sealed the nomination but the convention was no less bitter. Rockefeller provoked riotous boos and catcalls when he denounced the conservatives in an impassioned speech, equating them with extremists.[39] Goldwater pushed back, asserting that "extremism in the defense of liberty is no vice," and "moderation in the pursuit of justice is no virtue," a pointed criticism of the Rockefeller wing.[40]

The ensuing 1964 presidential race between Barry Goldwater and Lyndon Johnson—directly challenging the New Deal consensus once more—presented America with its first true clash of rival visions in years.[41] Goldwater's message that the New Deal state should actually be rolled back electrified a growing grass roots, and a legion of young activists flooded into the party to elect him. To many in the general public, however, Goldwater's attacks against the now near-universally accepted New Deal consensus sounded like dangerous nuttery. Goldwater pronounced that he might favor making Social Security voluntary and privatizing the Tennessee Valley Authority, the popular New Deal electrification and economic development agency for the Tennessee Valley.[42] He seemed to suggest he might consider employing nuclear weapons in Vietnam or Cuba, comments much disputed but upon which Democrats eagerly seized.[43] Democrats naturally portrayed Goldwater as a crazy, far-right, warmongering lunatic whose election would destroy the country.[44] When Goldwater campaigned on the slogan "in your heart, you know he's right," Johnson countered with "in your gut, you know he's nuts."[45] Johnson even aired a famous campaign commercial in which a little girl was incinerated on camera by a nuclear weapon unleashed because Goldwater was elected president.[46] The general election against President Johnson ended in one of the more lopsided blowouts of American political history—Goldwater took only six states and 52 electoral votes, while Johnson won 486.

Goldwater's campaign wasn't, as it's sometimes portrayed, a forerunner of the culture wars battles of the 1960s and 1970. Indeed, the pro-choice, gay-friendly, libertarian Goldwater wasn't even a cultural conservative, dedicating a good part of his latter Senate career to denouncing the growing influence of the Religious Right.[47] As a vehicle of the anti–New Deal conservative movement of the 1950s, the Goldwater campaign focused on the same core New Deal issues over which Republicans had fought since

FDR—the size of government, federal power, constitutional limits, regulation, political liberty, and taxes. The Goldwater revolt wasn't the first chapter of the cultural politics that would soon tear the stability of postwar America apart, but simply another front in the classic New Deal debate ongoing since the 1930s. That said, the cultural battles that would rock America were already rumbling, and they played out through the campaign, most powerfully through the issue of the 1964 Civil Right Act.

The 1964 election took place directly after Johnson helped force the 1964 Civil Rights Act through Congress, which ended official segregation and the Jim Crow regime across the South. Even Goldwater's worst critics don't believe he was personally a racist by the standards of his era. He had been a founding member of the Arizona NAACP, bravely integrated his family's department stores long before anyone required it, and as a general in the Arizona National Guard chose to desegregate its Air National Guard.[48] Although his mother was Episcopalian and Goldwater was raised in that faith, his father was also Jewish at a time in which many American institutions openly discriminated on that basis.[49] Goldwater had, however, also voted against the Civil Rights Act on the grounds that it was unconstitutional for the federal government to order a private individual to do business with someone with whom he didn't want to interact.[50] As Goldwater famously said about it, "You can't legislate morality."[51] Goldwater and Johnson agreed not to campaign on the heated issue of race, now rattling both parties, but it nonetheless rumbled and pulled underneath the campaign.[52] Goldwater didn't voice support for segregation during his campaign or repeat racist sentiments—in fact, much the opposite—and specifically sought to avoid the issue of racial politics whenever possible as too "explosive" and treacherous for the nation to discuss at that moment.[53] Seeing opportunity, however, Goldwater also made courting the South a priority in his campaign strategy, spending more attention on the region than Republicans before him, and he certainly understood the backlash playing out in national politics and how it might benefit him.[54] Democrats fought to hold onto their long-standing Southern bastion—not always honorably themselves[55]—but many segregationist voters, believing Goldwater a more likely ally, still bolted. Goldwater won five states across the "Solid South," largely due to segregationist voters bitter at Johnson for his "betrayal."[56]

After the 1964 election, the establishment seized back control of the Republican Party, and Goldwater soon faded from relevance. For the next fifteen years, the narrative around Goldwater's campaign was that it had been a strange epic disaster and a cautionary tale of what happens when the crazies on a party's wing seize a nomination and terrify America. The Republican Party the establishment recaptured, however, wasn't really the same party as before. Goldwater's campaign brought a flood of new foot soldiers into the party—a new generation of young conservative activists loyal to the ideas of Buckley's conservative movement and committed to waging a great war against New Deal liberalism.[57] Through Goldwater's nomination, Buckley's band transformed their small intellectual movement into a powerful grassroots political movement, the "New Right." Over the following years, these New Right conservatives founded institutions to hone and promote their ideas, establishing think tanks, advocacy organizations, and fundraising operations.[58] Young Americans for Freedom, founded at Buckley's house in 1960, blossomed into a powerful New Right youth organization.[59] News magazines and media enterprises arose to trumpet the movement's cause. In 1965, Buckley ran for mayor of liberal New York City and won a surprising 13 percent of the vote.[60] In 1966, public television offered Buckley an opportunity to host a television program, *Firing Line*, to debate ideas and promote his perspective. The Goldwater campaign also brought forward new conservative personalities like Phyllis Schlafly, whose self-published book promoting Goldwater, *A Choice Not an Echo*, brought her national prominence. These new soldiers networked, organized, and integrated into local Republican organizations to create an entire generation of future leaders inspired not by organizational Republican politics but conservative movement activism.[61] Goldwater's campaign transformed Buckley's philosophy from the abstract pages of a magazine into a political army. This army, drawing now on decades of direct experience with the New Deal consensus, hoped once more to reform it and push it back using the ideology Buckley's conservative movement had developed, "movement conservatism."

For the next fifteen years, on the surface of politics, New Deal liberalism remained the overwhelming operating assumption of American government. Through Lyndon Johnson's Great Society, the protest movements, the Vietnam War, the Nixon presidency, Watergate, Jimmy Carter, and more, the New Deal consensus would continue to hold. Yet the debate over the New Deal had now cracked back open. A New Right had emerged eager to fight the war for which Dewey and Eisenhower had declared a cease fire. The Goldwater campaign also left its mark in another important way. Close to the end of the 1964 campaign, Goldwater asked one of his celebrity endorsers to give a televised speech echoing themes of liberty, called "A Time for Choosing."[62] The speech made an impassioned case for limited government based on the ideals of personal freedom. It became so nationally popular that it changed America's perception of the celebrity who gave it, transforming him in the nation's eyes from just another aging actor to a politician and potential leader.[63] That celebrity, of course, was Ronald Reagan.

REAGAN AND THE CONSERVATIVE MOVEMENT TRIUMPHANT

In 1964, Ronald Reagan wasn't yet a politician. He had only recently even become a Republican. For most of his life, Reagan considered FDR a personal hero, and he long supported liberal causes in Hollywood. Yet, over the 1950s, both through his union work as president of the Screen Actors Guild and his work hosting GE Theater, Reagan immersed himself in the serious study of politics and gradually became a *National-Review*-reading movement conservative.[64] When he gave his televised "Time for Choosing" speech, he was still in America's eyes just another Hollywood actor endorsing a candidate. The speech, however, was such a powerful and compelling articulation of Reagan's newfound beliefs that it almost instantly transformed him from a minor Hollywood celebrity into a full-fledged politician.[65] It also revealed he was pretty good at politics. As soon as the 1964 election was over, people began courting Reagan as a potential candidate for office.

In 1966, Reagan ran for and won the governorship of California.[66] Given his obvious political skills, rising from actor to governor in just a few years, the conservative grass roots conferred upon him the mantle of leader of their movement. Reagan was widely considered the conservatives' favored candidate at the 1968 Republican National Convention, but he discovered Nixon had already neatly secured the nomination.[67] Reagan, therefore, instead spent two terms in Sacramento building a political resumé.[68] His next opportunity came in 1976, when he challenged Gerald Ford, the sitting president of his party, for renomination. It was another great proxy war between the conservative and establishment wings, and both candidates went into the Republican National Convention just shy of a majority of the delegates.[69] The establishment again held off the conservative insurgency, but this time just barely. Finally, in 1980 the path was clear, and Reagan became the presumptive frontrunner. This time the establishment had to run as the insurgent campaign, rallying around George H. W. Bush. Bush ran as an establishment moderate, taking a pro-choice position on abortion, supporting the Equal Rights Amendment, and emphasizing his disdain for Reagan's supply-side "voodoo economics."[70] Reagan easily sewed up the nomination, making Bush his vice-presidential candidate as consolation prize. The conventional wisdom was the Republican Party had yet again committed political suicide, just as it had with Goldwater.

America in 1980, however, was in a dour mood. Since 1964, the country had traveled through years of instability—a string of high-profile political assassinations; disruptive protests; urban riots; the Vietnam War; a spike in crime and slowdown in the economy; the rise of the counterculture, the Great Society, and the New Left; Watergate and Nixon's resignation. By 1980, the American economy was trapped in stagflation, a dreaded mix of a stagnant economy and painful inflation.[71] Another oil shock in 1979 had Americans once again waiting in gas lines.[72] Many Americans had grown angry at federal spending, and citizens in places like California even broke out in defiant "tax revolts."[73] Iran had taken American hostages, and the American government floundered powerlessly to free them.[74] In 1979, President Carter unsettled the nation in a nationally televised speech claiming America was locked in "paralysis and stagnation and drift," and that the "erosion of our confidence in the future is threatening to destroy the social and the political fabric of America."[75]

After the hard years of the 1970s, what many perceived to be over-reach from Johnson's Great Society and its aftermath, and dismay at the radicalism at the farther fringes of the New Left that had grown out of the protest movements and the counterculture, many Americans had lost faith in the national consensus. It had even become an item of faith that the American government had become nearly ungovernable and that the presidency was too complicated for any one person to manage.[76] Americans were open to a message of decisive change. Reagan offered it. Reagan pledged to repair the stagflation economy with supply-side economics—making it easier for people to produce and invest instead of spending money to boost national demand. He would slash national tax rates. He would prune federal regulations. He would cut federal spending, especially on Great Society social programs he believed wasteful and inefficient. He pledged to balance the federal budget. He would push government responsibility from the federal government to the states. He would boost support for the military to more directly confront the Soviet Union.[77] While most of Reagan's platform is now unremarkable Republican boilerplate, at the time it was shocking. Reagan had essentially pledged to begin dismantling the New Deal, replacing it with Buckley's movement conservatism.

Reagan won in 1980 in a national landslide, winning forty-four states. With Reagan topping the ticket, the Republicans also took back the Senate for the first time since Eisenhower. Reagan's win and the size of his coattails came as a thunderclap to the American political establishment.[78] The establishment—including a significant number of Republicans—were sure Reagan's presidency would be a disaster.[79] They thought Reagan's supply-side economic policies would wreck the economy.[80] They thought his attacks on welfare programs would throw millions into poverty. They thought his methods of fighting the Cold War would trigger World War III.[81] Republican leaders initially set out to control and contain him for the good of the party and America. Then Reagan actually began to follow through with his pledges, and the American establishment howled.

In his inaugural address, Reagan shocked the establishment when he famously proclaimed, "In this present crisis, government is not the solution to our problem. Government *is* the problem."[82] Reagan distributed to his cabinet copies of a 1,093-page book called *Mandate for Leadership*, prepared by a then small conservative think tank, The Heritage Foundation. The book set out a comprehensive blueprint for conservative policy changes in every corner of government.[83] Reagan then started to actually carry out this vision. He successfully pushed a major tax overhaul through Congress in his first term, slashing top marginal tax rates and reducing complexity in the tax code.[84] In his second term, he pushed through another tax cut.[85] Reagan fought for budget cuts.[86] His administration labored to eliminate government regulations it found burdensome or pointless or that didn't meet a strict cost-benefit analysis.[87] When Reagan faced an illegal strike by the federal air traffic controllers' union, he stunned most everyone by not just firing them but banning them from further federal employment—changing the assumptions behind labor-management disputes across America.[88] For the first time since the New Deal, Republicans weren't simply slowing the New Deal's advance or attempting to run New Deal programs more efficiently. The New Deal was actually going backward.

After decades of unquestioned dominance, Democrats had grown to assume the New Deal could only go forward, that every program passed and policy implemented was a permanent victory. Now Republicans were taking their achievements apart. Democrats were shaken and demoralized.[89] More remarkable, the predicted disasters didn't come. The economy took off again, and the "me generation" started making money. The runaway inflation was tamed. The nation shook off the tragedy of Vietnam and began to feel safe and strong once more. There were no new national humiliations like the Iranian hostage crisis, and no more crazy disruptions to ordinary economic life like the gas lines of the oil shock. American confidence soared. While many in the 1970s feared the nation was tumbling ever downward, it now seemed to be rising upward. Reagan called his 1984 reelection campaign "Morning in America," asking the rhetorical question of whether Americans believed they were better off now than four years before.[90] He won a national landslide, taking 525 electoral votes and forty-nine states.

In retrospect, what's remarkable about the Reagan Revolution wasn't its specific achievements. When placed in context of what came later, they actually look quite small. After cutting taxes, Reagan later agreed to raise taxes in exchange for budget cuts.[91] The Reagan administration ramped up deregulation in federal agencies, but the reduction was ultimately merely a dent.[92] America never adopted Reagan's supply-side philosophy, which had never even been popular in a Republican Party dominated by free-marketers who mostly went along in the belief that "starving the beast" of government was nevertheless a worthy goal.[93] While Reagan promised to balance the federal budget, deficits ballooned under his presidency.[94] The reason Reagan's presidency was a revolution wasn't the weight of the specific policies enacted but what they represented for the nation's frame of reference. After Reagan's eight years in office, America shifted its baseline assumptions about the role of government. The national consensus moved toward free markets. The momentum shifted from government growth to deregulation. The perspective on the Cold War changed from a permanent standoff to a conflict America could resolve—as Reagan put it, "We win, they lose."[95] Reagan had begun to turn the battleship of America's political debate away from the assumptions of New Deal liberalism.[96]

Just as importantly, the Reagan administration transformed the Republican Party. Although his most senior appointments came out of the old experienced Republican establishment by necessity, many of the Republicans who streamed into Washington to work for him were from a new generation of young movement conservatives. Under Reagan, institutions like the Heritage Foundation and American Enterprise Institute, once scorned and shut out of power as radicals, could now get the ear of people in positions of power. William F. Buckley, not so long ago a young antiestablishment radical yelling stop, was now a warm personal friend of the president of the United States.[97] After eight years in office, Reagan transformed the conservative rebellion of Buckley and Goldwater into the base of a new Republican establishment that had enacted a movement-conservative agenda out of the pages of *National Review*, and the American people reelected the conservatives in a landslide. With the weight of that revelation, the old Rockefeller establishment wing of the party—its foundational belief against challenging the New Deal proved wrong—collapsed. Apparently, taking on the New Deal wasn't political suicide after all. After Reagan, most every Republican of any standing would proudly claim to be a Reagan Republican. Even George H. W. Bush, the establishment's candidate of 1980, became a Reagan movement conservative, pledging never to raise taxes and taking new positions on social issues.[98]

By bringing the conservative movement to power within the Republican Party, the Reagan presidency launched the last act of the Fifth Party System debate. For decades, New Deal liberalism was unquestioned as the foundation for American government. When Democrats won elections, they advanced their New Deal philosophy with the American people's consent. Now, for the first time since the 1930s, a Republican Party energized around its countervision of government was driving the nation's political debate. As Washington journalists Jack Germond and Jules Witcover wrote in 1985, "The guiding light of half a century—the New Deal of Franklin D. Roosevelt and its successor mutations from Truman through Carter and Mondale—had been all but snuffed out by the voters as the preferred framework for government policy at the national level."[99] It was no longer sufficient for Democrats to pit their New Deal against the pre–New Deal world of Herbert Hoover. They now had to debate a conservatism pointing out the New Deal's wrong turns and proposing limits. Before Reagan, it was radical to suggest the programs and structures the Democrats had built since the 1930s could ever be unwound. After Reagan, it was foolish to think they couldn't be. As columnist George Will wrote, Goldwater actually won in 1964, but "it just took 16 years to count the votes."[100] What followed was a fifteen-year struggle to resolve the New Deal debate for good.

THE END OF THE FIFTH PARTY SYSTEM DEBATE

For Republicans, the Reagan Revolution was like breaking free from a sterile white room and stumbling into Willy Wonka's Chocolate Factory. Republicans had decades of frustrated pent-up energy and an agenda to discover and implement. For the first time in a half century, all the policy white papers and think-tank reports that conservatives had spent decades designing could suddenly become actual government policy. Republicans launched an onslaught of energetic policy experiments to take apart or reform longstanding Democratic policies and programs. After Reagan, movement-conservative ideas quickly spread throughout the Republican Party at every level of government. A new generation of Republican executives rose up outside Washington in states and cities, many in jurisdictions Democrats traditionally controlled. Executives like Tommy Thompson in Wisconsin, John Engler in Michigan, Rudy Giuliani in New York, and Richard Riordan in Los Angeles launched new ideas questioning core New Deal governing assumptions, policies like community policing to fight crime, charter schools and school choice to reform education, and welfare-to-work programs to reform entitlements. They also began eliminating New Deal style programs in efforts to balance budgets, reduce taxes, cull regulations, and cut red tape. They slashed taxes, cut programs, reduced regulations, and on various fronts took apart the institutions Democrats had spent decades building. No one was talking about expanding New Deal programs any more, much less creating new ones. They were talking about eliminating them.

By the early 1990s, many Democrats, tired of losing the momentum to Republicans, had come to believe their party had lost touch and overreached during the 1970s. These "New Democrats," believing Democratic Party excesses had caused moderate voters, independents, and "Reagan Democrats" to abandon them, founded institutions like the Democratic Leadership Council to recalibrate their party. They emphasized ideas like "common-sense solutions," moving from "redistribution to growth," and pursuing liberal ideas through values like patriotism and religious faith.[101] In 1992, Arkansas governor Bill Clinton, a leader of this movement, won back the White House while campaigning on a platform based around blunting the conservative critique of New Deal liberalism. Clinton promised a middle-class tax cut, to "reinvent government" by streamlining agencies and cleaning up needless regulation, and a proposal to "reform welfare as we know it."[102] Once in office, however, Clinton abandoned his campaign promise of a middle-class tax cut, proposing and championing a significant tax increase instead.[103] He devoted great energy to a healthcare reform initiative that stoked significant national opposition and ultimately crashed in failure.[104] He plunged himself into contentious culture war issues for his time.[105] The new Democratic administration had interpreted the victory as permission to once again advance their party's previous priorities. In 1994, voters, dismayed at the backtracking, particularly replacing a promised tax cut with an increase, dramatically swept the Democrats out of both houses of Congress.

For the 1994 midterm election, an ambitious congressman named Newt Gingrich designed an agenda of reforms with the Conservative Opportunity Society, seeking to take the Reagan Revolution into the final bastion of the New Deal—Congress.[106] Congress was the bulwark of the New Deal state because it's the institution of government that can actually change laws, create programs, or abolish them. Gingrich's "Contract with America" promised a flurry of concrete ideas and policy proposals, nationalizing what was normally a collection of hundreds of local elections. It promised a welfare reform bill, term limits for members of Congress, a balanced budget constitutional amendment, criminal procedure reform, a small business incentive package, and a per-child tax credit, along with reforms to House procedures to break the power of House committee chairs.[107] Between the outraged backlash at Clinton's reneging on promises and the popularity of Gingrich's Contract, America swept out the Democrats in what came to be called a "Republican Revolution."[108] The Democrats had controlled the House for over forty years, so long people had come to assume Democratic control of Congress was a structural reality of American government. America was stunned.

For Democrats, losing the House was worse than a disaster. It meant losing the committee chairs, budget authority, and majority power that backstopped the institutions of New Deal liberalism—putting every program Democrats had enacted over decades at risk. The new Republican House rapidly passed a stream of ambitious proposals from a line-item veto bill to empower the president to eliminate pork-barrel spending, a tax reform bill to slash the capital gains tax rate and provide exemptions on the sale of a home, an anticrime bill limiting how freely prisoners could file habeas corpus appeals, term limits for federal office, and a constitutional amendment to balance the budget.[109] Most ambitious was a comprehensive welfare reform bill that traded the cash-entitlement system for one requiring work, job training, and education to obtain benefits, and a package of federal spending bills with significant cuts sufficient to balance the federal budget. Republicans were actively undoing what Democrats had spent decades building, achievements Democrats assumed would never be undone. The bewildered Democrats went into a panicked shock.

Over the next two years, on issue after issue, Republicans brought fresh ideas into the arena, proposing radical changes based on their conservative countervision of government while Democrats met them with a vigorous defense. These competing agendas crashed one into the other as each party was forced to justify to America what they hoped to accomplish and why. In these debates, Democrats and Republicans were implicitly debating the limits of the New Deal. They debated which parts of New Deal liberalism had worked and which parts might work better. They debated which initiatives Americans no longer wanted and they reformed others. The synthesis of Republican proposals and Democratic pushback unleashed a remarkably productive moment of substantive government reform. Republicans got their crime bill and their welfare reform bill.[110] After intense negotiations and political hardball, including a nasty government shutdown, the parties temporarily brought the federal budget into balance after years of deficits.[111] On issue after issue, as the parties fought, they began to reach a rough consensus about the New Deal and its limits, what government might do and what it shouldn't do. Then, around 1996, this brief moment of reform slowed to a halt.

Two significant turning points occurred in the latter half of the 1990s that Americans have yet to fully appreciate. First, in his 1996 State of the

Union address, President Clinton made a shocking proclamation—that "the era of big government is over."[112] In case anyone missed the importance, he said it twice. Clinton had just spent the last two years negotiating with Republicans about ending programs his party had authored and giving up on long-held Democratic items of faith, while a Republican Speaker of the House, declared *Time*'s "Man of the Year," was essentially driving the government.[113] Conventional wisdom held that his presidency had failed. With a tough reelection looming, Clinton was desperate to seize back his mantle of "New Democrat." His speech wasn't just important, however, because it recommitted him to the New Democrat mode. "Big government" is just the pejorative name Republicans use for the New Deal state. In promising "the era of big government is over," the leader of the Democratic Party had proclaimed in a formal address to America that his party had given up on further advancing the New Deal.

Not so long afterward, the Republicans made a similar concession. By the end of the 1990s, Gingrich's Contract with America was crashing. While initially popular when talking about slashing government in the abstract, Republicans were now threatening things America wanted them to leave alone. Republicans since 1980 had systematically dismantled parts of the New Deal and Great Society Americans disliked. They reversed the growth of the regulatory state and began imposing cost-benefit thinking to future regulation. They reformed welfare. They popularized markets as tools for regulating business and discredited top-down methods of command and control. They reversed the growth of taxes. Now, they were encroaching on parts of the New Deal that America liked. When Republicans bragged about slashing government, Democrats argued they would wreak heartless havoc by cutting popular programs like Pell Grants and Head Start, eliminating the government's ability to reduce pollution leading to unclean air and water, and cutting off needy families from food stamps. America didn't want to cut Medicare or allow it to "wither on the vine" through a voluntary move to a private program. They didn't want to privatize Social Security or abolish the Department of Education. When Democrats picked up seats in the election of 1998—helped along by the widespread belief that Republicans, in addition to policy errors, went too far pushing for Clinton's impeachment when it was revealed he had engaged in a sexual affair with a White House intern— the Republicans pushed the now deeply unpopular Gingrich and his revolution overboard.[114] Informed his reelection as Speaker was unlikely, Gingrich resigned from Congress and the Republican House went into the care of Tom DeLay and a new Speaker, Denny Hastert, who restored the traditional model of the Speaker as a dealmaker instead of would-be visionary.[115] The Republican Revolution was over.

These two turning points stand as milestones at the end of an epoch. The fifteen years of debate and reform that followed Reagan's election brought the Fifth Party System to its finale. Democrats now knew if they ever again moved away from defending the existing New Deal to actively advancing New Deal liberalism, the American people would strike them down as they had Clinton's Democrats. The era of big government really was over. Democrats would continue to talk about advancing New Deal liberalism, campaign on it, and write policy white papers about it, but in practice accepted they would never again actually seek to do it. There would also be no more Republican crusades to dismantle the remaining institutions New Deal liberalism created. Republicans likewise knew if they were to ever again actively seek to unwind any more of the New Deal, the American people would strike them down as they had Gingrich's revolutionaries. Republicans would continue to talk about dismantling government, campaign on it, and write policy white papers about it, but they would never again actually seek to do it in any lasting way. Few yet realized it, but both parties in the middle of the 1990s reached the logical end of their agendas.

In the first chapter of the Fifth Party System story, Democrats proposed New Deal liberalism in the midst of crisis as a solution to America's problems. America implemented it, kicked the tires, and decided which parts it liked and which parts it didn't. In the next chapter, the conservative movement launched a great ideological pushback against the New Deal. For years, Republicans challenged New Deal liberalism, pointing out its excesses and proposing its limits. The American people listened, adopting some of the Republican critique and rejecting other parts. Now, in a final chapter, after decades of lived experience with the New Deal,

America had resolved the debate. The American people listened to what each party said, accepted some of it, rejected other parts of it, and reached a final judgment. America decided this was how far the New Deal would go and no farther. The debate was over. With the era's great debate now essentially resolved, the Fifth Party System began unraveling.

THE UNRAVELING OF THE FIFTH PARTY SYSTEM'S NEW DEAL DEBATE

The Fifth Party System has essentially been a debate over how to adapt America's institutions to the industrial modern world after a horrific depression and global war. The purpose of that debate wasn't ever to fully implement all the ideas of liberalism or conservatism. It was for the American people to think through difficult problems and eventually reach a synthesis taking wisdom from both sides. It was to identify the ideas it liked, toss out the ones it didn't, and place the proper limits on whatever it chose to keep. By the middle of the 1990s, that debate was complete. After decades of experience, the American people decided they wanted their government to take on substantial responsibility for matters of health, safety, and welfare that it hadn't assumed before 1932. They also decided these new responsibilities weren't limitless nor was central planning always the best way to carry them out. The American government would have regulatory agencies responsible for supervising various areas of the economy and society. It would have a welfare state with programs like Medicare and Social Security. It would intervene in the private economy to reduce the effects of unfair discrimination. At the same time, those new powers would be strictly limited so as not to step too harshly on individual freedom or the market economy. There would be no more National Industrial Act cartels, no more vast new Great Society programs or "Soak the Rich" federal tax rates. America had decided how to adjust the institutions of its republic to work within the twentieth-century industrial-era world. There was nothing left to debate.

In rhetoric, America continues to organize its political life around the ancient New Deal battle. It's what our parties claim to believe. It's what their campaigns center around. It's the framework around which they organize their agendas. Democrats continue to believe in the New Deal, campaign on it, and defend what the party has already accomplished under it. In practice, Democrats mainly defend old programs while seeking a few small tweaks to existing policies. Republicans continue to philosophically oppose the New Deal, campaign against it, and rally to stop it from going further. In practice, Republicans would no longer actively take apart bedrock twentieth-century government institutions if they could. While some pundits and activists still passionately believe in the same old fights, and while both coalitions still contain a fair share of committed old warriors dedicated to fighting old New Deal battles decades after the Great Depression, in practice it's all theater. Democrats implicitly understand they can push the New Deal no further. Republicans implicitly understand they can't abolish the rest of the New Deal state without proposing something better. The fight around which we organize American politics is in reality a bushel of archaic platitudes. The country has moved on.

Like the debate of any party system, the great debate of the Fifth Party System was one neither side was ever meant to win. In every party system debate, America tests the ideas of both parties over time and ultimately finds a middle ground. It takes Hamilton's Federalist agenda but sprinkles it with Jefferson's ideas. It adopts Jacksonian Democracy and the Whig American system at the same time. It works through the resentments of the Civil War while taking into account the perspectives and interests of North and South. It breaks up the Gilded Age with a Populist and Progressive Era, taking ideas from both. The New Deal Party System was always destined to end with America implementing parts of New Deal liberalism tempered by conservative objections, reforming the American government for the modern age while taking into account the best ideas of the conservative countervision. The Fifth Party System was never a great tug of war pulling government left and right toward victory. It was never a battle either conservatives or liberals were meant to win. It was a decades-long discussion in which America tested rival ideas and listened to objections until it reached a consensus drawing from both about how best to solve one specific set of problems at one moment in its history.

As the importance of an era's debate declines at the cusp of a realignment, politics and government stagnates and decays. Public officials and political elites invoke by rote the comfortable boilerplate of a prior age, ignoring the constant arrival of unfamiliar problems worrying the rest of the nation. Listless parties coast by on old slogans. Elections get reduced to mere entertainment instead of debates about real issues. There's corruption, both the seedy kind with bribes and profiteering and the accepted kind with money and politics and power bleeding together without regard for the good of America as a whole. Government gets reduced to a stagnant machine of maintaining power while politics becomes a vast circus for loyalty-signaling and emoting. Campaigns become a meaningless show centered around personality and identity. Citizens get frustrated at governments that seem useless, unsure of who to blame but sure no one in power is making things better. This was true of the Era of Good Feelings.[116] It was true as America moved into the 1850s.[117] It was true of the Gilded Age.[118] It was true of the Jazz Age of the 1920s.[119] The abandonment of substance and ideas in government in fact is the most reliable indicator a realignment may be around the corner. For years, the American political system has mainly focused not on ideas and policies but the machinations of the political system, obsessing about daily "messaging," raising money from K Street, winning elections, and engaging in gimmicky short-term policy "ideas" geared to winning cable news cycles and clickbait headlines but not carrying out the concrete agenda of real policy ideas the parties claim to represent. Political debate has become less a clash of ideas and more a clash of symbolic stands and micro-scandals that make the other party look bad.

Between the Great Depression and the mid-1990s, American government was constantly doing important things—the New Deal, postwar rebuilding, massive new infrastructure, civil rights, the Great Society, major tax reform, antidiscrimination laws, deregulation, or welfare reform. In between was a constant stream of less glamorous but no less important work, whether the Peace Corps, the Clean Air Act, airline deregulation, the Americans with Disabilities Act, or adjustments to entitlement programs. Every few years between the New Deal and the middle of the 1990s brought another new idea or great political achievement of the kind of which historians take note, whether Democrats moving the New Deal forward or Republicans reforming and refining government according to their countervision. At the end of the 1990s, that all stopped and a rot set in. Government has continued functioning. Officials responded to crises. After the September 11 attacks, America put everything on hold to respond to a new threat. When an economic crisis in 2008 plunged the world economy into a tailspin, America responded. Yet responding to erupting crises and keeping the machinery of government operating is different from mapping out a proactive strategy to face the longer-term problems that shape the nation's future. For almost two decades, little of real significance has happened in American politics or government outside crisis management.

As we remain caught in the fights of our own era, it can be hard to accept the degree of the stagnation. It's tempting to credit the intentions of the politicians you support and blame the failures on those you didn't. Yet, for almost an entire generation, there's been no truly significant achievement in government of the kind that regularly existed before. The Bush administration launched a few small-scale experiments—a tax reduction, a quickly abandoned Social Security reform proposal, the No Child Left Behind education initiative, faith-based initiatives, and expanding the Medicare entitlement with Medicare Part D.[120] The Obama administration threw its weight behind a national health insurance bill, the Affordable Care Act, which benefits a great many people. Despite the howls of Republicans who denounced it, and the satisfied cheers of the Democrats who celebrated it, however, it was also a bill—a series of important administrative tweaks to existing law rather than a major structural change, something of the historical significance of perhaps the Clean Air Act or the Americans with Disabilities Act—that in any other political era would be considered meaningful but small.[121] It only seemed so major because it was the only significant law passed in over a decade. None of this is the sort of achievement that historians looking back a century hence will likely even note. There hasn't even been a great and noble failure in which officials sought to solve hard new problems with an innovative new idea and failed. Few appreciate the irony. Despite the sincere belief across America that the other tribe is wrecking America with terrible policies and ideas, for years nothing much has actually happened at all.

The resolution of the great debate of the Fifth Party System is the first powerful force leading America toward a realignment. It's not that the nation doesn't have real and distressing problems it desperately needs to solve. It's not that liberals and conservatives don't have worries and ideas about how to address them. Nor is it even that the individual officials in government no longer care. Idealists and wonks keep devising policies, writing op-ed columns, and drafting white papers in the hope someone with influence might listen. Every once in a while, some agency announces some minor victory or an idealistic politician proposes a real effort to solve a difficult problem that inevitably fails to get traction. The problem is the framework of our debate. All our parties know how to do—all they were designed to do—is to fight about the world of Franklin Roosevelt. The fight between New Deal liberalism and conservatism pits against each other two ideologies designed to solve problems decades in the past for an America that's no longer here. It channels our collective worries and ideals through an anachronistic system never designed for the problems of the world we live in now. Our parties, working off out-of-date playbooks, are fighting over policies nobody ever really intends to pursue over the problems of an industrial manufacturing economy that hardly even exists in light of a depression more than half a century in the past.

America's two major parties continue on like automatons making the same old arguments over the same old issues as if by rote, while in reality there's little to debate. The Democrats have enacted all the parts of New Deal liberalism the American people want. The Republicans have unwound all the parts of New Deal liberalism the American people didn't want. Neither party is built—through their ideologies, their ideas, their orthodoxies, or the structure of their coalitions—to pick up and address the new and unfamiliar issues that exist today. The New Deal debate is over and most of what remains is just the kabuki theater of campaigns, politics for the sake of politics, symbolism, and spoils. We've reached the long empty part of a party system in which an era's great debate is done but the next one has yet to start.

CHAPTER 13

THE PENDULUM OF GREAT AWAKENINGS

American culture rocks back and forth like a pendulum between pragmatic eras and moralistic ones. Sometimes America is a practical country focused on negotiating over interests, policies, and results—concrete things people can horse trade and thereby compromise over. Other times, America is a messianic country obsessed with moral crusades over questions of right and wrong. Sometimes Americans care most about breadbasket issues of stability and prosperity. Other times Americans eagerly sacrifice practical concerns to make America more just and more fair, eager to burn old institutions down in the hope of building better ones from the ashes. Back and forth it goes about once or twice a century. These repeating eruptions of moralism are called great awakenings, and they're one of the most important and least discussed phenomena of American culture and politics.

When the awakening spirit strikes America, it sparks a lightning strike of major reform that affects everything. Americans who once believed the nation's most important task was to uphold good order and provide for everyone's needs suddenly cast off such pragmatic concerns, convinced the nation must be urgently reformed and uplifted. Awakenings trigger great religious revivals. They create bursts of charity and volunteerism. They trigger new interest in spiritualism. Most important, nearly every great cause in American history traces back to an awakening. The abolition of slavery. Women's suffrage. Temperance. Public schooling. The ban of child labor. Antipoverty activism. Anticorruption and good government efforts. Health safety laws. Great awakenings are the hidden driver behind many of the greatest social and cultural reform movements in the history of America. Yet few of us know, or are taught, much about this undisputedly important force running through America's culture and politics. It's a tragedy because we live in an awakening era now, one that has shaken the foundation of the Fifth Party System since the 1960s—and is helping to drive the next realignment to come.

AMERICA'S CYCLE OF GREAT AWAKENINGS

America's great awakenings are wholly uncontroversial textbook history. Many American children learn all about them in school, albeit from a corner of their textbook, tucked in the back, which they study and soon forget. Despite their well-documented importance to the history of America, great awakenings don't really make it into America's national narrative. They're often pigeonholed as simply "religious history" ancillary to the course of national events. America's first three great awakenings did indeed spark important Christian revival movements, ones that transformed the country's religious landscape and brought Christian activists into politics as they swept across the nation. These awakenings were also, however, a great deal more. They were great national moral revivals, ones in which Americans both secular and religious plunged into crusades for reform—a national moral spirit that many Americans naturally channeled through their Christian beliefs. Each time this awakening spirit arose in a new generation, it changed people's priorities. It created new social and political issues. It seeped deeply into every nook of the culture and overwhelmed everything.

The original Great Awakening struck America in the middle of the 1700s and ran through to the American Revolution's dawn. It began when a flood of itinerant preachers like George Whitefield started traveling up and down the colonies spreading a religious revival that directly challenged traditional authority and spread new ideas about the individual's relationship with God. A Second Great Awakening began around the 1820s and ran up through the Civil War. It saw tent revival meetings burn over the landscape, encouraging Christians to reform society to bring about Christ's return and putting fire into a movement to abolish slavery. It helped along the Second Party System's collapse. A Third Great Awakening broke out in the 1880s and ran into the early twentieth century. This one inspired religious reformers, newly drawn back into the church, to reform society according to the ideals of the Social Gospel. They became foot soldiers in the Progressive Movement that fought to, among many other things, ban alcohol, end industrial abuses like child labor, educate poor children through new public schools, extend charity to the poor and to new immigrants crowding into America's booming cities, and grant the vote to women.

In each awakening, Americans who had grown secular and disinterested in spiritual matters suddenly refilled the churches and went on quests for spiritual renewal. Each saw a nationwide revival in enthusiastic religion, particularly among Protestants. These revivals united around a great nondenominational Christian identity and saw religion mix with entertainment and community, whether through itinerant preachers preaching to emotional crowds in fields during the eighteenth century, carnival-like tent revival meetings in the early nineteenth century, or the educational and entertainment chautauqua circuit of the turn-of-the-twentieth century. Each awakening created new religious movements, new religious institutions, and new charitable endeavors, and a corresponding decline in the less-enthusiastic established churches. They also drew some Americans down alternative spiritual paths, inspiring them to search for meaning through beliefs like occultism, transcendentalism, or personal improvement. These religious eruptions, however, were merely the most noticeable part of something greater—national outbursts of crusading moral reform.

With each awakening, a pragmatic America suddenly threw off material obsessions over jobs, opportunity, and security, for questions of morality, spiritual renewal, and reform. In America's pragmatic ages—like the early republic, the Civil War's aftershock, or the 1920s through World War II—Americans wanted stability, peace, and prosperity. During awakenings, they were willing to tear everything down to rebuild something better. From the First Awakening's challenge to traditional authority, to the Second's abolitionists and temperance crusaders, to the Third's progressive reformers, every awakening has sparked significant movements to uplift and improve America. Awakenings are crusading and rowdy eras of powerful reform movements and energetic politics. They're eras of conflict, where compromise becomes impossible over stark and urgent matters of right and wrong. They're eras of turmoil as zealous crusaders burst into the center of the national debate demanding radical change, willing if necessary to see the world burn down. When the awakening spirit washes over America, it seeps into every pore of society, touching not just religion and politics but also culture and entertainment, spilling over everyone and everything.

There's little agreement about why awakenings come and go. Historians have theories to explain each individual awakening—changes in religious theology, changes in the economy, the ideas and campaigns of different people, and so on. Yet there's little consensus around why awakenings happen at all, what causes them to fade, or why they keep coming back again and again. The best explanation is they're simply the result of the inevitable shifts between prosperous and stable eras and harder times. Generations who live through difficult times value peace, prosperity, and strong institutions because they know the wolves of war, economic panic, depression, or the collapse of safety and order are never far from the door. Americans who grow up in stable and comfortable times worry less about how bad things can get, dreaming more about how much better they might be. When they look at stable, sturdy institutions, they don't see bulwarks against danger but imperfect systems locking in injustices and wrongs. As America moves between bad times to good ones, and back again, it leaves the ripples of awakenings in its wake. When danger and chaos loom, awakenings disappear and the culture turns pragmatic. When the danger ends and good times resume, awakenings come roaring back.

Awakenings are wholly separate phenomena from realignments, yet the two powerfully interact. Awakenings supercharge society with moral fervor. They cause people to see politics not in terms of disagreements but in terms of good and evil or right and wrong. They make it harder for people to split the difference or compromise. They also change people's priorities, making issues that weren't important during a party system suddenly the most important questions to resolve. When America is immersed in the spirit of an awakening, Americans charge into crisis with the moral certainty of crusaders, demanding immediate and sweeping changes that rip old alliances down. Although independent forces driven by completely different factors, awakenings inevitably interact with politics, parties, and party systems. America's continual shifting back and forth between a pragmatic culture and a moralistic one is an important part of the story of how party systems come to be and why they then break down.

As the Fifth Party System now prepares to break as America heads into its next realignment, awakening fervor seems poised to play an important role again—because a Fourth Great Awakening is almost certainly already underway.

THE GREAT AWAKENING

People often think of the American colonies as a hotbed of enthusiastic religion. The famous European settlers of New England, after all, were religious pilgrims who fled the Old World due to their zealous and nonconforming brand of Protestant Christianity. When we remember colonial America, we remember the world of the *Scarlet Letter*, preachers in town hall meetings, and the witch trials of Salem. Yet, by the 1740s, that fervent colonial religion had long since cooled.[1] When colonists went to church, reverends read their bored congregations dry and pedantic sermons more like academic lectures on theology.[2] Most colonists continued to profess religious belief, but that religion now played merely a perfunctory role in their lives. American religion, from the Congregationalist churches in New England to the Church of England further south, and all the other diverse denominations of colonial America scattered among them, had become mainly a formal enterprise of ritual and rote. Amid all this formal religion, however, were the early rumblings of revival. Many colonists yearned for a more meaningful and personal religious message, one not based in cerebral theology but in salvation. A few preachers were already stirring up new religious passion and triging small passionate revivals, the most famous of which was Jonathan Edwards, author of the famous sermon "Sinners in the Hands of an Angry God."[3] The American colonies were dry tinder waiting for the right torch. Then, in 1739, a young preacher arrived in the colonies from England and he set this timber of revival alight.[4]

While few Americans today have heard of George Whitefield, in the decades before the American Revolution he was without doubt the greatest celebrity of the American colonies. Whitefield first found religion as a poor student at Oxford—a "servitor" who paid for his education in exchange for often humiliating personal service to higher-status students—where he fell in with Charles and John Wesley, who ran an organization they called the "Holy Club." Believing mankind ought to submit every hour to God, they drew up a strict regime of religious rituals carving out specific time for prayer, Bible study, meetings, and spiritual reflection. Other students, who found it all absurd, labeled them "methodists."[5] Whitefield so threw himself into religious devotion and the Holy Club—failing to eat and sleep—he made himself gravely ill. When he recovered, he believed it had been a miracle in which he was spiritually reborn.[6] As he declared it, it was a "new birth." After his ordination in the Church of England and graduation from Oxford, and while waiting for a ship to join the Wesleys as missionaries to the then remote American colony of Georgia, Whitefield began preaching locally and something remarkable happened.[7] Word began to spread about his extraordinary sermons about spiritual rebirth and a conversion experience to God. Crowds started to pack into the churches to hear him. Whitefield wrote that at one of his appearances "people clung onto the rails of the organ-loft, climbed upon [the] roof of the church, and made the church itself so hot with their breath, that the steam would fall from the pillars like drops of rain."[8] By the time he left for Georgia, still in his early twenties, Whitefield was famous.

Whitefield spent less than a year as a missionary before returning to England. Back home, his powerful sermons continued to attract attention. And then bigger crowds. Whitefield's sermons were unlike anything anyone had heard. He was a small man with crossed eyes, but his booming voice carried across the fields. He had an actor's skills and expressive voice that the famous actor David Garrick famously said could make a crowd convulse simply by saying the word "Mesopotamia."[9] To accommodate more listeners—and because church officials uncomfortable with his unorthodox message and style closed the doors of their churches to him— Whitefield began preaching outdoors in the open air.[10] He preached to high and low alike, preaching in the prisons and to coal miners outdoors.[11] As he preached, Whitefield would shake and cry as his roaring voice told of the joys of salvation and the pains of damnation. His crowds would, like him, experience his religion as a deep emotional and personal experience, and they, like him, would shout out and moan and cry as he preached.[12] The crowds grew to the tens of thousands.[13] It wasn't just his dramatic and impassionate style. Whitefield offered an astounding message of personal redemption unlike anything anyone had ever heard. Like most of the preachers who followed in his wake, Whitefield was formally a Calvinist who believed in an elect predestined for salvation. Yet his Calvinism was highly unorthodox, emphasizing the possibility of salvation through a conversion experience from God's grace.[14] According to Whitefield, all men and women, rich or poor, were equal in pursuit of salvation because they could all connect directly to God and experience His grace for themselves. It was a direct challenge to privilege, nobility, and authority, leveling social class and rejecting established religious authority as the key to salvation. As Whitefield traveled around England, he stirred up controversy and enthusiastic religious revival everywhere he went.

In 1739, Whitefield made his first tour of the American colonies, sparking a colonywide religious revival.[15] His first trip began in Philadelphia, where Whitefield's remarkable preaching brought out unheard of crowds who clustered to hear him speak. Benjamin Franklin, a deist and not a particularly religious man who nonetheless became one of Whitefield's greatest supporters, wrote this about Whitefield's arrival:

> In 1739 arriv'd among us from England the Rev. Mr. Whitefield, who had made himself remarkable there as an itinerant Preacher. He was

at first permitted to preach in some of our Churches; but the Clergy taking a Dislike to him, soon refus'd him their Pulpits and he was oblig'd to preach in the Fields. The Multitudes of all Sects and Denominations that attended his Sermons were enormous and it was matter of Speculation to me who was one of the Number, to observe the extraordinary Influence of his Oratory on his Hearers, and how much they admir'd and respected him, notwithstanding his common Abuse of them, by assuring them they were naturally half Beasts and half Devils. It was wonderful to see the Change soon made in the Manners of our Inhabitants; from being thoughtless or indifferent about Religion, it seem'd as if all the World were growing Religious; so that one could not walk thro' the Town in an Evening without Hearing Psalms sung in different Families of every Street.[16]

Franklin sought to calculate how many actually came out to hear Whitefield. As he wrote, "Being among the hindmost in Market Street, I had the Curiosity to learn how far he could be heard. . . . I computed that he might well be heard by more than Thirty Thousand. This reconcil'd me to the Newspaper Accounts of his having preach'd to 25,000 People in the Fields."[17]

As Whitefield traveled across the American colonies north and south, his sermons became great events where tens of thousands gathered to experience his unique message of redemption. He sparked new interest in religion everywhere he went. After Whitefield's first visit to America, an army of similar preachers soon appeared modeling themselves on him bearing similar messages.[18] Like Whitefield, they preached in the open air to passionate crowds, offering a similar message that anyone could experience God and be saved. They, too, preached to rich and poor alike, unwilling to subordinate themselves to the local religious authorities of the communities in which they traveled.[19] In fact, they made little distinction between religious denominations at all, preaching to mixed groups of Congregationalists, Anglicans, Quakers, Baptists, and anyone else alike. Established religious authorities or "Old Lights" across the colonies panicked at this outbreak of "enthusiastic" religion among these "New Lights."[20] They didn't like open-air preaching, the emotionalism, or the shaking and sobbing and groaning. They feared the dismissal of their authority and the careless mixing of denomination. They didn't like the social leveling of the Awakening message and loathed the splitting of their churches as the inspired broke away to form their own churches and sects.

The Great Awakening burned for years, with outbreaks hotter at some times and places. Before his death in 1770, Whitefield made seven similar trips to preach in the American colonies, each a major event like a concert tour by a rock star. By the eve of the American Revolution, the Awakening had profoundly transformed colonial culture. American religion was no longer dry and academic but passionate and emotional, putting personal experience and conversion over scripture and hierarchy. The churches refilled with a surge of new attendance. The splintering of churches, new denominations, and pan-denominational preaching inspired for the first time a new spirit of pan-Christian religious tolerance under an umbrella of evangelical identity.[21] Enslaved Africans, who previously mainly still followed the religious traditions of their homelands, converted to Christianity in large numbers in response to Awakening preachers who preached to them that all men were equal before God.[22] Most important, the Awakening's social leveling and challenge to church authority created a new democratic spirit among the colonists of America.[23]

The Great Awakening is usually discussed today as a major religious movement. It was, but it was also more. As the Awakening swept across the colonies, it elevated questions of morality, righteousness, and reform above pragmatic concerns. When Awakening preachers challenged church authorities, leveled social class, and preached about the individual's personal relationships to God, they openly challenged fundamental social structures in the name of righteousness and morality. This assault sent a shiver of social and political activism throughout American society, one that took decades to fade away. Historians still debate the extent to which the Great Awakening brought about the American Revolution. To be sure, many of the revolution's leaders were stridently secular Enlightenment liberals or deists who prized rationalism, rejected religious authority, and embraced overt secularism. Many of the revolution's foot soldiers, however, were deeply religious, and many preachers in the model of Whitefield inspired their flocks to challenge King George's authority from the pulpit just as they had his bishops.[24] Most important, the Great Awakening sent a new national spirit swirling about the air, one that shifted the nation's focus from what was wise toward what was right and wrong, moralizing everything.

The Great Awakening inspired a generation of Americans to ponder how they might help make their society better, more fair, and more just. It created a national culture that encouraged public passion and emotion, that encouraged Americans to be more strident and uncompromising against immorality and injustice. The Awakening's open defiance of state-sanctioned bishops and pastors inevitably led to people questioning other traditional authorities, like nobles and kings.[25] Perhaps most important, the Awakening imparted to Americans across the colonies the motivation and resolve to risk their safety and livelihoods to fight for what they believed was moral and right. It thereby transformed a political dispute between mother country and its colonies into a moral war in which Britain wasn't just wrong but corrupt and immoral, and the colonies' pursuit of liberty not just beneficial but sacred and just—the sort of fight that could never be negotiated or compromised, only won.[26] The American republic, it's fair to say, was forged in the fire of an awakening.

THE SECOND GREAT AWAKENING

In the years after the American Revolution, America settled down into the hard work of building its new republic. By then, the moral fires of the Great Awakening had long burned out. The churches that filled to bursting emptied again. Americans were no longer crusading over utopias and dreams because they had already seized their revolution and won it. People who had just fought a hard and often terrible war now wanted to restore what that revolution cost—stability, order, opportunity, and prosperity—as they built a new nation from scratch.[27] America once again became a pragmatic country, one wrapped up in the concerns of building a new nation in hope of peace, prosperity, and stability.[28] The spiritual landscape of America thus turned back to something like it had been before the Great Awakening, more dutiful and formal than passionate.

As America moved deeper into the nineteenth century, however, a thirst for meaning and morality started to creep back into the culture, especially among younger Americans who had grown up long after the smoke and fire of revolution had cleared. This rising generation of Americans, having lived their entire lives in the newly stable and prosperous republic, looked at their imperfect society with its flawed institutions, compromises, injustices, and immoralities, and wondered how much better things might become. A few religious revivals broke out around the turn of the nineteenth century in the newly settled hinterlands—what we now call the Midwest and Appalachia—such as the explosive Kentucky camp revivals of preacher James McGready.[29] As America headed into the 1820s, similar camp revival meetings began to spring up across rural America as if some great moral bubble suddenly burst. Soon, these revivals broke out everywhere, with epicenters in places like what was then rural western New York state, earning it the name of the "Burned-Over District" because the fire of religious revival had swept through so powerfully and so often there was no fuel left to burn.[30] Passionate traveling preachers "rode the circuit" from little town to little town, spreading the revival spirit. These multiday affairs mixed religion, community, and entertainment. Preachers took turns delivering sermons and then everyone would sing hymns. People would gather from all the local homesteads—normally isolated and starved for activity—to socialize, celebrate, and newly embrace their religion.

The religion of the Second Awakening was a lot like the first. Itinerant preachers, many without formal theological qualifications, toured the nation spreading awakening religion.[31] They embraced an emotional Protestant evangelicalism, shaking and crying out and emphasizing one's personal and emotional connection to God. Listeners sometimes acted out in spasms and ecstasies as they felt this new spiritual connection.[32] The revival was again multidenominational,[33] and it again flourished and swelled the ranks of more enthusiastic denominations like the Methodists and Baptists at the expense of more traditional ones like the Congregationalists, Presbyterians, and Episcopalians. New religious denominations sprang up such as the Latter-day Saints, the Shakers (named because they would shake in moments of religious ecstasy), the Seventh Day Adventists, and the communal and free-love Oneida Community.[34] A flurry of organizations like the American Bible Society sprang up, placing themselves above sectarian divisions to serve Christians as one common faith.[35] Preachers once again made great efforts to preach to the enslaved in the belief that every soul belonged to God, further spreading Christianity among enslaved Americans. As this national spirit washed over America, others threw themselves into alternative spiritual quests for meaning. The Unitarians transformed from a minor movement into a large, established, powerful church.[36] The philosophical and spiritual movement of transcendentalism flourished, seeking to merge rationalism with spirituality and romantic emotionalism.[37] Interest in the occult exploded as Americans began to experiment in séances.[38]

The Second Awakening, however, was also an important theological evolution. While the First Great Awakening was heavily Calvinist in its theology, the Second emphasized perfectionism and millennialism.[39] Second Awakening preachers spread the idea across America that if mankind continued to perfect human society to establish God's Kingdom on Earth, they could trigger Christ's return and thousand-year reign. In other words, if Americans transformed America into a nation sufficiently just, good, and moral to serve as God's Kingdom, they could bring about the Second Coming.[40] Second Awakening Christians therefore believed they had a special duty to create a moral nation through a combination of saving souls, moral citizenship, and political efforts for national reform.[41] Newly energized Christians, eager to earn their place in heaven or bring about the Millennium, threw themselves into charitable projects such as campaigns for education and charitable work in prisons, among the mentally ill, and with the poor, intended to help those in need and morally reform those they believed farthest from God.[42] They decried the immorality of public figures and the lack of virtue in a party politics fighting over mere offices and ambition—they often found party politics itself inherently immoral.[43] Most important, they launched three great crusades for national reform that changed the face of America—the abolition of slavery, temperance, and women's suffrage.

When popular history tells the story of America's road to civil war, it rarely mentions the role of the Second Awakening. It's usually noted that many abolitionists and activists were preachers or devout, but it's then presumed everyone was "just more religious back then." The religious enthusiasm that bathed America in the decades before the Civil War was in fact new and disruptive, a burst of revival that convinced a new generation of passionate Christians that slavery wasn't just wrong but a moral sin that had to be urgently rooted out to bring about the Millennium.[44] The abolition movement that flourished before the Civil War was mainly a religiously driven crusade and outgrowth of the Second Awakening. Most of the critical figures in the abolition movement were either awakening-driven Christians or in some way intertwined in the revival. The abolitionist Charles Grandison Finney, perhaps the most important abolitionist, was the preacher whose religious revivals were most responsible for creating the Burned-Over District in New York.[45] Abolitionist Lyman Beecher was another major preacher of the revival. His son, preacher Henry Ward Beecher, also became a major figure in the abolition movement from his activism against the Compromise of 1850, his raising funds to purchase freedom for slaves, and his financing weapons and supporting arms for antislavery forces in Bleeding Kansas— the rifles called "Beecher's Bibles" since some supposedly arrived in boxes marked "books." Beecher's daughter, Harriett Beecher Stowe, wrote the book that helped galvanize opposition to slavery, *Uncle Tom's Cabin*.[46] William Lloyd Garrison, publisher of the abolitionist (and later women's suffrage) *Liberator* newspaper, had deep ties to the revival movement and spoke and wrote of the issue through the lens of morality and God. The early antislavery Liberty Party was so overwhelmingly evangelical it was described as "a religious brotherhood."[47] The Free Soil Party, too, drew heavily from evangelical support.[48] John Brown, the abolition warfighter who fought in Bleeding Kansas and led a raid on the federal armory in Harper's Ferry to arm a slave revolt, was a zealous Christian activist.

It was this religious and moral energy that transformed the fight against slavery from one America sought to avoid to one it was now eager to wage. At the height of the Second Great Awakening, over 90 percent of American Protestants had become evangelical, making it the most significant cultural force in the country before the Civil War.[49] Nor did the Second Awakening's influence stay only on one side of the fight over slavery. As the abolition cause grew, slavery's defenders increasingly invoked religious arguments in support of slavery as well to fend off the powerful religious arguments against it. Slavery's defenders stopped claiming slavery was simply an unfortunate institution justified by necessity that would eventually fade away; they started making religious arguments that slavery was a positive good and a scripturally sound institution ordained by God.[50] On both sides, slavery increasingly became an urgent moral battle.

Out of the activism over abolition sprang the other two great moral crusades of nineteenth-century America, temperance and women's suffrage. During the Second Awakening, women in particular flocked to the church, and from there into social activism, often becoming leaders in the movement.[51] Revivalist preachers spread the message that alcohol was a moral evil, which resonated strongly with many women who believed alcohol abuse a serious threat to women and families as working-class men (particularly Catholic immigrants from Ireland and Southern Germany) squandered the little money they had drinking in saloons, coming home to their families late, drunk, and sometimes violent.[52] Christian women organized to eliminate alcohol from America, not only to morally uplift individuals but also to encourage men to support their wives and children. The abolitionist crusade also attracted a large number of evangelical activists like Susan B. Anthony and Lucretia Mott, who built networks, learned to organize politically, and developed a language to articulate the desire for political liberation.[53] Women like the Grimke sisters began speaking to mixed groups of men and women in public, sparking a contentious debate within the abolition movement about the propriety of women directly participating in the public arena.[54] As the influence of women in the abolition movement grew, it eventually began accepting women as more than simply axillaries, with the Anti-Slavery Society accepting women as full members in 1840. It wasn't far for abolitionist women to extend their agenda of demands into more rights for women, most importantly suffrage, with the support of some (although not all), of their awakening and abolition allies.[55] In 1848, a group of abolitionist and temperance activists finally made their demands for suffrage at Seneca Falls.[56] Abolition, temperance, women's suffrage, and awakening religion were thus tied together as related and overlapping movements with overlapping participation, each outgrowths of the same religious awakening. It's no accident the Seneca Falls Convention took place in the heart of the Burned-Over District.[57]

The Second Great Awakening transformed a pragmatic America into a nation of moral crusaders and reformers eager to feed their souls, discover meaning, and transform society. They sincerely believed their religious beliefs, morality, and public action were intricately linked—as Charles Finney argued, "Politics are a part of religion in such a country as this."[58] As America became more moralistic and zealous, political debate became more confrontational and heated, and disputes became urgent moral crusades over justice, sin, and righteousness. Political violence in the cause of morality ironically became a new norm, such as the religious abolitionists like John Brown who poured into Kansas in the 1850s to stop the spread of slavery and got caught up in a bloody frontier war. Without question, this national moral fervor was the major force turning slavery from a question America wanted to bury to a battle of moral urgency demanding resolution now. Americans marched into the Civil War on a holy crusade for righteousness, as the Civil War mainstay "Battle Hymn of the Republic" put it, "He died to make men holy, let us die to make men free, while God is marching on!"[59] More than any other influence, the Second Awakening helped tear America's Second Party System down.

THE THIRD GREAT AWAKENING

The Second Awakening died out amid the carnage of America's Civil War. The war ripped America apart, decimated families, and left hundreds of thousands of bodies shredded on the battlefield. Exhausted, many Americans lost their fervor for religion and the nation turned its attention back to practical questions—how to pull a nation back together after it had been so violently severed, and how to restore prosperity in the aftermath of such destruction.[60] As America gave up on Reconstruction and entered the new prosperity of the Gilded Age, the nation mainly focused on pragmatic things like making fortunes. Politics was no longer moral but transactional, not a place to change the world but one where political machines sent candidates to bring back spoils. There were no more causes. Graft and corruption flourished.

It wasn't long, however, before the awakening spirit came roaring back, making the practical years of Reconstruction appear a temporary lull as Americans caught their breath. At first, revivalists like Dwight Moody, a Massachusetts preacher who settled in Chicago, began organizing great revivals that looked a lot like the revivals of the Second Awakening. These revivalists preached a similar brand of religion as that of the Second Awakening, with a millennialism that encouraged Americans to do good works for the destitute and championed the great causes the Second Awakening left undone, like temperance.[61] As America moved into the 1880s, however, a new wave of revivalists emerged with an altogether different focus. America was becoming an industrial power, and its rapidly swelling cities brought staggering new social problems that a prior generation of independent farmers couldn't have imagined, such as rampant child labor; overcrowded tenement housing; and poor women, many of them immigrants, working brutal hours in horrific conditions. Focusing on the social problems of the booming cities, these reformers weren't interested in tent revivals. They adopted a new theology about what a good Christian should to do to bring about God's Kingdom on Earth—the Social Gospel.

According to the Social Gospel, the only true way to bring about God's Kingdom on Earth was to re-engineer the social institutions of society so they collectively produced just and moral results.[62] Social Gospel reformers thereby hoped to engineer away the evils and abuses of nineteenth-century industrialization, ushering in God's Kingdom whether or not they could personally redeem every American. We most closely associate this Social Gospel Christianity with pastor Walter Rauschenbusch and his bestselling 1907 book, *Christianity and the Social Crisis*,[63] but the ideas Rauschenbusch put into words were dominant long before his book.[64] Social Gospel Christianity was deeply influenced by modernity and the new tools of social science, which it sought to harness to remake America into a more godly nation. With new knowledge from social science, reformers believed they could, through moral social policy, override the natural tendencies of people toward depravity in a fallen world of imperfect souls. They could plan and design a more just and moral society whether or not individuals were themselves just or moral, reversing the ills and evils of the new industrializing world. Social Gospel Christians became a driving force behind the Progressive Movement.

As the Third Awakening gained steam by the end of the nineteenth century, Americans turned back toward religion and the Social Gospel boomed. Energized Christians, many of them middle-class women for whom social activism provided both a social activity and an opportunity to assume leadership in the public square, flooded into cities to take up charitable projects, particularly among the working poor, immigrants, and the mentally ill. They joined forces with more secular reformers caught up in the same national spirit, merging the Social Gospel's desire to usher in God's Kingdom with the drive of secular reformers who wanted to remake America for reasons of good government, decency, and efficiency. A new generation that mainly came of age in prosperous homes amid national stability after the trauma of the Civil War became a new political force, the Progressive Movement.[65] Whether or not they were caught up in the religious revival, these progressives were all caught up in the same moral revival, one channeling the same national spirit through different means.

The progressive reformers of the Third Awakening built parks in cities so children had healthy green places to play. They promoted the conservation of nature and created the National Parks. They mobilized to pass laws that eliminated child labor, eradicated abusive sweatshops preying on working women and children, imposed maximum work hours, and implemented minimum wages. They won "blue laws" requiring businesses close on Sunday. They created and expanded public schools to give poor and immigrant children access to a modern education. They fought back against fly-by-night schemers harming people with scam products, creating the Food and Drug Administration to ensure contaminants didn't enter the industrial food supply and to eliminate quack remedies from medicine. They pushed antitrust laws to stop Gilded Age anticompetitive behavior like price fixing, which unfairly drove smaller competitors out of business to seize monopoly profits. To break up patronage and machine boss politics, they fought against corruption and graft, pushed parties to pick candidates through primary elections, and passed a constitutional amendment to allow citizens to directly elect their senators to break up political machines. Most notably, they pushed into the mainstream the two great uncompleted crusades of the Second Awakening, temperance and women's suffrage, winning constitutional amendments for both.

The Third Awakening, just like the First and Second, saw a new national enthusiasm for religion and the churches filled once more. More enthusiastic Protestant denominations like the Pentecostals and the Holiness Movement grew in significance.[66] New religious denominations sprang up, like Christian Science and the Jehovah's Witnesses; new religious concepts took root, like dispensationalism; and new interest in alternative forms of spiritual exploration such as occult spiritualism flourished once more.[67] Christian activists founded or greatly expanded institutions like Bible colleges, the YMCA (which grew and took on prominence), and the Salvation Army (which arrived in America from England and flourished). In other ways, however, the Third Awakening was again an evolution. Preachers proclaiming religion to their flocks drove the moral agendas of the First and Second Awakenings. Progressive reformers of the Third quoted social science and reason, with religion now mostly serving as their motivator and support. In place of religious tent revivals, Third Awakening reformers created standing retreats called chautauquas—educational and entertaining gatherings to which people would travel to hear speakers give lectures and tell stories on a mixture of religious messages, politics, entertainment, and comedy, combining cultural improvement with a revival camp meeting.[68] Enthusiastic Christians entranced by the Social Gospel flooded into missions of charity and reform out of religious and moral duty, but then justified their missions not through scripture but reason and expertise.

The Social Gospel, however, wasn't the only Christian movement of the Third Awakening. As America moved into the twentieth century, an alternative Christian theology also arose, one challenging the Social Gospel as a wrong turn. This vision, personified by the former professional baseball player turned preacher Billy Sunday, believed religion's purpose wasn't restructuring society but saving individual souls. Sunday called himself a "rube" committed to the fiery "old-time religion" as he preached to massive crowds in the old camp-revival style, violently rejecting well-to-do progressives and Social Gospel innovations.[69] Sunday supported many progressive reforms—temperance, ending child labor, helping the poor, and women's suffrage, among others—but rejected the idea that Christians had a duty to remake America instead of simply reforming themselves. After a wealthy California businessman published a widely successful set of essays that echoed a similar back-to-basics religious philosophy called *The Fundamentals*, this alternative movement got a name—fundamentalism.[70] These fundamentalists emphasized new ideas like biblical inerrancy and fought against the teaching of evolution, inciting the famous "Scopes Monkey Trial."[71]

The spirit of this Third Awakening, however, began to fade as America entered the Jazz Age world of the 1920s. Most of the progressive agenda was now in place, and Americans began turning their attention back to more practical concerns. Then, in 1929, the economy crashed and an economic catastrophe began—the Great Depression—and thoughts of great nationwide moral and social reforms vanished.

THE FOURTH GREAT AWAKENING

Throughout its history, America has repeatedly plunged into these eras of moral reform called awakenings. Each time, these awakenings wrought profound changes to America's parties, its culture, and its politics. Some awakenings supercharged new ideas with manic energy to build new parties better suited to constructing a better future, like the Third Awakening that helped build the Fourth Party System's parties of the Populist and Progressive Era. Other awakenings drove new conflicts that ripped party systems down, such as the moral crusades of the Second Awakening that helped destroy the Whigs and America's Second Party System. American party systems rise and fall through cyclical realignments independent of awakenings. Yet the moral fervor awakenings create when they occur still profoundly affect the course of party systems and realignments. The role awakenings can play in the evolution of party systems is particularly important today, since we're almost certainly living in the middle of America's Fourth Great Awakening.

When America emerged from the Second World War, the country was again mainly secular and pragmatic, concerned with restoring prosperity and stability. Americans were naturally in a pragmatic state of mind. Around the middle of the 1960s, however, something burst and Americans suddenly threw themselves into national projects of moral reform and renewal once more. Across culture and politics, Americans shifted their priorities from pragmatic matters like jobs, labor, and national regulation to moral issues like social equality, environmental purity, personal morality, and abortion. As the baby boom generation, which grew up amid great stability and wealth, came of age, they enthusiastically embraced these new crusades. Some young Americans embraced a new counterculture and joined a New Left, one interested in moral questions like fairness and justice and taking up causes like the end of racial discrimination, the advancement of civil rights, the equal treatment of women, the end of war, and the purification of the natural environment. Others headed back to church, leading to another revival that energized the modern evangelical movement, taking up causes like the defense of traditional morality and culture. A new crusading moral spirit seeped into America's culture, launching a great national culture war.

We're not in the habit of describing our own era as an awakening, but it bears every hallmark of one. With good times restored, a new generation arose dreaming of how much better America might be. A mix of clashing social activists, both secular and religious, rushed into public debate, embarking on crusades to transform America into a more just and moral nation. America began another national era trading a pragmatic politics and culture for one of crusading reform—a Fourth Great Awakening.[72] As William McLoughlin, a professor of history and religion who studied great awakenings wrote:

> Great awakenings (and the revivals that are part of them) are the results, not of depressions, wars, or epidemics, but of critical disjunctions in our self-understanding. They are not brief outbursts of mass emotionalism by one group or another but profound cultural transformations affecting all Americans and extending over a generation or more. Awakenings begin in periods of cultural distortion and grave personal stress, when we lose faith in the legitimacy of our norms, the viability of our institutions, and the authority of our leaders in church and state. They eventuate in basic restructurings of our institutions and redefinitions of our social goals.
>
> Great awakenings are not periods of social neurosis (though they begin in times of cultural confusion). They are times of revitalization. ... Without them our social order would cease to be dynamic; our culture would wither, fragment, and dissolve in confusion, as many civilizations have done before.[73]

Like in every awakening, a new generation of reformers uprooted America's political debates, substituting the old pragmatic politics of consensus for fresh moral crusades. The Fourth Great Awakening they launched has burned across American politics ever since.[74] It's certain to play a key role in the next realignment to come.

CHAPTER 14

THE FOURTH GREAT AWAKENING AND THE 1960s

I n 1964, President Lyndon Johnson announced his intention to embark on a bold agenda of national reforms to create what he declared would be a "Great Society." Over his presidency, his Democratic Party would push through a dramatic burst of initiatives, moving into new areas like civil rights, poverty, environmental protection, and education. These initiatives came to symbolize a new Democratic Party, replacing a party of economic policy and labor unions with one crusading to reform and remake America. In 1968, Richard Nixon also announced a new direction for his party. He would push back against the "permissiveness" leaking into the culture as a growing counterculture attacked cultural norms. Nixon would promise to restore national stability after a surge in violent crime, an outbreak of riots in major cities, and the rise of angry protest movements. Speaking in his own moral terms based in concepts like patriotism, tradition, and personal morality, Nixon pledged to restore law and order for the benefit of the "Silent Majority" he believed the Democratic Party had abandoned.

At the start of the Fifth Party System under Franklin Roosevelt, the Democratic Party was a party of workers. It was the party of city machines run by recent generations of immigrants, and organized labor, and working people across the economically struggling Solid South. The Republicans were a party of corporate magnates, professionals, business people, and the well-to-do. Today, we define professionals, college professors, and educated activists as the Democratic Party base. We assume rural and working people to be Republicans. The once Democratic Solid South is now solidly Republican, and the former Republican base in the

Northeast is the heartland of the Democrats. We trace the source of this political transformations to the 1960s, since it's during the 1960s when these worlds began to flip. It's when America's parties started talking differently and attracting different people. It's when they started taking on new issues they hadn't cared about before. It's when the anger, the polarization, and the culture war began creeping into the politics and the culture of America. It was the start of America's Fourth Great Awakening, and it changed everything.

HOW THE 1960s TURNED THE WORLD UPSIDE DOWN

When America elected John Kennedy president in 1960, the country was at the height of its postwar boom. This was the America of housecoats, neat suits, pillbox hats. At the end of the Second World War, many Americans feared that, when the nation demobilized, it would fall back into depression.[1] Instead, the economy soared, delivering to ordinary Americans an extraordinary degree of peace and prosperity they would have never dreamed possible during the Depression and the war. Many Americans came to assume a level of comfort they would have found unthinkable in the hard times of their youth—a middle-class house in the suburbs with new appliances and a car in the garage.[2] America was now a global superpower and world leader. During Kennedy's presidency, America even decided to build a rocket to the moon—imagine Franklin Roosevelt announcing such a thing during the Great Depression! After several harrowing decades of desperation and war, America was happy and hopeful. The country was safe, society was stable, and the future looked bright. Then all that peace and prosperity vanished and America descended into a scary new era of economic troubles and social instability.[3]

America through the 1960s and 1970s tumbled through a series of shocking events, national crises, and eruptions of social discontent. Popular political figures were assassinated one after another—John Kennedy, Bobby Kennedy, Martin Luther King. Crime suddenly spiked. Racial discontent flooded into the open, and riots broke out in the streets of major cities, burning neighborhoods to the ground. Anger over the Vietnam War shook the nation with sometimes violent protest. Young political radicals claimed to declare war against the United States and celebrated "Days of Rage." In 1968, young protesters crowded the streets of Chicago to protest at the Democratic National Convention. They wore long hair, shouted slogans, and had complete disdain not only for the political establishment of the party they supported but for the establishment of every institution in America. Chicago's mayor, the boss Richard Daley, a product of the traditional working-class Democrats of Chicago, held these rowdy protesters in contempt and sent thousands of police to repress and neutralize them. The two armies clashed, sparking the Battle of Michigan Avenue, in which a flurry of police batons battered angry protesters, along with anyone else unlucky enough to get in their way. Americans watching the political convention on television witnessed this "police riot" and saw the forces of the establishment breaking the bones of protesters who refused to recognize their authority. The confident and stable America of the early 1960s had turned into a nation in social turmoil within less than a decade.

The Democratic Party in 1960 was still a party of unions and labor regulations fighting for Franklin Roosevelt's industrial policy. By 1968, it was fast becoming the party of the raucous young protesters preoccupied with issues like opposing the war in Vietnam, cleaning up the environment, empowering women, and advancing civil rights. When Nixon first ran for president in 1960, he ran as the heir of Eisenhower. In 1968 he ran on a new law and order agenda centered around issues like crime, welfare spending, supporting the military, and curbing social "permissiveness." Over the following years, the Democrats changed from a lunch-pail party of autoworkers and shop clerks into the party of Silicon Valley CEOs, professors, and college-educated professionals. The Republicans changed from a country-club party of doctors, lawyers, and bankers into a party of blue-collar workers and small-business people from the heartland. The Solid South gradually transformed from a Democratic Party bastion into a Republican one. The once Republican Northeast became the new Democratic base. It was as though the nation flipped over.

The dramatic changes in the way America's parties looked, talked, and presented themselves over the 1960s and 1970s are so astounding they have obsessed us ever since. Except that so much also stayed the same. The Democrats never abandoned their old issues or Franklin Roosevelt's ideology of New Deal liberalism. They merely expanded on it, adding new issues and priorities, like the status of women, the importance of the environment, and the expansion of civil rights. Republicans never gave up on anti-big-government conservatism. They maintained their old commitments—indeed, they doubled down on them—while adding new ones, like crime, welfare, and the breakdown of traditional cultural rules and social order. So much had changed, and yet the basic framework of our parties' ideological debates remained essentially the same.

The 1960s mark an important change in America, one that affected its parties profoundly. America's political culture shifted from pragmatism to moralism. It happened because, in the middle of the 1960, America's Fourth Great Awakening began. It's perhaps the most misunderstood event in American politics—and a driving force of the realignment that's inevitably to come.

LYNDON JOHNSON AND THE GREAT SOCIETY

In May of 1964, in advance of his coming presidential campaign, President Johnson announced his intention to usher in an ambitious new program to rival that of Franklin Roosevelt. He announced in a speech at the University of Michigan his plan to create a "Great Society." Johnson claimed such a society "demands an end to poverty and racial injustice."[4] It would be "a place where every child can find knowledge to enrich his mind and enlarge his talents." It would be "a place where the city of man serves not only the needs of the body and the demands of commerce but the desire for beauty and the hunger for community." It would be "a place where man can renew contact with nature" and "a place which honors creation for its own sake and for what it adds to the understanding of the race." The speech, reflecting the work of Johnson's residential intellectual,

Princeton professor Eric Goldman, was an intentional shift in tone and priorities.[5] Goldman, whom Johnson brought into the White House to discover new policies in a role similar to Kennedy's Arthur Schlesinger, had reached out to liberal intellectuals in the beginning of 1964 to distill a new direction for the Johnson administration.[6] Their overwhelming answer was to cast off worries about material progress for questions of values. As Goldman came to believe, "the nation had reached a general affluence that permitted it to give attention not only to the quantity but also to the quality of American living."[7]

The agenda we call the Great Society actually began before Johnson's speech gave it a name, almost as soon as Johnson assumed the presidency in November of 1963 after John Kennedy's shocking assassination. Johnson's first priority upon becoming president was to pass the stagnant legislative efforts that Kennedy had sent to Congress but couldn't or wouldn't get Congress to pass—most importantly a tax cut and a civil rights bill.[8] Johnson's decision to actively push civil rights was startling because his entire public career to that point had been as an avowed racist and segregationist. Johnson was known as a strong segregationist and champion of the Southern Senate Old Bulls, who had installed him as Senate leader expressly to protect the South's interests.[9] Just a few years before, Johnson led the effort to defang Eisenhower's 1957 civil rights bill by stripping out its enforcement provisions,[10] letting the toothless and watered-down bill pass because, as he said to Doris Kearns Goodwin, he and the Senate segregationists thought, "These Negroes, they're getting uppity these days" so "we've got to give them a little something, just enough to quiet them down, not enough to make a difference."[11]

In contrast to his image and the mythology surrounding him, Kennedy had done very little for civil rights during his presidency beyond symbolic gestures. His focus had mainly been administering the New Deal apparatus, fighting the Cold War, and championing a tax cut. As a Northern liberal, Kennedy supported civil rights in his public pronouncements, but he did little to advance it throughout his career. In Congress, he even quietly cooperated with the campaign of Southern Democratic leaders to strip the most meaningful provisions out of the

1957 Civil Rights Act.[12] As president, he told civil rights leaders that, while he supported them in principle, he couldn't afford to alienate Senate segregationists whom he needed to pass other priorities. As his friend and close advisor Arthur Schlesinger wrote, Kennedy "had at this point, I think, a terrible ambivalence about civil rights. While he did not doubt the depth of the injustice or the need for remedy . . . he had a wide range of presidential responsibilities, and a fight for civil rights would alienate Southern support he needed for other purposes (including bills, like those for education and the increased minimum wage, of direct benefit to the Negro)."[13] Needing to win over Northern liberals before he faced a renomination battle in 1964, maybe one against Bobby Kennedy, Johnson resolved he "had to produce a civil rights bill that was even stronger than the one they'd have gotten if Kennedy had lived."[14]

Whatever the reason behind his public conversion on segregation, Johnson's decision to push through a major civil rights bill was a significant milestone for America. At first, Johnson attempted and failed to convince segregationist leaders in the Senate to accept a strong civil rights bill, arguing it would eventually happen anyway. "We're friends on the q.t.," Johnson told Southern senators, "Would you rather have me administering the civil rights bill, or do you want to have Nixon or Scranton?"[15] They rejected his offer, so Johnson put the full weight of his office behind the single most important civil rights bill in American history since Reconstruction. The bill would finally end segregation; end restrictions used to stop African Americans from voting; prohibit state and local governments from denying access to facilities to people on the basis of race; prohibit private hotels, restaurants, theaters, and public accommodations from discriminating on race; and prohibit racial discrimination in employment.

Outraged at Johnson's perceived betrayal, the segregationists resolved to fight Johnson's bill with everything they had. Needing more votes, Johnson turned to the Senate's Republican leader, Everett Dirksen of Illinois, to spearhead his effort in Congress. Dirksen had a strong civil rights record and controlled the votes of thirty-seven Republican senators key to breaking the inevitable segregationist filibuster.[16] In winning

Dirksen's support, Johnson had enlisted the Republican Party as a critical ally for his bill. Johnson maneuvered a strong bill through the obstruction of segregationists in the House, winning the support of 80 percent of House Republicans and 61 percent of House Democrats. West Virginia Democrat Robert Byrd led an epic fifty-four-day filibuster on the Senate floor—a significant event in an age in which filibustering meant actually talking day after day to continually hold the legislative floor. The bill's supporters rallied the necessary votes to break the filibuster by a vote of 71–29, with 82 percent of Senate Republicans voting to break the filibuster as well as 66 percent of the Senate Democrats. It was a long overdue but important national achievement.

After passing his Civil Right Act, Johnson won reelection and then over the next two years initiated and passed through Congress one of the most ambitious packages of federal-government-led initiatives and programs in American history. Johnson launched a federal "War on Poverty," spending billions of dollars on new programs to expand welfare benefits for the poor, improve education, and train people from poor communities for jobs. He emphasized improving education, traditionally an area left to states, creating new funding, new educational programs like Head Start, and aid for bilingual education. He created new environmental laws such as the Clean Air Act and Endangered Species Act. He spearheaded new federal initiatives for consumer safety, passing new laws and programs for cigarette labeling, food packaging, child safety, and consumer lending. He increased spending on infrastructure and mass transit projects, created a cabinet-level Department of Transportation, and strengthened motor vehicle safety. He sponsored new cultural spending, creating the National Endowment for the Arts and the National Endowment for the Humanities, as well as the Corporation for Public Broadcasting. In perhaps the most famous Great Society achievement, Johnson created Medicare.

Both the scope and the raw number of Johnson's Great Society reforms was staggering. Mixed within the well-known major efforts were also a stream of less notable policies and programs of real significance. A few other Great Society efforts included: Medicaid; the Office of Economic Opportunity and its related antipoverty efforts, like Job Corps, Community Health Centers, Upward Bound, Indian Opportunities, Migrant Opportunities, and Food Stamps; national volunteering agencies, like VISTA and the Legal Services Corporation; the National Highway Transportation Safety Administration; chemical labeling; national meat inspecting agencies; the Truth-In-Lending Act; environmental efforts, like the Endangered Species Act; the Aircraft Noise Abatement Act; the National Historic Preservation Act; and the National Environmental Policy Act.[17] Just as Goldman said, the Great Society was a coordinated push to move the Democratic Party away from questions of economic policy into areas of moral policy. It took interest in new issues—the environment, consumer protection, poverty, education, health, and civil rights—and wrapped them in a new moral urgency. The earth needed to be saved, the poor needed to be uplifted, the powerless needed to be educated, and the marginalized needed to be brought fully into the national community.

The question that ought to perplex us is why Lyndon Johnson, of all people, launched this revolution in the Democratic Party. Johnson was an old school, hardscrabble, rural, socially traditionalist Democrat who had made his career on economic populism and segregation. He was the protégé and champion of the segregationist Old Bulls of the South, with a long record of disgustingly racist views continuing long past his public conversion on civil rights.[18] He wasn't young, a social progressive, a dreaming visionary, a hippie, or a liberal intellectual. Not only were the young protesters of the New Left not his political base, the New Left loathed him for expanding the Vietnam War.[19] It's now well-established that he was corrupt, having used his influence in politics to build a lucrative radio empire in his wife's name, winning his first Senate election almost certainly with the help of fraudulent votes, sitting at the center of the Bobby Baker scandal, and more.[20] He was often cruel, demanding, and a kiss-up kick-down sort of guy.[21] He was personally crude, flagrantly cheated on his wife and bragged about it, and liked to humiliate aides by taking meetings while seated on the toilet.[22] Johnson wasn't even looking for a new direction for his party; he didn't even like the name "Great Society," which people criticized as naive and utopian.[23] As he saw things, his Great Society wasn't a break with Democratic tradition but simply a second New Deal applying the New Deal philosophy to his own era's problems.

Johnson didn't change the face and direction of his party because of who he was. He did it despite of who he was. His administration and his party got caught up in a new spirit in the air, one that was nudging it along whether Johnson and his staff realized it or not. That spirit arrived through the counterculture and its political vehicle, the New Left.

THE COUNTERCULTURE AND THE NEW LEFT

In the middle of the 1960s, a dramatic movement erupted among America's youth. It seemed to come out of nowhere. When the postwar generation finally settled down after the hell of the Depression and Second World War, with the specters of starvation, desperation, and death burned permanently in their minds, they built a neat world of predictability and order. When their children, the baby boomers, came of age in the middle of the 1960s, they found that stability and order stifling.[24] In 1960, while America was still enjoying the national stability of the postwar boom, young people dressed neatly, cut their hair short, and were expected to call their elders sir and ma'am.[25] This new movement of young people refused to dress up, with men wearing their hair long and growing scraggly facial hair while women wore flower-power dresses.[26] They rejected buttoned-up mainstream culture, embracing message songs and attending lively rock festivals like Woodstock that attendees treated like religious events.[27] Many embarked on quests for meaning, flirting with new-age spiritualism and declaring the "Age of Aquarius." Their parents built a stable, orderly, prosperous society to protect against how horrific the world could be. Their children dreamed about how much better it could become. The very order and predictability their parents valued as a means to stave off the wolves of the world, their children believed locked in injustices and wrongs.

In a few short years, a new, radical, and rowdy youth culture burst onto the scene, committed to turning America upside down. The changes combusted spontaneously, with no obvious leader, occurring with no clear cause and flowering among countless interrelated leaders, thinkers, organizations, and social movements, who all demanded that society change. It was a wild new spirit in the air that flourished just as the children who had grown up amid unprecedented stability and prosperity after the Second World War came of age. People called this generational rebellion the "counterculture."

The young Americans of this counterculture visibly, and often ostentatiously, rejected the postwar society their parents built. They rejected its manners, trading in housecoats and neckties for clothes that emphasized casualness and individuality.[28] They rejected its cultural tastes, seeking out entertainment and music that emphasized meaning and novelty instead of easy fun and tidy tunesmithing.[29] They questioned the middle-class economic order of nine-to-five jobs, corporations, and men in gray flannel suits and traded in the establishment middle-class values of getting married and securing stable jobs to undertake personal quests for meaning. They rejected older notions of sexual morality, becoming increasingly open to casual sex and a more sexualized culture.[30] Some explored Eastern religions like Buddhism and Hinduism and practices like yoga and meditation.[31] Others delved into astrology and New Age mysticism, leading to the popular label the "Age of Aquarius."[32] Still others flirted with the occult, sparking the growth of neopaganism and Wiccan religion. Some embraced an ethic of "free love," looking for meaning by giving themselves to others in sexual experiences.[33] Others joined the "Jesus Movement"—often derided as the "Jesus Freaks"—who saw the hippie lifestyle's ethos of peace and love as a purer reflection of Christ's message.[34] Many sought enlightenment through psychedelic experiences, creating an explosion in the popularity of drugs such as hallucinogenic mushrooms and LSD.[35] They followed the advice of psychologist Timothy Leary, advocate for the use of psychedelics, who famously suggested they "turn on, tune in, drop out."[36]

Most important, this new generation questioned the values of the society their parents defended. They questioned America's commitment to fairness in its acceptance of racial discrimination. They questioned its compassion, resolving to fight poverty. They questioned its humanity, with its Cold War, nuclear weapons, and military interventions in places like Vietnam.[37] They questioned its purity, insisting society do more to "save the earth to reverse what they believed the ravages commercialism and industrialism had inflicted on the earth's environment."[38] They questioned the fairness of traditional gender roles, committing to women's liberation and a sexual revolution.[39] They created new rights movements, such as the gay rights movement and the Native American rights movement.[40] They founded movements against nuclear weapons and nuclear power. They took up causes like poverty, advocating for more active government assistance for those living in the poorest slums in the nation's urban core.[41] They picked up the civil rights torch from their elders, advocating for racial equality in areas beyond anything the original civil rights generation had imagined. These "hippies" and their counterculture asserted that the entire postwar American social order was, in almost every aspect, unjust and immoral.[42]

Out of this new spirit grew a new force in politics called the New Left. It had its roots in counterculture-aligned activist movements, from student groups to the antiwar movement. In 1960, the Student Nonviolent Coordinating Committee formed as a student organization, which acted as ancillary support to the broader civil rights movement and later grew into a major civil rights organization. The students of the SNCC helped organize sit-ins and the "freedom rides" against segregated busing, supplementing the actions of older civil rights activists like Martin Luther King Jr.[43] In 1962, a young college group called Students for a Democratic Society, which had evolved from an earlier socialist organization interested in Old Left issues of labor and workers, held its first convention at a United Autoworkers camp in Port Huron, Michigan.[44] They set out a vision in a manifesto called the Port Huron Statement that proclaimed an intention to remake both the Democratic Party and America. It declared that while "many of us began maturing in complacency" young Americans should now, given the injustices and troubles of the late twentieth century, particularly racial segregation and the Cold War, seek to renew democracy to "replace power rooted in possession, privilege, or circumstance by power and uniqueness rooted in love, reflectiveness, reason, and creativity."[45] As SDS rose in prominence to become the heart of the New Left movement, the Port Huron Statement came to be seen as the movement's founding principles.[46] Among its chief goals from the beginning was to remake the Democratic Party into a more "liberal" party, driving away elements it found wanting to create a demographic realignment.[47]

As more members of the baby boomer generation reached political adolescence and maturity, student activism became a stronger force. Young activists took up the new issues and joined the new movements springing up around them. In 1962, Rachel Carson published her book *Silent Spring*, which helped to launch a new environmental movement.[48] In 1963, Betty Friedan published *The Feminine Mystique*, which served as a rallying point for a modern feminist movement.[49] Within a few years she helped found the National Organization for Women, which fought "to bring women into full participation in the mainstream of American society now, exercising all the privileges and responsibilities thereof in truly equal partnership with men."[50] By the end of 1964, after Johnson significantly escalated the war in Vietnam in response to the Gulf of Tonkin incident, an explosion of war protests broke out among students and other young Americans. In 1965, racially charged riots broke out in the Watts section of Los Angeles that left thirty-four dead and wrecked portions of the city with looting and arson.[51] Over the next few years, similar destructive riots broke out in cities across America, mainly in Northern industrial cities like Detroit, Newark, and Washington, DC.[52]

After 1965, student activism became not only more widespread but more confrontational and radical. Many student activists, enraged by an escalating and in their view immoral and unjust Vietnam War, and furious at the draft that could force them to risk their lives fighting in it, increasingly believed that aggressive, confrontational, and even extreme methods were morally justified, if not essential, to advance their causes and remake a debased America. In 1966, in the wake of the Watts riot, Stokely Carmichael replaced John Lewis as the leader of the SNCC, representing a significant change in the organization's approach. Carmichael preached a total reform of society, sought direct confrontation with racism, and broke with his organization's prior commitment to nonviolence. The activists called their new approach "black power."[53] Around the same time, after a fierce internal battle, a new faction rose to the leadership of SDS. The new leaders counseled direct action, confrontational politics, and more militant activism.[54] This new faction eventually evolved into more radical groups, including the violent radicals who called themselves the Weathermen and who declared formal war against the United States, staging "Days of Rage" in which young radicals rioted and destroyed property.[55] New groups favoring this new approach to politics formed, too, such as the Youth International Party or "Yippies," which formed in 1967 to advance the spread of the hippie culture and engaged in confrontational protests combined with performance art like running a pig named Pigasus as a candidate for president.[56]

By 1968, when New Left protesters flooded Chicago for that year's Democratic National Convention, Lyndon Johnson was now deeply unpopular due to the escalation of the Vietnam War. Johnson was personally bewildered by his liberal critics and the rowdy young protesters of the New Left who had come to despise him. "What in the world do they want?" Johnson would complain.[57] What, he wondered to the people around him, would make the favored children of America's middle and upper classes, after he had accomplished so much that was important to them, rebel and riot? Johnson declined to run for reelection, knowing he would certainly lose the nomination. The Democrats would instead nominate Johnson's vice president, Hubert Humphry, once known as a bold and forward-thinking liberal—in 1948 he bravely led an unsuccessful demand for civil rights at the Democratic National Convention— but whom the New Left protesters now viewed as an establishment crony complicit in Vietnam. Chicago's mayor, Richard Daley, a creature of the Old Left, found the young protesters who poured into his city distasteful. The protesters hated Daley in return. They saw him, and his entire labor-Democrat machine-politics part of the party as the very problem they hoped to defeat. Daley first sought to discourage protesters from coming to the city. When they arrived anyway, Daley hoped to sideline them to maintain public order. Rowdy protesters, some like Abbie Hoffman's

Yippies hoping to stir trouble, crowded into Grant Park. Scuffles broke out. Daley unleashed the police, creating a "police riot." Open warfare broke out in the streets. The police beat protesters with nightsticks. Young protesters threw bricks and bottles, fighting back. As the Democratic Party made its presidential nominating speeches, America watched on television as policemen loyal to a Democratic mayor beat young Democratic activists bloody.[58]

That clash in Chicago became a symbol of a new power struggle, a literal war for the soul of the Democratic Party. On one side, the Old Left of Daley's unions and labor and working-class politics. One the other side, this New Left of student activists. The Old Left was pragmatic and focused on interests. The New Left was moralistic and interested in dreams. As the 1960s and 1970s progressed, the Great Society and its ideals would spread through an entire generation of Democratic activists. They would gradually, as they came of age, capture the party's institutions, first nominating candidates of their choice like McGovern in 1972, and later becoming the candidates themselves.[59] Before long, this rowdy group of activists in Chicago would succeed in their desire to push the Old Left off center stage. The Democratic Party would no longer be a pragmatic party of labor. It would be a moral party led by a new generation of zealous crusaders looking to change the world and defeat their enemies.

The counterculture was a great moral revival. The New Left was its political arm. As a new generation came of age, it turned away from pragmatism for new moral questions. It embraced a new movement linking spiritual revival, creating a nationwide community mixing its beliefs with entertainment, socializing, and art. It embraced a new agenda of social and moral reforms it believed were essential to remake America into a more just and moral nation. Then it marched off to enact those reforms on the political battlegrounds of America.[60] As New Left leader Tom Hayden wrote, "Like the American revolutionary period, the awakening of the early sixties was a unique ingathering of young people—many of them potential leaders—to proclaim and then try to carry out a total redemptive vision. . . . The gods of our parents had failed or become idols. Then a new spiritual force came in 1960, to move the world. We felt ourselves to be the prophets of that force."[61] While the movement flourished with these young Americans, the spirit it embodied quickly spread across America. The ideas and priorities it introduced seeped into the culture of the liberal political coalition, carrying along politicians, intellectuals, and public officials—even those as far from the counterculture's ideals as Lyndon Johnson.

That's why the intellectuals Eric Goldman surveyed suggested the Great Society and why Johnson and his administration embraced its ideals. We're not accustomed to thinking about the activism and unrest of the 1960s this way, but it looks just like an awakening.[62] It was only getting started.

NIXON AND THE RISE OF THE SILENT MAJORITY

When Richard Nixon ran for president for the second time in 1968, he faced a country in a very different mood from the one he faced in 1960. In 1960, Nixon campaigned against John Kennedy as a Republican in the mold of Eisenhower, the president he had served as vice president.[63] This younger Nixon presented himself as a moderate, traditional, establishment Republican like Tom Dewey and Nelson Rockefeller. He promised to continue the peace and prosperity of the Eisenhower years and campaigned hard for the African American vote as a member of the NAACP. He was a strong supporter of Eisenhower's pioneering 1957 Civil Rights Act, and a vocal proponent of *Brown v. Board of Education*.[64]

By 1968, however, the country had changed. The effortless peace and prosperity of the postwar boom had suddenly begun to fray. After years of growth, jobs, and increasing wages, the economy began to slow, an economic slide that would continue into the 1970s.[65] Adding to that worry, there was the ever-increasing stream of violent incidents and threats to national stability. Over just a few years, America had stumbled through a seemingly unending string of shocking political assassinations. Violent crime had inexplicably spiked to alarming levels.[66] America had entered a bloody and unpopular war, spurring sometimes violent protest. The 1965 Watts riots shook America, and many similar racially charged riots followed it, with protesters breaking windows, smashing storefronts, and setting things alight.[67] Violent and radical groups like the Weathermen declared their "Days of Rage." Over the next few years, some young radicals even joined terrorist groups, staged robberies, planted bombs, kidnapped people, and murdered police officers. America had also, all of a sudden, curtly brushed aside ancient social norms over sex, drugs, and family roles. Drug use went from a hidden vice to an increasingly open one. Adultery and divorce went from hidden and rare events to an accepted practice, if not a new norm. In a few short years, America had become a nation fearful of rising crime, national assassinations, declining opportunity, and unpredictable social change. Many people felt that the very fabric of the nation was rapidly coming undone.[68]

From where we all now stand, it's hard not to look back at the middle of the twentieth century without recognizing all the positive changes and the reforms everyone agrees made things better—the end of segregation, the pushback against racism and gender discrimination, the cleanup of industrial pollution in our shared air and water. We all know, however, how the story ends. We know the economy that slowed in the middle of the 1960s would eventually get better, that the go-go 1980s were right around the corner, and the stable and prosperous 1990s were soon to come. We know crime would fall again in the 1990s, and the graffiti-spattered subway cars would once again be clean. We know most of the young rabble rousers would age and mature, becoming a new middle class raising families in suburbs and holding office-park corporate jobs. Most of all, we know the social disruptions of the 1960s and 1970s would leave behind positive changes because some of what America ripped down over those years needed to go. It's easy to forget that people then had no way to know whether the breakdown in postwar stability and prosperity would end, or whether the rapid disintegration of social stability would just get worse.

Throughout his pre-1968 political career, Nixon was known as a moderate, neither part of the conservative movement like Goldwater and Reagan nor part of the Eastern establishment like Rockefeller. He won the Republican nomination in 1968 mainly because, after turmoil of the Goldwater campaign, he had the rare ability to move between both groups without alienating either of them.[69] Nixon also wasn't a conviction politician, a policy wonk, or an ideologue. He was an insider who always felt like an outsider. He was obsessed with winning to prove he deserved the respect he craved, and willing to use whatever strategy worked. Looking at the electorate in 1968, Nixon saw two interrelated things. First, many ordinary Americans were now worried about the turbulence rocking the country—the student protesters, the crime, the Vietnam War, the riots, and in certain parts of the nation fierce backlash to federal intervention to create integration and advance civil rights. Second, many traditionally Democratic groups were alienated from their party and potentially open to a Republican campaign. Nixon had on his staff a young lawyer named Kevin Phillips who wrote a widely circulated memo to the campaign titled "Middle America and the Emerging Republican Majority," which in 1969 he would develop into a blockbuster book, *The Emerging Republican Majority*.[70] Supporting Nixon's instincts, Phillips argued that various groups traditionally part of the Democratic base—rural voters, blue collar laborers, Southern voters, and recently "bourgeoisified" "white ethnics" such as Irish and Italian Catholics—were poised to drift into the Republican Party over the coming years. His analysis was supported by another Nixon advisor, political scientist Harry Jaffa, who believed America was at the tip of its next major political realignment.[71]

Recognizing the country was changing, and the Republican Party with it, the Nixon team in 1968 devised a different electoral strategy, one on which Nixon would build throughout his presidency. Nixon recognized that many Americans—particularly those from the generations finally enjoying peace and stability after some hard years—were scared. It was more than the weight of so much social change battering society. Nor that such vast change happened so fast. It was that the change came laced with radicalism, unpredictability, and violence. Nixon and his team saw constituencies that had long voted Democratic had grown alienated from their party and might be open to a Republican message. If he and his campaign could develop a message speaking to their concerns, Nixon believed he was poised to lead a national realignment, becoming the next FDR. In a landmark May 1968 radio address titled "New Alignment for American Unity," Nixon set out his vision. He proclaimed that five distinct groups—traditional free-enterprise Republicans, "new liberals" like Daniel Moynihan, a "new South" that wanted economic growth, "black militants" who wanted opportunity, and a "silent center" who disliked social radicalism—were, despite their disagreements, poised to become the base for a new Republican party. They would unite under a new agenda, fighting against not only the economic big government of Frankl in Roosevelt but also against the social big government of Lyndon Johnson.[72] Of these, the most important to Nixon were the silent center, the people whom he, in his acceptance speech at the Republican National Convention, called "the great majority of Americans, the forgotten Americans, the non-shouters, the non-demonstrators," who "are not racist or sick" and "are good people, they are decent people, they work and they save and they pay their taxes and they care."[73]

In his 1968 campaign, Nixon would build a new Republican theme of "law and order," pushing back against crime, radicalism, and perceived social breakdown. He promised to return America to prosperity, stability, and strength by reinforcing traditional American values. This wasn't Nixon's idea alone, but the theme of most American politics in the unsteady air of 1968. As political reporter Theodore White wrote:

> Wherever candidates paused to speak, wherever people gathered to listen, there could be no doubt in any bystander's mind that law-and-order was indeed a legitimate issue. The two surest applause lines in any candidate's speech were always his calls for "law-and-order" at home and "peace" in Vietnam. This is what the American people—poor and rich, white and black—wanted to hear.[74]

Nixon left the Deep South to Alabama governor George Wallace, who was running a third-party segregationist campaign. Nixon instead concentrated his attention on the states of the Upper South, which had already proved more willing since the 1950s to consider voting Republican. Eisenhower won several Upper South states in 1952 and most of the region in 1956.[75] While losing the Deep South to Wallace, Nixon ultimately beat the now unpopular Hubert Humphrey in 1968 taking most states outside the Northeast.

Early in Nixon's first term, his new strategy began to solidify. In 1970, two Democrats, Ben Wattenburg and Richard Scammon, wrote a book called *The Real Majority*, warning Democrats they were losing a significant part of their coalition due to "The Social Issue."[76] The book became central to Nixon's thinking in the 1970 and 1972 campaigns.[77] Nixon and his staff believed the Democratic Party's new social policies and cultural positions had opened a door for Republicans to peel off important constituencies. Between the expensive and ambitious experiments of the Great Society, the brash young radicals of the New Left declaring revolutions, and the stream of controversial rulings from the liberally aligned Warren Court, the Democratic Party seemed increasingly in the hands of people cheering as progress changes that other Americans believed signs of the very breakdown in stability they feared. Many Americans after 1968 were genuinely troubled that the nation was coming apart, that social disorder was growing, that the postwar boom was ending, that order and stability were under assault, that the country was becoming more dangerous, that radicals were seeking power, that powerful groups were seeking untested policies in every area with unknown consequences, and that the Democratic Party as an institution was cheering it all on as a fair cost for progress. Nixon would now pitch his appeal to the people he famously called in a 1969 speech America's "Silent Majority." To court them, Nixon remained committed to the traditional Republican message against "big government," favoring lower taxes and less regulation, and opposing the expansion of New Deal–style programs. He would simply add new issues centered around the rise of what he called "permissiveness."

Nixon's new message would define the rest of his presidency. Going forward, Nixon's chief rhetorical enemies would no longer be socialists or economic centralizers but rampaging criminals, angry war protesters, and disorderly counterculture hippies. Nixon would decry permissiveness, meaning the abandonment of rigor and decline of moral duty, which he blamed for the spike in crime, the violent protests, the rise in drug use, and the spread of pornography and obscenity. He would talk about crime, values, and the breakdown of social stability. He would talk about drugs and protesters. He would talk about welfare and spending that ignored the needs of the middle class. His rhetoric would become more resolutely patriotic, voicing strong support for the military and national institutions. He would attack the wastefulness of Democratic social welfare programs and talk more about devolving power to the states. Nixon promised to push back against the social upheaval and to restore prosperity and stability though an agenda of law and order.[78] In a 1973 book, Nixon advisor Patrick Buchanan explained the approach like this:

> There exists a range of issues, a panoply of concerns and attitudes, where the President and socially conservative Democrats are aligned on one side, and liberal Democrats on the other.... On and on, the issues could be enumerated. The ideological fault that runs beneath the surface and down the center of the Democratic Party is as deep as any political division in America. From their respective views on the military, marijuana, school prayer, welfare, campus disorders, the "Greening of America," George Wallace, civil disobedience, foreign aid, the United Nations— the Catholic and ethnic and Southern conservative foot soldiers who gave FDR those great landslides are in fundamental disagreement with the isolated, intellectual aristocracy and liberal elite who now set the course of their party. While the Nixon landslide was a victory over McGovern, it was also a victory of the "New American Majority" over the "New Politics," a victory of traditional American values and beliefs over the claims of the "counter-culture," a victory of "Middle America" over the celebrants of Woodstock Nation.
>
> This reality makes the long-projected realignment of parties a possibility and could make Mr. Nixon the Republican FDR.[79]

This rhetoric was an assertion of a moral vision completely counter to that of the New Left. While it, too, claimed to want to create a more moral America, it defined morality in starkly different terms, such as patriotism, tradition, and the responsibilities of citizenship.

Nixon wasn't the only person campaigning on these themes. Seeing the same trends, Wallace, in his 1968 segregationist campaign, mixed his open racism with Nixon-like demands for law and order, attacks against hippies, disdain for elites, contempt for out-of-control judges, and populist appeals lionizing the working class. When he ran again in the 1972 Democratic primary, Wallace downplayed the open racism but continued these social themes to great success. Wallace won the Michigan primary and placed well with more than 20 percent of the vote in states like Wisconsin, Pennsylvania, Indiana, and Maryland, before a would-be-assassin put him in a wheelchair for life, ending his campaign. (Nor was it the first time Wallace had done well among Northern Democrats, having won about a third of the vote in the 1964 Democratic primaries in Wisconsin, Indiana, and Maryland.)[80] Nixon's campaign explicitly hoped Wallace might serve as a waystation for unhappy Democratic voters concerned about the Social Issue. They hoped these voters might, over time, turn to a Republican Party that echoed similar themes but without the overt racism of Wallace's segregationist brand.[81]

Nixon's law and order agenda remains highly controversial under the name that came to define it, the Southern Strategy. It's a somewhat misleading label because, while cracking the Democratic Solid South was the great prize, Nixon's goal was just as much to win working-class and rural Democrats in Northern cities and suburbs as in the South. The idea of a Southern strategy was controversial at the highest realms of Nixon's Republican Party at the time.[82] Everyone understood that a significant number of Southern voters in 1968 were angry about federal intervention in civil rights—not just the dismantling of official segregation in the South, but also newer issues like school busing to end school segregation. The issues of social breakdown, national turmoil, permissiveness, and backlash were thus intricately intertwined. For some voters, issues like enforced integration, school busing, urban riots, and radical movements were in fact parts of what they perceived as social breakdown. When Republicans campaigned on restoring law and order, opposing radicalism, reducing spending on Great Society social programs, and pushing back against permissiveness, some voters associated those themes with policies like school busing, integration, civil rights protests, and the urban riots.

Nixon never campaigned directly on racist themes—quite the contrary, he insisted in public that he continued to support expanding civil rights. His administration took some positive actions to advance civil rights, including defending racial quotas in the Philadelphia Plan, creating minority small business programs, and expanding the power of the EEOC,[83] and Nixon strongly championed policies to encourage African American small business—"black capitalism," as he called it—even though he knew it wouldn't help him or his party, because he genuinely believed in it.[84] At the same time, Nixon's administration dragged its feet on school desegregation, fired HEW's Leon Panetta when facing strong Southern opposition to Panetta's efforts to desegregate schools, and sought to appoint a Supreme Court nominee later exposed to have a segregationist past.[85] After 1968, moreover, Nixon was unwilling to invest much time on civil rights, particularly after his bitter disappointment in 1960 when he failed to win more than thirty percent of the African American vote against Kennedy despite what he saw as his clearly superior civil rights record.[86] Nixon judged the African American vote lost forever to the Democrats, given the mixture of Democratic economic policies and New Left civil rights activism.[87] He was also pessimistic about his own generation's ability to help solve it at all.[88] Most important, campaign operatives knowing the dark beliefs lurking within some voters' hearts also cynically sought to exploit the backlash against civil rights for votes.[89] Kevin Philipps, in the belief that politics mainly turned on "who hates who," openly promoted the idea that African American support for Democrats would benefit Republicans as white Southern voters angry about desegregation drifted toward the Republicans in response, without regard to policy.[90]

Americans have fiercely debated ever since the extent to which voters responded to Nixon's law and order strategy due to the issues it directly raised, or due to racist sentiment. It remains a subject of great partisan and academic debate.[91] While the facts aren't in much dispute, the narrative and interpretations one finds within them greatly depend on how you weigh those facts, the moral standards you expect from people living then, whether you choose to accept at face value what people said about their intentions, and what you suspect lurked unsaid in millions of people's hearts. Whether people were responding to social breakdown, rising crime, worries about the moral values of a changing country, backlash, or whether those were all just related aspects of the same thing, is a question on which our generation, still immersed in our era's partisan loyalties, will likely never reach agreement. Regardless of the narrative you accept, however, it's impossible to say Nixon's Social Issue actually changed his party ideologically. Moreover, whatever weight you assign these issues in your narrative, they all ultimately flow from something else looming over America—the national shift toward the moral politics of an awakening.

Nixon's Social Issue ultimately didn't change the core ideology of the Republican Party any more than the Great Society changed the ideological foundation of the Democrats. The Republican Party before Nixon united around an ideology fighting New Deal big government. After Nixon, the Republicans were still organized around fighting the same "big government." What Nixon's new approach had done, just like the Democrats' Great Society had done, was adapt the party's agenda drawing on the political language of morality—in the Republicans' case, values like fairness, patriotism, and guardianship. Nixon's Republicans thereby added a second agenda of social issues to their existing economic causes like taxes and regulation, just as Johnson's Democrats had added a second moral agenda to their economic and labor agenda. Johnson, in his Great Society, had launched a new moralistic platform for the Democrats. Nixon then proposed a moralistic platform of counter-reforms to fight what Great Society Democrats had sought to do.

America's shift toward moral politics in the 1960s and 1970s still had profound effects. As Americans grappled with new issues in a changing country, and as each party emphasized new issues and policies, the principles and values that spoke to different demographics changed over time. It was a process that played out over a generation or more, driven less by people changing their own views than by younger generations forming different allegiances than their elders, which over time caused national demographic changes as one cohort replaced another.[92] Nor is it a surprise that people might prioritize different principles and values in light of changing issues. It's hardly a surprise, for example, that people looking for federal protection from institutional discrimination would, over time, gravitate toward the party ideologically committed to social changes that benefit the least well off. Neither is it surprising that people unhappy with federal interventions might over time move toward a party whose ideology was wary of active government interventions on principle. These things happened not because America's leaders changed their parties' ideologies, but because they left them intact in the midst of such a major shift in the nation's priorities. It wasn't the parties that changed, but America.

Nixon's Social Issue was ultimately a mirror of Johnson's Great Society. As an awakening spirit swept across the country, America took new interest in morality, reform, and spiritual questions. Each party responded, employing their existing ideologies to these new moral concerns, developing new moral agendas to add to their existing economic ones. As America moralized its politics and new issues came to the fore, each party focused on new issues and concerns. Democrats leveraged New Deal liberalism to create a reform agenda to create a more moral America. Republicans leveraged conservatism to do the same, just emphasizing a different and clashing set of moral values, like patriotism, respect for authority, and tradition.[93] There was no sharp break, much less a realignment. Republicans and Democrats both simply took their existing ideologies and unleashed them on questions of culture, morality, and what sort of nation they wanted America to become. The Democrats extended New Deal liberalism to create social New Deal liberalism. The Republicans went from opposing economic "big government" to also opposing social "big government." In embracing the Social Issue, Nixon was just responding to the effects of an awakening. Nor did it stop there.

THE AWAKENING OF THE EVANGELICAL RIGHT

When Nixon adjusted the Republican Party's message and agenda toward themes of morality, he unwittingly welcomed another new movement into his party. While America was paying attention to the hippies of the counterculture, a second spiritual movement was quietly building under the surface. Every past awakening has sparked a revival of religious passion among American Protestants. These revivals see the sudden growth of more enthusiastic denominations and the decline of more establishment churches, the growth in a Christian faith community that intermingles worship with entertainment and community, and most importantly the influx of committed Christians in the public arena committed to a new agenda of morality and reform. This awakening was no exception. Along with the counterculture that grew out of the 1960s and 1970s, America's Fourth Great Awakening also birthed the evangelical movement, which gave rise to the "Religious Right."

Throughout the 1930s and 1940s, as national religious enthusiasm burned out at the end of the Third Awakening, the fundamentalist movement that struggled under the shadow of the Social Gospel retreated from public view. This was the countertradition of Billy Sunday and *The Fundamentals*, which rejected social reformist Christianity, socialism, secularism, and modernism, while strongly defending the doctrine of biblical inerrancy—the belief that the Bible is the divine word of God without error.[94] After the Scopes Monkey Trial in 1925 caused national ridicule and backlash, the fundamentalists retreated from the hurly-burly of politics to live according to a stricter interpretation of biblical law. Then a group of dissidents broke off to form their own faith community, which would build on fundamentalist teachings while believing it also important for Christians to engage with the culture and other denominations and faiths.[95] They took on the name "evangelicals," which before was a term used interchangeably within fundamentalism.

During the 1950s and 1960s, this evangelical community grew in visibility under pastor Billy Graham. While Graham maintained a mainly fundamentalist theology, he built a national constituency for his Christian message that crossed denomination and tradition through a series of revivals he called crusades. Without abandoning his strict biblical message, Graham engaged directly with the culture to minister to fellow Christians and convert minds. Graham became a national celebrity, ministering to and becoming close friends with presidents of both parties, such as Eisenhower, Johnson, and Nixon. Graham's brand of evangelicalism, however, still stayed out of direct politics.[96] Evangelical leaders might weigh in on weighty public matters from time to time, but they didn't advocate for laws, politicians, or political parties.

Then, in 1976, evangelical Christians poured into the public square to elect fellow-evangelical Jimmy Carter president.[97] The rest of America had no idea what to make of it. Out of nowhere, evangelicals who long believed it improper for Christians to muck about in Caesar's realm had jumped forth to exercise their collective muscle for a political cause. *Newsweek* magazine famously ran a cover story dubbing 1976 the "Year of the Evangelical."[98] After the election, these newly visible evangelicals didn't go away. Over the next few years, they threw themselves into political causes as if making up for decades of lost time. They took up opposition to legalized abortion, the defense of prayer in schools, and the maintenance of tax exemptions for religious organizations. They worried about the decline of the traditional two-parent family, the spread of the sexual revolution, the mainstreaming of pornography, and the secularization of public institutions. In 1979, popular preacher and televangelist Jerry Falwell founded a national organization to coordinate the political action of evangelicals, called the Moral Majority, and in 1980, soured on Carter due to his failure to fight for their moral causes, these evangelicals threw their full weight behind Ronald Reagan.[99] A new powerful force had entered American politics and the Republican Party.

It's hard to remember that as recently as 1970, evangelical Christians played almost no visible role in American political debate. Neither political party courted evangelical Christians, or even considered them an important voting bloc. Organizations like the Moral Majority, the Christian Coalition, the Family Research Council, and Focus on the Family hadn't yet been formed. The pro-life movement didn't yet exist. In fact, many evangelical Christians were ambivalent about or even supported legalized abortion—people perceived it a Catholic issue.[100] No one considered evangelical Protestantism to be either left or right, nor did they believe evangelical belief had anything to do with political liberalism or conservatism. Yet, by 1980, when the Moral Majority helped push Ronald Reagan into the presidency, the "New Christian Right" had suddenly become among the most important voting blocs in America, and its goals had become important signifiers of conservative politics.

This alliance between these newly active evangelicals and the Republican Party was hardly inevitable. The midcentury religious revival had flourished among many demographics that were traditionally Democratic. It was also in ways deeply populist, promoting issues and causes that America's national elite dismissed, like traditional family structures, space for religious teachings in the public square, pro-life policies, and traditional sexual morality. Upon entering politics, evangelicals initially supported Democrats and the evangelical Jimmy Carter. It's possible to imagine a universe in which evangelicals became a powerful constituency of moralistic and populist Democrats, sparring alongside the counterculture like fundamentalism had alongside the Social Gospel. By moralizing the Republican Party, however, Nixon had opened a door. When Nixon translated the Republican Party's anti-big-government agenda into one opposing the social "big government" of the New Left and the Great Society, he created a new moral language that intersected with the priorities of the religious revival. Nixon's Social Issue implied the values and concerns of the religious revival were a form of national virtue—not Burke's virtue that had strongly influenced the Republicans during the New Deal's early days, but the virtue of national reform. When evangelicals became disappointed with Carter, an influential group of Republican political activists, including Richard Viguerie, Howard Phillips, and Paul Weyrich, began building the infrastructure to court them. In 1978, they built one of the first "Christian Right" organizations, the Christian Voice, and in 1979 they convinced Jerry Falwell to start the Moral Majority. In 1980, evangelicals shifted their support to Reagan.[101] They never looked back.

The year of the evangelical, however, hadn't actually come out of nowhere. While America stood mesmerized by the counterculture awakening during the 1960s and 1970s, an evangelical Christian revival had also been growing quietly as its counterpart.[102] In the middle of the 1970s, about when its most enthusiastic members reached adulthood, it finally burst into public view. This revival looked a lot like the religious revivals of prior awakenings. New interest bloomed across America for enthusiastic Christian religion. Evangelical Protestants united under a cross-denominational identity. They formed new organizations to serve this new community, like Christian publishers and service organizations— by the mid-1990s America had over 2,500 Christian bookstores.[103] They created new forms of worship, like megachurches, televangelism, and Christian rock music.[104] They took new interest in religion in their daily lives, becoming involved in things like Bible studies and mission trips. American evangelicals built an entire evangelical subculture, with its own businesses, music, well-known stars, movies, music, book series, and community connecting them together across America.[105] New and more enthusiastic denominations boomed, like the Charismatic movement.[106] Most important, as in every awakening, this community plunged into America's political and cultural debates on a mission of national moral reform. The only key difference between this revival and previous ones was theological. The evangelical revival wasn't founded on the Social Gospel or the millennial ideas of the nineteenth century, but rather on ideas that originated with fundamentalism, like biblical inerrancy.[107]

As the boomers grew into full adulthood, this evangelical movement grew in power. After the first wave of evangelical political organizations, such as the Moral Majority, faded during the 1980s, a new generation of even more powerful organizations rose to take their place, including the Christian Coalition, Family Research Council, and Focus on the Family.[108] With their growing influence, openly evangelical candidates with platforms trumpeting their faith—people like Mike Pence or Mike Huckabee—became commonplace. In 1988, a genuine evangelical minister, Pat Robertson, even made a credible run for the Republican nomination for president, winning the Iowa caucuses.[109] By the early 2000s, evangelicals had become so influential within the Republican Party that their issues had graduated from factional ones to core party positions. Just as the Democrats had allowed an awakening movement to bring new moral issues into their party, so had the Republicans.

WHY A FOURTH AWAKENING

The cultural uprising of the 1960s and 1970s is strangely familiar. It exploded out of nowhere just as a new generation came of age. It rejected the status quo as immoral and wanting. It created new interest in spiritualism and sparked new spiritual movements. It gave birth to new social reform movements. It supercharged rowdy protests movements that sought to purify society and create a new order that was more just and moral. It dismissed worries about stability and order. It birthed new political issues based not around interests over which people might compromise but in stark clashes of morality. It celebrated ripping down imperfect and defective features of society to replace them with a more moral and just order. Most important, it bathed society in a new spirit of moral reform that replaced a largely pragmatic political era with a new one obsessed over moral questions. The era, in other words, looks exactly like the start of a great awakening.

America's Fourth Great Awakening, like every awakening, has been disruptive to politics. Awakenings infuse every debate with moral urgency and charge the entire society with the electric energy of possibility and change. They can inspire Americans to do amazing and difficult things prior generations believed impossible. They also, however, encourage citizens to take on divisive issues that tear at society's most painful spots. Compromise becomes difficult when those with whom we agree aren't simply allies but the righteous and those with whom we disagree aren't simply opponents but evil. Crusading zeal brought many of America's most important reforms, but it also helped break the Whigs and drove the nation into a civil war. Most of the common complaints about how American politics has become more angry, polarized, and unstable in some way trace back to the beginning of this awakening.

What has made this awakening particularly disruptive is it also hurled two competing moral visions into each other, igniting the clash we call the culture war. Two independent awakening movements, the counterculture and the religious revival, each took up its own brawling crusade for reform. One threw itself into a vast project of moral reform to tear down the postwar social order, which it thought oppressive. Its counterpart threw itself into a counterproject of moral reform to shore up those same institutions, which it thought upheld the nation's virtue. Each rival moral movement attached itself like a passenger to the party it believed best represented its interests, although neither was a perfect fit. The counterculture was based in progressive ideas, but it was also uneasy with the party's Old Left populists and, given its belief in self-expression and freedom from authority, was often comfortable with liberty. Evangelical reformers made uneasy allies with a liberty faction they sometimes saw as libertines but were comfortable with populism in its resentment of cultural elites. As these rival movements gradually gained in power, their feud—ancillary to and sometimes even clashing with the core New Deal debate—seeped everywhere into the culture and even into people's personal lives.

As the awakening spirit spread and the parties applied their ideologies to new issues, the sorts of people who responded to those ideologies and agendas also changed. In the 1940s and 1950s, the sorts of people attracted to populist and progressive arguments included a lot of working-class Americans and Americans across the Solid South. Then young progressives from the New Left flooded into the party, many from wealthy, educated, and professional backgrounds. Republicans in the 1940s and 1950s included a lot of wealthy and educated professionals. Then working- and middle-class Democrats from Nixon's Silent Majority and young evangelicals responding to new Republican positions on moral virtue flooded into the party. People who in one era might have grown up to become populists began thinking instead of virtue. People who in one era might have grown up to be liberty conservatives instead became progressives. As these issues played out over the 1970s and 1980s, the sorts of people we assumed to be Democrats or Republicans gradually changed— and not because the parties changed their ideologies or because the older generation abandoned prior allegiances. Younger voters focused on different issues and formed different attachments.

Weak and anachronistic parties can linger on for years going through the motions until some disruption shakes American politics hard enough for them to collapse. The Fourth Great Awakening is potentially that sort of disruption. America now has two crusading reform movements embedded in its parties, committed to tearing each other down. They seek to push and pull people across the normal New Deal political divides around a second set of issues that sometimes sits uneasily within the baseline New Deal debate. A political culture once pragmatic and interested in making deals is now almost completely a moralistic one, inspired to save the world, impose justice, and vanquish opponents seen as corrupt and evil. As it overwhelms the Fifth Party System, Americans become more eager to rip institutions down, charge into the fray, and tear each other apart in the name of the greater good.

The Fourth Great Awakening, like every awakening, was a revolution for America. It plunged the nation into significant projects of moral revival, social justice, and national reform. The civil rights revolution, the pro-life movement, the sexual revolution, the environmental movement, the late twentieth-century religious revival, the war on poverty, and nearly every other major social revolution over the last few decades is in some way connected to the Fourth Awakening. Many of these revolutions, just like those of prior awakenings, will without doubt leave a legacy of important and positive reforms that make America a better nation—one that is indeed more just, more fair, and more moral. Just as with prior awakenings, the Fourth Awakening has also destabilized American politics. It has made our disputes angrier, more zero-sum, and more unresolvable. It shifted the nation's attention from the sorts of pragmatic questions around which we can compromise to solve and toward the sorts of moral questions that we can only win or lose. It destabilized our party coalitions, not only by changing their demographic makeup but also by moving people into both parties who were not truly loyal to the ideology they adopted. It polarized not only our political debate but the entire culture, as its zealous uncompromising values seep slowly into everything.

That's why so much changed in America during the 1960s and 1970s. It's why the nation embarked on so many vital crusades for national reform. It's why our parties began to talk about new issues, attract different sorts of people, and often speak in different voices. It's why there was a political revolution even though our parties ideologically remained fundamentally the same. America began its Fourth Awakening, and it's still ongoing now. While this awakening significantly altered our parties' agendas and priorities, it also left them, for now, philosophically intact. That doesn't mean, however, that the Fourth Awakening wasn't also ultimately a destabilizing influence on our politics. Like every awakening in America's history, the Fourth Awakening also planted seeds that, as they grow, can crack the very foundations on which our party system stands.

CHAPTER 15

THE END OF THE INDUSTRIAL ERA AND THE AMERICAN CENTURY

In 1981, Democratic senator Daniel Patrick Moynihan noted that "of a sudden, the GOP has become the party of ideas," thereby coining a powerful phrase that has resonated through American politics ever since—the "party of ideas."[1] The Democrats were a party of ideas during the 1930s through the 1960s, offering America a constant stream of big new plans, from the New Deal through the Great Society. Between the 1970s and the 1990s, the Republican Party was a party of ideas, conceiving one after another paradigm-shifting reform: welfare reform, tax policy restructuring, empowerment zones, school choice, term limits, community policing, and entitlement reform. Both parties today, however, offer essentially the same policies they developed decades ago, served with a generous helping of platitudes and boilerplate. It's been two decades since either party was spitting out a stream of reforms, groundbreaking policies, bold experiments, and innovative new ideas. Hardly anyone would call either party a true party of ideas.

Our present moment looks a lot like the last days before every realignment. One of the signs of declining parties is just this kind of political stagnation and drift. It's hard for people in public life to admit this, but everything is changing and nobody knows exactly what to do. Not only do we face a flurry of new and unfamiliar problems, we frequently lack a solid framework that allows us to even think about or understand our changing world. The old formulas are no longer working, yet no one has developed new ones we think might work. America desperately needs innovation and ideas so it can develop new policies, solve challenging new problems, and renew its politics around a compelling vision of tomorrow. Yet our national political culture no longer values substance, governing, or ideas much at all. This situation is both dangerous and unsustainable. As we know from history, if our leaders refuse to take this moment seriously, lunging into new problems with innovation and ideas, it's only a matter of time until someone or something comes along who will.

THE END OF INDUSTRIAL-ERA AMERICA

Imagine you're the chief of a tribe of hunter gatherers. You spend your days worrying about the problems of your known universe, like whether the herds are thinning in your hunting grounds, whether a rain ritual is needed to please the spirits, or whether your brother might be plotting against your rule. One day a nuclear submarine pops up on your shores and strange men with laser rifles get out looking to trade iPads for squash, and asking whether your people would like to work in the factory they've opened further up the coastline. Understandably, you have no conceptual framework to deal with these demands because the entire situation is completely outside your understanding of reality. Until that moment, your universe didn't include nuclear submarines, laser rifles, iPads, or factories. Your response to this threat or opportunity is bound to be disastrous because you can't really comprehend what's happening, given your mental picture of the world.

As the world changes, it often moves faster than our mental picture of the universe can adjust. The French court of Louis XVI found it difficult to understand a world in which wealth and power no longer came from heritable land worked by peasants but from enterprises owned by untitled commoners. Turn-of-the-century farmers found it difficult adjusting to a world in which agricultural prices were falling while better wages were now on offer in cities. The music industry found it impossible to adjust to quick and cheap digital distribution. The first instinct of people when faced with this sort of disruption to the traditional order is normally inaction and an angry resistance to change they don't want but can't prevent. It takes people time to reorder their thinking and then reorder their affairs to adjust. The end of the industrial era is a similar disruption to the traditional order in America.

Once upon a time, we Americans lived in an industrial-age economy in which one high-school educated worker could support a family in a middle-class lifestyle with a skilled manufacturing job. That worker's paycheck (usually a husband's) could buy a house in the suburbs, a car or perhaps two, a television, and new appliances, while his nonworking spouse stayed home to raise the family full-time. He likely belonged to an industrial union, and his workplace was probably highly regulated. The America he lived in was not only the strongest nation in the world and the greatest military superpower on earth but, for a time, the only fully functioning modern economy on the planet. Europe and Asia were in rubble after a devastating war, and the remainder of the earth was divided between the inefficient command-and-control economies of the Soviet bloc and the developing "third world." The United States disproportionately supplied the economic and cultural output of the entire globe.[2] It invented and exported the world's automobiles, its appliances, its music, and its movies. It was spectacularly rich, with a middle and lower class that often lived better and consumed more than wealthy people elsewhere.[3] It was secure both economically and militarily. Its culture was the world's culture, its values the world's values, its currency the world's currency, and its economy the world's economy. For many of us, this is what America is supposed to look like.

Henry Luce wrote an article in *Life* magazine in 1941 about the beginning of what he called "The American Century."[4] That name for this extraordinary era of American prosperity and influence, the American Century, has come to represent this exceptional moment in the decades after the Second World War. The America of this age was the keystone of the world economic system. For years, it provided the world with the goods only its booming and untouched economy could produce, or produce in sufficient quantities.[5] In the immediate aftermath of the war, America made up about half of the entire world's gross national product and still made up well over a quarter into the 1950s.[6] Europe and Japan were in rubble, Eastern Europe was trapped behind an Iron Curtain, and the rest of the world was stuck in dysfunctional postcolonialism. When the world finally recovered from the war, it produced an economic boom in which America was perfectly positioned to flourish.[7] America was the world's most productive economy by a significant margin, a position it maintained for decades—many people worried in the mid-twentieth century that Europe's economies might never again catch up.[8] America faced no real competition for its cars, music, movies, refrigerators, televisions, or dollars, exporting not only its goods but also its culture to the world.[9] America also benefitted from a cooperative market system with its European allies and Japan, in which it imported cheaply and exported its bounty, creating net investment abroad.[10] Real medium income in America doubled in the quarter century after the war, the proportion of families with incomes above the comfortable range increased by a factor of six, and the percentage of Americans in poverty fell from 32 percent to only 11.[11] There was a golden age in the growth of manufacturing wages.[12] America became astonishingly rich by global historical standards, and its middle class came to take for granted unprecedented personal wealth as a middle-class birthright.

Not only was the America of this American Century historically rich and productive with a flourishing middle class, it was also the leader of one side of a worldwide ideological struggle between liberal democratic capitalism and communism in which every nation around the globe was forced to take sides. America knew who her friends and enemies were, what they wanted, and from where new threats were likely to come. Half the nations of the world came to believe their national survival depended on American success. America was expected to lead, and when she did she could trust half the world would follow. America therefore took the lead in designing and enforcing the trade regimes, financial rules, and even cultural habits of the world. The astounding advantages of getting to reshape the world for its benefit flowed back to its people and economy. This great wealth and power—wealth and power that trickled down in a comfortable lifestyle for most of its people—was in part the result of

America's unique political system, institutions, and values, but also in part because of its accidental position as the planet's sole standing economic powerhouse. When we Americans picture the natural state of the world, we picture this world of middle-of-the-twentieth-century America. We picture the industrial might, devastated globe, modern industrial economy, and unquestioned and unchallenged American leadership, influence, wealth, and economic dominance of the American Century. Yet, like any historical era—Roman Europe, medieval France, or Civil War America—this version of America isn't "normal" in any historical sense. It's a snapshot of a particular time and place in world history, one in which America's fortune rested in large part not only on its own policies but also on potent forces outside its own doing or control.

It's more than just America's good fortune during the postwar boom. The vision of industrial-era America that we take for granted as "normal," in fact, is grounded in a specific and unique economic system, cultural system, and international system unlike anything that came before or anything that will come again. Its backbone was the economic system we all take for granted but that's actually historically unique—the industrial manufacturing economy. Twentieth-century America meant massive organizations mass-producing physical objects, from automobiles to refrigerators to music records to Ovaltine to transistor radios. Americans today have a hard time even envisioning an economy that didn't mainly involve people getting hired into jobs at large corporations to perform some small part of making something to be sold to others. Yet, for most of human history, people didn't have "jobs." They worked on little family farms or ran a little store or performed a service like medicine or law for the people in their own communities. They worked for themselves, with their families or maybe a few business partners.

When we transitioned from an agricultural to a modern industrial economy, we rearranged our entire way of life to accommodate the new economic model that supported us. Building cars or steel or television shows takes massive investments of capital that few can get, and needs specialized workers who cooperate to succeed, so we built a unique economic and social infrastructure to support it. We moved from little towns around America to sell our labor to large enterprises that mass-produced things or sometimes services. Since many of us no longer owned little family businesses, but depended instead on salaries, we needed pensions and retirement funds to support us once we aged out of the labor market. Medicine moved from small-town practitioners to impersonal hospital corporations with industrial MRI machines, so now we needed health insurance. Since we no longer depended on intergenerational family farms, we began to live in households consisting only of one immediate family. We needed bigger houses to store our new industrial inventions, particularly the cars in our garages, so we built cul-de-sacs in the suburbs where we could commute to our corporate urban jobs. We became more egalitarian with sex roles, particularly after women joined the workforce during the war, although we still mostly expected men to be breadwinners and women to get married and maintain the homestead.

All our debates today take for granted that America is now, and always will be, industrial America as it existed between 1945 and 1995. We continue to think of work life in terms of the industrial labor relationship. We think of family life in terms of the nuclear unit, with one wage-earner and one domestic worker in charge of child care. We think of foreign policy as if America were naturally a colossus fighting for freedom and producing the output of the world. We think it right and natural that the world watch American movies, buy American cars, and use American dollars as their reserve currency. We think it right and natural that our middle class ought to be richer than the middle classes of most other nations, or even their rich. Over decades, we built our institutions, both informal and through government, assuming that these things are true because, for most of our lifetimes, they were. These assumptions quietly stand behind the Medicare system. They stand behind the Social Security system. They're the assumptions supporting America's military commitments. They're the assumptions of its education system. They're the assumptions behind America's environmental laws, its labor laws, and its health and safety laws. They're the assumptions supporting the commitments in the federal budget. They're the assumptions behind everything.

Not only are our institutions grounded in the assumptions of midcentury industrial America, but the politics of our Fifth Party System is as well. This lost world thus continues to frame the thinking of both Republicans and Democrats, who often don't even realize they're presuming the long-gone world of the middle twentieth century is America's natural order. The primary debate in the middle twentieth century was how best to manage and distribute the staggering fortune and wealth America's industrial economy was then producing. We fought over the most practical way to do it—whether the system would be more efficiently managed by a group of carefully selected experts or by markets and bottom-up choices. We disputed the fairest way to do it—whether the fruits of Americans' labors should be distributed to citizens based primarily on those who produced them or otherwise, and if so how that could be fairly accomplished. We disputed the ideological underpinnings of it—how our cultural assumptions impacted the system and how change would affect us. Using the industrial-era model of the world in our heads, we built institutions to do these things—from Social Security to Medicare to the EPA to our tax code, to family medical leave laws, and so on—dividing our political system into two camps, each taking a different side.

America's economy, culture, and position in the world, however, are increasingly different from the industrial-era models existing in our heads as "normal" because industrial-era America is almost gone, rapidly transforming into information-age America. The new economy is a fast, digital, service economy with global competition coming from places that Americans recently called the third world. One high-school educated adult no longer can expect to support a middle-class lifestyle with a factory job in Michigan. Americans no longer can expect to work at one great American industrial firm for forty years, receiving at retirement a pension, a gold watch, and the company's thanks. The new model of American life is not safe, stable, or effortlessly prosperous. It's fast, mobile, disruptive, and unstable. Workers rapidly get laid off and change jobs. New technologies emerge every few years, disrupting new economic sectors. Cultural norms change constantly. Manufacturing and industrial-era jobs are replaced with service and information jobs. Americans compete against former subsistence farmers equipped with laptop computers and mobile phones from halfway around the globe. Competition comes from everywhere—not only from China, India, Brazil, Russia, and Europe, but also from places many Americans don't think much about like Indonesia, Vietnam, and Bangladesh. American culture increasingly competes with other cultures. People migrate across continents for opportunity and safety. Former Cold War allies no longer feel threatened enough to unquestionably follow America's lead, and they look to rising powers everywhere who are seeking to take its place.

Although we're not sure what it all means for the future, we know the industrial-era economy is gone. We'll always manufacture things, but the world is no longer organized around mass-producing industrial goods. The economy is now organized around a mix of manufacturing, services, and information. Workers no longer expect to spend lifetimes at one firm, acting instead as free agents of their own careers. Digital upstarts have disrupted traditional industries. Robots and algorithms have replaced jobs with routine components. National markets are now international markets. New technologies are reordering the basic underpinnings of society, from how we communicate to our expectations of privacy to the capabilities of firms and governments to sift through troves of data that would have been unimaginable a mere generation ago. It's common, if not expected, for couples to both work outside the home and share domestic duties. Nontraditional families are becoming traditional families. Changing attitudes are redefining basic questions like what a family is, how we parent, how we separate home from work, and what our spouse and children expect from us. Just as disruptively, America faces the rise of the rest of the world. Europe recovered from war by the 1960s, and Japan followed soon after.[13] Just as America was adjusting to competition from the resulting Mercedes and Toyotas, the Cold War ended, freeing Eastern Europe. Soon thereafter, the former "third world" began to adopt a more market-oriented economic model, adding massive nations like Brazil, India, and China to the global economy. People from every corner of the globe now compete with Americans for jobs, sales, and economic innovations. What started with manufacturing jobs moving to Mexico turned into computer programming jobs moving to Bangalore. Gone are the days where America stood alone as the only working modern economy, exporting its bounty to the world.

America faces new and daunting challenges well outside the scope of the New Deal framework. We face new friction with our European allies. We face the rising power of China, which would like to push American influence out of its Asian backyard. In certain parts of the world, we face a complete backlash against capitalist democracy, reversing a long global trend away from autocracy. We face additional disruption from ever-evolving information-age technologies, creating new capabilities and threats among both friends and enemies. We face asymmetric foreign policy threats, from Islamic extremist groups to aggressive dictatorships armed with nuclear weapons. In addition, we confront countless unsolved political questions inside America's healthcare system, its national resources and environment, its budget and priorities, its national infrastructure, its education system, its immigration laws, and its culture. Those are just the most dramatic changes, and this new era has barely begun.

What's more, even more disruptive changes are surely waiting for us in the coming years, which we can no more imagine now than a nineteenth-century farmer looking at a cotton gin could appreciate the long-term economic implication of the technological breakthrough it represented— the coming world of trains, motors, factories, telegraphs, steam engines, and booming urban populations. We don't yet fully understand the future we're already living in, much less where things are headed. The only thing we can say for certain is that the world for which we designed our institutions and politics no longer exists. The world of the early twentieth century is as similar to our world as the world of agricultural Civil War America was to the world of the Roaring Twenties. Our entire political party system is organized around a program that becomes more irrelevant with each year to the problems Americans want and need addressed. Our parties' ordinary toolkits simply aren't designed for our new concerns. Citizens become angrier with a political system that seems trapped in stale old debates, unable to address the most important questions about their lives. With each passing year, the glue that once bound our parties together becomes weaker, leaving the parties dependent on inertia and rhetoric to sustain them as relevant political forces.

One of the harbingers of a coming realignment is the rise of urgent, compelling, and dangerous new issues that America's parties can't or won't address. Our parties remain stuck in the New Deal debate we created them to resolve, but we no longer live in that New Deal era world. The American Century is over. The world has changed. We're facing unfamiliar new challenges in the middle of an economic and cultural revolution. Yet all of our national policy remains rooted in a world that no longer exists. Worse, our politics is unable to even conceive of the new world up ahead. As that new world brings greater and greater change, with a political system trapped farther and farther in the past, eventually something has to snap. Ask yourself this: If, for some reason, our two major parties collapsed tomorrow, would we choose to reinvent them in the same way? If we were to recreate our parties today, at this historical moment, with this set of challenges, would we create two political parties divided by this particular set of issues? Would we reconstruct two parties tailor-made to argue the policies of Franklin Roosevelt?

THE DECLINE OF SUBSTANCE IN POLITICS

It's become a common complaint that America's political culture is broken. It often seems America's government is wholly incapable of getting even the most basic and noncontroversial things done. The American government has implemented only a handful of significant new initiatives in over a generation, and even those pale when compared to the groundbreaking ideas of the previous era like Social Security, Medicare, moon rockets, and welfare reform. It's been years since America's parties were offering innovative and bold ideas, and we've come to take for granted as a nation that governing is just an extension of campaigning and that federal policy is a campaign promise in a stump speech. Our political culture is obsessed with shaping narratives, embarrassing the opposition, campaigning, and winning without regard for the actual purpose of holding public office. We've come to accept that every legislative fight is a carefully selected wedge issue meant to energize one party's base while dividing the coalition of its rival. We accept that high officials mainly focus on the mechanics of politics, such as raising money to position themselves for the next election. It's considered naive to take seriously that democratic government should primarily focus on ideas and governing. We live in a permanent election campaign in which the actions of government serve the interests of elections, instead of elections serving the interest of getting difficult agendas enacted. It's comforting to think politics in America has always been this way. In fact, it's reasonable to be alarmed.

All administrations care about winning elections and shaping opinion. Even America's most celebrated statesmen were also politicians who gave their historic speeches with an eye on manipulating public opinion, who threw nasty mud at each other through partisan campaigning, and whose greatest policy achievements were meant to help their authors win elections. Since the republic's earliest years, politics has incorporated parades, slogans, patronage networks, campaign finance, soundbites, and political cheerleading as if government was a sport. Yet for most of the Fifth Party System, the politicians who ran America's government also took substance and ideas deadly seriously. Franklin Roosevelt organized his presidency around a collection of brilliant minds from Columbia and Harvard Universities, a brain trust who constructed the meat of the New Deal from nothing. The most powerful advisers in Roosevelt's administration whose roots were in the hurly-burly of politics, like Harold Ickes and Frances Perkins, were also people of deep substance who personally rolled up their sleeves to design and implement ideas. Eisenhower administered the details of government as he administered the army that won the Second World War. John Kennedy assembled the whiz kid advisers of Camelot who asked what they could do for America. Lyndon Johnson, a crude master of political hardball, empowered deeply political men and tough operators like Bill Moyers, Jack Valenti, and Joe Califano, who all also knew and cared about actual policy. The biggest stars in the Nixon administration included Henry Kissinger, a controversial champion of realpolitik but also a deep substantive thinker, and Daniel Patrick Moynihan, an academic and Democrat whose role in crafting major domestic policy ultimately landed him in the Senate. Ronald Reagan brought the entire conservative movement's intellectual shop into government, where it rolled up its collective sleeves to reverse the direction of federal policy. Their accomplishments weren't simply symbolic stands and signals meant to endear themselves to swing voters or the base. They were real achievements that affected people's lives, like the New Deal, like Medicare, like civil rights legislation, like new infrastructure, like important treaties, like landing a rocket on the moon, like paring back regulation, and like tax reform.

The more recent Washington experience of White House adviser John DiIulio, the original head of the White House Office of Faith Based Initiatives during the George W. Bush administration, offers a sad contrast. Professor DiIulio, a well-respected scholar, one of the most creative minds working in public policy, and a font of new ideas, resigned in frustration after less than a year in Washington after meeting a policy caste more interested in communications and spin than ideas. As he wrote in a well-publicized letter to journalist Ron Suskind for an article in *Esquire* magazine:

> In eight months, I heard many, many staff discussions, but not three meaningful, substantive policy discussions. There were no actual policy white papers on domestic issues. There were, truth be told, only a couple of people in the West Wing who worried at all about policy substance and analysis, and they were even more overworked than the stereotypical, nonstop, 20-hour-a-day White House staff. Every modern presidency moves on the fly, but, on social policy and related issues, the lack of even basic policy knowledge, and the only casual interest in knowing more, was somewhat breathtaking—discussions by fairly senior people who meant Medicaid but were talking Medicare; near-instant shifts from discussing any actual policy pros and cons to discussing political communications, media strategy, et cetera. Even quite junior staff would sometimes hear quite senior staff pooh-pooh any need to dig deeper for pertinent information on a given issue.[14]

At the highest level of government, DiIulio found innovation and policy ideas simply weren't valued by the political operatives running the nation.

Nor is DiIulio's experience somehow unique to the Bush administration, as similar complaints could be lodged at every other recent administration, Democratic or Republican, for over twenty years.

Our current era is increasingly looking as empty, if not perhaps worse, than the Era of Good Feelings or the Gilded Age. This decline in substance is about far more than just our government officials. It's everywhere throughout our political culture. It's in the media. It's our public debate. It's in how we, the American people, discuss and participate in our nation's politics. It's in us all. If you want a shock, go to a place like YouTube that archives old media. Watch a few political speeches, interviews, or even network talk shows from just a few decades back. Watch Reagan debate Carter or Mondale, or Bush debate Dukakis, or even the famously political Clinton debate Bush. Watch pundit-focused television shows like *Firing Line*, or even popular network talk shows like the *Dick Cavett Show*, in which pundits, scholars, and Hollywood celebrities discuss policy issues. The modern viewer will be startled at the serious discussions of national policy at a level of detail far beyond anything on television today. Even the celebrities talked politics in a way that was smarter, more substantive, and more interesting than most high government officials do now. America's political culture really has declined.

Political commentators blame various boogeymen for this alarming decline in substance. Today's elected officials do squander an absurd amount of time on tedious fundraising, making it almost impossible for them to properly focus on their actual job governing America. Donors do have great influence on what actually happens in government. Cable news, and now social media, have created a vast media machine constantly looking for political stories, rewarding the silly, the trivial, the divisive, and the bombastic. None of that, however, is as new as we pretend. Money has been part of politics since Mark Hanna built his epic war chest for McKinley because campaigns are expensive and government affects people with money, and not so long ago nearly every major town in America had at least two partisan newspapers chasing readers and smearing opponents. The problem isn't structural. It's cultural. The American political system is operating on autopilot. Its parties continue fighting over power so politicians can advance their careers, and the nation must continue holding elections because we have to have a government, but since our parties no longer have fresh visions to sell, the only things that remain are campaigns and power. The Democratic and Republican Parties are no longer parties of ideas.

RENEWING OUR PARTIES WITH IDEAS

In his masterwork *On War*, written after Napoleon humiliated the best European militaries of his era, Prussian general Carl von Clausewitz famously explained the difference between tactics and strategy. Before Napoleon, too many generals wrongly believed their job was to win battles and take cities. Napoleon taught them that the real point of war is to strategically use battles to force the enemy to capitulate to your nation's demands.[15] It's a lesson as important to the boardroom and campaign trail as the battlefield, and one leaders too often fail to learn, mistaking tactical thinking for strategy. Winning battles, like winning elections, is just tactics. Choosing the right battles to achieve your objectives, like shaping parties with agendas and ideologies, is strategy.[16] We often misleadingly label the political tacticians who think in terms of winning news cycles, constructing wedge issues, raising money, and breaking down the electorate with math as "political strategists." Real political strategists, however, are the people who construct political parties out of raw ideas from the vast symphony of factions and principles at play in a society. Like Henry Clay, Franklin Roosevelt, or William F. Buckley, they understand America's current political divides aren't permanent or stable, that "Democrat" and "Republican" are temporary categories that can change, and then they set out to change them.

It's a dirty secret of American politics that ideas don't help much to win elections. During the long stable era of a party system, most votes are cast before the election even starts. The vast majority of voters already identify as a Republican or a Democrat, or strongly lean that way while claiming to be independent, and nothing that happens during the campaign can ever change their mind.[17] Those votes that are up for grabs in an election, moreover, are rarely cast based on detailed policy pronouncements from candidates—few believe half those promises will ever come to fruition anyway. They're cast because voters come to believe that a candidate and party shares their principles. Voters select candidates and parties who they believe see the world as they do, trusting them to get right the details of all the policies those voters lack the time, the inclination, or the expertise to understand themselves. So that's what tactically minded campaign operatives supply—symbolism that communicates to voters that the candidate and party shares their view of the world.

Real policy ideas are terrible for campaigning. They often require highly technical scientific, legal, and industry knowledge. They inevitably force tough choices and hard compromises. Even the best ideas disrupt someone's expectations. Political opponents can easily take new and unfamiliar proposals, twist them, and make them sound radical and dangerous. The media, operating on tight deadlines and usually lacking the means to understand the details of complicated policies much better than any other group of Americans, has an incentive to focus on the entertaining sparks of political conflict rather than informing people of the substance of debates. When politicians do take on the hard work of wrestling with knotty problems and devising complicated and messy real solutions, they're more likely to get punished than rewarded for it politically. So candidates and parties craft symbolic "policy solutions" that are simple, easy to understand, represent clear values, and are vague enough in their details to not create an easy target for opponents. They sound like policy, but they're in reality communication efforts to signal priorities, factional loyalties, and how a candidate might approach problems— empty proposals for "change," pledges to "create jobs" without a plan to do it, pledges to "strengthen education" without proposing real changes, "50-point economic plans," sweeping reform proposals no one would ever dare implement, tiny pilot initiatives, and unrealistic proposed constitutional amendments no one will ever seriously push.

That doesn't mean, however, that policy substance is a luxury or waste of time. Ideas are the only thing that hold the multitude of people within a party together in the first place. People aren't born Democrats or Republicans, but rather choose to become Democrats or Republicans because they believe those parties will advance an agenda of ideas they like. The sole purpose of a political party is to carry out an orderly debate about solving the most pressing issues in America. A political party that can't produce a useful agenda of ideas about how it intends to fix the problems of its members is useless. Without its ideas to bind them around a common agenda, a party's fractious factions would eventually desert it and the party would fall apart. It's just that we take the importance of those ideas for granted because we all already know before the campaign starts what agenda Republicans favor and what agenda Democrats favor, based on each party's well-known identity and brand. Nobody has to listen to hours of candidate speeches or wade through fifty-point economic plans to roughly understand what ideas each party hopes to implement. The only reason ideas don't seem to matter to individual election outcomes is because people factor them in before the election starts.

The ideas supporting America's two major parties, however, are now staggeringly old, haven't been adjusted for the better part of a century, and were designed to address a completely different world. America's parties haven't simply failed to develop answers to our new problems. They lack even the framework to think about those problems. Nothing in New Deal liberalism or fighting big government tells you how to approach the rise of China. Nothing in that debate explains how to address the disruption to the economy and society of mass automation and artificial intelligence. Nothing in the New Deal fight explains what to do about the disruptions of globalism. Nothing tells you how to properly respond to an increase in migration. You can't take either New Deal liberalism or modern conservatism as a starting point and develop a coherent and comprehensive answer to these or any other of the vast new problems America faces as a nation. The New Deal debate provides no instructions for how to address the problems of today. No wonder everything has stagnated.

If America hopes to break out of this stagnation and to begin to address the new challenges of a changing world, it needs to restore a political culture of innovation and ideas. Politics isn't just an entertaining spectator sport, nor is it a place to validate our identity. It's the way we work together to solve the problems of our republic. If we're going to move confidently into the next era, we need political leaders advancing new and exciting agendas that speak directly to Americans' greatest hopes and most terrible worries. We need political activists as interested in concrete plans for change as they are in winning rhetorical battles and gaining influence. We need a national media fascinated by the details of what America's parties do as much as whether it's likely to be popular or attract votes. Perhaps most important, we need to put our policy entrepreneurs back in charge. Many of the stars of politics today—people like James Carville, Karl Rove, and David Axelrod—are pure political operatives. Their expertise and interest aren't in crafting innovative policy ideas to better govern America but in winning elections and power for their party machines, with policy important only to the extent it provides deliverables to influential factions that will generate enthusiasm and thus deliver votes. Policy entrepreneurs are the people who actually discover and implement new policies, people like Daniel Patrick Moynihan and John DiIulio. Policy entrepreneurs, not communicators, are the core function of government, and they're supposed to be the highest-status members of government and the most important people in any room. Communications staff and campaign operatives are supposed to be helpers communicating to others whatever the policy entrepreneurs decide.

Delegating so much real government power to campaign operatives is abnormal. Traditionally, campaign operatives like Lee Atwater weren't also influential people in White Houses but supporting players, people important during campaign season to help secure elections who then faded back into the woodwork of politics. Not so long ago, even presidential campaign managers tended to be respected policy figures moonlighting in election campaigns, not the other way around. Reagan's campaign manager William Casey became the director of the CIA. George Bush's campaign manager was James Baker, a treasury secretary and secretary of state. Letting communications people run a White House is like Goldman Sachs putting its human resources department in charge of proprietary Wall Street trading. What the political operatives and communicators know and care about—winning elections on the back of established ideologies and platforms—is tactics. What America needs now is true strategic thinking to redefine those ideologies and platforms for the future out of raw ideas. We need a William Jennings Bryan or Franklin Roosevelt, who will develop a new innovative agenda not around the problems of yesterday but the problems of tomorrow.

If our existing parties can't or won't address the new problems America faces, it's simply a matter of time before others come along who can and will. If we want our parties to transform themselves in a renewal, instead of simply waiting for a collapse, we need them to throw off their tactical obsessions and reembrace a culture of substance and ideas. They need more than crafty communications plans, clever wedge issues, better fundraising, or more likeable candidates. They need wholesale innovation and reform, building new political coalitions with fresh ideologies capable of solving new problems looking forward instead of back. Our parties have to once again become true parties of substance and ideas. Each election cycle they fail to deliver competent and substantive government loosens the bonds that hold their factions together. Eventually, something will strike the system hard enough and those floundering parties will crack. If our parties don't embrace the ethic of a Bryan or a Roosevelt, refreshing their agendas around the new problems of America, it's only time until they collapse in disaster like the Whigs.

CHAPTER 16

AMERICA UNRAVELING: OBAMA AND TRUMP—
THE LAST PRESIDENTS
OF THE FIFTH PARTY SYSTEM

Americans are baffled and worried about the direction of our politics. For most of us, throughout our entire lives we essentially understood how American politics was supposed to work. We knew what it meant to be a Republican or a Democrat. We knew what to expect from our leaders. We didn't always like our politicians, and we didn't like every Congress or presidential administration, but we felt confident that, although they might enact some policies we didn't like, they'd keep the country moving forth on the same expected course. Whichever party and whichever candidate won, we felt secure that everything would be okay. Now we're not so sure. The nation faces an ever-increasing array of difficult challenges, but very little is getting done. Our national political culture is mainly defined by fierce anger, political polarization, and tribalism. There's the slow seepage of scary outrage, hate, and resentment into the culture, where political opponents aren't mere friendly adversaries but immoral enemies to destroy by any means possible. There's the near extinction of the moderate wings of both parties. There's the sudden abandonment of once unchallenged norms. There's the never-ending battles over the culture war, the raw resentment of Red America against Blue America, and vice versa. American politics seems broken. We have good reason to be concerned.

What everyone can sense is we stand at an important turning point in history. We're ready as a nation to move past the old debates that have defined our politics for as long as any of us remember. We're ready to throw away the tired partisan divisions that presently define us, building new coalitions looking not backward but toward the problems of today. We're ready to embrace new solutions to our problems—not symbolic ones, but a flurry of real reforms that can rebuild and remake our nation. We're ready to renew our parties, our politics, and America. We have been for some time. Yet so far, no one has stepped forth to do it, leaving a vacuum at the center of our politics for everyone's worst impulses to fill. Instead of leading America toward renewal and reform, everyone seems eager to ride on top of the crest of a wave that's about to crash into the shoreline.

An era really is ending. Our party system actually is nearing its conclusion. The problem is, we seem completely unprepared to build America's next party system and launch our next great debate. Instead of seizing the challenge before us to lead America into a new era, we seem trapped instead in patterns and ways of thinking that make it difficult, if not impossible, for us to revitalize our politics. Unhappily, unless something changes soon, we know how this will end. Our era isn't heading toward a new era of forward-looking reform as we all hope. It's going to end like the Whigs.

THE LAST PRESIDENTS OF THE FIFTH PARTY SYSTEM

The American people enthusiastically elected Barack Obama in 2008 in an election unlike any recent campaign. Obama captured the nation's attention on a promise of "Hope and Change" ushering America into a new era of postpartisan politics.[1] He talked about how there was no Red or Blue America, only the United States of America.[2] That yes, we could change everything that troubled us about the stagnation in American politics.[3] That the future would be dramatically better than the present if we only cast off the outmoded thinking holding us back and moved forward together. Republicans complained that people treated Obama not like a politician but a celebrity, but that was always wrong. Every major presidential candidate is a celebrity. Obama inspired a commitment and exhilaration usually reserved for religious figures and rock stars. There were those iconic posters by artist Shepard Fairey.[4] There were the fan videos, like the popular "Obama Girl."[5] An estimated 1.8 million people flooded into Washington to see Obama inaugurated, packing into the National Mall for a ceremony that uncharacteristically felt more like a national festival than the sober swearing in of a president.[6] The Nobel Committee awarded him nothing less than the Nobel Peace Prize less than a year into his first term on the strength of what he was expected to do.[7]

By the time Obama ran for reelection, that euphoria was gone.[8] Not only wasn't the country united, it was more divided than before. The Tea Party movement had exploded across America.[9] Republicans shouted furiously that Obama was a socialist working to destroy the country. Progressive activists, believing Obama had continued many Bush-era policies and governed like a moderate Republican, felt betrayed.[10] America hadn't suddenly started solving all its problems. For the most part, Republicans in Congress and the Democrats in the White House refused to work together at all. Not only hadn't America entered a new age of transformation and national redemption, everything had gotten worse.

Pundits have come up with a lot of explanations for why the Obama euphoria happened—from Obama's superior campaign team to social media to Americans thrilled to elect the first African American president—and why it so quickly burst—from united Republican opposition against him to a struggling economy to racial animus. There's truth in all those explanations, but none of them really explains the strange national eruption of jubilation nor its calamitous collapse. The key to understanding the Obama phenomenon lies not in conventional explanations but in what Obama promised and what he was actually able to deliver. Without realizing it, Obama promised America he would be the first president of America's next party system. Instead, he governed as one of the last presidents of the system that was falling away.

As president, Obama claimed three great accomplishments. First, he managed the aftermath of the 2008 financial crisis, stabilizing the banking system, implementing industry "bail-outs," and passing a large stimulus bill.[11] Second, he worked to withdraw American troops from Iraq.[12] Third, he threw his weight behind the dream of every Democratic president since the 1960s, passing a national health insurance bill.[13] In addition to these three larger efforts, Democrats under Obama spearheaded various efforts in federal agencies; sought to raise the federal minimum wage; rhetorically supported the failed "Arab Spring"; and supported immigration reform to provide a path to citizenship for many of those who had entered the country illegally.[14] When all was said and done, the Obama administration in practice—whether you like its accomplishments or not, and whether you judge it competent and successful or not—looked a lot like every Democratic administration of the last fifty years. Its legacy amounts to stimulus spending on traditional Democratic priorities, expanded access to health insurance, pulling back forces from a foreign war, and administering the agencies of government in accordance with traditional Democratic priorities. These weren't major philosophical shifts. They weren't unexpected bold ideas. The record of the Obama administration turned out to be the traditional Democratic agenda one had come to expect from post–New Deal Democrats.

It's not surprising that the Obama administration hadn't broken with conventional politics. Obama's White House included the same power brokers, the same think tanks, the same staff, and the same interest groups who had traditionally supported Democrats. None of them were intellectual radicals looking to forge new unfamiliar ideologies, and few were political radicals looking to explore unfamiliar new ideas. They naturally did the same things they had done over their entire careers. They championed the same issues. They listened to the same voices. They fought the same battles. Democratic elites essentially read the mass enthusiasm for Obama and the strong Democratic majorities in Congress not as a mandate to rethink new challenges but as an opportunity to politically advance the traditional Democratic Party wish list. Yet Obama hadn't promised to govern as a traditional Democratic politician. He promised to throw away old ways of thinking, break through the walls of Red and Blue America, and usher in new solutions—"yes we can"—to update and renew his party. America didn't know exactly what they expected hope and change to mean, but, whatever it was, politics didn't really change. The same groups of people were still fighting about the same issues and employing the same ideologies as before.

Without realizing it, Obama implicitly promised America he would bring about the next great political realignment. He promised he wouldn't just be a good administrator of government, or a champion of New Deal liberalism, but he would forge a new agenda from scratch like Franklin Roosevelt, Henry Clay, or William Jennings Bryan—and he probably had a fair chance to do it. Without knowing it, the American people were eager for the realignment Obama implicitly promised. They too wanted to move away from the tired New Deal debates. They also hated the stale Red State–Blue State divisions. They too wanted a "post-partisan" government—not a government that stopped operating with two clearly distinct political parties but one that debated different ideas in a different way. What Americans hoped for, often without realizing it, was that Obama would be the first president to move past *these* partisan divisions, ushering in a government that finally left behind the debates of the Great Depression. When that didn't happen, Americans hoping for a new future naturally felt angry and cheated. No wonder the national mood was frustrated, let-down, and a little bit scared.

The window is open and has been for years. America is ready for a realignment. The only question is whether America's leaders will deliver a realignment through a party renewal or whether they ignore the pressures long enough so that it happens on its own in a collapse.

THE CONDITIONS FOR A REALIGNMENT

All three conditions that signal a coming realignment are in place. First, the great debate of the Fifth Party System era—our debate over New Deal liberalism—is over. Sometime in the middle of the 1990s, the American people reached a consensus over the New Deal debate. They agreed with Franklin Roosevelt that the American state would now take on new responsibilities in economic management, health, safety, welfare. They agreed with the conservatives that those responsibilities had limits. Despite the wild political rhetoric to the contrary, in practice the New Deal debate is over and has been for the better part of twenty years.

The New Deal debate and the agendas it created are anachronisms. The America they address no longer exists. Its economy is completely different, no longer centered around mass-producing factories employing armies of unskilled men. Its cultural landscape is different, the one-earner and one-homemaker nuclear families of the middle twentieth century replaced with today's more varied conception of families. Its society is different, with increased diversity and more openness to difference. Its geostrategic situation is different, with the Cold War now a memory and an unstable multipolar world emerging in its place.

Second, a legion of new issues and concerns has risen to which no one yet has answers. New technology, new economic models, vast cultural transformation, new ideas, changed global competitors, and more all combine to create new issues that Americans want and need to be addressed. Few yet understand these new concerns, fewer have solutions to problems that are still unclear, and no one has a framework to properly think about this transformed world. The world is changing and no one in authority seems to have a plan, much less a solution. Our parties, constructed to debate the problems of a world that no longer exists, are ill equipped to debate the problems of the current world. They increasingly hold fractious coalitions together by force of habit, inertia, and tribal loyalties. There are no great projects on the horizon because Americans demand solutions to problems the parties can't even begin to think about, much less solve.

Third, America increasingly faces national disruptions. The most powerful among them is the furious great awakening coursing through the nation. Awakenings always turn politics more divisive. People immersed in awakening fervor see politics not as a field for negotiating over differences, but rather as a great crusade to transform the nation according to one's conception of morality. Awakening crusades denigrate the idea of politics as a series of imperfect negotiations. They celebrate the idea of politics as total war, with elections becoming opportunities to wrest control of the state from enemies. In the grip of an awakening, American culture becomes moralistic, agitated, zealous, and confrontational. America elevates moral and symbolic issues to the highest importance while it neglects practical matters as too boring and prosaic, since the battle between good and evil outweighs the importance of simply making things work. Awakenings encourage radically ripping things down to rid them of evil, clearing ground to build new utopias. Awakening fervor helped bring down the Whigs. It inspired the populist revolt and progressive reforms. It helped fuel Jacksonian Democracy. Awakenings are the ultimate complicating factor leading to realignments.

The awakening may be the greatest disruptive force now acting in politics, but it's not the only one. As America's parties stopped offering compelling answers to new problems, others crowded into public view with their own new answers. A new "Alt-Right" emerged, one that sounds nothing like traditional conservatism. A new equity movement often called the "social justice left" emerged, a confident and confrontational movement with a different perspective and different priorities than traditional New Deal Democrats. A new movement has emerged seeking to curb mass immigration. So has a countermovement rejecting the morality of abstract borders. A resurgent socialism may be emerging, one rejecting capitalism as a just economic system. More new movements, moreover, are certain to come. What makes these movements disruptive is they're not the usual interests or advocacy groups fighting for public agendas within the traditional New Deal debate. They have completely different philosophical foundations, and therefore sit completely outside it. As they gain traction, they batter the traditional divides themselves.

Added to all that are the disruptive political figures that inevitably emerge as the walls of a party system begin coming down. Few figures have been as disruptive of late—triumphantly rejecting the traditional divisions of American politics and its norms—as the current president, Donald Trump.

SCRAMBLING COALITIONS AND COURTING COLLAPSE

America's political leaders aren't blind. They can see the discontent across America just as well as everyone else. They, too, know America is changing.

They can see Americans are worried about new issues. They can see new movements taking form. In response to these existential pressures, you would expect them to be working desperately to innovate new agendas, combat the trends dividing their coalitions, and locate new allies to sustain majorities. Yet they've done the opposite. Instead of adapting their agendas and ideologies to address a changing world, they've sought to leverage these disruptions as political fuel in order to generate a short-term advantage within the crumbling Fifth Party System. To the extent they address new issues, it's to cram new concerns into familiar party frameworks. To the extent they address new groups and movements, it's to coopt them as foot soldiers in the fading debate between New Deal liberalism and modern conservatism. To the extent they address people's fears and anger at an increasingly unstable and unpredictable world, it has been to harness the discontent for a few immediate votes not to actually solve their problems.

One of the greatest symptoms of the deterioration of our politics has been the decline of the people we call political moderates. Through the beginning of this century, both the Democrats and the Republicans included many of these supposed "moderates" in their ranks. These moderates won elections, influenced their parties, and played key roles at the highest levels of government. Then came years of campaigns of marginalization by both party activists and party leaders—denouncing the moderates as traitors, weak, unprincipled, RINOS (Republicans in Name Only), neoliberal sellouts, or worse. Over time, the moderate wings in both parties that once flourished dwindled until, today, they're widely considered at best beleaguered remnants and at worst extinct. Many presume the moderates faded into irrelevance because American politics has become more "polarized," and they were "centrists" at a time in which both parties were moving "farther" to the "left" and the "right." The problem with this explanation is, as we know, the left-right spectrum doesn't actually exist. Since there's no single spectrum of human political opinion, there's also no middle point between liberalism and conservatism for "centrists" to occupy. Nor is it compelling to say our parties have moved "farther" to the left and right since we don't even know what it means for something to be "left" or "right," other than its something the people we've already labeled "left" or "right" happen to support. Something else is going on.

One of the defining features of a realigning era is drift. The existing party ideologies increasingly become ineffective vehicles for maintaining active coalitions, yet nothing compelling has yet arisen to replace them. Parties, however, must continue to win elections so they can maintain their status and power, so they have no choice but to discover new means to attract voters to the polls—which can mean campaign hullabaloo, popular personalities, appeals to identity, and the airing of resentments. Among the tools on which our parties have increasingly relied to attract and energize votes are appeals based in partisan identities outside the core New Deal debate. These appeals aren't based on principles, policies, or ideas. They're not attempts to solve new problems or found a new debate. They're attempts to harness raw emotions like anger and identity to drive voters to the polls, most often not even to support the party but to vote against its opponents. Increasingly, many of us have even begun to believe these ancillary partisan identities are in fact the true core of our parties and thus the definition of their "base." The most potent of these are the culture war and tribal Red and Blue identity politics.

Among the reasons the Fourth Great Awakening has proven particularly divisive is it splintered into two opposing movements, each drinking deeply of the same awakening spirit yet holding starkly different visions of what morality requires. Most awakenings create one interlocking movement to reform America. This one created two, one countercultural and the other of Christian revival, and then sent them to war against each other. Each side saw its agenda as not just better but as the foundation of justice and morality. Each saw its opponents as not simply people with different priorities, but as actual advocates for evil. Each was eager to take on divisive issues tearing at society's most painful spots, willing to rush into the maw of crisis in the belief that hard times today were a fair price for a better tomorrow. Neither was willing to compromise because they were fighting over matters of good and evil. The Fourth Awakening essentially lit two rockets, each racing toward the other, launching a great "culture war."

For years, these two moral crusades rode like passengers on top of America's parties. The parties chiefly fought over the issues of the Fifth Party System's great debate, concrete policies like tax rates and budgets and regulations that Americans could debate, compromise, and resolve. These matters were the ones America had to get right so people had work, food, a place to live, personal safety, healthcare, and care for their children. On top of this pragmatic debate over the core issues of government, however, this secondary culture war debate engaged over more exciting and morally affirming battles—reforms, crusades, and dreams, along with people's deepest anger and resentments. It was almost as if America's parties had two competing identities, one official—the two great ideologies of New Deal liberalism and modern conservatism—which governed the core issues of government, and then, lurking underneath, a growing shadow identity—the culture war divide that grew out of the awakening. So long as the New Deal debate dominated, these awakening movements promoted their issues and supported their chosen party as auxiliaries. Then the New Deal debate faded, clearing the political field for these remaining issues, the stark moral culture war disputes.

The culture war is about two clashing moral crusades, so it rewards the intense, zealous, crusading, passionate, furious energy that tears party systems down without concern for what comes next. By its nature, it's a zero-sum fight that can never be resolved, only won or lost. As the culture war replaces normal politics, it has turned it angry, zero-sum, moralistic, and destructive—while also discouraging the sorts of pragmatic and innovative reforms that renewing our parties would entail. The culture war debate, invested in a narrow but powerful set of moral beliefs and issues, can't sustain a party system alone because it isn't interested or capable of addressing the full scope of bread and butter issues a party system ideology requires. Its crowding out regular politics, however, has made it difficult, if not near impossible, for America's political leaders to engage in the messy and pragmatic experimentation and negotiation necessary to develop any other new agenda of ideas. Much of what we've falsely labeled "polarization" is in reality just the growing influence of this awakening moralism since the core Fifth Party System debate was essentially resolved.

For many Americans, what now marks you as part of the liberal or a conservative tribe isn't your attachments to the official Fifth Party System's New Deal philosophical commitments but rather your position on culture war issues like abortion, environmental purity, social justice, or personal morality. This is increasingly true at even the highest level of our party councils and among powerful party activists, particularly those who became involved in politics not through regular party organizations but through the awakening movements. Having risen to power and authority, they sincerely believe their parties are, and ought to be, coextensive with the awakening movements to which they're truly loyal. The problem is, while sometimes these two identities, New Deal and cultural warrior, match, often times they don't. While each awakening movement made its home inside one of the New Deal parties, each also sometimes draws on ideas from outside them. The "liberal" side of the culture war, based in moral progressivism, sometimes clashes with populism and is friendly to liberty. The "conservative" side, based in a moral conception of the virtue of national improvement, sometimes clashes with liberty and is friendly to populism. Defining conservatism and liberalism around the culture war unwittingly elevates some voters who don't even fully agree with their party's formal ideological commitments as more "pure" than voters who actually do. Put plainly, some of those who consider themselves part of each party's most committed "base" don't actually believe fully in their party's official ideology—and then seek to enforce their alternative version as the true one.

The culture war, however, isn't the only alternative identity that has risen to take the place of our great debate. Others have begun to define their political identity less in terms of ideologies and ideas and more in terms of the identity politics of "Red" and "Blue" America. For many, as the New Deal debate has declined, conservativism and liberalism have become not rival political philosophies but rival cultural attitudes. What makes you a conservative or a liberal isn't your views on public policy, but rather your lifestyle choices—whether you watch PBS or NASCAR, whether you prefer a Prius or a truck, whether you listen to country or indie rock, whether you eat kale or prefer Chick-fil-A, and whether you admire the Ivy League and France or despise them. These stereotypes are broadly useful in defining likely supporters. These markers, however, have nothing to do with one's views on politics, issues, agendas, or approaches to government. At best, they conform to cultural stereotypes of rural and Southern versus urban and Northern culture, and one's position on the culture war.

The sorts of cultural traits we associate with conservative politics—rural, traditional, religious, sensitive to perceptions of East Coast snobbery, and glorifying "real American" tastes in music, sports, and hobbies—are in reality just identity markers of traditional working-class America. The traits we associate with liberal politics—urban, secular, socially conscious, and glorifying the "refined" tastes in music, sports, and hobbies common to the educated and wealthy—are lifestyle habits of the modern professional and executive class. Defining liberalism and conservatism this way means dividing America around the age-old resentments of regionalism and social class while pretending the divisions are about principles and ideas. Worse, substituting cultural markers to define who is a conservative and who is a liberal for philosophical ones—people who look like "us," act like "us," live where "we" live, and live like "we" do— prevents America's parties from acting as institutions meant to govern— to ensure that we're safe, that we have jobs, that we have enough to eat, that our children get educated, that our medicines are safe, that we have working roads and bridges and airports to allow us to thrive—and turns them into expressive performances for airing trivial resentments that have nothing to do with running the country.

Our parties have only reinforced these troubling tendencies through today's dominant mechanism for thinking about electoral tactics, the "base strategy." Until fairly recently, the conventional wisdom was that American elections were fought over the "center." Political campaigns believed their most important task was persuading undecided "swing voters" in the political "middle" to trust them with the government. There is, however, another way to win a majority of the votes cast— changing the composition of the electorate in your favor by increasing the number of your partisans who actually show up at the polls. Under this base strategy theory of elections, the best way to win campaigns isn't to persuade the uncommitted, but to identify your party's most committed "base" and ensure they cast a vote.[15] Get-out-the-vote efforts are as old as politics, of course, going back to the days of precinct captains from political machines ensuring their patronage-blessed residents turned up to pull the lever. In recent years, however, base mobilization has come to dominate the thinking of campaign operatives across politics, shifting the goal of political organizations from persuasion to reliability and accountability.[16] The base strategy can only guarantee a few extra percentage points, so it can't help when a party nominates a bad candidate or runs in a bad year or runs a bad campaign. In an election with two pretty evenly balanced parties—which a stable party system is structured to create—it can, however, statistically guarantee the few extra points that can turn a losing campaign into a victory.[17]

The base strategy is tactically smart. Persuading people is an art and therefore unpredictable. Many voters don't even pay much attention to politics—particularly voters with weak partisan identities—picking candidates for reasons wholly unrelated to governing, such as with whom they would prefer to share a beer. Months of campaigning to the uncommitted can be destroyed by a bad photograph or poorly timed news event creating "bad optics"—a widely distributed video showing a candidate bobbing about in a tank wearing a silly helmet, or windsurfing in a tight wetsuit, or jubilantly shouting into a microphone. Identifying committed partisans and encouraging them to show up on election day, on the other hand, is the kind of management science a campaign can execute reliably, statistically *guaranteeing* a certain percentage of additional votes. The base strategy reduces the importance of things a candidate can't control, giving the candidate a path to victory the campaign can regulate and manage.

Although it may be tactically effective, the base strategy is also dangerous because it actively discourages desperately needed innovation and ideas. You persuade undecided people to support you with issues and arguments. Policy and ideas of substance aren't how you create urgency among people who already don't care enough about politics to vote. You inspire partisans too unmotivated to vote with strong emotions like fear, anger, and alarm. Traditional campaigning was about convincing people with policies and ideas. Base thinking prioritizes making people angry, outraged, and scared. The widespread adoption of the base strategy has changed the way our parties speak, the way they argue, and the way they relate to the entire electorate. It changed the message our parties send America about for whom they stand and what they represent. While the base strategy might be an effective short-term method for chasing votes in an era in which traditional issues are losing power, it's yet another force making America's political culture more angry, tribal, and irrational while encouraging political leaders to disregard the issues and ideas that could lead toward a party renewal. It actively discourages parties from doing the hard work they need to do to renew themselves for a new era, pushing instead toward the sort of raw anger and antagonism that can rip party systems down.

A larger problem with the base strategy, however, is it also falsely presumes that parties have a "base" at all. We don't know what "liberalism" or "conservativism" even mean other than whatever the people we call liberals and conservative tend to like. Parties therefore don't actually have a "base" consisting of more "pure" partisans to energize. What parties have are pockets of voters they can more easily identify as likely supporters using the available tools of analysis—cold statistics, generalizations, and numbers. In the modern campaign, these tools are often very sophisticated and accurate. Parties through "microtargeting" can enhance voter files with other databases, mailing lists, public records, and consumer marketing data collecting individual purchases and preferences to predict likely supporters.[18] These tools work, however, through generalizations, demographics, and data. They therefore overvalue supporters who are most visible and easily identifiable and undervalue supporters more difficult to demographically stereotype and thus identify. It's almost impossible to use these methods to accurately identify what people philosophically believe or why they care about the issues they do, much less at a time in which those ideologies are already losing power. They're quite useful, however, to identify people active in the politics of the culture war or who reflect the stereotypes of Red and Blue identity. The dominance of base thinking in our parties further encourages them to define their "base" around these alternatives—and then to act on it, encouraging these alternative definitions to become true.

The people we've labeled moderates, ultimately, aren't actually moderates. They're mainly people who philosophically belong in one party but align differently on the ancillary politics of the culture war and the Red-Blue cultural divide, and so they're getting pushed out of the party in which they properly belong. The Republican "moderates" who once thrived in the party were generally urban, upper class or close to it, perhaps from the Northeast or West Coast, and, as it's conventionally put, "economically conservative and socially moderate." They believed in free markets, limited government, and low taxes, yet often showed discomfort with parts of the Republican cultural agenda.[19] They were, in other words, ideologically committed to fusion conservatism—mainly liberty conservatives (thus "economically conservative") who liked tax cuts, wanted "smaller government" with reduced regulation, while supporting Burkean calls for personal responsibility and caution toward social radicalism. They showed discomfort with parts of the Republican cultural agenda (thus "socially moderate") that sprang from the awakening religious revival. They also often lived among Blue State Democrats in suburbs and urban areas, sharing Blue cultural tastes in products, music, sports, and media.

The Democratic "moderates" who flourished in the Democratic Party until quite recently—now increasingly marginalized within the party as hated "neoliberals"—were usually pro-business and Wall Street–friendly Democrats from the professional class who strongly supported progressive social policies but were uncomfortable with populist rhetoric demonizing corporations, attacking business, or valorizing the working class.[20] They weren't sure about labor unions, found too much top-down regulation problematic, and believed business can be a good partner to government. "Blue Dog" Democratic moderates, once popular in rural districts and the collapsed Solid South, alternatively believed in a Democratic agenda supporting working people but were uncomfortable with parts of their party's social agenda.[21] They supported the traditional New Deal agenda, diverging only on culture war issues like same-sex marriage, traditional family structures, abortion, or climate change. These "moderates" usually lived among Republicans in rural areas from the collapsed Solid South and shared Red lifestyles and tastes.

The people labeled Republican moderates and Democratic Blue Dogs are essentially people in the correct party based on the New Deal debate who disagree with their party on the ancillary issues of the culture war. The people labeled neoliberal "moderates" are the reverse, people philosophically at odds with some of their party's beliefs based in the New Deal debate, yet who accept all of its positions on the culture war. As the core Fifth Party System debate fades, leaving these secondary movements to drive votes, people have been leaking into the "wrong" party. Populists and people open to populism are leaking into the Republican Party based on the issues of the awakening religious revival. Liberty conservatives and people open to liberty politics are leaking into the Democratic Party due to the moral politics of the New Left. New Deal liberals with Red State tastes are leaking into the Republican party based on cultural identity. Fusion conservatives with Blue State tastes are leaking into the Democratic Party for the same reason. As the parties chase "base" voters in a tactical effort to win a few more short-term campaigns, they're reinforcing this pushing and pulling of voters out of the party in which they philosophically belong. Most alarming, many, including those within party leadership, appear to believe these wrongly sorted voters are in fact more "pure" members of the party's "base" than the correctly sorted ones they carelessly dismiss as "moderate" sell-outs.

This drift is further amplified by generational misunderstandings. Many people have come to presume younger voters—the millennial generation and now also post-millennials—are rising New Deal liberals who will increasingly empower the traditional Democratic Party agenda through the "coalition of the ascendant."[22] It's true that younger Americans strongly stake out what most Americans not so long ago considered radically "liberal" positions on many contentious social issues, such as same-sex marriage, marijuana legalization, and politics that foster social inclusion.[23] They support a more active government and tipped the issue of same-sex marriage from unthinkable to the law simply by coming of age. Younger Americans also report a significantly more favorable impression of the Democratic Party than the Republican Party—a party brand they disproportionately seem to viscerally dislike. Yet younger voters also disproportionately lack faith in most institutions, including government, and hold business in surprisingly high regard as a potential problem-solver.[24] Millennial culture seems to revere start-up companies, entrepreneurship, and disruptive innovation. It's not obvious that, just because younger voters disproportionately dislike Republicans and support the liberal view on the most-visible social policy questions, they necessarily also support New Deal liberalism as a governing ideology. Just like any generational cohort, what younger voters share isn't a common political philosophy but a shared life experience.[25]

American politics today is still mostly defined by the perspective of the baby boom generation. The baby boomers have dominated American culture since they came of age in the 1960s, and they continue to control the heights of many institutions today, including America's parties. Generation X, on the other hand, as a small generational cohort, had no choice but to adapt themselves to a boomer-dominated world when they came of age. It's therefore sometimes easy to forget that the baby boomer worldview, which has influenced the way we frame American politics so strongly for decades, isn't the universal American experience. Boomers presume the normal state of America is a nation with strong institutions, broad-based prosperity, and the cultural norms of post-Second-World-War America. Younger voters grew up in a different America, one less dominant with weaker institutions and more political disorder. Boomers remember America before the civil rights movement, but younger Americans only know an America in which bigotry is ugly and reviled. Baby boomers hear war and think Vietnam, but to younger Americans war means Iraq and Afghanistan. Younger Americans don't remember pensions and lifetime jobs; their Dad's job got outsourced to Asia. Younger Americans don't remember trusting Walter Cronkite; their news anchors were models who cared about pop stars and "news you can use." Because they grew up in different times, baby boomers and younger Americans live with a completely different mental picture of the "normal" state of America.

Younger voters holding the exact same principles as their elders often reach radically different conclusions about policy because they apply their principles assuming different facts about the world. What to older Americans looks like radical "liberalism" is often to younger voters simply observing basic facts about life in the more tolerant and multicultural America they've always known. At the same time, younger Americans are also less trusting of national institutions because authority in their lives has appeared less competent and less trustworthy. Younger voters are less interested in ripping down institutions than building stronger competent ones that actually work and that function with integrity. While they might be open to a stronger and more competent government, that doesn't mean they trust government implicitly to solve problems. In their lives it's been pioneers behind companies like Microsoft, Google, Facebook, and Apple who actually changed the world and made things better, not politicians or agencies and departments beholden to powerful market incumbents. It was a private risk-taking entrepreneur, Elon Musk, who demonstrated the possibility of a real-life network of electric vehicles while also restoring humanity's push into space—feats we might think government ought to have pursued, but didn't.

America's parties too often mistake ideological allies from this generation for opponents because they reach different policy conclusions than older voters might. Just because younger voters disagree on some policy questions doesn't mean they disagree on philosophical principles. Sometimes it just means they're applying common principles to what they see as a different version of the facts. Republicans are repelling philosophical conservatives from this rising generation, while Democrats are welcoming supporters who don't actually believe in New Deal liberalism. Millennials are projected to soon become the largest generational cohort in America.[26] Without realizing it, both parties are further pushing voters out of the coalition in which they naturally belong and further destabilizing the party system.

All these various ideas and ways of thinking that have seized control of our politics in recent years are cooperating to push us away from a political revitalization and toward a difficult decline. They're encouraging angry zero-sum political thinking. They're causing us to fear opponents and catastrophize what ought to be normal disagreements. They're discouraging leaders from exploration and innovation. They're causing us to obsess over deeply personal and emotional issues we can never conclusively resolve, and to ignore all the festering problems that we can and must. They're pushing Americans out of the proper coalitions in which they officially belong, thereby destabilizing the existing party system. Together, they're encouraging us to do everything we can to rip the guardrails of our existing party system down, yet without providing new frameworks necessary to solve our problems in the future. What's frustrating is everything America's parties are doing is tactically smart to win immediate electoral advantages. Yet it's also a long-term strategic disaster almost perfectly designed to push an already-crumbling and irrelevant system toward a catastrophic collapse.

Our parties are drifting. The ideological binds that hold our political coalitions together are weakening. America is waiting for someone, some group, or some movement to come along offering a fresh ideology sufficient to produce a compelling agenda for the future, thereby launching America's next great national debate. Yet instead of developing a new agenda of ideas and new ideological commitments that might reunite people around a new great debate, our parties are seeking instead to win votes through short-term mobilizations that are pushing people out of their proper alignment. They're behaving as if our present disruptions are mere opportunities to seize the advantage for one side or the other in this decaying debate. They're eagerly encouraging the anger, distrust, and radicalization in the system, not as motivations to devise new solutions but as opportunities to drive empty turnout. In the chase for short-term votes, they're destabilizing the old system that sustains them without providing something new that might launch a new system for the future.

We know how this all ends. Instead of shoring up and bolstering the crumbling walls of their party coalitions, our parties are blindly chipping away at their foundations. At a time of deep instability, America's parties refuse to innovate. Instead of renewing themselves for the future, they remain trapped by their past. They ignore the new issues obsessing Americans, choosing instead to tactically maneuver under the old rules to win elections. Oblivious or indifferent to the long-term strategic consequences, they encourage the strong social forces already pushing their parties toward collapse. They're acting like parties too often act near the end of party systems, treating politics as an empty game for capturing offices instead of as a mechanism for debating the problems America wants and needs to have solved. The present situation in America looks a lot like the politics of the 1840s and 1850s, right before the traumatic Whig collapse. Which brings us to the destabilizing administration of Donald J. Trump.

THE AGE OF DONALD TRUMP

Donald Trump's campaign in 2016 was, in many ways, the mirror image of Barack Obama's 2008 campaign. Obama had been hopeful. He spoke of uniting Red and Blue America. He drew a picture of a positive future for America. Trump in 2016 drew a picture far more grim. He attacked his enemies harshly as the cause of all America's problems. He drew a negative picture of America as a failing nation in need of "Making America Great Again." Where Obama was calm and measured, Trump was brash and unpredictable. Where Obama embraced America's institutions and navigated its traditional channels of power, Trump attacked them. Where Obama worked within the existing party structures and orthodoxies, Trump worked outside them and assaulted them. Trump, a man with no real political record, defeated a field that included many of the best-known and most accomplished politicians in America, people with lifetimes of high-level political service between them. He dismissed them all as losers and failures and promised to fix their mistakes as only he knew how.

Trump was no rote Republican politician railing against big government as Republicans had done since 1932. He had little interest in the old New Deal debate at all. He promised a total revolution. He would throw out every political blueprint, all the dogma and orthodoxy that had supported generations of Republicans and Democrats, and he would experiment with radical new approaches based solely on his instinct. He would break all the old rules down, throw out all the expectations, and directly upturn issues no other politicians even wanted to touch—immigration, global trade, the rise of China, America's foreign commitments, and more. Trump promised to throw out the New Deal Party system and start anew. His supporters loved him for it, and he won an election that no one thought he could, not based on his charisma or background but despite of them.

Trump's campaign was, on its surface, completely unlike Obama's. Yet, in the ways that mattered most, both campaigns tapped into the same political energy. Both recognized that Americans were unhappy with the status quo. Both saw new issues and movements the rest of the political class had neglected and understood they could harness them politically. Both saw a hunger in America for something different from the traditional Republican-against-Democrat debates, and both offered people the hope that something major would change, without ever specifically explaining what or how. Without even recognizing it, both implicitly promised to toss away the New Deal Party System and lead a realignment. Yet neither had a plan as to what that realignment would be, nor was either truly prepared to bring it about.

After his election, some thought Trump could be another Andrew Jackson. He would lead a populist revolt from the executive branch, throwing out the elites and governing with strength for the benefit of the ordinary people who adored him. His campaign and his rhetoric drew on a seemingly new coalition, one capable of designing a new Republican ideology supporting a drastically changed Republican Party. Trump even put a portrait of Jackson up in the Oval Office at the suggestion of his then advisor Steve Bannon, who hoped Trump's presidency might be the spearhead of a top-down revolution remaking American government and its role within the world.[27] If Trump were a different sort of man, that might even have been a possible outcome of his presidency. He attracted a potentially disruptive electoral coalition emphasizing different issues and speaking in a new voice. Franklin Roosevelt, moreover, who wasn't himself an intellectual or a wonk, didn't know what his New Deal would be upon his election either, and yet in office he led a comprehensive revolution of government that reshaped his party and his nation. Had Trump been a man obsessed with the substance of governing, or had he been an ideologue committed to a vision for America, or had he simply been a man seeking the immortality that comes from leaving behind a legacy of national change, he might have empowered others in his administration to lead the top-down revolution some in his orbit hoped he would lead. That isn't, however, who he is.

Trump, it turned out, had no interest in the yeoman's work of party reform or political renewal. While campaigning, Trump promised his supporters to address neglected issues they cared about. In office, he has so far mainly managed urgent issues while seeking to maintain his popularity and power. Instead of harnessing the discontent to push through new policies, he has leveraged that anger for tactical political advantage. As new ideas and movements bubbled up, he has stoked their fury without offering concrete change. Instead of reforming the system in a fundamental way, he has surfed the rising discontent to maintain influence, power, and popularity with his supporters. Instead of designing innovative policies, he has emphasized divisive symbolic issues tapping into people's deepest passions, but without actually improving things. He has alarmingly disregarded fundamental political norms that have governed America for generations, which has in turn prompted his opponents to violate even more norms in opposing him. While disruptive in tone and style, he left his party's entire Fifth Party System ideology completely intact. What's more, he has intensified the polarization, the Red-Blue identity politics, the moral crusading, and the politics of culture war. He has further pushed Republican moderates and younger Americans toward the Democratic Party, while pulling populist Democrats toward the Republicans. He has embraced every trend destabilizing America's parties and then lit a match.

The conditions disrupting American politics are obviously much bigger than Trump. These forces have been at work for many years. Many of America's leaders have done their part to contribute to them. Trump's election was simply the most recent result of these long-running trends, not their cause. Nor is Trump the only figure exacerbating the situation. Leaders across politics have long encouraged these trends in the short-sighted short-term desire for tactical victories. This has been a joint effort across both parties for years. Nor has anyone else emerged to innovate and renew our parties as they have slowly broken down. In fact, we have all contributed to the decline. Short-term tactical political decisions only work because we collectively reward them. We the people create and reward the activists, the new movements, and the public climate that has led to the politics of this moment. This is not just on one leader, or even the entire political leadership class. It's on us all. Trump, those rallying around him, his opponents, and their supporters—none of them are seeking to innovate or build anything new. In our blinded short-term focus on the battles of the moment, we're all working together to burn everything down.

The present moment doesn't seem headed toward a national renewal like the Populist and Progressive Era. Neither does it look like the heady days of the New Deal. At the moment, it looks a lot like the last days of the Whigs. New issues are unsettling politics. New movements are forming and moving into the public arena. Politics is getting hotter, people are getting angrier, and old norms are falling away. An awakening is coursing through the nation's veins, charging activists with moral certainty and the will to destroy their enemies in the name of justice and morality. The president is encouraging disruption within America's old party coalitions that's pulling people out of the existing party alignment without actually providing a new ideology or agenda that could support a new one. At every level of politics, from the grass roots, through the political class, up to the highest office, everyone is recklessly working together to pull the old system down—and no one with sufficient influence is yet working on innovating or building something new that's capable of sustaining a new party system to replace it.

Americans are eagerly marching toward political disintegration like the Whigs. Party system collapses are, of course, completely unnecessary tragedies. We can, if we had the foresight and the will, reform our parties before our party system implodes. As of now, however, it appears there's little appetite for such transformation. Everyone is throwing gas into the flames and frolicking in the heat. When the collapse comes, what happens next won't be easy. With the old parties shattered, disorder will rush in. A new era of national turmoil will begin, and it may last years. Extreme movements and ambitious provocateurs with radical ideas are likely to rise. Political battles may get messy, constitutional crises could arise, and violence might even break out once more. It's impossible to know for sure what will follow, which is exactly the point. Anything could happen. Party collapses open the doors to whatever forces—good or malevolent—choose to push through. Whatever happens, things will surely get worse before they get better. Worse can last a long time. Our near-term future looks to be many hard years of instability and turmoil unless we quickly change our course. We have a choice. This is what we're choosing.

CHAPTER 17

WHAT HAPPENS NEXT

Imagine a world that divides humanity into two classes, Alphas and Betas. No one in this world has more social or political rights than anyone else and every citizen is equal before the law. However, the class to which you're assigned during your education determines your job, your salary, and your opportunities. Alphas do intellectual and managerial work—they're the leaders, the professors, the scientists, and the CEOs. They see their role as their society's guardians, obliged to use their superior educations and opportunities to guide society toward a better future. In return, they believe their hard work, extraordinary ability, and superior skill has earned them a right to a better lifestyle. Betas do hands-on work—manual labor, service jobs, and desk jobs that involve executing orders. Betas receive a modern education sufficient to become good workers, employees, and citizens, although without a detailed understanding of the fields in which they will never work, such as economics, science, history, or foreign policy. Betas live comfortably, although not as well as Alphas. Naturally, they resent the Alphas who give them orders and get things and opportunities Betas don't.

Every two years, this society elects a governing council. Council candidates court one of society's two natural voting blocs, the Alphas or the Betas. Alpha candidates prize efficiency, rational policy, progress, and good government to expand and create new opportunities. Beta candidates care most about fairness, focusing less on expanding opportunities and more on who gets what. As one might expect, elections get nasty. Alphas resent the "backward" Betas, secretly wondering why Betas even get to vote at all since the uninformed policies Betas support will inevitably break complex systems Betas don't understand. Betas think Alphas are soft, decadent, and greedy. For Betas, prosperity doesn't come from Alpha schemes but the fierce work of the Beta hands actually implementing what Alphas order. Betas fear Alpha plans for "good government" and "progress" will, in reality, entrench the wealth and status of Alphas, leaving Betas like them farther behind. Alphas don't understand Beta resentment, since they support policies meant to improve life for everybody. Betas don't understand Alpha priorities. As Betas see it, Alphas treat Betas as insignificant workers too ignorant to govern themselves, while the Alphas act morally superior for their "help."

To most Americans, this is an ugly society. Americans don't like distinctions of social class. They believe anyone, with a little hard work and luck, should be able to achieve their dreams. Instead of a world where everyone pulls together to design a fair system in which everyone can do well with luck and hard work, this is a world in which some hate others as they fight over scraps. Yet this ugly world that violates our deepest values is much like the one this realignment will create if we fail to prevent it.

HOW TO JUDGE A PARTY SYSTEM

You can't judge a party system based solely on whether one of its parties would govern the way you like. The American system is one of power sharing, checks, and balances. Neither party ever governs alone. No party wins all the time. While one party controls some branches of government, the other party controls others. Even when a party wins control of some branch of government, the other party still exerts influence in the minority. No party ever gets to fully govern the way it would like, and given the fierce backlash that would crash down on its head if it did cram through its agenda during a momentary opportunity, few parties would even try it if they could. The agenda of no single party ever controls what actually happens during a party system, but rather it's the clash *between* the competing agendas of the parties through an era's great debate that determines how an era ultimately turns out.

The great debate between its parties determines how America relates to the political issues of its era. It determines which issues become highly charged and partisan, and which become uncontroversial and depoliticized. It determines which issues become visible and prioritized, and which get neglected as "boring." It determines which issues fuse together because the people who care about them get grouped together in the same coalition, and which get arbitrarily separated because their advocates wind up on different teams. How America is divided determines which people find common ground because they're forced to cooperate and which people look for arbitrary reasons to disagree because they support opposing sides. It's how America gets divided into parties and the debate between them that determines how America is governed during a party system, what policies it implements, and what issues it resolves.

During the First Party System, America made national finance and foreign relations into national obsessions because those issues were now partisan under the terms of that era's great debate. During the Second Party System, issues like infrastructure spending, tariff rates, and a national bank became pitched ideological battles over which the nation obsessed, while important issues like slavery got ignored. In the Third Party System, America was divided between North and South, so issues like Reconstruction transfixed the nation. In the Fourth Party System, America was split over competing paths to modernization and reform, so ideas for economic and social reform burst to the front of the nation's consciousness. Today's Fifth Party System turned issues like taxes, regulation, and social welfare programs—policies that directly impact the size and power of the federal government—into highly charged and partisan issues that therefore gripped the nation. As Americans sorted themselves into "liberals" and "conservatives," they channeled their cultural and political passions through this lens.

Changing the composition of political coalitions changes the fault lines around which we organize everything. New alliances change the narratives and assumptions we take for granted. They make possible ideas that were formerly impossible given the cold hard political realities, while other ideas that were formerly possible now become impossible because of new party power dynamics. They change the issues we talk most about, since parties focus on issues over which everyone inside their tent agrees. They change the issues we neglect, since parties neglect issues about which members disagree. Where we draw the fault lines dividing America into its two great political coalitions impacts what we talk about, what we value, and even how we see ourselves throughout a historical era. How America's next political coalitions divide society will set the terms for our next great national debate. That debate will control how we talk about our problems, where we place our focus, which issues become polarized, and which issues we devalue and ignore. Those divisions will frame every political issue, as well as the obsessions of our culture, for decades. As we grapple with the problems of information-age America, the clash between our two political coalitions—whatever they turn out to be—will determine how we view those problems and how we go about discovering solutions.

The question is never just what new parties we think we might prefer, but rather what's the next great debate America needs. To properly evaluate the effectiveness of such a new debate, moreover, we have to understand the issues it will be debating. Only by examining the problems we as Americans face ahead, can we judge how a national debate over those issues might play out. America in fact faces a worrying list of pressing and neglected challenges. Depending on your personal politics and priorities, you likely have a list that keeps you up at night. Maybe you worry about the decline of American manufacturing, the outsourcing of jobs, the constant plague of underemployment, or the inability of a significant portion of Americans to find meaningful work. Maybe you worry about the sinking fortunes of the middle class. Maybe you worry about national security or Islamic terrorism or the potential threat of a rising power like China or threats to civil liberties. Maybe you worry about failures in America's healthcare delivery system or the complexities of the health insurance system or threats to medical innovation. Maybe you worry about the environment and the risk of global climate change. Maybe you worry about national economic policy or the ever-increasing debt. Maybe you worry about the scope of data and surveillance that new technology places into the hands of governments, corporations, and dangerous non-state actors. Maybe you worry about the flood of global migration, both refugees fleeing instability and economic migrants from dysfunctional areas seeking security and prosperity unavailable at home. Maybe it's something we can only glimpse much farther up ahead, like robots replacing so many jobs a significant portion of humanity becomes chronically unemployable, the coming birth of an artificial superintelligence, or the risk of a global pandemic. Or maybe it's something else. America faces serious challenges in almost every major area, some new and some that have been festering for years. It often seems as if the world we know is falling to pieces and no one has any idea what to do next.

Looking at each problem in isolation, it may seem America is suddenly beset with a swarm of completely unrelated issues. However, most of the looming problems frequently worrying us are in fact related tremors from just three large disruptions now shaking the world.

THE ISSUES OF THE FUTURE

America faces three powerful disruptions currently shaking its foundations that any new party system will have to somehow address. The first of these disruptions is the decline of the industrial era and America's transition toward a global information-based economy. The industrial era was a dream for America. The nation had available to it every ingredient necessary for industrial success—vast natural resources, a large population, and a political culture well suited to fostering large-scale industrial production. America found itself a respected global superpower and virtually the only modern industrial economy left standing after the devastation of the Second World War. With the right tools and limited competition, America became the economic engine of the world, inventing, designing, growing, and manufacturing for everybody around the globe. For decades, almost anyone in America from any background could, if they were willing to work hard and follow the rules, find a lifetime of stable work supporting a comfortable lifestyle with minimal risk. That produced a large and prosperous middle class that was, by world historical standards, extraordinarily rich. As it rose to unrivaled prosperity and global power, America constructed new institutions to govern this novel world. America over the twentieth century constructed a complex web of institutions to govern a country of urban industrial producers. America created regulatory agencies—a new concept not part of the nation's original constitutional design. It created executive organs like national security councils and domestic policy councils, while vastly expanding the scope of old ones like the Internal Revenue Service and the Federal Reserve System. It created Social Security, Medicare, social welfare programs, business regulation, labor rules, antidiscrimination laws, environmental rules, a new tax code, and more.

All the while, Americans reorganized their lives around the assumptions of the wage-earning and urban industrial world. They moved to the suburbs and bought cars to commute to industrial jobs in the cities. They set up 401Ks and insurance policies to protect them from the day they could no longer earn a wage. They had fewer children. Every institution of American society—in government, in private industry, and in the culture—was designed to help citizens thrive within America the industrial superpower. Society promised that, if you worked hard and played by the rules as it defined them, you might not get rich, and your life might have setbacks, but you would be okay. For most citizens, the system delivered on its promise of a life with a limited risk of ever confronting catastrophe, if not a good chance for a suburban house with two cars in the garage and a sufficient college fund left over. These assumptions, around which our entire society was built, remains for most Americans the baseline of what life in America is supposed to be like. However, this portrait of America no longer exists, except in our minds.

In the new information-age economy, firms no longer refine processes to cheaply mass produce good-enough results. They analyze the flood of data around us to quickly serve smaller groups exactly what they want. This new economic order is more dynamic and disruptive. Incumbent giants crumble, while new firms pop up from nowhere to become new giants. Firms of any size, located anywhere, can compete on nearly equal terms with the largest firms of the largest nations. The working and middle class is under increasing pressure in this new economy. Two college-educated workers today can often barely support a contemporary middle-class lifestyle, when not so long ago one high-school educated worker could thrive. Industrial-era stability is gone.

These changes to our society's structure are also changing how we live—in marriage, child rearing, healthcare, education, and leisure expectations. Social media is changing how people communicate, and even changing the nature of relationships. We're weaving new technologies like smart phones, tablets, and virtual home assistants into the way we live, even into the most private areas of our lives. Richer Americans are moving back into the urban core, while the suburbs are getting poorer. Car ownership is in decline among younger Americans. Childrearing has become more supervised. People are more concerned about what they eat. Social tolerance has become a core value, and formerly marginalized groups are entering the mainstream. These are just the first rumblings of the unpredictable changes that will inevitably come as the global information economy takes further hold. We're only at the beginning of the transition, a moment somewhat like when the people of the late nineteenth century watched railroads and factories springing up around their family farms.

The shift from the industrial to the postindustrial economy is as significant and disruptive as was the shift from an agricultural economy to an industrial, and ultimately no one yet knows how this massive shift will pan out. For some, it will provide new opportunities. Great fortunes will be made. For others, it will be a traumatic disruption from which they may never fully recover. Moreover, with the economic model and the temporary conditions that produced mass prosperity gone, America—while still a rich country—may not be as comparatively rich in the postindustrial age as it was during the industrial. It's possible this new economy may not continue to support the mass prosperity we've come to believe is "normal," with a comfortable middle-class suburban existence in reach of most Americans. For many Americans, the path to success in the new economy also may be less stable and more uncertain. Instead of finding a job with a stable firm and climbing its ladder, Americans are now encouraged to embrace risk, actively manage their careers, switch jobs often, and court disruption. No one expects to stay at one firm for thirty years, nor does anyone expect employers to reward such loyalty. In today's economy, it's understood that some people work hard and do good work but still get downsized. Labor markets are global. Smart people with internet connections from poor nations often can do a comparable job for less. In this new economic world, no one really knows what the rules to a stable and prosperous life will turn out to be. The only thing we know for certain is that the industrial-era economic and social model appears to be dead and new rules are in the making. The increase in economic inequality and the decline of the American middle class may not be temporary artifacts from recent events. They may be the start of a permanent adjustment toward a more historical version of what's "normal."

The first big challenge for the parties of America's next party system will be to usher the nation through this profound transformation. Systems that worked in the industrial world won't all continue to work in the very different postindustrial world. Significant economic transformations and technological transformations always bring cultural transformations, so as people work differently, and as the world works differently, people will live differently. In this new era, people will move to different places, buy different sorts of houses, and structure different sorts of families to support the new ways in which they earn their living. As new technologies embed themselves in our lives, they inevitably alter power dynamics—changing how people relate to each other, how they relate to institutions, and how they relate to government. Industrialization strengthened the state, giving it better tools to manage the economy and society while also increasing its scope and responsibilities. Postindustrial-era technology will have similar effects, whether through self-driving cars, powerful artificial intelligences, social media, automated drones, or technologies we still can't imagine. Just as people did during the industrial transition of the late nineteenth century, many Americans who worked hard and played by the old rules will increasingly find those rules no longer work. Our parties will have to manage the nation's transition to this new era, ensuring people understand the new rules and that playing by them works again. That will mean rethinking every national institution built around the assumptions of industrial-age life. Every program, law, regulation, and agency built around dead assumptions will have to be overhauled or replaced with new ones custom built to create success in the new reality of American economic, social, and cultural life.

A second challenge relates to the first, what some in the liberal-democratic West might call "the rise of the rest of the world." At the end of the Second World War, the world was organized around two great ideological alliances. America led the liberal-democratic nations of "the West" as they faced off against the communist bloc of the Warsaw Pact and "the East." The rest of the planet, from India to Asia, Africa, and Latin America, became pawns of those two great power blocs. As the strongest nation and the leader of the richer alliance, America became a military and economic superpower, with nations around the world, who believed American strength contributed to their safety and success, tacitly working to support it. Nations across the globe that once depended on American strength for their own security and prosperity no longer do. America remains the most powerful nation on the earth, but its economy no longer dominates the way it did during the postwar boom when every other industrial nation was either devastated by war, locked behind an Iron Curtain, or relegated to the status of postcolonial "third world." Countries like India, China, and Brazil, with immense resources in both raw materials and human capital, once pawns in a great power struggle, are now global leaders. American allies across the liberal-democratic West remain allies, but independent ones aware of where their values and American interests conflict. Many nations have even come to resent America and would like to see its influence and power weaken. Russia and China have become true rivals seeking to challenge America economically, militarily, and geostrategically, and they will exert power in the following decades with unknown intent. Older ideas like nationalism and religion have risen again to the top of the international agenda. Technology has enabled radical groups, multinational corporations, and popular movements to play roles that once only nation states could play. The world is more unpredictable than it was and less accepting of American power.

Every aspect of the global leadership America has come to take for granted—its currency as the world currency, its language as the world language, its movies and music as world entertainment, and its priorities becoming world priorities—is now open to challenge. There's no reason to think America will abandon its position as the most powerful nation in the world anytime soon. At the same time, powerful nations and non-state actors hope to knock her off her pedestal economically and as a global power. Some in America are eager to see America's role in the world retract, whether due to its cost or from a sense of morality. America's power and global influence, however, contributed to America's relative wealth during the twentieth century. It opened markets to America's products; provided a comparative advantage to American firms; spread English as an international language; enshrined the dollar as a global currency; allowed America to construct and police international agreements and norms designed to benefit America; and spread American culture, providing markets for American cultural exports. America's relative decline in global status, whether by geostrategic change or the design of its competitors, could bring about a corresponding decline in its wealth and prosperity—and a decline in its citizens' standard of living with it, bringing the American middle class closer to the living standards of a "normal" country without the superpower privileges Americans didn't even know they were enjoying.

A third problem relates to the first two—the legacy of the current institutions in place. Almost every government institution, program, and regulatory scheme in America was created specifically for the modern industrial economy at a time when American government was relatively small. Before the New Deal, America didn't have a large regulatory apparatus, didn't have much in the way of administrative agencies, and didn't have large and expensive programs like Social Security and Medicare to administer. The New Deal's architects only had to design institutions to usher America into a new economic age. As we seek to design new policies and programs today, we're no longer essentially working from scratch. The government programs and institutions America has created since the New Deal are now deeply embedded into society. People depend on them, building their lives around the expectation that they exist. We therefore have to design any new policies and institutions necessary for success during the next age while still burdened with the costs and needs of the existing ones.

Everyone in America knows that the government for decades has spent far more than it raises in taxes. The specific numbers jump about from year to year based on tax receipts and interest rates, but for decades the government programs and services Americans demand have simply cost far more than Americans are able or willing to pay in taxes, so year after year the government borrows the difference and adds it to the national debt. Our national debt is currently, at the time of this writing, a little over $21 trillion.[1] (A trillion dollars is a lot of money, even for the United States government. A million seconds is 12 days. A trillion seconds is 31,709 years.) In fiscal year 2017, America spent about $4 trillion and only took in $3.4 trillion in revenue, leaving a deficit of about $665 billion.[2] In fiscal year 2018, it's estimated that the deficit will be about $833 billion.[3] While politicians like to pretend we can someday balance this budget by simply cutting out "waste, fraud, and abuse," we can't—and not because there's no waste or abuse in government. Roughly 45 percent of our national budget is just Social Security, Medicare, and Medicaid—politically untouchable. Roughly 15 percent is defense. Somewhere around 6 percent is the interest payments on our existing debt. Just to stop borrowing more we would have to cut about half or more of everything else the government does—the courts, the FBI, the FDA, the EPA, the CIA, and the rest—which is far more than any amount of inefficiency and waste we'll ever find. No one in Washington really talks about paying down the debt America already has because realistically it can't ever generate the surplus necessary to pay down $21 trillion with $3.3 trillion in revenue and trillions in non-negotiable costs. The problem is utterly unsolvable mathematically without reforms so dramatic they will devastate people and the economy, which nobody wants. Not all economists believe America's national debt is a problem so long as the government can always afford its interest payments. Others find America's deficits and debt of grave concern, since if the interest on borrowing were to suddenly and sufficiently spike because people across the world stopped wanting to buy American government securities, or due to American political instability, or for some other reason, the American government and economy would tumble into a severe crisis.[4] Regardless of which you believe, the situation unquestionably makes our transition into the next age far more difficult. America must somehow reform its institutions to adapt to the era ahead, while it already can't really afford the government it already has at a tax rate it's willing to pay.

America is moving into a new era with staggering legacy costs from legacy institutions. To build anything new, the next era's architects have to work around their predecessors' efforts, a government that already consumes every available resource. Nor is it simply the cost. It's impossible to build anything fresh without taking into account all the laws, programs, and regulations that already exist and on which people have invested expectations. It's difficult, and frequently impossible, to change such powerful, vast, and entrenched programs and institutions without severely disrupting the expectations and plans of innocent people who now depend on them. Unlike the world Roosevelt's brain trust faced, reformers today can't build or create anything from scratch thinking solely about the needs of the moment. Before we can adapt our institutions for tomorrow, we first have to wrestle with the web of what we already created to address the world of yesterday.

When you evaluate potential political parties for tomorrow, you have to do it in the context of these three issues—the end of the industrial economy, the rise of the rest of the world, and the legacy costs of our existing institutions. You have to consider how those parties would manage a nation with battered middle and working classes confronting significant disruption in their expectations, the need to navigate great social and economic change, vast difficulties matching fiscal reality to priorities, and new competitors rising all around with deep interests in reversing America's dominance. These same three challenges will play out over countless other issues—employment and the economy, aging national infrastructure, increasing environmental concerns and the threat of climate change, clashes of interest with other global powers, threats of terrorism, policy affecting immigration, and an often-inadequate education system, among many more. America can no doubt succeed in navigating this daunting situation, but if it bungles the task it could also damage the country, plunging Americans into difficult times.

THE NEW COALITIONS WE DON'T WANT

Disruptive realignments are, of course, unpredictable. When the seals of society fall off, no one can say for sure what will rush through. Yet standing on the cold eve of a realignment, we have a pretty good idea— if nothing else intervenes—what's likely to happen next. We can't yet know, of course, how exactly the next realignment will arrive. No one ever knows until just before it happens. The next realignment might come after a punishing election, or a third-party campaign, or the walkout of factions from one of our existing parties. It might come through a disruptive leader, or an external shock, or an unanticipated economic crash that plunges America into agony and takes the old parties down. Or it could be something else. The specifics of the collapse, however, don't much matter. Whatever course of events sees the old party system crumble, we already have a fair idea of where that path inevitably will lead. If we simply look at what people are doing and where their interests lie, we can fairly deduce—if no one intervenes to alter the course—what, in the wake of the next party collapse, will likely follow next.

When America's parties finally break, their constituent factions, the principles and ideas they draw on, the people who vote for them, and the interest groups that support them, will all continue to exist. America may no longer be a country of conservatives and liberals working through our familiar Republican and Democratic Parties, but it will still be a nation of Americans who care about the same issues as before. America will still have Northerners, Southerners, urban dwellers, suburbanites, and rural communities. It will still have citizens who identify as different races, ethnicities, and religions. It will still be a nation of office workers, farmers, factory workers, service workers, computer programmers, and professionals. Most important, it will still be a country with populists, progressives, liberty conservatives, and virtue conservatives. The fall of a political party doesn't destroy its political principles or permanently silence the people who believe them. The only things that change when parties break are America's political alliances. The people who work together on each side of the political divide will no longer work together as allies and the ideologies that bound them will dissolve.

When faced with the problems of 1932, America's coalitions grouped together people who shared common interests, concerns, and perspectives. New Deal liberalism offered working-class populists—mainly working people, often rural, many Southern, who traditionally supported Democrats—material benefits to protect them from ruin along with the dignity and power they craved against prevailing Republican elites. It offered progressives—mainly educated, cosmopolitan, middle or upper-class professionals, often urban, many from the Northeast, who traditionally supported Republicans—a framework to employ the expertise and social science they valued to design better national institutions to combat the crisis. The coalition of ideological conservatism also made great sense in the middle of the twentieth century. Liberty conservatives were worried about the New Deal's increase in the power of the American state. Virtue conservatives worried the New Deal would erode the culture and character necessary for the republic to thrive. Sharing a common interest, their alliance was practical and sensible. Yet given the issues and demographic situation today, these coalitions no longer make sense in the same way.

Were America's parties to break, leaving each faction at play in America's current party system—populists, progressives, liberty conservatives, and virtue conservatives—free to form new alliances, it would be more logical today for virtue conservatives to form a political alliance with populists. Populists and virtue conservatives thrive within the same communities—mainly rural, suburban, and "Red State" America. Both are suspicious of elites—the financiers, professionals, Hollywood celebrities, academics, C-suite occupants, and meritocrats eager to move America into new global economy and leaving many working Americans behind. Most important, they each worry about the same postindustrial changes, economic and cultural, that disproportionately harm people like them. Populist resentment at elites and virtue conservative notions of protecting culture increasingly lead to the same place. While yesterday's populists had no reason to trust cautious and elitist Burkean virtue conservatives worried about maintaining stability, today's virtue conservatives are more likely to be revivalists following the virtue of national reform who don't see America's elites as guardians of the traditional order but threats to it leading the nation into decline. It makes sense today for virtue conservatives and populists to unite around their shared anger at elites over disruptive information-age economic and social change and a desire to restore traditional American virtue to preserve the republic.

It's also more logical today for liberty conservatives to forge an alliance with progressives. Demographically, liberty conservatives increasingly come from similar cultural backgrounds as progressives—highly educated suburban and urban professionals from the upper-middle class and economic elite who are "economically conservative and socially moderate." They live in similar communities, share common backgrounds and cultural tastes, and are similarly positioned to take advantage of the opportunities this emerging world provides. Most important, liberty conservatives and progressives share a common approach to the disruption of the postindustrial era—they embrace it. During the New Deal era, liberty conservatives and progressives were natural enemies. Progressives wanted to tame and control the industrial economy to help the working class, while liberty conservatives saw such elite-driven social planning as a dangerous infringement on liberty. Today's progressives, however, are less interested in governing through top-down planning and regulation and more comfortable with market-based approaches that manage incentives and conflict less with liberty. It makes sense today for liberty conservatives and progressives to unite around their mutual belief that, with modernization, rational policy, and good-government efficiency, America can continue to prosper in the emerging globalized world.

These new alliances would provide the foundation for two new political coalitions, each with its own new ideology. A coalition of virtue conservatives and populists would rally under a banner of reversing the nation's rush toward the global postindustrial world. Its ideology would be dedicated to preserving the nation's virtues for the benefit of ordinary Americans. It would cherish the values of traditional America—patriotism, hard work, Judeo-Christian values, and traditional cultural conservatism—and fight against the power of both economic and cultural "elites" pushing changes harmful to the "people." It would celebrate the virtue of ordinary working people. It would denigrate "out-of-touch elites" living in rich communities as dangerous "others" more loyal to the global elite than working America. It would launch populist attacks against college professors, ivy league schools, and residents of upscale neighborhoods in "creative class" cities, but also against CEOs, hedge fund managers, and venture capitalists benefiting from the changing economy while "the people" do worse.

A coalition of progressives and liberty conservatives would unite under the banner of advancing human progress. It would draw on the progressive impulse to employ planning and expertise to create the conditions necessary for national progress. It would seek to help working people but not to empower them. It would hope instead to improve them through education and cultural change to nudge them into becoming more like the professional and upper classes. It wouldn't worry about the power of "the corporations" or "the rich" so long as some of the excess could be redistributed to those in need and general conditions improved. It wouldn't view the world through the lens of nationalism but multinationalism, hoping to integrate the American economy into global opportunities while viewing it as a moral duty to assist non-Americans in need equally to Americans. It would be a party that was technocratic and meritocratic looking something like "Third Way" neoliberalism, something like moderate libertarianism, and something like the ethos of Silicon Valley. It wouldn't worry about elites but seek to harness expertise and elite power for the benefit of the human race at large.

America's leaders have in fact been reaching out toward these new coalitions for some time. Republican Party leaders have long reached toward this sort of populist-virtue fusion. Republican pollsters and consultants regularly propose the party concentrate on an agenda offering more to working Americans—now a significant part of the party's base—and throw off its image as the party of the rich. Populist-leaning Republicans often demand the Republican Party divorce Wall Street and the Chamber of Commerce, while business Republican groups openly gripe about the party's populist direction. Fusing virtue conservatism with populism is at the heart of the war against the Republican "establishment." It's the idea behind Republicans courting "Sam's Club voters." It's the coalition behind much of culture-war conservativism that has long imported populist themes into the Republican Party while marginalizing liberty-conservative "moderates." It's the coalition lurking behind Donald Trump's populist Republican pledge to "Make America Great Again." Democrats have similarly reached toward a technocratic liberalism seeking not to empower poor and working people but to instead improve them. For years, Democratic party leaders have embraced business-friendly "neoliberal" progressivism that fuses liberty with progressivism divorced from traditional Democratic populism. Wealthy national elites that in a prior era would have been natural business-class Republicans—Silicon Valley moguls, Wall Street bankers, and powerful CEOS—have drifted toward the Democrats. Democrats increasingly include not just the nation's cultural elites but also its economic elites, supporting policies that advance and support the integration of the multinational economy. At the same time, it's been years since Democrats truly sought to actually empower and represent traditional Democratic populists.

While the liberty and virtue coalition currently appears quite certain, some evidence, however, suggests the progressive and liberty coalition could also go in a slightly different direction. Over the last few years, momentum has built in parts of America behind a movement with a conception of equality often called equity or social justice—whose supporters are sometimes derided as "Social Justice Warriors. It holds the chief sin of modern America is the privilege it unfairly grants certain groups at others' expense—women, racial minorities, immigrants, sexual minorities, and others. This zealous and egalitarian movement believes it has a duty to overturn the current hierarchies of power in American society, either to abolish or to reverse them. Presently, this movement is mainly considered a modern adaptation of the moral progressivism that has played an important role in American politics for decades. It's not yet clear, however, whether this truly is the case, or whether this equity movement—with its new moral claims, emphasis on identity, and even hints of economic socialism—isn't perhaps a new movement introducing novel principles and ideas into America's politics. Nor is it even clear whether the movement's adherents know themselves, or whether the movement might in fact consist of two separate ideological factions, progressivism and equity, working on a common project but with beliefs grounded in different ideals.

While it's too early to know for sure what the equity movement will mean, and therefore which partners it might seek out in the next era, if it turns out it represents new principles, America's second coalition would likely be different. The strong egalitarian ethic of the equity movement would naturally interest it in radical projects to alter what it believes are unfair structures of power, making liberty—unwilling to tolerate the more intrusive state interventions necessary to create such cultural transformation—an unwilling partner. Equity's moral worldview would make true populists impossible partners as well. It would thus likely find itself in an alliance with progressivism—leaving liberty conservatives without a dedicated party and forced to join one of the other parties around secondary principles in which they believed. While an equity and progressivism party would follow a different ideology and propose different solutions than a liberty-progressive party, it would nevertheless look demographically similar. It would still attract the middle and upper classes and the meritocracy. It would still believe in technocracy, embracing the global economic and cultural change of postindustrialism and seeking to integrate America into the multinational world. It would still seek to uplift and benefit not just Americans but also the poor and struggling across the world. Despite the sometimes harsh rhetoric equity and progressivism both sometimes direct at the wealthy and corporations, it would also most naturally draw a distinction between the immoral wealth of the few, of the corporations and billionaires, and the moral and earned wealth of the meritocracy—exactly as prosperous turn-of-the-century progressives who railed at the trusts and John Rockefeller also once did. It would, in other words, still be a party with a vision to benefit all society but mainly appealing to cultural and economic elites. While ideologically different than a liberty and progressivism party—one focused more on systems of power and identity—it would ultimately attract the same types of people and have a similar perspective on the problems we currently face.

Shuffling America's ideological factions in this way, into a virtue-populism coalition and either a liberty-progressivism or progressivism-equity one, would lead to some unfamiliar combinations that unsettle expectations. An alliance between virtue and populism, for example, would mean virtue conservatives who classically opposed "big government" supporting economic populism. There's no reason, however, why the sorts of virtue conservatives who support a strong government protecting cultural values and warning against the government touching their Medicare couldn't be convinced to support an economic agenda that benefited virtuous working people at the expense of immoral elites. An alliance between virtue and populism might put Southern evangelicals into an alliance with factions like organized labor and poor urban minorities. Given historical anger and hard feelings, that at first seems unlikely—except the same could be said of African Americans joining the Party of Dixie in 1928. America has a long history of uniting political coalitions with histories of distrust when their interests later aligned. An alliance of liberty conservatives and progressives would put western don't-tread-on-me libertarians inside the same party as social reformers seeking to harness government. One can, however, pursue progressive goals like a safe and fair society, clean environment, and social tolerance through bottom-up market-based reforms instead of top-down ones.

What's most striking is the political map these new coalitions would create. Dividing America into a virtue-populist and a liberty-progressive or progressive-equity party would roughly recreate America's political arrangement during the Third and Fourth Party Systems. The virtue and populist political party would do well in rural areas, small towns, industrial areas, urban cores, and the South. Its base would be the South and the rust belt, and socioeconomically it would be the party of the poor and working class. The liberty and progressive party, or alternatively the progressive and equity party, would dominate the suburbs and exurbs. Its base would be on the coasts, the West, and the North. It would socioeconomically be the party of business, professionals, white-collar America, the upper half of the middle class, and the "meritocracy." It would effectively recreate the political map of the pre–New Deal era. The virtue-populist party would win states Democrats used to win. The liberty-progressive or progressive-equity party would win states Republicans used to win. These arrangements aren't only possible, they're well-tested. Far from creating something novel, this realignment would restore a political order that ruled America just outside our personal memories.

For most of American history prior to our era, it was the wealthy and educated—not the working classes—who supported progressive modernizing policies. Wealthy businessmen and social reformers drew from the same demographics and supported the same political party, the "pro-business" Federalists, Whigs, or pre–New Deal Republicans, who attracted support from the wealthy, professionals, and the upper classes. At the same time, it was the working classes and new immigrants who usually supported populist parties of social traditionalism that opposed modernizing plans. The Democratic-Republicans, Jacksonian Democrats, and Bryan Democrats were all deeply suspicious of banks, business, and the aristocratic pretensions of wealth. They had little faith in the plans of the elites, suspecting them to be Trojan horses intended to subvert America's republican values to better profit off their backs. Having demographically rearranged its political coalitions to address the industrial age, America may be falling back into old habits now that those industrial-era problems have faded.

The new party system these new coalitions would create would actually be positioned to address the new problems America faces. Unfortunately, if you match the specific problems we face over the coming years against the ideologies and interests of the new coalitions that appear to be taking shape, something disturbing jumps out. They divide America not around clashing ideas but zero-sum battles for spoils. They set the stage for a bitter and angry era obsessed over fighting who in America deserves more rather than how we might best strengthen it together. At a dangerous moment in history, the political coalitions that seem likely to emerge are a recipe for acrimony, conflict, failure, and national decline. Whatever you think of the national parties today, these parties would be worse. We should stop this new party system from forming while we can.

THESE ARE THE WRONG PARTIES FOR AMERICA

For everything that's wrong with our existing political coalitions, at least they're organized around ideas—"conservatism" versus "liberalism." Some people claim our current parties are principally divided on wealth and class, but that's never actually been the truth. Republicans draw both from wealthy investors and working- and middle-class traditionalists, while Democrats draw both from economic populists and socially advantaged progressives. What actually divides America's parties today isn't class or wealth but ideology. Both parties take for granted that the purpose of politics is to help every American live in a better, richer, freer, and safer nation. They simply disagree about what that means, and how to best go about achieving it. Democrats prefer to empower government to shape America into their version of a better future. Republicans want to empower people to decide for themselves how to get us to that better future. Even when acting parochially, and whether or not it's always carried out in practice, at least both parties justify and think about their ideas in terms of what will make the nation better for everyone.

This new party system that appears ready to emerge would exchange a politics of clashing ideas for one of clashing interests. It would concentrate those who benefit most from the information-age economy into one party while concentrating working-class and poorer Americans who benefit least into another. The virtue and populism party would represent the working class and those most displaced in the global economy. It would be a party of anti-elitism, disproportionately representing those most harmed by disruptive economic and social change. Its opponent would be considered the party of the economic and cultural elite. It would disproportionately represent people benefiting from disruptive economic and social change.

These new political coalitions would almost certainly respond to our challenges in predictable and troubling ways. The party that welcomed postindustrial changes would naturally focus on integrating America's elite into the new opportunities of the global economy. Its instinct would be to manage the relative decline of the United States so America's elite would continue to harness global opportunities to generate global wealth—not ensuring middle- and working-class Americans retain their relative prosperity to the global middle class. Its perspective would be postnational, viewing the world as one great community and questioning whether it's even appropriate to wield state power to advantage American workers over the poor citizens of other nations. Its opponent, fearing postindustrial changes, would naturally focus on economic and social resentment. In a fruitless attempt to preserve a fading position, it would lash out at change while targeting those it perceived as unfairly flourishing. Its instinct would be to wall America off from the world to stop the inevitable. Each coalition would be trying to preserve what's best for its team without concern for the other. One coalition would be looking out for the mobile global economic class and the other for the less-mobile economically disrupted. Politics under these new parties would no longer be about what we believe but who we're for. Debates would no longer be about methods of governing but whether our politicians can deliver an agenda for *us* against *them*. It's about our group getting ours and your group not taking yours. It's zero-sum politics pitting half of America against the other half. It would be a very ugly era for America.

America has frequently experienced outbursts of class politics, which in part is why populism has long played a role in American party politics. America has also lived through various incarnations of identity politics, whether urban versus rural, Northern versus Southern, Eastern versus Western, immigrant versus "native," or other categories, such as gender or race. America's parties during the Populist and Progressive Era, although divided around ideology, also roughly divided Americans based on prosperity and class, unleashing exactly the sorts of ugliness, anger, identity politics, and corruption one would expect. These fights however always took place in the background of booming long-term national prosperity, in which new groups could claim new opportunities and resources without anyone losing out. They fought over how to fairly divide a growing national pie, how best to manage an economic system of exploding opportunity and complexity, and how best to leverage increasing national wealth and power in the world. In a world in which prosperity is no longer growing so quickly—in which for one group to gain another group has to lose more—the effect of this style of politics will be far worse.

This realignment is a recipe for destructive policies on countless issues, including trade, immigration, taxes, cultural differences, not to mention countless unknown issues with which we will have to struggle as we adapt to a fast-developing future. One party would fight for policies benefiting the elite economy without regard to its impact on the working and rural people whom they considered backward. The other party would punish elites they believed had stolen their prosperity and dignity with rigged systems and elite-driven policies. One party would patronize, dismiss, and seek to reeducate those they believed ignorant. Another would rage and resent those they believed criminal and out-of-touch. Each party would be inclined to fight for policies that made their constituents better off at the expense of the Americans they didn't represent—that they saw not simply as opponents but as enemies. This zero-sum debate over resentments and spoils dangerously escalates the stakes of our disagreements. In this hypothetical era, every opportunity would have to come at the expense of a rival and every lost election would become a personal tragedy. In this new politics, losing an election wouldn't just mean new policies that violate your values. It would mean your enemies stripping away your means to live—threatening your savings, job, home, and opportunities for your children.

Such a realignment would be a recipe for corruption as the party in power rewarded its own while punishing rivals. It's a recipe for unfairness, with the wealthy seeking to protect their wealth and treating the lower and middle classes as tragic reclamation projects. It's a recipe for protected elites and national decline, as those who are thriving have no reason to care about the fates of those who aren't. It's a recipe for contempt, as each half of America gains hard reasons to hate and fear the other. It's a recipe for drastic

Gilded-Age level inequality, as no one would be looking out for what's best for everyone, only what's best for their own. It's a recipe for creeping authoritarianism, as parties wield power carelessly and tyrannically to coerce and punish those whom they resent and fear. Most worrying, it's a recipe for staggering instability. Losing an election would impose an intolerable cost—allowing those who resent you to strip away resources, opportunities, and the means to your family's future. It would mean standing aside so that people who hate you could hurt you. It's a political world seeming to require any action, no matter how radical, to seize and maintain power to avoid the punishing cost of losing to your enemies.

This is not a realignment we want. No one wants to live in a country like this. It's against every American's hopes and dreams. We don't want a zero-sum class-based politics. We don't want public officials to wield power corruptly, rewarding friends and crushing enemies. We don't want parties driving up further inequality, encouraging political tribalism, or engaging in an aggressive tit-for-tat for power that gradually erodes democratic norms until the safeguards of the republic crumble. What everybody wants is a national political debate that seeks the solutions that are best for everybody. We want parties and a government that treat us all with dignity. We want public officials who wield power carefully and with the interests of everyone always in mind, even those who voted against them. This realignment is a potential disaster for America.

We can choose a better future if we want it. Instead of allowing the winds of history to tear our party coalitions apart, we can harness those winds for a national renewal.

REBUILDING A BETTER PARTY SYSTEM FOR AMERICA

If we simply wait for America's existing party system to collapse, we have a good idea what happens next. At first, America will fall into a period of political instability and chaos. America's factions and interests, thrown cold into the wild, will wander blindly through the Fifth Party System's rubble for a time looking for new alliances to build new majorities. Eventually, they will form new coalitions out of the wreckage, but those coalitions will likely be ones we don't want. They'll divide us in destructive ways, leading America into a difficult and angry new era of zero-sum politics. We can do better. We can create our own new party system, reshaping politics by choice into a new alignment we like. We can launch a political renewal instead. To do it, we simply have to choose a new great debate that addresses the issues Americans now want and need addressed. From there, we can rebuild new parties prepared to actually discover solutions to our problems, unleashing a fresh era of national reform. The key is to define the message.

Not all parties are the same because not everybody joins a political party for the same reason. Sometimes people band together into a party because they share a similar vision for the future. They may disagree about many things, but they stand united in their desire to see a particular dream achieved. Other times people join a political party because they share a common fear. Their members may also disagree about other things, but they're committed to fighting against this mutual threat. When people unite around a common vision, they create an agenda party—a group of people united around a shared agenda. When they unite around a common threat, they create an opposition party—a group of people united to fight against a mutual danger. What separates an agenda party from an opposition party isn't whether the party promotes an agenda or opposes one, but which of the two is the thing that unites its members. Every political party has policy white papers on countless issues, hundreds of programs they'd like enacted, regulations they'd like changed, programs they'd like funded, and issues they'd like addressed. Every party hopes to stop the agenda of their opponents. The difference between an agenda party and an opposition party is which of the two came first—whether the agenda built the party, with the opposition following from it, or whether the opposition built the party, with the agenda following from it. The Fifth Party System Democratic Party is an agenda party. The Republican Party is an opposition party.

Most party systems begin with an agenda party proposing a new and disruptive program. In response, those alarmed with that program either unite into an opposition party to stop that agenda, or they create their own rival agenda party presenting America with an alternative program. The Federalists and the Democratic-Republicans were both agenda parties united around the clashing visions of Hamilton and Jefferson respectively. Andrew Jackson's Democrats were an agenda party united around Andrew Jackson's vision of Jacksonian Democracy, but the Whigs were an opposition party united around a shared distrust of the other party's agenda. The Whigs had beliefs and a strong agenda, including the supremacy of Congress, support for a national infrastructure plan, and opposition to wars of expansion, but what really united the fractious Whigs was a deep distrust for "King Andrew" Jackson. Lincoln's Republicans were an agenda party united around the Republican anti-slavery agenda and the ideal of the sanctity of every man's labor. The Civil War Democrats were an opposition party united around shared anger over the Republican program and Republican Party domination after the war. The Civil War Democrats had a clear agenda of fighting Reconstruction, opposing tariffs, and deference to state authority, but what really united Democrats was opposition to the Republican Party and its vision for America. Bryan's Democrats and Theodore Roosevelt's Republicans were both agenda parties battling over clashing visions of populism and progressive modernization.

The Fifth Party System Democrats are a classic agenda party. Democrats disagree on many things, but since the 1930s the one thing common to every Democrat is support for the ideology of the New Deal—the idea that experts, given the right resources, can design a better America that serves working people and the least well off. Modern Democrats oppose the policies and programs of the Republican Party—a party with ideals that stand in direct opposition to the Democratic agenda—but the Democratic Party wasn't designed to stop Republicans. It was designed to promote New Deal liberalism. The Republican Party, on the other hand, is a classic opposition party. It's a collection of people united to fight a common threat, New Deal liberalism. Republicans have always had a long list of policies they hoped to implement, whether revising tax codes, unwinding regulation, reforming entitlement programs, limiting abortion, preserving the traditional definition of marriage, strengthening defense programs, restructuring welfare, tightening crime controls, or encouraging charter schools. Yet these items didn't create the Republican Party, and they're not what really unites Republicans. Republicans are united around a shared conviction that New Deal liberalism is harmful and thus the Democratic Party must be stopped. Many Republican policy ideas, in fact, are just plans to undo things post–New Deal Democrats have already done.

To launch the next great debate, someone has to create a new agenda party. They need to unite half of America around a new compelling agenda to address the problems ahead. To do that, they need to build a party ideology distilled into a message—a sentence explaining how the party's principles and ideas will create a better future. The raw principles that make up party ideologies are unspecific, and there's always disagreement about how to apply them at any specific time and place. The ideas that make up a party's agenda—all the rules and regulations, programs and plans, budgets and legislative bills that are specific plans for government—are messy and complex in their specificity. A message is the link explaining how the party intends to turn its principles and ideology into tangible plans for change. In the language of corporate marketing, a party's message is its "brand," summing up how the party's beliefs and agenda will actually improve people's lives. During the Fifth Party System, the Democratic Party message was that Democrats would deliver mass prosperity and national progress through the New Deal's expert-led social planning and reforms. The Republican Party's message was that Republicans would defeat this New Deal style "big government," defending and preserving America's traditional liberties and its virtue. In one easy-to-understand sentence, these messages linked the principles each party supported to the agendas of ideas they proposed.

A successful party message has to offer a positive vision about the future that inspires people. To bind people together in a joint enterprise, you have to give them something honest in which to believe. Americans are a can-do people, a nation of pioneers and entrepreneurs. Americans carved a modern nation out of untouched wildness. They invented the electric lightbulb, the airplane, the automobile, rock and roll music, and the Hollywood blockbuster. They built a rocket ship, fired it off into space, and sent people to hit a golf ball on the surface of the moon. It's in the American character to believe there's no problem we can't solve with hard work and ingenuity. A successful party message in America can't just rage at enemies and voice resentments. You can win some elections by preying on people's cynicism, offering the right incentives, or bashing your opponents as worse than you are. People might vote for you without believing in you, but they won't join you. Nor can a successful party just buy off constituencies with a random hodge-podge of policies and issue papers. It has to offer a narrative explaining how all those policies and issue positions contribute to something larger and more important. It has to demonstrate that the party recognizes the nation's problems, has identified their cause, and has real plans to address them.

It isn't difficult to discover the right message for our current moment in history. We know the issues Americans care about, and we know their worries and their fears. They worry about declining opportunity. They're battered from all quarters by change. They fear the nation is declining. They think unfair barriers are erected in certain people's way. They have a sinking feeling that working hard and playing by rules will no longer be rewarded, because the rules have changed but nobody told them. They worry there are people who control their fate who aren't looking out for them, and who don't even like them. They think corruptions and dishonesties have overwhelmed the system at every level and they no longer have a fair chance. These, and nearly all the other worries seeping into politics, all come down to different variations of the same concern: Americans fear the American Dream is vanishing.

As we move into the Sixth Party System, that's the most compelling message around which we can build new parties. We should renew America's parties around restoring, defending, and protecting the promise of the American Dream.

CHAPTER 18

THE PARTY OF THE AMERICAN DREAM

So, then, to every man his chance—to every man, regard-
less of his birth, his shining, golden opportunity—to every
man the right to live, to work, to be himself, and to become
whatever thing his manhood and his vision can combine to
make him—this, seeker, is the promise of America.
　　　　　—Thomas Wolfe, *You Can't Go Home Again*

In 1931, the historian James Truslow Adams invented one of the most powerful phrases in America's history. In his best-selling history *The Epic of America*—a sweeping narrative explaining how America's history made it unique among nations—Adams wrote of "The American Dream." As he wrote:

> But there has been also the *American dream*, that dream of a land in which life should be better and richer and fuller for every man, with opportunity for each according to his ability or achievement. It is a difficult dream for the European upper classes to interpret adequately, and too many of us ourselves have grown weary and mistrustful of it. It is not a dream of motor cars and high wages merely, but a dream of social order in which each man and each woman shall be able to attain to the fullest stature of which they are innately capable, and be recognized by others for what they are, regardless of the fortuitous circumstances of birth or position.[1]

Adams gave a name to what was, in 1931, already a very old idea, one with origins stretching back to before even the foundation of the American republic. America is supposed to be the land of opportunity where anyone with hard work and a little luck can become anything they dream.

The American Dream is America's national narrative and has been for a very long time. It's so embedded into the American psyche that most Americans today believe the American Dream is the heart of what America is supposed to be. It's something uniquely rooted in the culture and history of America, a national story unlike that of any other country on earth. No other nation has a comparable idea of a "national dream"—there's no concept of a Canadian dream or a German dream or a Brazilian dream or an Indian dream. When people around the world think of what makes America different, they think first of the promise of this American Dream.

Yet this powerful belief in an American Dream is something many Americans fear is fading away. It's a national promise that many Americans see as under threat, or even a myth that's long gone. To renew America's parties, we ought to start with this battered national ideal of the American Dream.

THE AMERICAN DREAM

From the very start, America was created around the idea of citizens throwing off the burdens of social class or stigma to pursue new lives without the limits that kept the Old World's inhabitants locked in place. Before America was a nation of immigrants, it was a nation of colonists, many of whom were the Old World's most hated and marginalized people. They bravely set out to build new lives in what was then a harsh wilderness, longing to cast off the chains limiting how they could live, what they must believe, or what they could become. When those colonists rebelled against their king and formed a new republic, they didn't only create a government in which every free man was in theory equal before the law. They encoded the idea of social mobility deep into their new republic— the idea that citizens had the right to pursue not only life and liberty but also their own idea of happiness, without interference from the state, social tradition, or the whims of others. This new government would ban titles of nobility and its chief executive would be no duke or king or consul or emperor but a mere "president," a title that at the time had the connotation of the simple leader of a meeting.[2] From the very beginning, America was created as a nation in which anyone could become anything. In reality, of course, not every American was yet included in this dream— slavery, the non-inclusion of Native Americans, traditional gender roles, and historical divisions excluded many Americans from the full promise of these ideals. Yet America still purposely embedded this dream in the new republic's culture and institutions, at a time when even holding out such ideals was radical compared to the rigid divisions that had reigned across the rest of the world throughout the entirety of human history.

There's no doubt that material prosperity is, and has always been, part of the American Dream. But the American Dream isn't, and has never been, just a dream about a house in the suburbs, a college fund, and a two-car garage—much less a dream of getting rich. The world is full of wealthy nations with broad middle classes. In most of them, talented people can, with a little luck, get rich. Many have liberal democratic governments, and many open their borders to immigrants coming from across the globe looking to build better lives. In none of these countries do we call this access to opportunity or wealth a national dream. That's because the American Dream isn't just about wealth or jobs or the ability to strike it rich but social equality. It isn't a dream about, much less a guarantee of, success. It's a guarantee of a fair chance at success. The American Dream promises every American an equal chance to achieve whatever he or she desires, no matter the circumstance of their birth. Even if you're not born rich or connected. Even if you don't come from the right stock. No matter whether you were born in a poor urban neighborhood, a tiny rural town, or a nameless suburb far from the centers of power. Even if you weren't born in America at all. No matter your religious beliefs, your skin color, or your accent. The government isn't supposed to block your way, and your fellow citizens are supposed to offer you a fair chance to compete and, with luck, prevail. Whatever your dream, and no matter who you are, with enough hard work, ambition, grit, talent, and luck, you're supposed to have a fair shot at achieving anything you want to accomplish in America. Prosperity and economic opportunity are just the most potent byproducts of the American Dream, not its heart.

With time, the American Dream's details have changed with the nation, but this core promise of social equality never has. When James Truslow Adams first wrote of the American Dream, he had in mind the America of immigrants and the frontier. During this era of the American Dream, the frontier promised endless opportunity for settlers without property to achieve independence and prosperity. At the same time, new immigrants continued streaming into the young republic to escape the limitations of their old societies, eager for the fresh opportunities America provided them. The American government opened free land for settlement to any American willing to farm it, so generations of struggling workers from the East could always move west to become the owners of independent family-farming businesses. As new towns sprouted around those new farms, tradespeople and professionals continued to move west out of crowded and competitive cities to open new shops, newspapers, and medical practices. This expanding frontier came at a heavy cost to the Native Americans pushed off their ancestral lands. It also created unprecedented social mobility, allowing poor workers, who in any other place could never have hoped to escape the life into which they were born, to become landowners and businesspeople.

Later, when the nation reached the Pacific Ocean and there was little new land to settle, the American Dream didn't die despite the "closing of the West." It transformed into the American Dream of the Horatio Alger story, in which a young man could come to America with nothing and rise as high as his hard work and imagination could take him. In this late nineteenth-century version of the dream, a hired laborer could trek to California and strike gold, or a penniless Scottish immigrant like Andrew Carnegie could start life as a telegraph messenger boy and end up with a steel empire. As the nation grew into the modern industrial age, and especially after the Second World War, the American Dream shifted to the modern dream of a stable job, prosperity, and the opportunity for achievement and leisure. It became the postwar dream of a large middle-class home in the suburbs near good schools with two cars in the garage and savings toward retirement. For some, it became the slightly bigger version, the dream of founding a new business or rising to the top of an organizational hierarchy or finding fame and recognition in a chosen profession. America is where a poor kid from Arkansas like Bill Clinton can get himself into Yale Law School and eventually rise to become his nation's president.

We Americans never had a real aristocracy. We don't have a landed nobility and never did. We never believed it necessary that a son should follow the profession of his father. We don't celebrate living an entire life in the town in which you were born. We don't think it noble to give a job to your cousin when a better candidate exists. We like self-made people and distrust the idle children of wealth. We get outraged when a powerful person gets a speeding ticket erased, and we loath the phrase "don't you know who I am." We work hard to shatter glass ceilings, and we celebrate the people who break them down. We celebrate people who came from nothing to achieve great things—Walt Disney, Albert Einstein, Andrew Carnegie, Abraham Lincoln, or Steve Jobs. We know that human nature often works against these beliefs, but we still hold them dearly as key parts of the American character. That's the American Dream. We're supposed to be free people and social equals who each get to define ourselves how we choose. If we work hard and are smart and ambitious, we're supposed to have a fair shot at living the good life no matter where we started. If we're lucky, we can achieve anything.

To keep this promise, several things are supposed to be true in America. First, everyone in America is supposed to get the opportunity to pursue the life they want. Neither your parents nor your community chooses your path, but you do. You can try crazy things no one thinks will work. You can disrupt comfortable systems you think you can improve. Neither the state nor your fellow citizens get to stop you in the name of tradition or stability. No one gets to place arbitrary barriers or classifications in your path. Second, the doors to success in every field in America are supposed to be open to everyone, no matter your background or beliefs. Society is supposed to offer a fair playing field where advancement is based solely on grit and merit. Jobs, promotions, and opportunities aren't supposed to turn on who you are, where you come from, or the influence of your parents. Third, no one in America is supposed to get special treatment based on social identity, wealth, or influence—promotions you didn't earn, privileges others don't get, or exceptions made to rules others have to follow. We aren't all economic equals, but we're supposed to be social equals who all have to wait in the same line at the DMV.

America hasn't always completely kept these promises. Whether it be the Irish, African Americans, rural people, women, Catholics, or Jews, countless groups have at different times found arbitrary barriers erected before their success. The rich and famous have always received some unearned privileges, whether they be elite school admissions, jobs, restaurant tables, or club admittances. Tales abound of American visionaries ignored, inventions stolen, and small operations unfairly strangled by bigger and better-connected rivals. Even though it's never been perfect, it's important that America believes these things ought to be true and that Americans demand their country live up to these beliefs. As a result, America has historically gotten closer to these ideals than any other place on earth at any time in history.

The American Dream is what so many Americans today believe is failing. A mix of changes, events, disruptions, and beliefs have cooperated together to collectively erode Americans' faith in this foundational ideal. The irreversible shift to a postindustrial economy has destroyed large swaths of the settled order in America. Some have found themselves well equipped to take advantage of these disruptive changes to succeed beyond their imaginations. Others have worked hard and doggedly pursued their dreams but found the rules to success changed midstream. At the same time, some groups, such as women, African Americans, and new arrivals, who in the past had unfair barriers placed in front of their dreams, still don't trust America to live up to its promises. Disputes over equity, fairness, culture, and change have left Americans throughout the nation concerned, for different reasons, that the people in charge neither like them nor intend to give them a fair shake. Disruptive change is taking from people what they once had, and few trust they will receive a fair opportunity to get back something better, or even just as good. People

THE PARTY OF THE AMERICAN DREAM

don't know who or what to blame. Maybe the problem lies with foreign immigrants taking over good jobs. Maybe it's multinational corporations who don't care about workers. Maybe it's national elites selling out American values. Maybe it's the politicians and K Street lobbyists and big campaign donors selling out the country. Maybe it's just a symptom of America's national decline. Whatever the cause, many have come to believe the American Dream is fading into myth. All these feelings are variations on a theme—a changing world is destroying the promise of the American Dream.

The American Dream is what defines America. The American Dream is what Americans fear is lost. The message of any renewed American party system should revolve around restoring the American Dream. This is the debate America needs to begin, and it's the debate America wants to have. What exactly does the American Dream promise, and how can we ensure America fully lives up to this central vow? What can we do as a people to protect the American Dream, and indeed bolster it? The next great political debate in America, the one that will define the era that's to come, ought to center around this great question: How we can restore, extend, and protect America's sacred promise to its citizens, the American Dream? That's the key to renewing our parties into vibrant engines of government that can keep America strong and prosperous throughout the new age ahead.

REBUILDING PARTIES AROUND THE AMERICAN DREAM

You can't create a viable party just by stringing together a collection of policies you favor, or arbitrarily tossing together voting blocs you like. We're never designing political parties in isolation. We're designing a new party system. We're choosing the terms of the divisions that will separate America into two new coalitions dominating American politics and culture for decades. The issues and concerns we choose to create those new divisions will define the social rifts dividing the American people into two political tribes. They will decide which issues we make national priorities, and which issues we neglect. They will decide which issues become easy to solve, and which solutions become impossible because the people who support them are scattered across political coalitions. Most important, they will create the framework through which we think about our problems. The defining feature of a party system isn't the issues for which each party purports to stand but the great debate it creates. The question isn't which abstract parties you think might better serve America, but what debate, at this moment in our history, is the one America needs to have.

Nearly every major issue worrying Americans today comes back in some way to this question of the American Dream. Workers concerned about the impact of automation and globalization are worried about the decay of the American Dream. Americans worried about rising economic and social inequality are worried about the American Dream. Women, African Americans, new immigrants, and others, who believe unjust barriers stand in their way, believe they're unfairly blocked from pursuing the American Dream. People worried about the impact of mass migration on their jobs and communities are worried about the slipping away of the American Dream. Americans worried about the power of multinational corporations, about the power of new technologies, or about the end of American power and prestige abroad are in different ways worried about the American Dream. Across the nation, Americans with different concerns, living in different communities, based in differing political perspectives, are all worried about the loss of the American Dream. They're afraid it's no longer enough if they work hard and play by the rules. They think there's corruption across the system, giving certain people all the opportunities while people like them don't have a chance. They think power is falling into the hands of people who don't care about them or even like them. They fear their future looks bleak and that things won't get better.

This decline in belief in the American Dream has caused a national breach in trust. Much like the farmers and workers of the Gilded Age who believed they were cheated when the family farm economy imploded but the Rockefellers and Carnegies got rich, Americans who lived their lives according to an implicit social bargain are understandably angry when the terms of that bargain don't seem to have been met. They don't trust America or its institutions because they feel they haven't kept their word.

They don't trust politicians to tell the truth. They don't trust those with power to play fair. They don't trust the media. They don't trust corporations not to cheat. They don't trust employers who demand their loyalty to provide them loyalty in return. They don't trust elites not to abuse their status. They don't trust that the rules they follow will be honored by the people who make them, announce them, and guard them. If they work hard and abide by the rules they're told to follow, they end up feeling duped. Reestablishing trust in the American Dream would go a long way toward reestablishing the social trust that has been draining away.

We need a new national debate about how to expand opportunities for everyone. We need to talk about how to clear paths that are unfairly blocked. We need to talk about how we can ensure every American has a fair chance with a level playing field to live whatever life they dream of living, so long as they're willing to work at it and perhaps win a bit of luck. We need to talk about how to ensure everyone has access to the tools, networks, and opportunities they need to have a fair shot at achieving their ambitions. Rebuilding confidence in the American Dream is the most important task and issue America now faces. If we're going to figure out how to ensure that the American Dream remains true in America, we need a national debate to discuss how to protect and extend this dream together.

What America needs right now is some individual, movement, or group of leaders working together to break through politics with a new agenda based around new ideas. It needs leaders wanting to follow in the footsteps of William Jennings Bryan and Franklin Roosevelt. They need to throw away the archaic messages about New Deal liberalism or fighting big government and instead construct a completely different message from scratch. They need to design a new party ideology that can create a new agenda that actually speaks to the problems that keep Americans up at night. Ideally, they need to step up before our existing parties break. Instead of allowing our parties to collapse and waiting to see what new parties emerge from the rubble, they need to spark a party renewal that moves America into its next age without the turmoil and devastation of a traumatic party collapse. America needs someone to refresh our parties with a new agenda and launch this new great debate.

A message built around the American Dream would recognize the fears most Americans share about their future. It would explain what exactly is broken in America and thus propose what must be righted to fix it. Most important, it would provide a framework to build a positive agenda of ideas to make the future better. If our leaders were to embrace the message of the American Dream, they could seize this transition in history and ride through the realignment, yielding two parties stronger and better than they were before. Tossing industrial-era political battles into the past, they could usher in a new era of American political history based around renewal and reform. They could launch a new American party system dedicated to a new national debate over how to preserve and extend the promise of the American Dream. But what specifically does that mean?

THE AMERICAN DREAM AGENDA

The ideology of every political party in America is ultimately an answer to a question. That question is the core of each party system's great debate. The ideologies of the Federalists and the Democratic Republicans offered answers to the question of how we ought to construct a new and untested republic. The ideologies of the Democrats and the Whigs offered answers to the question of how to adapt that republic to the America of the frontier. The ideologies of our Civil War parties offered answers to the question of how to rebuild the republic after a nation-shattering war. The ideologies of the Populist and Progressive Era parties offered an answer to the question of how to address the disruptions and abuses and early industrialization. The ideologies of our New Deal parties also offered answers to a question: How to adapt the institutions of the republic to the realities of a complex and modern industrial economy after a depression and then world war? The Democratic Party answer was New Deal liberalism, harnessing expertise and planning to benefit working people and the least well off. The Republican Party answer was that we could do better by simply allowing the republic's existing institutions to evolve. Our coming Sixth Party System will have to answer a question too.

The American Dream ought to be at the center of our next debate. Our next party system ought to address this question: How do we once more adapt the institutions of our republic, given the changes of the global postindustrial world, to preserve the promise of the American Dream? There are many possible answers to that question, and many possible agendas of reforms that could achieve that goal. One could unite a multitude of different coalitions of people, drawing on an assortment of different principles, each of which offer a different answer to the question of the American Dream. Each such coalition would create a slightly different party ideology, and each could lead to varied proposed agendas. A party built around the American Dream message could in theory even draw on all the same principles—liberty, virtue, populism, and progressivism—as the parties that exist today. It could also even promote many ideas and policies taken from our New Deal era. Both parties have achieved their share of real and lasting policy successes during the industrial era, and many of these policies remain just as relevant now. Depending on the figure, movement, or party that sparked the renewal, an American Dream party could mean very different things.

Different people with different priorities will no doubt disagree about what policies and plans are most urgent for an American Dream Party to pursue, and what problems are most critical to attack. We each might have different preferred allies and certain groups we would rather our coalition oppose. All of that is fine. In fact, we don't ever have to all agree. Right now, all we have to agree on is the problem. If we can agree on America's next great national debate, we can start to build new frameworks. We can start weighing ideas, developing policies, and reaching out to potential allies to someday soon unite half the nation around new ideals. That said, there are nonetheless three things any form of an American Dream party would absolutely have to do.

First, the chief goal of any American Dream party would have to be to update America's institutions for this emerging new America. We built America's institutions for the industrial era of the middle twentieth century. Those institutions rely on the assumption that mid-twentieth-century America is still the reality of America, when that's no longer true.

An American Dream party would rethink every American institution, program, and law that was developed for a different time and place, to ensure they make sense in the postindustrial world ahead—creating new programs, abolishing others, updating regulations, and changing national priorities. It would further seek to unleash this national burst of major and often disruptive reform to ensure the reformed institutions support every American having a fair shot at pursuing their dreams. The specifics of the policies the party embraced might be different depending on the specific priorities of the coalition that emerged, but under any version the party would undertake a decades-long mission to refresh the aging institutions of America for the world as it exists today.

Second, any American Dream party would have to assume an affirmative responsibility to help people gain the skills, tools, and opportunities they need to become whatever it is they want to become. The American Dream isn't a guarantee of success or complete equality, but it is a guarantee of social equality and a fair shot at chasing dreams. An American Dream government wouldn't see itself as a guarantor of success but a guardian of opportunity. It wouldn't tell people what dreams to pursue. It also wouldn't just get out of the way, allowing people to chase dreams if they could. As it reformed America's laws and institutions, it would do it with the goal of ensuring that every American has the tools and opportunity to unleash their own potential and achieve success on their own terms. An American Dream party would therefore adapt the philosophy of the old proverb, "If you teach a man to fish, you feed him for a lifetime." Depending on the specifics of the coalition and its priorities, teaching America to fish might mean different things. It might mean not just education but helping people gain access to networks and skills. It might mean helping people acquire capital to start businesses or take risks. It might mean helping people with childcare or medical burdens. It might mean breaking up social, institutional, or government impediments that stop people from following their dreams. What any version of an American Dream party would have in common, however, is it would assume an affirmative responsibility to ensure everyone is socially equal and that everyone has a fair chance to pursue their ambitions, whatever they are and however they define them, regardless of who they are or where they start in life.

Third, any American Dream party would have to prioritize sweeping away the dishonesties and corruption we increasingly take for granted. It would make sure that powerful institutions actually played fair and kept their word. It would work to eliminate grift and graft across society, from government to Wall Street, corporate boards, advertising, law enforcement, and politics. It would seek to ensure that powerful institutions are honest. That they honor their commitments. That they don't cheat their workers or their customers. That they don't use clever spin when they ought to tell the truth. That they don't just honor their narrow legal obligations but also their moral obligations to be fair and loyal. The party would undertake to make certain the entire system works the way it claims to work, in order to shore up the gaping lack in trust that's corrosive to the republic.

Once this new American Dream party formed, America would have its new agenda party. It might build this party around the existing demographic coalitions of our existing party system, or it might instead build a brand new demographic coalition unlike anything we've seen before. It would, however, be a new ideological coalition binding Americans around a new agenda of reform. In response, those who opposed this vision would inevitably come together into a new opposition party. Perhaps they would simply unite to oppose the new agenda party, ensuring its policies are thoughtful and reasoned, stopping utopian overreach, protecting political minorities, and holding the new agenda party accountable. Perhaps instead they would discover their own new agenda to restore the promise of the American Dream, offering America a second alternative to protect and defend America's promise. Then we would have a new great debate.

With the birth of a new Sixth Party System, America would begin a decades-long discussion about how to protect, preserve, and extend the American Dream for years to come. Through that discussion, we would reform our institutions. We would discover new policies. We would surely get some things wrong but other things right. We would respond to a flurry of new technologies, economic disruptions, global events, and disruptive new ideas. Eventually, after years of experiments, debates, and contested elections, we would reach conclusions about what the future of America ought to be. Through it all, we would be discussing the question that most needs addressing: How can we assure that every American has a fair shot at pursuing America's sacred promise, the promise of the American Dream?

Another quote from Thomas Wolfe bears on our present moment:

> I think the true discovery of America is before us. I think the true ful-
> fillment of our spirit, of our people, of our mighty and immortal land,
> is yet to come. I think the true discovery of our own democracy is still
> before us. And I think that all these things are certain as the morning,
> as inevitable as noon. I think I speak for most men living when I say
> that our America is Here, is Now, and beckons on before us, and that
> this glorious assurance is not only our living hope, but our dream to be
> accomplished.[3]

The time for us to accomplish it is now.

THE CHOICE

We stand at another key turning point for America, like the foundation of the republic, the collapse of the Whigs and the outbreak of Civil War, the rise of the populist and progressive reform movements, or the political collapse of the Great Depression and the start of the New Deal. The decisions we make in the coming years will shape America more significantly than we comprehend. As we choose our path, we're not only choosing how the little political battles of our day resolve, but also reshaping the most fundamental divisions of America for decades to come. No one knows for sure what will happen next. What we do know is that we can either stay on our current path and simply let the future happen to us, or else we can embrace the future and shape it for the benefit of us all. We still can choose, renewing our parties rather than seeing them collapse, rebuilding their coalitions around fresh ideas for the future. We can create the debate America needs without the breakdown, disruption, and clashing interests of a party collapse. If we choose it, we can rebuild tomorrow without allowing today to crumble first.

We should take events firmly by the hand and guide America toward the future we prefer. We should take charge of our collective destiny. It's not too late. We should rush forward as Americans, optimistic and resolved with the future in our hands, and renew our parties, renew our politics, and renew once more the United States of America by restoring our nation's greatest promise—the American Dream.

ACKNOWLEDGMENTS

This book is the product of many years, over which the ideas it contains have changed and evolved as I continued to learn. I have the greatest appreciation for all the people who stood by me on what I'm sure often seemed a quixotic quest, particularly in its early days when there was no guarantee it would ever come to fruition. I cannot thank enough my mom and dad, Nat Edmonds, and Mike Signer for believing in the project. I particularly can't express enough gratitude to my father, who over the years acted as a sounding board for my ideas, a cheerleader for the project, and a coach pushing me to do my best possible work and then get it over the finish line.

I am also grateful to those who took the time to read various drafts of the book, providing me with marvelous feedback, including Frank Lovett, Chris Stark, Mike Signer, and my father. Above all, I cannot possibly repay Lucy Hornby for taking the time to provide me with detailed and brilliant notes that proved invaluable. I also thank those who helped to connect me with other people and resources that contributed to the project, particularly Bill Zumeta and Alice Ayres.

I would also like to thank my agent, Don Fehr of Trident Media, for seeing the promise in the project. I also thank the wonderful people at Prometheus who shepherded the book into the world, including Steven L. Mitchell, Cate Roberts-Abel, Hanna Etu, Lisa Michalski, and particularly my editor Sheila Stewart whose skill and patience made this a better book. I couldn't dream of a better publisher with which to work.

I also thank Liz Mills for creating the wonderful cover art, and Jennifer Hardy for her exceptional photography. I am also grateful to Georgetown University for opening their library to me, a place which over the course of researching the book almost become a second home.

Finally, I need to thank everyone who over the years listened as I worked through and developed the ideas that found their way into the book, particularly Aaron DiStefano, Michelle DiStefano, and Liam Hardy. I also wish to express my appreciation to my nephews Nathan and Noah, whose enthusiasm for American history is inspirational.

NOTES

CHAPTER 1: INTRODUCTION

1. V. O. Key Jr., "A Theory of Critical Elections," *Journal of Politics* 17 (February 1955): 3–18.

2. Key further explored the ideas of realignments as gradual changes in a later work. (V. O. Key Jr., "Secular Realignment and the Party System," *Journal of Politics* 21 [May 1959].)

3. E. E. Schattschneider, *The Semisovereign People: A Realist's View of Democracy in America* (New York: Holt, Rinehart, and Winston, 1960), pp. 78–96.

4. Walter Dean Burnham, *Critical Elections and the Mainsprings of American Politics* (New York: W. W. Norton, 1970), pp. 2–3. See also Walter Dean Burnham, "The Changing Shape of the American Political Universe," *American Political Science Review* 59 (March 1965): 7–28; Walter Dean Burnham, *The Current Crisis in American Politics* (New York: Oxford University Press 1982) (collection of Burnham articles on realignments).

5. Burnham, *Critical Elections*, p. 10.

6. James L. Sundquist, *Dynamics of the Party System: Alignment and Realignment of Political Parties in the United States* (Washington, DC: Brookings Institution, 1973), p. 7.

7. Joel H. Silbey, "Beyond Realignment and Realignment Theory: American Political Eras, 1789–1989," in *The End of Realignment? Interpreting American Electoral Eras*, ed. Byron E. Shafer (Madison: University of Wisconsin Press, 1991), p. 3.

8. Burnham, *Critical Elections*, p. 181.

9. Theodore Rosenof, *Realignment: The Theory That Changed the Way We Think About American Politics* (Lanham, MD: Rowman and Littlefield, 2003), p. 121; John H. Aldrich, *Why Parties: The Origin and Transformation of Political Parties in America* (Chicago: University of Chicago Press, 1995), p. 262.

10. Kevin P. Phillips, *The Emerging Republican Majority* (New Rochelle, NY: Arlington House, 1969), pp. 36–37, 474.

11. Arthur Paulson, *Electoral Realignment and the Outlook for American Democracy* (Boston: Northeastern University Press, 2007), pp. 6–8. (The "dealignment" theory hasn't aged well, as America, in fact, moved into a new era of strong party "polarization.")

12. David Mayhew, *Electoral Realignments: A Critique of an American Genre* (New Haven, Yale University Press 2002), 43–68.

13. Jerome M. Clubb, William H. Flanigan, and Nancy H Zingale, *Partisan Realignment: Voters, Parties, and Government in American History* (Beverly Hills: Sage Publications, 1980), pp. 264–65.

14. Mayhew, *Electoral Realignments*, pp. 74–83.

15. Silbey, "Beyond Realignment," p. 3.

16. Everett Carll Ladd, "Like Waiting for Godot: The Uselessness of 'Realignment' for Understanding Change in Contemporary American Politics," in Schafer, *End of Realignment?*, p. 34.

CHAPTER 2: AMERICA'S FIRST AND SECOND PARTY SYSTEMS

1. Richard Hofstadter, *The Idea of a Party System: The Rise of Legitimate Opposition in the United States, 1789–1840* (Berkeley: University of California Press, 1969), pp. 10–39 (including survey of eighteenth-century thought).

2. James Madison, "Federalist No. 10," in *The Federalist*, ed. Jacob B. Cooke (Middletown, CT: Wesleyan University Press, 1961), pp. 56–57.

3. Hofstadter, *Idea of a Party System*, p. viii.

4. James Madison, "Federalist No. 51," in *Federalist*, ed. Cooke, p. 349.

5. The classical political theory the Founders studied barely mentioned parties at all. (Hofstadter, *Idea of a Party System*, p. 51.)

6. Gordon S. Wood, *Empire of Liberty: A History of the Early Republic, 1789–1815* (New York: Oxford University Press, 2009), pp. 35–36.

7. While most of the government, including Congress, consisted of Federalists, most Anti-Federalists quickly came to support the new constitutional government as well—of course while hoping for some amendments. (Wood, *Empire of Liberty*, p. 53.)

8. Hofstadter, *Idea of a Party System*, p. 51.

9. Ibid., p. ix.

10. Hamilton saw himself, and Washington often treated him, as a sort of a prime minister to Washington's presidency—Hamilton sometimes even referred to it as "my administration" instead of Washington's. (Wood, *Empire of Liberty*, p. 91.)

11. Ibid., pp. 90–91.

12. Ibid., pp. 95–103.

13. Ibid., pp. 103–105. The Federalist system was meant to bind national elites to a strong national government through relationships of interest and patronage, while allowing a natural meritocracy with the necessary talent and republican virtue to rise to national service. (Wood, *Empire of Liberty*, pp. 105–107.)

14. Lance Banning, *The Sacred Fire of Liberty: James Madison and the Founding of the Federal Republic* (Ithaca, NY: Cornell University Press, 1995), p. 63.

15. Ibid., p. 45. Democratic-Republicans believed these yeoman farmers had the combination of independence without aristocratic pretension that made them specifically important to maintaining the republican virtues necessary to maintain republican government.

16. Wood, *Empire of Liberty*, pp. 142–45.

17. Ibid., p. 157.

18. Ibid., pp. 176–81.

19. The disastrous mission of French diplomat Citizen Genet, who intentionally stirred up revolutionary sentiment around America in defiance of Washington, outraged the president and particularly turned him against the idea of intervening in the revolution. (Stanley Elkins and Eric McKitrick, *The Age of Federalism: The Early American Republic, 1788–1800* [New York: Oxford University Press, 1993], pp. 341–54.)

20. Wood, *Empire of Liberty*, pp. 162–64.

21. Philip S. Foner, ed., *The Democratic-Republican Societies, 1790–1800: A Documentary Sourcebook of Constitutions, Declarations, Addresses, Resolutions, and Toasts* (Westport, CT: Greenwood Press, 1976), pp. 3–40; Hofstadter, *Idea of a Party System*, pp. 93–95; Elkins and McKitrick, *Age of Federalism*, pp. 451–88.

22. George Washington, "The Farewell Address," in *Washington's Farewell Address: The View from the 20th Century*, ed. Burton Ira Kaufman (Chicago: Quadrangle Books, 1969), p. 23.

23. The Democratic-Republicans usually just called themselves Republicans, with later historians bestowing the name Democratic-Republican on them to differentiate them from the later Republican Party.

24. Wood, *Empire of Liberty*, pp. 166–73.

25. Elkins and McKitrick, *Age of Federalism*, pp. 513–28.

26. Herbert Agar, *The Price of Union* (Boston: Houghton Mifflin, 1950), p. 91.

27. John Adams to Thomas Jefferson, July 9, 1813, in *The Adams Jefferson Letters*, ed. Lester J. Cappon (Chapel Hill: University of North Carolina Press, 1987), pp. 350–52; Hofstadter, *Idea of a Party System*, p. 28.

28. Hofstadter, *Idea of a Party System*, p. 110; Elkins and McKitrick, *Age of Federalism*, p. 545.

29. War fervor was driven in significant part by outrage over the XYZ Affair, in which the revolutionary French government threatened the United States and then French ministers mistreated American diplomats seeking to negotiate neutrality, including by demanding personal bribes for negotiators and a large payment to France. That led to a "Quasi War" between the United States and France. (Wood, *Empire of Liberty*, pp. 239–47.)

30. Ibid., pp. 244–60.

31. Ibid., pp. 250–60.

32. Hofstadter, *Idea of a Party System*, p. x.

33. Wood, *Empire of Liberty*, pp. 260–62.

34. John E. Ferling, *Adams vs. Jefferson: The Tumultuous Election of 1800* (New York: Oxford University Press, 2004), pp. 136–74.

35. David McCullough, *John Adams* (New York: Simon and Shuster, 2001), p. 537.

36. Susan Dunn, *Jefferson's Second Revolution: The Election Crisis of 1800 and the Triumph of Republicanism* (Boston: Houghton Mifflin, 2004), p. 1.

37. Wood, *Empire of Liberty*, pp. 283–84.

38. Thomas Jefferson, "First Inaugural Address," in *The Papers of Thomas Jefferson*, ed. Barbara B. Oberg (Princeton, NJ: Princeton University Press, 2006), p. 149.

39. Hofstadter, *Idea of a Party System*, pp. 127–28.

40. Sean Wilentz, *The Rise of American Democracy: Jefferson to Lincoln* (New York: W. W. Norton, 2005), p. 101.

41. Wood, *Empire of Liberty*, pp. 292–93.

42. Ibid., 292.

43. Ron Chernow, *Alexander Hamilton* (New York: Penguin Books, 2004), p. 647.

44. Wood, *Empire of Liberty*, pp. 370–74.

45. Forrest McDonald, *The Presidency of Thomas Jefferson* (Lawrence: University of Kansas Press, 1976), p. 130.

46. Ibid.

47. Ibid.

48. Duverger's Law is named after French lawyer and scholar Maurice Duverger, who first explained the tendency for first-past-the-post systems to lead to two major parties, as opposed to multiparty systems. (Maurice Duverger, *Party Politics and Pressure Group: A Comparative Introduction*, trans. David Wagoner (New York: Thomas Y. Crowell, 1972), pp. 27–32.)

49. John Gerring, *Party Ideologies in America, 1828–1996* (Cambridge, UK: Cambridge University Press, 1998), pp. 6–7.

50. Gerring's system of ideological party eras differs in several ways from the generally accepted definitions of American party system. Gerring combined the Whigs, the Third Party System Republicans, and the Fourth Party System Republicans as ideologically similar, while marking an ideological shift as the Republicans moved away from economic protectionism during the 1920s. Gerring also noted a change in the Democratic Party's ideology during the 1950s, as the party moved toward universalism. (Gerring, *Party Ideologies in America*, pp. 15–18.) None of these deviations, however, meaningfully undermine the generally accepted party system configuration. As this book explores, the Whiggish American System tradition did indeed survive within both the Third and Fourth Party System Republicans as a part of the party's Yankee faction. The drift toward protectionism occurred during, and was a symptom of, the Fourth Party's System's Jazz Age stagnation, drift, and decline. The Democratic shift toward universalism was a result of the national shift toward moralism of the 1960s awakening.

51. Gerring, *Party Ideologies in America*, pp. 272–75.

52. The old idea of American parties (as opposed to European parliamentary parties) as inherently nonideological, an idea most associated with Louis Hartz as set forth in *The Liberal Tradition in America* (New York: Harcourt, Brace, 1955) has long been in decline. See, for example, Gerring, *Party Ideologies in America*, pp. 4–7, for a discussion of the changing view in political science. See also Mark Hulliung, ed., *The American Liberal Tradition Reconsidered: The Contested Legacy of Louis Hartz* (Lawrence: University of Kansas Press, 2010). The nonideological thesis appeared compelling in the middle of the twentieth century because America then was in the long stable portion of a party system. The parties appeared nonideological because the battle lines were already drawn, one party's ideas were dominant, and new ones hadn't yet arisen. As we approach the next realignment, ideological "polarization" has reemerged because the political framework is now once more up for grabs. It's increasingly clear American parties were always quite ideological indeed—it's just we didn't notice because their ideologies were so embedded into the system they became invisible to us. Like a musty smell in a room that seems to disappear after a few hours in its midst, we lost the ability to perceive the most powerful influence pervading politics.

53. For an example of the profound effect our partisan identification has on others' attitudes and judgments toward us, see Shanto Iyengar and Sean J. Westwood, "Fear and

Loathing across Party Lines: New Evidence on Group Polarization," *American Journal of Political Science* 59, no. 3 (July 2015): 690–707. See also Pew Research Center, *The Partisan Divide on Political Values Grows Even Wider*, October 5, 2017, http://www.people-press.org/2017/10/05/the-partisan-divide-on-political-values-grows-even-wider/.

54. For a discussion on the long-term stability of individual partisan preferences, see Donald Philip Green and Bradley Palmquist, "How Stable Is Party Identification?" *Political Behavior* 16, no. 4 (December 1994): 437–66; Philip E. Converse, "Of Time and Partisan Stability," *Comparative Political Studies* 2, no. 2 (July 1969): 139–71.

55. Wood, *Empire of Liberty*, pp. 312–13.

56. Madison accepted so much of the old Federalist program that the Federalist Party was "superfluous." (Arthur M. Schlesinger, *The Age of Jackson* [New York: Little Brown, 1945], p. 19.)

57. Donald R. Hickey, *The War of 1812: A Forgotten Conflict* (Urbana: University of Illinois Press, 2012), pp. 28–32, 41–44.

58. Wood, *Empire of Liberty*, p. 646.

59. Ibid., pp. 647–48.

60. Ibid., pp. 676–92; Hickey, *War of 1812*, pp. 66–99, 181–228.

61. Wood, *Empire of Liberty*, pp. 692–93.

62. Hickey, *War of 1812*, pp. 263–65.

63. J. C. A. Stagg, *Mr. Madison's War: Politics, Diplomacy, and Warfare in the Early American Republic 1783–1830* (Princeton, NJ: Princeton University Press, 1983), p. 481; Hickey, *War of 1812*, p. 278.

64. Hickey, *War of 1812*, pp. 279–82.

65. Wood, *Empire of Liberty*, p. 696.

66. "No one represented more stoutly than [Monroe] the conviction that the Federalist party, as a threat to Republican institutions, ought to be extinguished, and no one was more confident that the American system, whatever one might say of other systems, could be managed without a partisan opposition." (Hofstadter, *Idea of a Party System*, p. 188.)

67. This built on a longstanding policy going back to Jefferson that, while Democratic-Republicans might accept Federalist ideas and policies, they would never dare to put actual Federalists in positions of power in the belief that only an immoral person with dangerous ideas would ever identify with the Federalist Party. (Hofstadter, *Idea of a Party System*, pp. 186–87.)

68. James Monroe to General Andrew Jackson, December 14, 1816, in *The Writings of James Monroe: Including a Collection of his Public and Private Papers and Correspondence Now for the First Time Printed*, vol. 5, ed. Stanislaus Murray Hamilton (G. P. Putnam's Sons, 1901), pp. 345–46.

69. Daniel Walker Howe, *What Hath God Wrought: The Transformation of America 1815–1848* (New York: Oxford University Press, 2007), p. 93.

70. Ibid., pp. 94–95.

71. Ibid., p. 95.

72. Nobel E. Cunningham, *The Presidency of James Monroe* (Lawrence: University of Kansas Press, 1996), pp. 127–31; Hofstadter, *Idea of a Party System*, pp. 226–31 (explaining how the lack of a two-party contest led to the decline of effective government and the powerlessness of Monroe).

73. Agar, *Price of Union*, pp. 201–202.

74. Jon Meacham, *American Lion: Andrew Jackson in the White House* (New York: Random House, 2008), pp. 44–45.

CHAPTER 3: AMERICA'S SECOND AND THIRD PARTY SYSTEMS

1. John Quincy Adams, "Inaugural Address, March 4, 1825," in *The Selected Writings of John and John Quincy Adams*, ed. Adrienne Koch and William Peden (New York: Alfred A Knopf, 1946), p. 357; see also Richard Hofstadter, *The Idea of a Party System: The Rise of Legitimate Opposition in the United States, 1789–1840* (Berkeley: University of California Press, 1969), pp. 231–33; Daniel Walker Howe, *The Political Culture of the American Whigs* (Chicago: University of Chicago Press 1979), p. 50.
Adams was particularly slow to accept the necessity of parties, holding to the idea that parties were creatures of irrational passion long after they had become a reality of the republic. (Ibid., p. 52.)

2. Howe, *Political Culture of the American Whigs*, pp. 137–38.

3. Robert V. Remini, *Andrew Jackson and the Course of American Freedom, 1822–1832* (New York: Harper and Row, 1981), p. 111.

4. Remini, *Andrew Jackson*, p. 103.

5. The idea of Adams and Clay putting their own personal interests over the people's clear choice was itself a form of corruption and a betrayal of republicanism. (Remini, *Andrew Jackson*, p. 99.)

6. The allegation that the Whigs were just discredited Federalists under a new name would dog the Whig Party throughout its existence. (Michael F. Holt, *The Rise and Fall of the American Whig Party: Jacksonian Politics and the Onset of the Civil War* [New York: Oxford University Press, 1999], p. 2.)

7. While this was his well-earned public reputation, Jackson's rages were sometimes just for show and to gain a political advantage. In private he could reportedly be quite cool and self-possessed. (Arthur M. Schlesinger, *The Age of Jackson* [New York: Little, Brown, 1945], pp. 36–41.)

8. Gordon S. Wood, *Empire of Liberty: A History of the Early Republic, 1789–1815* (New York: Oxford University Press, 2009), p. 21.

9. Lance Banning, *The Sacred Fire of Liberty: James Madison and the Founding of the Federal Republic* (Ithaca, NY: Cornell University Press, 1995), p. 372.

10. Remini, *Andrew Jackson*, pp. 25–33.

11. "The force driving Jackson after 1824: a belief in the primacy of the will of the people over the whim of the powerful, with himself as the chief interpreter and enactor of that will." (Jon Meacham, *American Lion: Andrew Jackson in the White House* [New York: Random House, 2008], p. 46.)

12. Remini, *Andrew Jackson*, p. 130.

13. Meacham, *American Lion*, p. 4.

14. Remini, *Andrew Jackson*, pp. 173–80.

15. Most of the property restrictions were gone by 1828, leading to a large increase in popular involvement in politics. (Holt, *Rise and Fall of the American Whig Party*, p. 8.)

16. Schlesinger, *Age of Jackson*, p. 46.

17. Ibid., pp. 46–47.

18. Clay thought Jackson's election was "mortifying and sickening" to the "lovers of free Government." (Meacham, *American Lion*, p. 49.)

19. Howe, *Political Culture of the American Whigs*, p. 125.

20. James C. Klotter, *Henry Clay: The Man Who Would be President* (Oxford: Oxford University Press, 2018), pp. 64–69.

21. Klotter, *Henry Clay*, p. 69.

22. Schlesinger, *Age of Jackson*, pp. 74–75.

23. Ibid., pp. 75–76.

24. Remini, *Andrew Jackson*, p. 111.

25. Holt, *Rise and Fall of the American Whig Party*, pp. 15–17.

26. Andrew Jackson, "President Jackson's Veto Message Regarding the Bank of the United States; July 10, 1832," http://avalon.law.yale.edu/19th_century/ajveto01.asp (from *A Compilation of the Messages and Papers of the Presidents*, prepared under the direction of the Joint Committee on printing, 52nd Congress; New York: Bureau of National Literature, 1897).

27. Ibid.

28. Ibid.

29. Holt, *Rise and Fall of the American Whig Party*, p. 20; Meacham, *American Lion*, pp. 239–41.

30. Holt, *Rise and Fall of the American Whig Party*, p. 17.

31. Holt, *Rise and Fall of the American Whig Party*, p. 46.

32. The Anti-Masons seemed a natural National Republican constituency but Clay and his party refused to adopt a movement they found distasteful, and denounced them instead. (Holt, *Rise and Fall of the American Whig Party*, pp. 11–14.) They would often pick up these voters in later years as the Anti-Masons declined.

33. Remini, *Andrew Jackson*, p. 41.

34. Holt, *Rise and Fall of the American Whig Party*, p. 28.

35. Howe, *Political Culture of the American Whigs*, p. 15.

36. Whigs were less comfortable with the spoils system but ultimately practiced it nonetheless. (Howe, *Political Culture of the American Whigs*, p. 54.)

37. Holt, *Rise and Fall of the American Whig Party*, p. 119.

38. Holt, *Rise and Fall of the American Whig Party*, p. 113.

39. Whigs connected prosperity and growth as a tool of social and personal improvement, "believe[ing] that industrialization and improved technology held out great hope for the betterment of mankind." (Ibid., p. 9.)

40. To the Whigs, prosperity and economic progress was the first step to unleash personal and moral progress and reform. (Ibid., pp. 100–101.)

41. Ibid., pp. 20, 32.

42. Ibid., p. 113.

43. Holt, *Rise and Fall of the American Whig Party*, pp. 83, 117.

44. Ibid., pp. 116–17; Howe, *Political Culture of the American Whigs*, p. 13; Richard Carwardine, *Evangelicals and Politics in Antebellum America* (New Haven, CT: Yale University Press, 1993), p. 131; Howe, *Political Culture of the American Whigs*, p. 9.

45. Ibid., p. 685; Howe, *Political Culture of the American Whigs*, pp. 16–17.

46. Howe, *Political Culture of the American Whigs*, pp. 13, 16–17.

47. Harrison was in fact not a common hard-drinking man living in a log cabin at all. The Whig campaign for Harrison was a model of Jacksonian campaigns, with parades, songs, slogans, and hoopla such as rolling giant leather balls through the countryside with anti-Democratic slogan on them. (Holt, *Rise and Fall of the American Whig Party*, pp. 105–106.) The Democrats attacked the campaign as a carnival that insulted the people's intelligence. (Ibid., p. 111.)

48. Ibid., pp. 133–38.

49. The Second Great Awakening profoundly influenced Whig thinking, with many evangelical Protestant Whigs believing their policies were mean to bring a "collective redemption to society." (Howe, *Political Culture of the American Whigs*, p. 9.)

50. Ibid., p. 152.

51. Carwardine, *Evangelicals and Politics in Antebellum America*, pp. 1, 4.

52. James H. Moorhead, *American Apocalypse: Yankee Protestants and the Civil War 1860–1869* (New Haven, CT: Yale University Press, 1978), p. 11.

53. Sally G. McMillen, *Seneca Falls and the Origins of the Women's Rights Movement* (New York: Oxford University Press, 2008), pp. 52–54; William E. Gienapp, *The Origins of the Republican Party, 1852–1856* (New York: Oxford University Press, 1987), pp. 45–46; Holt, *Rise and Fall of the American Whig Party*, pp. 689–90.

54. Carwardine, *Evangelicals and Politics in Antebellum America*, pp. 6–14. "For these men and women slavery was far more than a social evil to be endured stoically until it naturally withered away. It was a sin that corroded the moral fiber of everyone it touched, directly or indirectly. Every individual, slaveholder or otherwise, had a compelling moral obligation to sever all ties with the institution and begin immediate work for its removal." (Ibid., p. 135.)

55. John R. McKivigan, *The War against Proslavery Religion: Abolitionism and the Northern Churches, 1830–1865* (Ithaca, NY: Cornell University Press, 1984), pp. 144–49. Some passionate abolitionists, frustrated at the Whig Party's unwillingness to risk dividing its voters by embracing their cause, formed the Liberty Party, which drew from a similar demographic of evangelical reformers and cut into the usual Whig base. (Holt, *Rise and Fall of the American Whig Party*, pp. 155–57.)

56. Holt, *Rise and Fall of the American Whig Party*, p. 686.

57. Ibid., p. 686.

58. Ibid., pp. 163–64.

59. Ibid., pp. 164, 170.

60. Ibid., p. 172.

61. Ibid., p. 173.

62. The Texas annexation issue was not the only thing that hurt Clay in the election; many abolitionists, who as evangelical Protestants would be expected to be Whigs, rejected the slaveholder Clay in favor of the Liberty Party. (Ibid., pp. 195–96.)

63. Ibid., p. 233.

64. Ibid., pp. 248–49.

65. Howe, *Political Culture of the American Whigs*, p. 273. Henry Clay was Lincoln's personal idol and model for statesmanship. (Ibid., p. 272.)

66. Holt, *Rise and Fall of the American Whig Party*, pp. 250–51.

67. Whig newspapers had claimed Taylor as a Whig during the war to claim military glory from the Democrats, even though Taylor had never even voted much less been a politically active Whig. (Ibid., p. 248.)

68. Ibid., pp. 271–72.

69. Ibid., p. 319.

70. There's good reason to believe that Van Buren's Free Soil candidacy didn't change the outcome of the election and Taylor would have won regardless. (Ibid., pp. 372–76.)

71. Slaveholder Taylor had a different plan in mind, one less friendly to the spread of slavery, in which the territory captured from Mexico would be admitted as two states, presumably free. The clash between President Taylor's plan, which Southern Whigs feared would be politically disastrous in the South, and Clay's Compromise became a battle of egos until Taylor's death. (Ibid., pp. 474–75, 517–19.)

72. The Fugitive Slave Act was so deeply unpopular among Northern churches, it drove evangelicals into political action. (Carwardine, *Evangelicals and Politics in Antebellum America*, pp. 178–80.)

73. Holt, *Rise and Fall of the American Whig Party*, pp. 606–607.

74. Gienapp, *Origins of the Republican Party*, pp. 16–17; Holt, *Rise and Fall of the American Whig Party*, pp. 682, 724–25.

75. Politicians at the time openly noted there was no real difference between the parties any more. (Holt, *Rise and Fall of the American Whig Party*, p. 688.)

76. Gienapp, *Origins of the Republican Party*, pp. 27–31.

77. Holt, *Rise and Fall of the American Whig Party*, pp. 753–55.

78. Ibid., p. 763. Or as Horace Greeley wrote, the party had been "not merely discomfited but annihilated." (Ibid., p. 766.)

79. Ibid., p. 765.

80. Gienapp, *Origins of the Republican Party*, p. 39.

81. Ibid., pp. 69–71; Holt, *Rise and Fall of the American Whig Party*, p. 806.

82. Nicole Etcheson, *Bleeding Kansas: Contested Liberty in the Civil War Era* (Lawrence: University of Nebraska Press, 2004), pp. 14–16; Gienapp, *Origins of the Republican Party*, p. 70.

83. Gienapp, *Origins of the Republican Party*, pp. 78–83.

84. Ibid., p. 161.

85. Holt, *Rise and Fall of the American Whig Party*, p. 190.

86. Carleton Beals, *Brass-Knuckle Crusade: The Great Know-Nothing Conspiracy: 1820–1860* (New York: Hastings House, 1960), pp. 121–45; Gienapp, *Origins of the Republican Party*, p. 92.

87. Holt, *Rise and Fall of the American Whig Party*, p. 845. The Know-Nothings believed Catholicism as a faith was naturally hostile to republicanism. (Ibid.) See also Sydney E. Ahlstrom, *A Religious History of the American People* (New Haven, CT: Yale University Press, 1972), pp. 555–68.

88. The nativists had long been a drag on the Whigs given their overlapping bases of support, perhaps helping cost the Whigs the 1844 election. (Holt, *Rise and Fall of the American Whig Party*, pp. 206, 212.)

89. Gienapp, *Origins of the Republican Party*, p. 95.

90. The party also benefited from the rising strength of awakening Christianity, with increasingly religious Protestants convinced Catholicism encouraged moral laxity, corrupted personal morals, undercut Christian education, and threatened the republican values of America ordained by God. (Carwardine, *Evangelicals and Politics in Antebellum America*, pp. 199–203.)

91. Ibid., pp. 240–48. Speaker Banks was in reality a true politician who believed whatever was most advantageous to him at the time. (Ibid., p. 243.)

92. Gienapp, *Origins of the Republican Party*, pp. 240–41.

93. For the first few years, what was to become the Republican Party functioned as an ad hoc alliance of movements and parties, often under names like Fusion, Independent, and People's instead of Republican. These smaller movements merged into a united Republican Party state by state over time. (Paul Kleppner, *The Third Electoral System, 1853–1892: Parties, Voters, and Political Cultures* [Chapel Hill: University of North Carolina Press, 1979], pp. 71–72.)

94. Carwardine, *Evangelicals and Politics in Antebellum America*, pp. 245–46.

95. Gienapp, *Origins of the Republican Party*, pp. 168–72, 296–99.

96. Etcheson, *Bleeding Kansas*, p. 135.

97. Gienapp, *Origins of the Republican Party*, pp. 297–99.

98. Stephen B. Oates, *To Purge This Land With Blood: A Biography of John Brown* (Amherst: University of Massachusetts Press, 1984), pp. 132–37; Etcheson, *Bleeding Kansas*, pp. 107–14.

99. Etcheson, *Bleeding Kansas*, pp. 121–22.

100. Ibid., pp. 98–99; Gienapp, *Origins of the Republican Party*, pp. 299–300.

101. Gienapp, *Origins of the Republican Party*, pp. 240–41.

102. Oates, *To Purge This Land With Blood*, pp. 274–358; Etcheson, *Bleeding Kansas*, pp. 207–18.

103. Gienapp, *Origins of the Republican Party*, pp. 305–306.

104. Ibid., pp. 316–46.

105. Ibid., pp. 441–43.

106. Kenneth M. Stampp, *America in 1857: A Nation on the Brink* (New York: Oxford University Press, 1990), pp. 293–322.

107. "Constitutional Union Platform of 1860," in *National Party Platforms, 1840–1957*, ed. Kirk H. Porter and Donald Bruce Johnson (Urbana: University of Illinois Press, 1956).

108. The "bloody shirt" metaphor came from the savage beating of a Mississippi schoolteacher in 1871 by vigilantes dressed in the white robes of the Ku Klux Klan. The mob demanded he leave the county for teaching African Americans, and when he refused they beat him mercilessly almost to death. A myth claimed that a Union soldier had transported his bloody nightshirt to Washington where a congressman waved it about in a speech denouncing Southern intransigence—which there is no record of having happened. Nonetheless, Southerners afterward would denounce Northern agitation against Southern resistance to Reconstruction, violence, and mistreatment of African Americans as demagoguery—"waving

the bloody shirt." (Stephen Budiansky, *The Bloody Shirt: Terror After Appomattox* [New York: Viking, 2008], pp. 1–10.)

Rum, Romanism, and Rebellion came from a campaign speech for James Blaine in 1888 by an obscure Protestant minister, Samuel Burchard, which the newspapers quoted as saying Republican would not "identify themselves with the party whose antecedents have been rum, Romanism, and rebellion." The speech damaged Blaine with Irish voters for the anti-Catholic slur, but also resonated over time. (Mark Wahlgren Summers, *Rum, Romanism, and Rebellion: The Making of a President, 1884* [Chapel Hill: University of North Carolina Press, 2000], pp. 281–88; H. Wayne Morgan, *From Hayes to McKinley: National Party Politics, 1877–1896* [Syracuse, NY: Syracuse University Press, 1969], pp. 232–34.)

109. Ben Wright and Zachary W. Dresser, introduction to *Apocalypse and the Millennium in the American Civil War Era*, ed. Ben Wright and Zachary W. Dresser (Baton Rouge: Louisiana State University Press, 2013), pp. 3–5.

CHAPTER 4: AMERICA'S THIRD AND FOURTH PARTY SYSTEMS

1. Jeremy Atack, Fred Bateman, and William N. Parker, "The Farm, the Farmer, and the Market," in *The Cambridge Economic History of the United States*, vol. 2, *The Long Nineteenth Century*, ed. Stanley L. Engerman and Robert E. Gallman (Cambridge: Cambridge University Press, 2000), pp. 245–47.

2. Sean Dennis Cashman, *America in the Gilded Age: From the Death of Lincoln to the Rise of Theodore Roosevelt*, 2nd ed. (New York: New York University Press, 1988), pp. 14–48; Nell Painter, *Standing at Armageddon: The United States, 1877–1919* (New York: W. W. Norton, 1987), pp. xvii–xxvii.

3. Cashman, *America in the Gilded Age*, pp. 17–29, 50–93.

4. Ibid., pp. 173–74.

5. Richard Hofstadter, *The Age of Reform: From Bryan to FDR* (New York: Alfred A. Knopf, 1974), p. 8.

6. Charles W. Calhoun, *Minority Victory: Gilded Age Politics and the Front Porch Campaign of 1888* (Lawrence: University Press of Kansas, 2008), p. 1.

7. Atack, Bateman, and Parker, "Farm, the Farmer, and the Market," p. 280.

8. Paul W. Glad, *The Trumpet Soundeth: William Jennings Bryan and His Democracy, 1896–1912* (Lincoln: University of Nebraska Press, 1960), p. 47.

9. H. Wayne Morgan, *From Hayes to McKinley: National Party Politics, 1877–1896* (Syracuse, NY: Syracuse University Press, 1969), pp. 366–79, 383–88; Glad, *Trumpet Soundeth*, pp. 47–48; Paolo E. Coletta, "Greenbackers, Goldbugs, and Silverites: Currency Reform and Politics, 1860–1897," in *The Gilded Age: A Reappraisal*, ed. H. Wayne Morgan (Syracuse, NY: Syracuse University Press, 1963), pp. 114–15 (on farmers' need for eastern banking due to national monetary policies).

10. Atack, Bateman, and Parker, "Farm, the Farmer, and the Market," p. 275.

11. Heather Cox Richardson, *West from Appomattox: The Reconstruction of America After the Civil War* (New Haven, CT: Yale University Press, 2007), pp. 161–64.

12. Stuart M. Blumin, "The Social Implications of US Economic Development," in *Cambridge Economic History of the United States*, vol. 2, pp. 848–49.

13. Mark Wahlgren Summers, *Rum, Romanism, and Rebellion: The Making of a President, 1884* (Chapel Hill: University of North Carolina Press, 2000), pp. 22–26.

14. Eric Foner, *Free Soil, Free Labor, Free Men: The Ideology of the Republican Party Before the Civil War* (New York: Oxford University Press, 1970), pp. 12–18.

Since Reconstruction of the South turned on forcing the region to accept the sanctity of free labor and contract—the alternative to abusive labor arrangements and slavery—it become impossible for Republicans not to honor those same principles in Northern labor arrangements. (Eric Foner, *Reconstruction: America's Unfinished Revolution, 1863–1877* [New York: Harper and Row, 1989], p. 482.) Republican business arguments over issues like monetary policy tariffs were also tied to a deeply reformist moralistic belief that special-interest regulations like tariffs were a form of corruption and abuse of power. (Andrew L. Slap, *The Doom of Reconstruction: The Liberal Republicans in the Civil War Era* [New York: Fordham University Press, 2006], pp. 96–107.)

15. Morgan, *From Hayes to McKinley*, p. 19; Horace Samuel Merrill, *Bourbon Leader: Grover Cleveland and the Democratic Party* (Boston: Little, Brown, 1957), pp. 44–50; Summers, *Rum, Romanism, and Rebellion*, pp. 108–109.

The name "Bourbon" most likely arose as a joke comparing them to the French Bourbon dynasty, who, when restored to power after the French Revolution, supposedly "had learned nothing and forgotten nothing." (Morgan, *From Hayes to McKinley*, p. 19.)

16. Foner, *Reconstruction*, pp. 125–28; Stanley L. Engerman, "Slavery and Its Consequences for the South in the Nineteenth Century," in *Cambridge Economic History of the United States*, vol. 2, p. 358.

17. Summers, *Rum, Romanism, and Rebellion*, pp. 111–12; Gustavus Myers, *The History of Tammany Hall*, 2nd ed. (New York: Boni and Liverright, 1911), pp. 211–83; James S. Olsen, "The World of George Washington Plunket," in *Honest Graft: The World of George Washington Plunkett*, by William L. Riordon (1905; St. James, NY: Brandywine Press, 1993), pp. 5–9; Painter, *Standing at Armageddon*, pp. xxx–xxxiv; Lawrence Goodwyn, *The Populist Moment: A Short History of the Agrarian Revolt in America* (New York: Oxford University Press, 1978), p. 4.

18. Foner, *Reconstruction*, pp. 31–32.

19. Ibid., pp. 66–67, 254–55, 446–48.

20. Ibid., pp. 68–71, 142–70.

21. Ibid., pp. 61–62, 228–39.

22. Ibid., pp. 333–37.

23. John Hope Franklin, *Reconstruction After the Civil War*, 2nd ed. (Chicago: University of Chicago Press, 1994), pp. 84–126; Foner, *Reconstruction*, pp. 276–77, 291–307; Gregory P. Downs, *After Appomattox: Military Occupation and the Ends of War* (Cambridge: Harvard University Press, 2015), pp. 68–86.

Republican control was, of course, always tentative on a local level, with Democrats and former Confederates in firm control of much of the South on a local level from the very start of Reconstruction.

24. Franklin, *Reconstruction After the Civil War*, pp. 150–69; Foner, *Reconstruction*, pp.

425–59. "In effect, the Klan was a military force serving the interests of the Democratic party, the planter class, and all those who desired the restoration of white supremacy." (Ibid., p. 425.)

25. Paul Kleppner, *The Third Electoral System, 1853–1892: Parties, Voters, and Political Cultures* (Chapel Hill: University of North Carolina Press, 1979), pp. 124–25; Foner, *Reconstruction*, pp. 512–24.

26. Foner, *Reconstruction*, pp. 575–83; Painter, *Standing at Armageddon*, pp. 1–8.

27. Calhoun, *Minority Victory*, pp. 15–16; Morgan, *From Hayes to McKinley*, pp. 166–70; Summers, *Rum, Romanism, and Rebellion*, pp. 91–107.

28. Kleppner, *Third Electoral System*, pp. 133–136; Morgan, *From Hayes to McKinley*, pp. 220–21.

29. Calhoun, *Minority Victory*, pp. 19–21; Slap, *Doom of Reconstruction*, pp. 40–42.

30. Summers, *Rum, Romanism, and Rebellion*, pp. 41–58; Goodwyn, *Populist Moment*, p. 4.

31. Henry Adams, *The Education of Henry Adams: A Centennial Version* (Boston: Massachusetts Historical Society, 2007), p. 230.

32. "For a generation after the Civil War, a time of great economic exploitation and waste, grave social corruption and ugliness, the dominant note in American political life was complacency." (Hofstadter, *Age of Reform*, p. 60; Jack Beatty, *Age of Betrayal: The Triumph of Money in America, 1865–1900* [New York: Alfred A. Knopf, 2007], pp. 192–99.)

The decline in fact began even before Reconstruction ended, with disgraces like the Credit Mobilier scandal—in which high officials, including the vice president, took bribes to allow vast government overcharges in constructing the Transcontinental Railroad—beginning during the Grant administration. (Foner, *Reconstruction*, pp. 468–69.)

33. Ibid., pp. 466–67.

34. Morgan, *From Hayes to McKinley*, pp. 29–31. While Republican reformers mostly fought over the corruption of the spoils system and bosses, they also fought against protective tariffs and railroad monopolies that they believed fostered elite corruption threatening republican government. (Slap, *Doom of Reconstruction*, pp. 96–107.)

35. Foner, *Reconstruction*, pp. 499–511; Morgan, *From Hayes to McKinley*, pp. 208–12; Summers, *Rum, Romanism, and Rebellion*, pp. 59–76 (on Stalwarts and Half-Breeds), 197–209 (on Mugwumps); Cashman, *America in the Gilded Age*, pp. 198–203; Gerald W. McFarland, "The New York Mugwumps of 1885: A Profile," in *The Mugwumps, 1884–1900*, ed. Gerald W. McFarland (New York: Simon and Schuster, 1975), pp. 62–80.

36. Glad, *Trumpet Soundeth*, pp. 22–23.

37. Ibid., pp. 28–29; Coletta, *William Jennings Bryan*, pp. 5–6.

38. Coletta, *William Jennings Bryan*, p. 19.

39. Ibid., p. 48.

40. Hofstadter, *Age of Reform*, p. 7.

41. Atack, Bateman, and Parker, "Farm, the Farmer, and the Market," pp. 245–47.

42. Kleppner, *Third Electoral System*, pp. 257–97; Goodwyn, *Populist Moment*, pp. 29–54; Foner, *Reconstruction*, pp. 474–75.

43. "People's Platform of 1892," in *National Party Platforms, 1840–1956*, ed. Kirk H. Porter and Donald Bruce Johnson (Urbana: University of Illinois Press, 1956), pp. 89–91; "People's Platform of 1896," in Porter and Johnson, *National Party Platforms*, pp. 104–106;

Glad, *Trumpet Soundeth*, p. 32; Caine, "Origins of Progressivism," p. 18; Richardson, *West from Appomattox*, pp. 255–56.

44. Hofstadter, *Age of Reform*, p. 62.

45. Ibid., p. 67.

46. Rockoff, "Banking and Finance," pp. 644–46.

47. Coletta, "Greenbackers, Goldbugs, and Silverites," pp. 118–19; Cashman, *America in The Gilded Age*, pp. 5–9; Morgan, *From Hayes to McKinley*, pp. 46–48; Painter, *Standing at Armageddon*, pp. 83–89, 129; Richardson, *West from Appomattox*, pp. 153, 158–60, 163–64; Rockoff, "Banking and Finance," pp. 661–69.

48. Coletta, "Greenbackers, Goldbugs, and Silverites," pp. 115–18; Nicholas Barreyre, *Gold and Freedom: The Political Economy of Reconstruction*, trans. Arthur Goldhammer (Charlottesville: University of Virginia Press, 2015), pp. 43–77.

49. Bland-Allison Act of 1878, 20 Stat. 25 (1878); see also Coletta, "Greenbackers, Goldbugs, and Silverites," pp. 119–22; Morgan, *From Hayes to McKinley*, pp. 8–51; Paulo E. Coletta, *William Jennings Bryan: Political Evangelist, 1860–1908* (Lincoln: University of Nebraska Press, 1964), pp. 63–64.

50. Sherman Silver Purchase Act of 1890, 26 Stat. 289 (1890); see also Coletta, "Greenbackers, Goldbugs, and Silverites," pp. 122–24; Coletta, *William Jennings Bryan*, pp. 65–66.

51. Hugh Rockoff, "Banking and Finance, 1789–1914," in *Cambridge Economic History of the United States*, vol. 2, pp. 669–72.

52. Morgan, *From Hayes to McKinley*, pp. 446–49; Stanley P. Caine, "The Origins of Progressivism," in *The Progressive Era*, ed. Lewis L. Gould (Syracuse, NY: Syracuse University Press 1974), p. 21.

53. Richardson, *West from Appomattox*, p. 283.

54. Coletta, "Greenbackers, Goldbugs, and Silverites," pp. 127–28, 133–36.

55. Merrill, *Bourbon Leader*, pp. 172–82; Charles W. Calhoun, *From Bloody Shirt to Full Dinner Pail: The Transformation of Politics and Governance in the Gilded Age* (New York: Hill and Wang, 2010), pp. 147–50.

56. Coletta, "Greenbackers, Goldbugs, and Silverites," pp. 137–38; Merrill, *Bourbon Leader*, pp. 184–85; Coletta, *William Jennings Bryan*, pp. 93–96. The outrage was that the government could have sold the bonds at the higher price itself, instead of allowing Morgan and his banker associates to reap that profit.

57. Glad, *Trumpet Soundeth*, p. 54.

58. Ibid., pp. 40–41.

59. "Bryan made no attempt to hide his kinship with Populists, and national known Populists came to his aid." (Ibid., p. 75.) Bryan claimed while campaigning, "I was born a Democrat but have strong Alliance [meaning Populist] tendencies." (Ibid., p. 73.)

60. Ibid., p. 86.

61. Ibid., pp. 67–72; Louis W. Koenig, *Bryan: A Political Biography of William Jennings Bryan* (New York: G. P. Putnam's Sons, 1971), p. 125; see also Coletta, *William Jennings Bryan*, pp. 86–89. "Cleveland was the choice of the gold men of the East, not of the farmers of the plains and deltas for whom Bryan himself spoke, and Bryan refused to lift even a little finger for Cleveland during the campaign." (Coletta, *William Jennings Bryan*, p. 72.)

62. Koenig, *Bryan*, pp. 155–58.

63. Ibid., pp. 109, 122.

64. Coletta, *William Jennings Bryan*, pp. 109, 114–15.

65. Ibid.

66. Ibid., pp. 132–33.

67. William Jennings Bryan, "The Cross of Gold Speech," in *William Jennings Bryan: Selections*, ed. Ray Ginger (New York: Bobbs-Merrill, 1967), pp. 45–46.

68. Ibid., p. 46.

69. Coletta, *William Jennings Bryan*, p. 141.

70. Ibid.; see also Koenig, *Bryan*, p. 198.

71. Coletta, *William Jennings Bryan*, pp. 175–76.

72. Ibid., p. 171.

73. Ibid., p. 151.

74. Ibid., p. 194.

75. Ibid., p. 193.

76. McKinley collected a campaign war chest of about $7,000,000 compared to Bryan's $300,000. With additional outside expenditures included, McKinley spent perhaps $16,000,000 compared to Bryan's $600,000. (Ibid., p. 198.)

77. Ibid., p. 199.

78. Ibid., pp. 153–54.

79. Ibid., pp. 156–58; Goodwyn, *Populist Moment*, pp. 256–63.

80. Coletta, *William Jennings Bryan*, p. 174.

81. Koenig, *Bryan*, pp. 385–98.

82. Ibid., pp. 493–502.

83. Koenig, *Bryan*, pp. 405–10.

84. Coletta, *William Jennings Bryan*, pp. 290–93.

85. Glad, *Trumpet Soundeth*, p. 59.

86. Coletta, *William Jennings Bryan*, pp. 415–16; Koenig, *Bryan*, p. 357.

87. George E. Mowry, *The Era of Theodore Roosevelt, 1900–1912* (New York: Harper and Brothers, 1958), pp. 18–24.

88. Arthur M. Schlesinger Jr., *The Crisis of the Old Order, 1919–1933*, vol. 1 of *The Age of Roosevelt* (Boston: Houghton Mifflin, 1957), p. 23.

89. Ibid., pp. 64–65 (Muckrakers), pp. 65–66 (settlement houses); Arthur S. Link and Richard L. McCormick, *Progressivism* (Arlington Heights: Harlan Davidson, 1983), pp. 72–84 (social activists), pp. 85–96 (experts).

90. Mowry, *Era of Theodore Roosevelt*, pp. 85–105.

91. "Progressivism had by no means been a Democratic monopoly before 1933; indeed, the term itself implied primarily a dissident Republican." (Arthur M. Schlesinger Jr., *The Politics of Upheaval: 1935–1936*, vol. 3 of *The Age of Roosevelt* [Boston: Houghton Mifflin, 1960], p. 595.)

92. In the history of the Progressive Movement, Teddy Roosevelt was the "greatest of them all in his public impact." (Schlesinger, *Crisis of the Old Order*, p. 18.)

93. Theodore Roosevelt, *The New Nationalism* (New York: Outlook Company, 1910), pp. 10, 28.

94. Ibid., p. 12.

95. Ibid.

96. The struggles between the Yankee business faction and the progressives dominated the Taft presidency and Roosevelt's 1912 Bull Moose rebellion until the party system faded into complacency in the 1920s, leaving the Yankees nominally in charge in an era of decay and inaction. (See, e.g., Mowry, *Era of Theodore Roosevelt*, pp. 226–73.) Yet these two dispositions still coexisted within the same party throughout the era much as any coalition alliance between two rival factions with different perspectives, much like our parties today.

97. Mowry, *Era of Theodore Roosevelt*, p. 85; Hofstadter, *Age of Reform*, pp. 132, 135.

98. Arthur S. Link, *Woodrow Wilson and the Progressive Era: 1910–1917* (New York; Harper and Brothers, 1954), pp. 8–10. Wilson first rose to prominence "as a spokesman of Democratic conservatism—as a foe of Bryanism, of governmental regulation, and of the restrictive practices of labor unions." (Ibid.)

99. Amos R. E. Pinchot, *History of the Progressive Party, 1912–1916*, ed. Helene Maxwell Hooker (New York: New York University Press, 1958).

100. Wilsonian progressivism was about empowering the individual and breaking up power both private and public. According to Wilson and the architect of his progressive program, future Supreme Court justice Louis Brandeis, "To bestow more power on men than they could endure was to change the few into tyrants, while it destroyed the rest. Centralization enfeebled society by choking off experiment and draining talent from the community into the center. Nor could one pin faith on government regulation: 'remedial institutions are apt to fall under the control of the enemy and to become instruments of oppression.'" (Schlesinger, *Crisis of the Old Order*, p. 30.)

101. As historian Arthur Link, widely considered the definitive biographer of Wilson, wrote of the Wilsonian "progressives" of the Democratic Party: "To the extent that they championed popular democracy and rebelled against a status quo that favored the wealthy, they were progressives. Actually, however, they were so strongly imbued with laissez-faire concepts that they were, strictly speaking, liberals in the nineteenth century English tradition instead of twentieth century progressives. They wanted impartial government with a modicum of federal regulation, rather than dynamic, positive federal intervention and participation in economic and social affairs. With their states-rights view of the Constitution, these liberal Democrats tended to suspect any attempts to commit the federal government to projects of social amelioration, because such intervention implied an invasion of the police power heretofore exercised almost exclusively by the states." (Link, *New Freedom*, p. 241.) Whatever Wilson's New Freedom was, and regardless of what its adherents claimed, it was not philosophically the progressivism of the Progressive Movement.

102. "The Democrats, [Wilson] thought, should wipe out the vestiges of special privilege in tariff legislation, liberate credit from Wall Street control, and rewrite antitrust legislation in order to restore the reign of competition in the business world. This, not the uplift of depressed groups by ambitious projects of federal intervention, was the mission of the New Freedom as he perceived it." (Arthur S. Link, *The New Freedom*, vol. 2 of *Wilson* [Princeton, NJ: Princeton University Press, 1956], pp. 241–42.)

103. Link, *New Freedom*, p. 243.

104. Wilson, in his 1916 reelection campaign, endorsed a much more aggressively

progressive program and won the support of many progressive leaders, although soon after he entered the First World War and then become incapacitated by a stroke, so little of it ever came to fruition. (Arthur S. Link, *Campaigns for Progressivism and Peace, 1916–1917*, vol. 5 of *Wilson* [Princeton, NJ: Princeton University Press, 1965], pp. 39–40, 125–30.) Wilson, however, made similar efforts to court African Americans in his 1912 campaign, only to become an enemy of equality as president. (Link, *New Freedom*, pp. 243–44.)

105. Link, *New Freedom*, pp. 254–56 (on resistance to social legislation and ending child labor), pp. 257–59 (on resistance to women's suffrage), pp. 259–60 (on resistance to prohibition).

106. Ibid., pp. 243–54 (on the mistreatment of African Americans), pp. 264–76 (on resistance to organized labor); Geoffrey R. Stone, "Mr. Wilson's First Amendment," in *Reconsidering Woodrow Wilson: Progressivism, Internationalism, War, and Peace*, ed. John Milton Cooper (Washington, DC: Woodrow Wilson Center Press, 2008), pp. 189–213 (on suppression of dissent and First Amendment violations).

107. "Populism and Progressivism were in considerable part colored by the reaction to this immigrant stream among elements of the native population." (Hofstadter, *Age of Reform*, p. 8.)

CHAPTER 5: THE FIFTH PARTY SYSTEM

1. Arthur M. Schlesinger Jr., *The Crisis of the Old Order, 1919–1933*, vol. 1 of *The Age of Roosevelt* (Boston: Houghton Mifflin, 1957), pp. 77–81.

2. Kenneth Whyte, *Hoover: An Extraordinary Life in Extraordinary Times* (New York: Alfred A. Knopf, 2017), pp. 204–206, 378–79. This point is a subject of some historical debate. Partisans and scholars closer to Hoover's own era, viewing him as a failed president in contrast to Roosevelt's heroic New Deal, tended to portray him as a pro-business conservative hostile to expansive government. A more contemporary account tends to challenge that old consensus. What can be said without controversy is Hoover's background was as a Republican progressive. To the extent a case can be made that he later matured into a "conservative," it was as a Calvin Coolidge Yankee and not a modern free-market libertarian.

3. "He had never been shy about federal interference in the economy. Hoover was especially comfortable with intrusive government in exceptional circumstances, and he did not view the nation's predicament as the usual course of business. . . . It followed, in his mind, that the country should mobilize all of its resources against the emergency, as it would in wartime." (Whyte, *Hoover*, p. 480.)

4. Ibid., pp. 407–10.

5. Ibid., p. 412.

6. "Each stage of the battle on a thousand fronts had pushed the national government further out into policy frontiers few had ever expected to visit. Each administration initiative to date, from Hoover's first confidence-building meetings in Washington, through his counter-cyclical spending, the drought aid, the moratorium, the unemployment agencies, the bankers' pool, had seemed, in its day, novel, momentous, and daring." (Ibid., p. 482.)

7. Unemployment had risen to twelve million Americans, one in four workers, and national income fell by about half. In Chicago, one in two workers was looking for a job. (Schlesinger, *Crisis of the Old Order*, pp. 248, 250.)

8. For a lively telling of ordinary America slipping into poverty during Hoover's presidency, see Schlesinger, *Crisis of the Old Order*, pp. 167–72; see also William E. Leuchtenburg, *Franklin Roosevelt and the New Deal, 1932–1940* (New York: Harper and Row, 1963), pp. 1–4.

9. Leuchtenburg, *Franklin Roosevelt and the New Deal*, pp. 3–4.

10. Glen Jeansonne, *Herbert Hoover: A Life* (New York: New American Library, 2016), p. 285.

11. On Roosevelt and his political philosophy: Arthur M. Schlesinger Jr., *The Politics of Upheaval: 1935–1936*, vol. 3 of *The Age of Roosevelt* (Boston: Houghton Mifflin, 1960), pp. 647–55.

12. Leuchtenburg, *Franklin Roosevelt and the New Deal*, p. 8.

13. Ibid., pp. 10–12.

14. Schlesinger, *Crisis of the Old Order*, pp. 399–401.

15. For a discussion of independents and progressives in key roles on the Roosevelt team, see Schlesinger, *Politics of Upheaval*, p. 412.

16. Ibid., pp. 418–20.

17. Arthur M. Schlesinger Jr., *The Coming of the New Deal: 1933–1935*, vol. 2 of *The Age of Roosevelt* (Boston: Houghton Mifflin, 1958), pp. 504–505; Schlesinger, *Politics of Upheaval*, pp. 412–13.

18. While economist John Maynard Keynes had sought to influence the Roosevelt administration, his influence on their policies was slight. (Leuchtenburg, *Franklin Roosevelt and the New Deal*, p. 36.)

19. Schlesinger, *Politics of Upheaval*, p. 236.

20. Leuchtenburg, *Franklin Roosevelt and the New Deal*, pp. 33–36.

21. Schlesinger, *Crisis of the Old Order*, p. 401.

22. This involved something of a dance to ensure price increases didn't outstrip rising wages and working conditions before the new system completely set in, making people temporarily worse off. (Schlesinger, *Coming of the New Deal*, pp. 122–23.)

23. Ibid., pp. 282–83. This was in addition to the public-works relief efforts of the Civil Works Administration that grew out of the Federal Relief and Construction Act.

24. "People identified the whole recovery effort with the NRA." (Ibid., p. 118.)

25. Ibid., pp. 45–46.

26. The AAA ordered ten million acres of cotton to be plowed in 1933, a quarter of the 1933 cotton crop, and slaughtered around six million pigs. It planned a similar intervention in the wheat crop until bad weather destroyed enough that it was deemed unnecessary. (Ibid., pp. 60–63.)

27. Ibid., pp. 114–15.

28. Leuchtenburg, *Franklin Roosevelt and the New Deal*, pp. 65–66.

29. Schlesinger, *Coming of the New Deal*, pp. 103–104.

30. Ibid., pp. 92–93.

31. The entire thrust of Wilsonian "progressivism" was to limit bigness, adapting Jeffersonianism to a more progressive purpose. (Schlesinger, *Crisis of the Old Order*, p. 30.)

32. Schlesinger, *Coming of the New Deal*, p. 92.

33. "The tenets of the First New Deal were that the technological revolution had rendered bigness inevitable; that competition could no longer be relied on to protect interests; that large units were an opportunity to be seized rather than a danger to be fought; and that the formula for stability in the new society must be combination and cooperation under enlarged federal authority." (Ibid., p. 179.)

34. Ibid., pp. 62–67.

35. Ibid., pp. 77–78, 376–79.

36. Ibid., p. 168.

37. Ibid., pp. 126–27.

38. Ibid., pp. 133–34.

39. John T. Flynn, *The Roosevelt Myth* (New York: Devin-Adair, 1948), pp. 44–45.

40. Ibid., p. 45.

41. "Rugged Individualism Loses Advocate as NRA 'Chiseler' Fights Tailors' New Code," *New York Times*, December 10, 1935, p. 2.

42. Schlesinger, *Coming of the New Deal*, p. 483.

43. Ibid.

44. Ibid.

45. T. Harry Williams, *Huey Long* (New York: Alfred A. Knopf, 1978), p. 677.

46. Richard D. White Jr., *Kingfish: The Reign of Huey P. Long* (New York: Random House, 2006), pp. 244–54.

47. Williams, *Huey Long*, p. 708.

48. Ibid., p. 693.

49. White, *Kingfish*, p. 198.

50. Early in Roosevelt's term, Coughlin had enthusiastically supported him on the radio and supported his New Deal programs because he believed government had a duty to limit the amount of profit acquired by any industry. (Schlesinger, *Politics of Upheaval*, p. 23.)

51. Charles Coughlin, "Two Years of the New Deal (Sunday, March 3, 1935)," in *A Series of Lectures on Social Justice* (Royal Oak, MI: Radio League of the Little Flower, 1935), pp. 193–206.

52. "Capitalism, as we know it, must depart! No better than communism, it seeks to identify all wealth in the hands of a few. The communist claims all for the State and none for the individual. The capitalist claims all for his class and none for the laborer or the farmer as he gains control over the State. Social Justice seeks and demands a just distribution of the nation's wealth and a just distribution of its profits for the laborer as well as for the industrialist." (Charles Coughlin, "Share the Profits with Labor [Sunday, December 2, 1934]," in *Series of Lectures on Social Justice*, p. 55; see also Charles Coughlin, "More on the National Union [Sunday, November 18, 1934]," in *Series of Lectures on Social Justice*, pp. 20–33; Schlesinger, *Politics of Upheaval*, pp. 24–25.)

53. Schlesinger, *Politics of Upheaval*, pp. 30–36.

54. Ibid., p. 550.

55. Long's actual plan was most likely to run an ally as a third-party "Share Our Wealth" candidate in 1936, combining his own support with Coughlin's and Townsend's in the hope of throwing the election to a Republican. Anticipating the Republican would fare no better, and likely make the Depression even worse, Long would then run himself in 1940 and win. (Williams, *Huey Long*, p. 844.)

56. Ibid., p. 795.

57. Schlesinger, *Politics of Upheaval*, pp. 392, 397.

58. Ibid., pp. 236–37. During the Second New Deal, members of the administration did sometimes talk with Keynes, who indeed encouraged them to spend. For this reason, commentators sometimes made a connection between New Deal policies and Keynes's theories at the time. The administration, however, although aware of Keynes didn't actually rely on his theories and were spending to meet the needs of the emergency and politics. (Ibid., pp. 407–408.)

59. Ibid., pp. 424–26.

60. Ibid., p. 637.

61. Ibid., pp. 448–63, 626–30.

62. Schlesinger, *Coming of the New Deal*, p. 82.

63. Leuchtenburg, *Franklin Roosevelt and the New Deal*, pp. 13–16; see also Schlesinger, *Crisis of the Old Order*, pp. 256–63.

64. "Whether revolution was a real possibility or not, faith in a free system was plainly waning. Capitalism, it seemed to many, had spent its force; democracy could not rise to economic crisis. The only hope lay in governmental leadership of a power and will which representative institutions seemed impotent to produce." (Schlesinger, *Coming of the New Deal*, p. 3.)

65. Schlesinger, *Crisis of the Old Order*, pp. 204–205.

66. R. J. Overy, *War and Economy in the Third Reich* (Oxford: Clarendon Press, 1994), p. 38.

67. Ibid., p. 42; Harold James, *The German Slump: Politics and Economics 1924–1936* (Oxford: Clarendon Press, 1986), p. 344.

68. The depression-ravaged Western economies and the Soviet economy of course still interacted, with depression conditions in the West bringing a mix of costs and benefits, the Soviets benefitting from the increased availability of cheap skilled Western advisors while suffering from reduced demand for Soviet exports.

69. J. D. Barber and R. W. Davis, "Employment and Industrial Labor," in *The Economic Transformation of the Soviet Union, 1913–1945*, ed. R. W. Davies, Mark Harrison, and S. G. Wheatcroft (Cambridge: Cambridge University Press, 1994), p. 84.

70. Hiroaki Kuromiya, *Stalin's Industrial Revolution: Politics & Workers, 1928–1932* (Cambridge: Cambridge University Press, 1988), pp. 139–72; Robert Conquest, *The Harvest of Sorrow: Soviet Collectivization and the Terror-Famine* (Oxford: Oxford University Press, 1986), pp. 225–59; David C. Engerman, *Modernization from the Other Shore: American Intellectuals and the Romance of Russian Development* (Cambridge, MA: Harvard University Press, 2003), pp. 154–55.

71. Engerman, *Modernization from the Other Shore*, pp. 153–93; Jennifer Burns, *Goddess*

of the Market: Ayn Rand and the American Right (Oxford: Oxford University Press, 2009), pp. 34–38.

72. Schlesinger, *Crisis of the Old Order*, pp. 219–23; Schlesinger, *Politics of Upheaval*, pp. 182–207 (on appeal of communism); Schlesinger, *Politics of Upheaval*, pp. 69–90; (on appeal of fascism); Leuchtenburg, *Franklin Roosevelt and the New Deal*, pp. 26–28 (on both).

73. Leuchtenburg, *Franklin Roosevelt and the New Deal*, p. 30.

74. Schlesinger, *Politics of Upheaval*, pp. 82–83.

75. Ibid., p. 89.

76. David M. Kennedy, *The American People in the Great Depression: Freedom from Fear, Part One* (Oxford: Oxford University Press, 1999), p. 117.

77. On how the New Deal restored faith in the American republic: Schlesinger, *Politics of Upheaval*, pp. 656–57.

78. Ibid., p. 6.

79. A. L. A. Schechter Poultry Corp. v. United States, 295 U.S. 495 (1935).

80. Ibid.; Schlesinger, *Politics of Upheaval*, pp. 281–83.

81. William E. Leuchtenburg, *The Supreme Court Reborn: The Constitutional Revolution in the Age of Roosesvelt* (Oxford: Oxford University Press, 1995), p. 89.

82. G. Edward White, *The Constitution and the New Deal* (Cambridge, MA: Harvard University Press, 2000), pp. 167–97, 302–12 (explaining legal-philosophical differences between the Horsemen and the Musketeers).

83. Schlesinger, *Politics of Upheaval*, pp. 458–60.

84. Ibid., pp. 460–62; Missouri v. Holland, 252 U.S. 416 (1920) (Justice Holmes on living Constitution).

85. Ibid., pp. 464–67.

86. Ibid., pp. 286–87, 453.

87. United States v. Butler, 297 U.S. 1 (1936).

88. Leuchtenburg, *Supreme Court Reborn*, p. 136; James F. Simon, *FDR and Chief Justice Hughes: The President, the Supreme Court, and the Epic Battle over the New Deal* (New York: Simon and Schuster, 2012), p. 317.

89. Edward A. Purcell, *Brandeis and the Progressive Constitution: Erie, the Judicial Power, and the Politics of the Federal Courts in Twentieth-Century America* (New Haven, CT: Yale University Press, 2000), p. 136.

90. Leuchtenburg, *Franklin Roosevelt and the New Deal*, pp. 237–38.

91. Ibid., p. 237.

92. Leuchtenburg, *Supreme Court Reborn*, pp. 143–54; Simon, *FDR and Chief Justice Hughes*, p. 327.

93. Leuchtenburg, *Supreme Court Reborn*, pp. 156–61.

94. Ibid., pp. 238–39; Susan Dunn, *Roosevelt's Purge: How FDR Fought to Change the Democratic Party* (Cambridge, MA: Belknap, 2010), pp. 214–17.

95. Leuchtenburg, *Franklin Roosevelt and the New Deal*, p. 239.

96. James T. Patterson, "A Conservative Coalition Forms in Congress," *Journal of American History* 52, no. 4 (March 1966): 757–72.

97. Schlesinger, *Politics of Upheaval*, pp. 525–27.

98. Ibid., p. 596.

99. "The image of the New Deal [according to its opponents] was that of the totalitarian state." (Schlesinger, *Coming of the New Deal*, p. 472.)

100. "As for the moral consequences, many conservatives earnestly believed that the New Deal was destroying the historic pattern of American life—a pattern of local initiative and individual responsibility." (Ibid., p. 475.)

101. Ibid., p. 486.

102. Schlesinger, *Politics of Upheaval*, pp. 530–36.

103. "Republicans: Going Places," *Time*, October 26, 1936.

104. Schlesinger, *Politics of Upheaval*, p. 624.

CHAPTER 6: THE LIBERAL AND CONSERVATIVE MYTH

1. William Doyle, *The Oxford History of the French Revolution* (Oxford: Clarendon Press, 1989), pp. 67–85.

2. Ibid., pp. 93–103.

3. Ibid., pp. 106–11.

4. Ian Davidson, *The French Revolution: From Enlightenment to Tyranny* (New York: Pegasus Books, 2016), p. 78; Geoff Eley, *Forging Democracy: The History of the Left in Europe, 1850–2000* (New York: Oxford University Press, 2002), pp. 17–18; Christopher Cochrane, *Left and Right: The Small World of Political Ideas* (Montreal: McGill-Queen's University Press, 2015), p. 10.

5. Lawrence Goldman, "Conservative Political Thought From the Revolution of 1848 Until the *Fin de Siecle*," in *The Cambridge History of Nineteenth-Century Political Thought*, ed. Gareth Stedman Jones and Gregory Claeys (Cambridge, UK: Cambridge University Press, 2011), pp. 691–719.

6. Eley, *Forging Democracy*, pp. 17–18.

7. Robert Wokler, "Rousseau's Two Concepts of Liberty," in *Lives, Liberties, and the Public Good: New Essays in Political Theory for Maurice Cranston*, ed. George Feaver and Frederick Rosen (Basingstoke, UK: Macmillan, 1987), pp. 61–68.

8. David Y. Allen, "Modern Conservatism: The Problem of Definition," *Review of Politics* 43, no. 4 (October 1981): 582n1; Goldman, "Conservative Political Thought," p. 691.

9. The revolutions were driven by a mix of liberals fighting for diets and parliaments and republican reforms; peasants upset at painfully high food prices during an economic downturn and discontent with landlords; urban workers and artisans during an era of early industrialization with labor grievances about working conditions; nationalists looking for national independence in an era of empires; and simply widespread resentment from the working classes looking to overthrow their lords and masters to better their lot. This multitude of causes got inevitably jumbled and mixed together into the cause of republican liberty at the hands of the Enlightenment liberal reformers negotiating in the courts of the monarchs. (Jonathan Sperber, *The European Revolutions, 1848–1851* [Cambridge, UK: Cambridge

University Press, 1994], pp. 105–47; Jacques Droz, *Europe Between Revolutions, 1815–1848*, trans. Robert Baldick [New York: Harper & Row, 1967], pp. 62–96; Peter N. Stearns, *1848: The Revolutionary Tide in Europe* [New York: W. W. Norton, 1974], pp. 46–50.)

10. Sperber, *European Revolutions*, pp. 148–53.

11. Jose Harris, "The French Revolution to *Fin de Siecle*: Political Thought in Retrospect and Prospect, 1800–1914," in Jones and Claeys, *Cambridge History of Nineteenth Century Political Thought*, pp. 893–933.

12. Geoff Eley, *Forging Democracy: The History of the Left in Europe, 1850–2000* (Oxford: Oxford University Press, 2002), pp.152–64, 176–84.

13. MacGregor Knox, *To the Threshold of Power, 1922/33*, vol. 1 of *Origins and Dynamics of the Fascist and National Socialist Dictatorships* (Cambridge, UK: Cambridge University Press, 2007), pp. 232–406.

14. Paul E. Gottfried, *Fascism: The Career of a Concept* (DeKalb: Northern Illinois University Press, 2016), pp. 24–25.

15. Walter Laqueur, *Fascism: Past, Present, Future* (New York: Oxford University Press, 1996), p. 15.

16. Roger Griffin, *The Nature of Fascism* (London: Routledge, 1993), pp. 49–51; Robert O. Paxton, *The Anatomy of Fascism* (New York: Alfred A. Knopf, 2004), pp. 11–12.

17. For a survey of some of the academic attempts to define the left and right, see Cochrane, *Left and Right*, pp. 14–21.

18. Alan S. Gerber et al., "Personality and Political Attitudes: Relationships across Issue Domains and Political Contexts," *American Political Science Review* 104, no. 1 (February 2010): 111–33; Alan S. Gerber et al., "The Big Five Personality Traits in the Political Arena," *Annual Review of Political Science* 14 (2011): 265–87; Gian Vittorio Caprara, Claudio Barbaranelli, and Philip G. Zimbardo, "Personality Profiles and Political Parties," *Political Psychology* 20, no. 1 (March 1999): 175–97.

19. Jonathan Haidt, *The Righteous Mind: Why Good People Are Divided by Politics and Religion* (New York: Vintage, 2012), pp. 153–79.

20. Italian philosopher Norberto Bobbio is the only thinker who has come close to determining a value separating political left from right that has gained any acceptance, proposing that what separates the two is one's view on equality. (Norberto Bobbio, *Left and Right: The Significance of a Political Distinction*, trans. Allan Cameron [Cambridge, UK: Polity Press, 1996]. See also Perry Anderson, *Spectrum: From Right to Left in the World of Ideas* [London: Verso, 2005], pp. 129–39.)

Equality alone, however, neither explains the actual policies left and right parties actually embrace, nor is it anything more than the recognition that the nineteenth-century "left" represented republicanism while the ideology of the modern "left" in part seeks to benefit the least well off.

CHAPTER 7: THE AMERICAN IDEAL OF LIBERTY

1. The Whigs, moreover, continued to campaign on liberty, attacking the Democrats as executive tyrants long after Jackson was gone. (Michael F. Holt, *The Rise and Fall of the American Whig Party: Jacksonian Politics and the Onset of the Civil War* [New York: Oxford University Press, 1999], pp. 109–10.)

The party defined itself around the "belief that the fundamental purpose of the Revolutionary experiment in republican self-government was to protect personal and popular (or public) liberty from concentrations of arbitrary and tyrannical power that would lead inevitably to the people's figurative 'enslavement' unless actively resisted." (Ibid., p. 952.)

2. John Henry, "Science and the Coming of Enlightenment," in *The Enlightenment World*, ed. Martin Fitzpatrick et al. (London: Routledge, 2004), pp. 10–11, 22–25; Paolo Casini, "Newton's 'Principia' and the Philosophers of the Enlightenment," *Notes and Records of the Royal Society of London* 42, no. 1 (January 1988): 35–52; Dorinda Outram, *The Enlightenment*, 2nd ed. (Cambridge: Cambridge University Press, 2005), p. 100.

3. Louis Dupre, *The Enlightenment and the Intellectual Foundations of Modern Culture* (New Haven, CT: Yale University Press, 2004), pp. 19–44.

4. Peter Gay, *The Enlightenment: The Science of Freedom*, vol. 2 of *The Enlightenment: An Interpretation* (New York: Alfred A. Knopf, 1969), pp. 27–45.

5. Ibid., pp. 140–50 (scientific method), pp. 344–68 (economics), pp. 396–405 (social tolerance), pp. 448–96 (republicanism).

6. Jean-Jacques Rousseau, *The Social Contract*, trans. Maurice Cranston (London: Penguin Books, 1968), pp. 72–74, 149–57; Peter McPhee, *Liberty or Death: The French Revolution* (New Haven, CT: Yale University Press, 2016), p. 170; Jonathan I. Israel, *Democratic Enlightenment: Philosophy, Revolution, and Human Rights, 1750–1790* (New York: Oxford University Press, 2011), pp. 455–57, 641–47, 897–933.

7. Israel, *Democratic Enlightenment*, pp. 443–79; James MacGregor Burns, *Fire and Light: How the Enlightenment Transformed Our World* (New York: Thomas Dunne Books, 2013), pp. 68–89.

8. Alexis de Tocqueville, *Democracy in America*, trans. and ed. Harvey C. Mansfield and Delba Winthrop (Chicago, University of Chicago Press, 2000), p. 239. As Tocqueville said of it, "Have men changed in character by being united? Have they become more patient before obstacles by becoming stronger? As for me, I cannot believe it; and I shall never grant to several the power of doing everything that I refuse to a single one of those like me." (Ibid.) Others, including John Adams and Edmund Burke, had used similar words to describe this concern before Tocqueville, but since Tocqueville's book spread the idea he usually gets credit for coining the phrase.

9. Gordon S. Wood, *Empire of Liberty: A History of the Early Republic, 1789–1815* (New York: Oxford University Press, 2009), p. 33.

10. In the fight to ratify the Constitution, Madison told Jefferson it was his fear that no majority driven by a "common passion" would ever be able to refrain from crushing the minority. (Michael Signer, *Becoming Madison: The Extraordinary Origin of the Least Likely Founding Father* [New York: Public Affairs, 2015], p. 197.)

11. James Madison, "Speeches in the Virginia Assembly, July 20, 1788," in *The Writings*

of James Madison: Comprising His Public Papers and His Private Correspondence, Including Numerous Letters and Documents Now For the First Time Printed, vol. 5, ed. Gaillard Hunt (New York: G. P. Putnam's Sons, 1904), p. 126.

12. Robert Nozick, *Anarchy, State, and Utopia* (New York: Basic Books, 1974), p. 26.

13. John Stuart Mill, "On Liberty," in *The Basic Writings of John Stuart Mill: On Liberty, The Subjection of Women, and Utilitarianism* (New York: Modern Library, 2002), p. 11.

14. Nozick, *Anarchy, State, and Utopia*, pp. 48–53, 297.

15. Tara Smith, *Ayn Rand's Normative Ethics: The Virtuous Egoist* (Cambridge: Cambridge University Press, 2006), p. 7; Jennifer Burns, *Goddess of the Market: Ayn Rand and the American Right* (Oxford: Oxford University Press, 2009), pp. 147–48.

16. Lanny Ebenstein, *Chicagonomics: The Evolution of Chicago Free Market Economics* (New York: St. Martin's, 2015), pp. 108–29; Bruce Caldwell, "The Chicago School, Hayek, and Neoliberalism," in *Building Chicago Economics: New Perspectives on the History of America's Most Powerful Economics Program*, ed. Robert Van Horn, Philip Mirowski, and Thomas Stapleford (Cambridge: Cambridge University Press, 2011), pp. 301–34.

17. Friedrich A. Hayek, *Individualism and Economic Order* (Chicago: University of Chicago Press, 1948), pp. 85–86.

18. Richard Pomfret, *The Age of Equality: The Twentieth Century in Economic Perspective* (Cambridge, MA: Belknap, 2001), pp. 185–86; Richard H. K. Vietor, "Government Regulation of Business," in *The Cambridge Economic History of the United States*, vol. 3, *The Twentieth Century*, ed. Stanley L. Engerman and Robert E. Gallman (Cambridge: Cambridge University Pres, 2000), 996–1011.

19. Angus Burgin, *The Great Persuasion: Reinventing Free Markets since the Depression* (Cambridge, MA: Harvard University Press, 2012), pp. 214–26.

20. S. G. Wheatcroft and R. W. Davies, "Agriculture," in *The Economic Transformation of the Soviet Union, 1913–1945*, ed. R. W. Davies, Mark Harrison, and S. G. Wheatcroft (New York: Cambridge University Press, 1994), p. 113.

21. Frank Dikötter, *Mao's Great Famine: The History of China's Most Devastating Catastrophe, 1958–1962* (London: Bloomsbury Publishing, 2010), pp. 58–61; Ian G. Cook and Geoffrey Murray, *China's Third Revolution: Tensions in the Transition towards a Post-Communist China* (Richmond, UK: Curzon, 2001), p. 55.

22. Nicholas Wapshott, *Keynes Hayek: The Clash that Defined Modern Economics* (New York: W. W. Norton, 2011), pp. 245–84; Pomfret, *Age of Equality*, pp. 131–50.

23. Al From, *The New Democrats and the Return to Power* (New York: Palgrave Macmillan, 2013), pp. 50–84.

24. Richard H. Thaler and Cass R. Sunstein, *Nudge: Improving Decisions about Health, Wealth, and Happiness* (New York: Penguin, 2008).

25. Thomas Hobbes, *Leviathan* (London, 1651), ch. 13.

26. James Madison, "Federalist No. 51," in *The Federalist*, ed. Jacob E. Cooke (Middletown, CT: Wesleyan University Press, 1961), p. 349.

27. Max Weber, *Weber's Rationalism and Modern Society: New Translations on Politics, Bureaucracy, and Social Stratification*, ed. and trans. Tony Waters and Dagmar Waters (New York: Palgrave Macmillan, 2015), p. 136.

CHAPTER 8: THE PROGRESSIVE PLAN

1. James Harding, *Alpha Dogs: The Americans Who Turned Spin Into a Global Business* (New York: Farrar, Straus and Giroux, 2008), p. 97.

2. These Second Awakening reformers, mainly Whigs, built public schools, funded mental hospitals, and sought to make prisons places of redemption as well as punishment, all as part of a mission to spread moral redemption. (Daniel Walker Howe, *Political Culture of the American Whigs* [Chicago: University of Chicago Press, 1979], pp. 36–37.)

3. Paul W. Glad, *The Trumpet Soundeth: William Jennings Bryan and His Democracy, 1896–1912* (Lincoln: University of Nebraska Press, 1960), p. 6.

4. James H. Moorehead, *American Apocalypse: Yankee Protestants and the Civil War, 1860–1869* (New Haven, CT: Yale University Press, 1978), pp. 11–12.

5. The pre–Civil War tradition of moral reform in America "emphasized the purgation of individual's sins as the key to transforming society." (Stanley P. Caine, "The Origins of Progressivism," in *The Progressive Era*, ed. Lewis L. Gould [Syracuse, NY: Syracuse University Press, 1974], p. 20.)

6. Howe, *Political Culture of the American Whigs*, pp. 28–29.

7. Peter Gay, *The Enlightenment: The Science of Freedom*, vol. 2 of *The Enlightenment: An Interpretation* (New York: Alfred A. Knopf, 1969), pp. 319–23; Lynn McDonald, *The Early Origins of the Social Sciences* (Montreal: McGill-Queen's University Press, 1993), pp. 145–46.

8. McDonald, *Early Origins of the Social Sciences*, pp. 295–300.

9. George E. Mowry, *The Era of Theodore Roosevelt, 1900–1912* (New York: Harper and Brothers, 1958), pp. 19–25.

10. Richard Hofstadter, *The Age of Reform: From Bryan to FDR* (New York: Alfred A. Knopf, 1974), pp. 165–67.

11. Mowry, *Era of Theodore Roosevelt*, pp. 25–30.

12. Ibid., p. 51.

13. "Progressivism was inspired by two bodies of belief and knowledge– evangelical Protestantism and the natural and social sciences." (Arthur S. Link and Richard L. McCormick, *Progressivism* [Arlington Heights, IL: Harlan Davidson, 1983], p. 22; Caine, "Origins of Progressivism," pp. 16–17.)

14. "While Progressivism would have been impossible without the impetus given by certain social grievances, it was not nearly so much the movement of any social class or group as it was a rather widespread and remarkably good-natured effort of the greater part of society to achieve some not very specified self-reformation." (Hofstadter, *Age of Reform*, p. 5.)

15. Mowry, *Era of Theodore Roosevelt*, pp. 88–89.

16. Ibid., pp. 86–88.

17. Ibid., p. 85.

18. Michael McGerr, *A Fierce Discontent: The Rise and Fall of the Progressive Movement in America, 1870–1920* (New York: Free Press, 2003), pp. 66–68; 84, 100–101; Arthur M. Schlesinger Jr., *The Crisis of the Old Order, 1919–1933*, vol. 1 of *The Age of Roosevelt* (Boston: Houghton Mifflin, 1957), p. 23.

19. Mowry, *Era of Theodore Roosevelt*, pp. 94–95, 98–99.

20. R. Laurence Moore, "Directions of Thought," in Gould, *Progressive Era*, p. 48.

21. Schlesinger, *Crisis of the Old Order*, p. 18.

22. Caine, "Origins of Progressivism," p. 14; Heather Cox Richardson, *West from Appomattox: The Reconstruction of America After the Civil War* (New Haven, CT: Yale University Press, 2007), pp. 262–68; Schlesinger, *Crisis of the Old Order*, pp. 23–24.

23. George Martin, *Madam Secretary: Frances Perkins* (Boston: Houghton Mifflin, 1976), pp. 76–121.

24. Hofstadter, *Age of Reform*, pp. 185–96; Ida Tarbell, "The History of the Standard Oil Company: The Oil War of 1872," in *The Muckrakers: The Era in Journalism That Moved America to Reform, The Most Significant Magazine Articles of 1902–1912*, ed. Arthur Weinberg and Lila Weinberg (New York: Simon and Schuster, 1961), pp. 22–39; see also Doris Kearns Goodwin, *The Bully Pulpit : Theodore Roosevelt, William Howard Taft, and the Golden Age of Journalism* (New York: Simon and Schuster, 2013).

25. Michael Kazin, *The Populist Persuasion: An American History* (Ithaca, NY: Cornell University Press, 1994), pp. 82–96.

26. Richard Hofstadter, *The Progressive Movement, 1900–1915* (Englewood Cliffs, NJ: Prentice Hall, 1965), pp. 7–8; Eric F. Goldman, *Rendezvous with Destiny: A History of Modern American Reform* (New York: Alfred A. Knopf, 1970), pp. 188–207; Herbert A. Croly, *The Promise of American Life* (1909; Cambridge, MA: Belknap, 1965).

27. Hofstadter, *Progressive Movement*, pp. 8–9; Walter Rauschenbusch, *Christianity and the Social Crisis* (Louisville, KY: Westminster / John Knox Press, 1991).

28. Thomas K. McCraw, "The Progressive Legacy," in Gould, *Progressive Era*, pp. 181–82.

29. Benjamin Parke DeWitt, *The Progressive Movement: A Non-Partisan, Comprehensive Discussion of Current Tendencies in American Politics* (1915; Seattle: University of Washington Press, 1968), pp. 162–72.

30. Ibid., 244–73.

31. Ibid., pp. 113–61; Hofstadter, *Age of Reform*, pp. 225–54.

32. DeWitt, *Progressive Movement*, pp. 189–243; Hofstadter, *Age of Reform*, pp. 254–69.

33. Hofstadter, *Age of Reform*, pp. 265–66.

34. Theodore Roosevelt, "Theodore Roosevelt on Conservation, December 3, 1907," in Hofstadter, *Progressive Movement*, pp. 69–72; James Penick Jr., "The Progressives and the Environment: Three Themes from the First Conservation Movement," in Gould, *Progressive Era*, pp. 115–31.

35. DeWitt, *Progressive Movement*, pp. 319–40.

36. McGerr, *A Fierce Discontent*, pp. 79–81, 102–103.

37. Hofstadter, *Age of Reform*, p. 184.

38. Louis W. Koenig, *Bryan: A Political Biography of William Jennings Bryan* (New York: G. P. Putnam's Sons, 1971), p. 357.

39. Mowry, *Era of Theodore Roosevelt*, p. 102.

40. Christine Rosen, *Preaching Eugenics: Religious Leaders and the American Eugenics Movement* (Oxford: Oxford University Press, 2004), p. 12.

41. Hofstadter, *Age of Reform*, pp. 179–83; Aileen S. Kraditor, *The Ideas of the Women's Suffrage Movement, 1890–1920* (New York: Columbia University Press, 1965), pp. 121–62.

42. Hofstadter, *Age of Reform*, p. 183.

CHAPTER 9: THE VIRTUE OF A REPUBLIC

1. James McHenry, "Papers of Dr. James McHenry on the Federal Convention of 1787," Philadelphia, May 14, 1787, available at Yale Law School, Lillian Goldman Law Library, http://avalon.law.yale.edu/18th_century/mchenry.asp.

2. Charles de Montesquieu, *The Spirit of the Laws*, trans. and ed. Anne M. Cohler, Basia Carolyn Miller, and Harold Samuel Stone (Cambridge: Cambridge University Press, 1989), pp. 156–66.

3. Ibid., pp. 22–24.

4. Ibid., p. 36.

5. Plato, *The Republic*, ed. G. R. F. Ferrari, trans. Tom Griffith (Cambridge: Cambridge University Press, 2000), pp. 268–74.

6. Ibid., pp. 252–54.

7. Ibid., pp. 274–84.

8. Gordon S. Wood, *Empire of Liberty: A History of the Early Republic, 1789–1815* (New York: Oxford University Press, 2009), pp. 7–8.

9. The Democratic-Republican lionization of yeoman farmers was based in the idea that small landowners with sufficient property, but without aristocratic pretensions, were sufficiently independent, free, and uncorrupted, to embody the virtues a republic specifically required. (Wood, *Empire of Liberty*, pp. 45–46.)

10. Gordon S. Wood, *The Creation of the American Republic, 1776–1789* (Chapel Hill: University of North Carolina Press, 1969), pp. 65–70.

11. Gordon S. Wood, *The Idea of America: Reflections on the Birth of the United States* (New York: Penguin, 2011), pp. 321–34.

12. Ibid., pp. 325–27.

13. James Madison, "Speeches in the Virginia Assembly, July 20, 1788," in *The Writings of James Madison: Comprising His Public Papers and His Private Correspondence, Including Numerous Letters and Documents Now for the First Time Printed*, vol. 5 (New York: G. P. Putnam's Sons, 1904), p. 223.

14. James Madison, "Federalist No. 51," in *The Federalist*, ed. Jacob E. Cooke (Middletown, CT: Wesleyan University Press, 1961), p. 349. See also James Madison, "Federalist No. 55," in Cooke, *Federalist*, p. 378. "Republican government presupposes the existence of these qualities [of virtue] in a higher degree than any other form. Were the pictures which have been drawn by the political jealousy of some among us faithful likenesses of the human character, the inference would be, that there is not sufficient virtue among men for self-government; and that nothing less than the chains of despotism can restrain them from destroying and devouring one another."

15. David Bromwich, *The Intellectual Life of Edmund Burke: From the Subtle and Beautiful to American Independence* (Cambridge, MA: Belknap, 2014), pp. 27–28; Richard Bourke, *Empire and Revolution: The Political Life of Edmund Burke* (Princeton, NJ: Princeton University Press, 2015), pp. 27–44.

16. Bromwich, *Intellectual Life of Edmund Burke*, pp. 30, 110–14; Bourke, *Empire and Revolution*, pp. 229–33.

17. Leslie Mitchell, *The Whig World, 1760–1837* (London: Hambledon, 2005), pp. 7–8. Whigs were not, however, radicals. They centered their beliefs around the importance of property, believing those with property had a special duty to restrain the monarch for the benefit of the people in defense of traditional liberty. (Ibid., pp. 135–74.) From the perspective of today's egalitarian left, the British Whigs in many ways look quite conservative.

18. It is of course difficult to classify either the Whigs or their opponents of the era, the Tories, the way we do coherent modern parties. They were poorly organized in a modern political sense and contained contradictory impulses and people. By Burke's time, moreover, Whigs had been in power for so long, working hand in hand with the Crown, that they had in practice lost much of their historic opposition to royal authority. Nonetheless, classic ideals remained those with which one would classify oneself as either a Tory or Whig. (Frank O'Gorman, *The Rise of Party in England: The Rockingham Whigs, 1760–82* [London: George Allen and Unwin, 1975], pp. 13–21.)

19. Burke, "Speech on Conciliation with America," pp. 120–21, 136; Burke, "Letter to the Sheriffs of Bristol," pp. 293–95, 299–300.

20. Edmund Burke, "Speech on American Taxation," in *The Writings and Speeches of Edmund Burke*, vol. 2, ed. Paul Langford (Oxford: Clarendon Press, 1981), pp. 406–63; Edmund Burke, "Speech on Conciliation with America," in *The Writings and Speeches of Edmund Burke*, vol. 3, ed. W. M. Elofson and John A. Woods (Oxford: Clarendon Press, 1996), pp. 102–69; Edmund Burke, "Letter to the Sheriffs of Bristol," in Elofson and Woods, *Writings and Speeches of Edmund Burke*, vol. 3, pp. 288–330.

21. Bromwich, *Intellectual Life of Edmund Burke*, pp. 252–60; Bourke, *Empire and Revolution*, pp. 298–99, 500–506.

22. Bourke, *Empire and Revolution*, p. 679.

23. Edmund Burke, "Reflections on the Revolution in France," in *The Writings and Speeches of Edmund Burke*, vol. 8, ed. L. G. Mitchell (Oxford: Clarendon Press, 1989), pp. 53–293.

24. Conor Cruise O'Brien, *The Great Melody: A Thematic Biography and Commented Anthology of Edmond Burke* (Chicago: University of Chicago Press, 1992), pp. 412–14; Thomas Paine, "Rights of Man: Being an Answer to Mr. Burke's Attack on the French Revolution," in *Selected Writings of Thomas Paine*, ed. Ian Shapiro and Jane E. Calvert (New Haven, CT: Yale University Press, 2014), pp. 172–261; Mary Wollstonecraft, "A Vindication of the Rights of Men," in *A Vindication of the Rights of Men and A Vindication of the Rights of Woman*, ed. Sylvana Tomaselli (Cambridge: Cambridge University Press, 1995), pp. 5–64.

25. Bourke, *Empire and Revolution*, pp. 741–819.

26. Ibid., pp. 763–68.

27. "Liberty" to Burke "is inseparable from order, from virtue, from morals, and from religion" and is "neither hypocritically nor fanatically followed." (Edmund Burke "Letter to a Noble Lord," in *The Writings and Speeches of Edmund Burke*, vol. 9, ed. Paul Langford [Oxford: Clarendon Press, 1992], p. 153.) As Burke wrote at the time of the American Revolution, "For liberty is a good to be improved, and not an evil to be lessened. It is not only a private blessing of the first order, but the vital spring and energy of the state itself, which has just so much life and vigour as there is liberty in it. But whether liberty be advantageous or not (for I know it is a

fashion to decry the very principle) none will dispute that peace is a blessing; and peace must in the course of human affairs be frequently bought by some indulgence and toleration at least to liberty." (Burke, "Letter to the Sheriffs of Bristol," p. 318.)

28. "A particular order or things may be altered; order itself cannot lose value." (Burke, "Letter to a Noble Lord," p. 161.)

29. Edmund Burke "An Appeal From the New to the Old Whigs," in *Edmund Burke: Reflections on the Revolution in France and Other Writings*, ed. Jesse Norman (New York: Alfred A. Knopf, 2015), p. 728.

30. Burke called these a "system of manners." "The law touches us here and there, and now and then. Manners are what vex and sooth, corrupt or purify, exalt or debase, barbarize or refine us, by a constant, steady, uniform, insensible operation, like that of the air we breathe in. They give their whole form and colour to our lives. According to their quality, they aid morals, they supply them, or they totally destroy them." (Edmund Burke, "First Letter on a Regicide King," in *Writings and Speeches of Edmund Burke*, vol. 9, p. 242.)

31. Ibid., p. 729.

32. Ibid., pp. 694–97.

33. Burke, "Letter to a Noble Lord," p. 156.

34. Gertrude Himmelfarb, *The Road to Modernity: The British, French, and American Enlightenments* (New York: Alfred A. Knopf, 2004), pp. 91–92.

35. Michael F. Holt, *The Rise and Fall of the American Whig Party: Jacksonian Politics and the Onset of the Civil War* (New York: Oxford University Press, 1999), p. 3.

36. Richard Carwardine, *Evangelicals and Politics in Antebellum America* (New Haven, CT: Yale University Press, 1993), pp. 199–204. These Know-Nothing fears of energized Protestants, of course, clearly overlapped with the Second Great Awakening.

37. Ibid., pp. 18–20.

38. "For the religious crusaders who led the temperance, peace, antislavery, missionary, and other benevolent societies, it was not enough to win individual souls to Christ; society as a whole must respond to His call." (Daniel Walker Howe, *The Political Culture of the American Whigs* [Chicago: University of Chicago Press, 1979], p. 9.)

39. Ibid., pp. 17–22.

40. Carwardine, *Evangelicals and Politics in Antebellum America*, pp. 6–14.

41. Ibid., pp. 134–39; A major argument within the early Republican Party was that the "Slave Power" was a direct threat to America's republican traditions and liberty. (Holt, *Rise and Fall of the American Whig Party*, p. 844.)

42. Russell Kirk, *The Conservative Mind: From Burke to Eliot*, 7th ed. (Washington, DC: Regnery, 1995), pp. 12–64.

43. George H. Nash, *The Conservative Intellectual Movement in America: Since 1945* (New York: Basic Books, 1976), pp. 68–69.

CHAPTER 10: THE FURY OF POPULISM

1. Cristobal Rovira Kaltwasser, "Explaining the Emergence of Populism in Europe and the Americas," in *The Promise and Perils of Populism: A Global Perspective*, ed. Carlos de la Torre (Lexington: University of Kentucky Press, 2015), p. 189; Paul Taggart, *Populism* (Buckingham, UK: Open University Press, 2000), pp. 3–4; Damir Skenderovic, "Populism: A History of the Concept," in *Political Populism: A Handbook*, ed. Reinhard C. Heinisch, Christina Holtz-Bacha, and Oscar Mazzoleni (Baden-Baden, Germany: Nomos Verlagsgesellschaft, 2017), p. 51.

2. Ernesto Laclau, *On Populist Reason* (London: Verso, 2005), p. 1; see also Margaret Canovan, *Populism* (New York: Harcourt Brace Jovanovich, 1981), p. 1; Ghita Ionescu and Ernest Gellner, *Populism: Its Meanings and National Characteristics* (New York: Macmillan, 1969), p. 1.

3. Ben Stanley, "The Thin Ideology of Populism," *Journal of Political Ideologies* 13, no. 1 (February 2008): 106; Cas Mudde, "The Populist Zeitgeist," *Government and Opposition* 39, no. 4 (2004): 544.

4. Reinhard Heinisch and Oscar Mazzoleni, "Analysing and Explaining Populism Bringing Frame, Actor, and Context Back In," in *Political Populism*, p. 105.

5. Mudde, "Populist Zeitgeist," p. 543; Jan-Werner Müller, *What Is Populism?* (Philadelphia: University of Pennsylvania Press, 2016), p. 23; Stanley, "Thin Ideology of Populism," p. 101.

6. Populism in this way makes a moral claim of representation, although one that cannot be disproved. Any outcome other than victory for the populist is considered evidence of corruption and thus illegitimate. (Müller, *What Is Populism?* pp. 29, 38–40.)

7. Carlos de la Torre, "Introduction: Power to the People? Populism, Insurrections, Democratization," in *Promise and Perils of Populism*, p. 8.

8. Ibid.

9. Margaret Canovan, *The People* (Cambridge, UK: Polity Press, 2005), pp. 88–90; Müller, *What Is Populism?* pp. 101–103.

10. Gordon S. Wood, *Empire of Liberty: A History of the Early Republic, 1789–1815* (New York: Oxford University Press, 2009), p. 41.

11. Jackson believed in "the primacy of the will of the people over the whim of the powerful." (Jon Meacham, *American Lion: Andrew Jackson in the White House* [New York: Random House, 2008], p. 46.)

12. Ibid., p. 52; Democrat saw banks and corporations as "privileged monsters," paper money as a "cheat and a fraud," and debt as "inducements to self-enslavement." (Michael F. Holt, *The Rise and Fall of the American Whig Party: Jacksonian Politics and the Onset of the Civil War* [New York: Oxford University Press, 1999], p. 685.)

13. This concern is sometimes expressed as "What's the Matter with Kansas?," a phrase taken from the title of Thomas Frank's 2004 book, *What's the Matter with Kansas? How Conservatives Won the Heart of America* (New York: Metropolitan Books, 2004) exploring the slipping away of the traditional Democratic Party populist base. The title is itself was taken from the title of a popular editorial at the time of the Bryan campaign, targeting the Populist Movement in the populist hotbed of Kansas.

14. This national shift from a pragmatic to a moralistic politics during the Fourth Great Awakening, and the new divisions it opened inside the Democratic Party coalition, is discussed in great detail in chapter 14.

15. In fact, the urban immigrant machines were usually at odds with the progressive reformers seeking to benefit their constituents. (Richard Hofstadter, *The Age of Reform: From Bryan to FDR* [New York: Alfred A. Knopf, 1974], pp. 181–84.)

16. For a good discussion of the difference between the American populist and progressive tradition see Hofstadter, *Age of Reform*, pp. 4–5; see also Arthur M. Schlesinger Jr., *The Crisis of the Old Order, 1919–1933*, vol. 1 of *The Age of Roosevelt* (Boston: Houghton Mifflin, 1957), p. 18.

CHAPTER 11: THE CHOICE: COLLAPSE OR RENEWAL

1. The correct quote is in fact: "It is not worthwhile to try to keep history from repeating itself, for man's character will always make the preventing of the repetitions impossible." (Mark Twain, *Autobiography of Mark Twain*, volume 2, ed. Benjamin Griffin and Harriet Elinor Smith [Berkeley: University of California Press, 2013], pp. 370–72.) Most appropriately, the quote came from an essay in which Twain worries about the inevitable collapse of the American republic into a tyranny due to corruption and the decline of republican virtue in its people. "For twenty-five or thirty years I have squandered a deal of my time—too much of it perhaps—in trying to guess what is going to be the process which will turn our republic into a monarchy, and how far off that event might be." (Ibid., p. 371.) The more popular ascribed quote, unfortunately for a fine writer like Twain, caught on because it sounded better.

CHAPTER 12: THE LAST HURRAH OF THE FIFTH PARTY SYSTEM

1. Some fierce opponents of Roosevelt and his New Deal refused to even use his name, calling him simply "that man" or "he." (William E. Leuchtenburg, *Franklin Roosevelt and the New Deal, 1932–1940* [New York: Harper and Row, 1963], p. 176.)

2. Michael Bowen, *The Roots of Modern Conservatism: Dewey, Taft, and the Battle for the Soul of the Republican Party* (Chapel Hill: University of North Carolina Press, 2011), p. 23.

3. Ibid., pp. 56–57.

4. Ibid., p. 23.

5. Ibid., p. 67.

6. "Dewey Defeats Truman," *Chicago Tribune*, November 3, 1948, p. 1.

7. Ibid., pp. 76–77, 82–83.

8. Ibid., p. 113. Eisenhower was particularly taken with the argument that he should run to save the Republican Party as a political entity, believing the collapse of one of America's major national parties would be a traumatic disaster for the nation. (Stephen A. Ambrose, *Eisenhower: Soldier, General of the Army, President Elect, 1890–1952* [New York: Simon and Schuster, 1983], p. 516.)

9. Ambrose, *Eisenhower*, p. 535.

10. Ibid., pp. 540–41.

11. Brown v. Board of Education, 347 U.S. 483 (1954).

12. The Civil Rights Act of 1957, 71 Stat. 634 (1957).

13. Lionel Trilling, *The Liberal Imagination: Essays on Literature and Society* (New York: Viking 1950), p. ix.

14. William F. Buckley Jr., "Reflections on Election Eve," *National Review*, November. 3, 1956.

15. William F. Buckley Jr., "Mission Statement," *National Review*, November 19, 1955.

16. William F. Buckley Jr., *God and Man at Yale: The Superstitions of "Academic Freedom,"* (Chicago: Henry Regnery, 1951).

17. Linda Bridges and John Coyne, *Strictly Right: William F. Buckley Jr. and the American Conservative Movement* (Hoboken, NJ: John Wiley and Sons, 2007), pp. 22–23.

18. Ibid., pp. 5–6.

19. William A. Rusher, *The Rise of the Right* (New York: William Morrow, 1984), pp. 43–53; George H. Nash, *The Conservative Intellectual Movement in America: Since 1945* (New York: Basic Books, 1976), pp. 145–48.

20. Nash, *Conservative Intellectual Movement in America*, pp. 148–49.

21. Chambers in 1948 testified in front of the House Un-American Affairs Committee that Hiss, a State Department employee and well-liked member of the American establishment, was known to him from his Communist activism as a Soviet spy.

22. Rusher, *Rise of the Right*, p. 82; Nash, *Conservative Intellectual Movement in America*, p. 155; Donald T. Critchlow, *The Conservative Ascendancy: How the GOP Right Made Political History* (Cambridge: Harvard University Press, 2007), pp. 13–26.

23. Nash, *Conservative Intellectual Movement in America*, pp. 156–58.

24. Whittaker Chambers, "Big Sister Is Watching You," *National Review*, December 27, 1957.

25. Buckley, "Mission Statement."

26. Nash, *Conservative Intellectual Movement in America*, p. 140; see also Bridges and Coyne, *Strictly Right*, p. 26. "Schools of thought that would soon be part of that movement existed here and there, but they seldom worked in concert with one another."

27. Bridges and Coyne, *Strictly Right*, pp. 56–57; Angus Burgin, *The Great Persuasion: Reinventing Free Markets since the Depression* (Cambridge, MA: Harvard University Press, 2012), p. 148.

28. Nash, *Conservative Intellectual Movement in America*, pp. 174–78.

29. Frank S. Meyer, "Freedom, Tradition, Conservatism," in *What Is Conservatism?* ed. Frank S. Meyer (New York: Holt, Rinehart and Winston, 1964), pp. 8–9.

30. Frank S. Meyer, "Why Freedom," *National Review*, September 25, 1962.

31. "*National Review* in its first years was dominated by the conviction that its preeminent intellectual enemy—and they insisted it *was* an enemy—was liberalism." (Nash, *Conservative Intellectual Movement in America*, p. 149.) Buckley's conservatives even vigorously opposed a popular Republican president like Eisenhower because, although he claimed to represent them on policy, he had made peace with the ideas they believed it urgent to fight. (Ibid., pp. 254–55.)

32. Bridges and Coyne, *Strictly Right*, p. 82.

33. Nash, *Conservative Intellectual Movement in America*, p. 207.

34. Rusher, *Rise of the Right*, pp. 135–59; Jonathan M. Schoenwald, *A Time for Choosing: The Rise of Modern American Conservatism* (New York: Oxford University Press, 2001), pp. 126–29.

35. Nash, *Conservative Intellectual Movement in America*, pp. 290–91.

36. J. William Middendorf II, *A Glorious Disaster: Barry Goldwater's Presidential Campaign and the Origins of the Conservative Movement* (New York: Basic Books, 2006), pp. 51–52.

37. Theodore H. White, *The Making of the President: 1968* (New York: Atheneum, 1965), pp. 262–65.

38. Lewis Gould, *Grand Old Party: A History of the Republicans* (New York: Random House, 2003), p. 357.

39. Robert Alan Goldberg, *Barry Goldwater* (New Haven, CT: Yale University Press, 1995), pp. 203–204.

40. Theodore H. White, *The Making of the President: 1964* (New York: Atheneum Publishers, 1965), 228.

41. Ibid., pp. 309–11.

42. Ibid., pp. 317–19.

43. Ibid., pp. 311–16.

44. Robert Dallek, *Flawed Giant: Lyndon Johnson and His Times, 1961–1973* (New York: Oxford University Press, 1998), pp. 170–78 (on Johnson's coordinated—and often dirty and unfair—tactics to discredit Goldwater in the media).

45. Ibid., p. 345.

46. Ibid., p. 339.

47. Goldberg, *Barry Goldwater*, pp. 328–34; Lloyd Grove, "Barry Goldwater's Left Turn," *Washington Post*, July 28, 1994, p. C01.

48. Timothy N. Thurber, *Republicans and Race: The GOP's Frayed Relationships with African Americans, 1945–1974* (Lawrence: University Press of Kansas, 2013), p. 123; Middendorf, *Glorious Disaster*, p. 106.

49. John W. Dean and Barry Goldwater Jr., *Pure Goldwater* (New York: Palgrave Macmillan, 2008), pp. 157–59.

50. Goldberg, *Barry Goldwater*, pp. 196–97.

51. Robert K. Vischer, *Conscience and the Common Good: Reclaiming the Space Between Person and State* (Cambridge: Cambridge University Press, 2010), p. 127.

52. Critchlow, *Conservative Ascendancy*, p. 72.

53. Schoenwald, *Time for Choosing*, p. 148; Thurber, *Republicans and Race*, pp. 196–203. He did, however, sometimes speak on issues like education, busing, and disorder that had racial implications.

54. Thurber, *Republicans and Race*, pp. 196–203; Goldberg, *Barry Goldwater*, pp. 197–98.

55. This included, among other things, Johnson at the 1964 Democratic Convention conclusively siding with the all-white segregationist Mississippi Democratic Party delegation, which had barred African Americans, over the integrated slate of the Mississippi Freedom

Democratic Party—actively employing the tools of the federal government to thwart civil rights activists, including Martin Luther King, all to appease segregationist Democrats to keep them loyal to him and his party. (Dallek, *Flawed Giant*, pp.162–63.)

56. Goldwater's campaign advisors were aware that racial backlash was helping their campaign whether they did anything to encourage it or not. They believed it was far too dangerous to touch the issue directly, and that they could only stand back and watch as it played out. (Thurber, *Republicans and Race*, pp. 183–84.)

57. Mark Hamilton Lytle, *America's Uncivil Wars: The Sixties Era from Elvis to the Fall of Richard Nixon* (New York: Oxford University Press, 2006), pp. 88–95.

58. Schoenwald, *Time for Choosing*, pp. 221–50; James Pierson, *Shattered Consensus: The Rise and Decline of America's Postwar Political Order* (New York: Encounter Books, 2015), pp. 175–93.

59. John A. Andrew III, *The Other Side of the Sixties: Young Americans for Freedom and the Rise of Conservative Politics* (New Brunswick, NJ: Rutgers University Press, 1997), pp. 53–74, 71–72; Lytle, *America's Uncivil Wars*, pp. 91–93; Terry H. Anderson, *The Movement and the Sixties: Protest in America from Greensboro to Wounded Knee* (New York: Oxford University Press, 1995), pp. 108–109; see also Young Americans for Freedom, "The Sharon Statement," in *America in the Sixties—Right, Left, and Center: A Documentary History*, ed. Peter B. Levy (Westport, CT: Praeger, 1998), pp. 46–47.

60. Nash, *Conservative Intellectual Movement in America*, p. 292.

61. With success, the conservative revolutionaries also began drawing more careful lines about what counted as respectable conservatism, with Buckley famously condemning the powerful John Birch Society for its paranoid conspiracy theories and extremism in order to excise it from his movement. (Ibid., pp. 293–94.)

62. Ronald Reagan, "Televised Address: A Time for Choosing," in Levy, *America in the Sixties*, pp. 117–23.

63. Sean Wilentz, *The Age of Reagan: A History, 1974–2008* (New York: Harper, 2008), p. 132.

64. Steven F. Hayward, *The Fall of the Old Liberal Order, 1964–1980*, vol. 1 of *The Age of Reagan* (New York: Forum, 2001), pp. ix–x.

65. Ibid., pp. x–xi.

66. Ibid., p. 102.

67. Rusher, *Rise of the Right*, pp. 195–202; Iwan Morgan, *Reagan: American Icon* (London: I. B. Tauris, 2016), pp. 113–14.

68. Wilentz, *Age of Reagan*, pp. 133–34.

69. Craig Shirley, *Reagan's Revolution: The Untold Story of the Campaign That Started It All* (Nashville: Nelson Current, 2005), pp. 297–331; Hayward, *Fall of the Old Liberal Order*, pp. 447–84.

70. Hayward, *Fall of the Old Liberal Order*, pp. 625–27.

71. Ibid., pp. 684–85; Richard H. K. Vietor, "Government Regulation of Business," in *The Cambridge Economic History of the United States*, vol. 3, *The Twentieth Century*, ed. Stanley E. Engerman and Robert E. Gallman (Cambridge: Cambridge University Press, 2000), pp. 995–97.

72. Hayward, *Fall of the Old Liberal Order*, pp. 572–74.

73. W. Elliot Brownlee, "The Public Sector," in *Cambridge Economic History of the United States*, vol. 3, pp. 1054–55.

74. Hayward, *Fall of the Old Liberal Order*, pp. 572–74.

75. Laura Kalman, *Right Star Rising: A New Politics, 1974–1980* (New York: W. W. Norton, 2020), pp. 327–30; Hayward, *Fall of the Old Liberal Order*, pp. 576–78.

76. Steven F. Hayward, *The Conservative Counterrevolution, 1980–1989*, vol. 2 of *The Age of Reagan* (New York: Crown Forum, 2009), pp. 14–16, 27–29.

77. Hayward, *Fall of the Old Liberal Order*, pp. 685–94.

78. John Ehrman, *The Eighties: America in the Age of Reagan* (New Haven, CT: Yale University Press, 2005), pp. 73–74; Hayward, *Conservative Counterrevolution*, pp. 22–23; Wilentz, *Age of Reagan*, pp. 125–26.

79. Hayward, *Conservative Counterrevolution*, pp. 31–33.

80. Ibid., pp. 59–72.

81. Ibid., pp. 97–109.

82. Wilentz, *Age of Reagan*, pp. 127–28; Hayward, *Conservative Counterrevolution*, p. 51.

83. Hayward, *Conservative Counterrevolution*, pp. 47–48.

84. William E. Pemberton, *Exit with Honor: The Life and Presidency of Ronald Reagan* (Armonk, NY: M. E. Sharpe, 1997), pp. 102–104; Hayward, *Conservative Counterrevolution*, pp. 155–66.

85. Hayward, *Conservative Counterrevolution*, pp. 470–78.

86. Hayward, *Conservative Counterrevolution*, pp. 150–56; Wilentz, *Age of Reagan*, p. 141.

87. Wilentz, *Age of Reagan*, p. 140; Ronnie Dugger, *On Reagan: The Man and His Presidency* (New York: McGraw-Hill, 1983), pp. 148–75.

88. Hayward, *Conservative Counterrevolution*, pp. 169–74; Wilentz, *Age of Reagan*, p. 143.

89. Wilentz, *Age of Reagan*, p. 144.

90. Hayward, *Conservative Counterrevolution*, pp. 376–80.

91. Ronald Reagan, "Inaugural Address, January 20, 1981," in *Debating the Reagan Presidency*, by John Ehrman and Michael W. Flamm (Lanham, MD: Rowman and Littlefield, 2009), p. 82.

92. Ibid., p. 82; William A. Niskanen, *Reaganomics: An Insider's Account of the Policies and the People* (New York: Oxford University Press, 1988), pp. 115–33.

93. Hayward, *Conservative Counterrevolution*, pp. 61–63.

94. Ibid., pp. 182–91.

95. H. W. Brands, *Reagan: The Life* (New York: Anchor Books, 2015), p. 254.

96. Ehrman, *Eighties*, pp. 206–207. "In 1980, no one knew whether conservatives could govern the country—they were small in number, and had little experience on the national stage or in managing large governmental institutions. Reagan proved conclusively that conservatives could govern effectively."

97. William F. Buckley Jr., *The Reagan I Knew* (New York: Basic Books, 2008).

98. Jon Meacham, *Destiny and Power: The American Odyssey of George Herbert Walker Bush* (New York: Random House, 2015), pp. 296–98; Herbert S. Parmet, *George Bush: The Life of a Lone Star Yankee* (New York: Scribner, 1997), pp. 339–41, 348–50, 359–60; Critchlow, *Conservative Ascendancy*, p. 222.

99. Jack W. Germond and Jules Witcover, *Wake Us When It's Over: Presidential Politics of 1984* (New York: Macmillan, 1985), p. 14; see also Ehrman, *Eighties*, pp. 87–88.

100. George F. Will, "The Cheerful Malcontent," *Washington Post*, May 31, 1998, p. C07.

101. Al From, *The New Democrats and the Return to Power* (New York: Palgrave Macmillan, 2013), pp. 49–65; Michael Nelson, "Redividing Government: National Elections in the Clinton Years and Beyond," in *42: Inside the Presidency of Bill Clinton*, ed. Michael Nelson, Barbara A. Perry, and Russell L. Riley (Ithaca, NY: Cornell University Press, 2016), pp. 29–30.

102. Steven M. Gillon, *The Pact: Bill Clinton, Newt Gingrich, and the Rivalry that Defined a Generation* (New York: Oxford University Press, 2008), pp. 101–102; Wilentz, *Age of Reagan*, p. 365.

103. Gillon, *Pact*, p. 144.

104. Nigel Hamilton, *Bill Clinton: Mastering the Presidency* (New York: Public Affairs, 2007), pp. 56–66, 300–304; Wilentz, *Age of Reagan*, pp. 332–34.

105. Wilentz, *Age of Reagan*, pp. 329–30.

106. Nicol Rae, *Conservative Reformers: The Republican Freshmen and the Lessons of the 104th Congress* (Armonk, NY: M. E. Sharpe, 1998), pp. 33–44; Gillon, *Pact*, pp. 123–28.

107. Newt Gingrich, Richard K. Armey, Ed Gillespie, and Bob Schellhas, *Contract With America: The Bold Plan by Rep. Newt Gingrich, Rep. Dick Armey and the House Republicans to Change the Nation* (New York: Times Books, 1994), pp. 3–22.

108. James G. Gimpel, *Legislating the Revolution: The Contract with America in Its First 100 Days* (Boston: Allyn and Bacon, 1996), pp. 1–30; Wilentz, *Age of Reagan*, pp. 349–50.

109. Gimpel, *Legislating the Revolution*, pp. 42–114; Elizabeth Drew, *Showdown: The Struggle between the Gingrich Congress and the Clinton White House* (New York: Simon and Schuster, 1996), pp. 93–112; Critchlow, *Conservative Ascendancy*, p. 248; Rae, *Conservative Reformers*, pp. 74–81.

110. Gillon, *Pact*, pp. 177–79.

111. Ibid., pp. 147–72, 200–203.

112. Hamilton, *Bill Clinton: Mastering the Presidency*, pp. 574–75; Wilentz, *Age of Reagan*, p. 364.

113. Gillon, *Pact*, pp. 140–41; *Time*, December 25, 1995.

114. Gillon, *Pact*, pp. 223–72; Wilentz, *Age of Reagan*, pp. 382–400.

115. Gillon, *Pact*, pp. 256–58.

116. "The country was experiencing such widespread corruption [during the Era of Good Feelings] that it worried many men for the safety of American institutions." (Robert V. Remini, *Andrew Jackson and the Course of American Freedom, 1822–1832* [New York: Harper and Row, 1981], p. 13.)

117. As some commentators said at the time, "These party names of Whig and Democrat now mean nothing and point to nothing." The parties had become solely "a means of political intrigue and an avenue for the attainment of office," and politics had become merely "a scramble for the spoils and a fight about Men rather than measures." (Michael F. Holt, *The Rise and Fall of the American Whig Party: Jacksonian Politics and the Onset of the Civil War* [New York: Oxford University Press, 1999], p. 772.)

118. "For a generation after the Civil War, a time of great economic exploitation and waste,

grave social corruption and ugliness, the dominant note in American political life was complacency." (Richard Hofstadter, *The Age of Reform: From Bryan to FDR* [New York: Knopf 1974], p. 60.)

119. Arthur M. Schlesinger Jr., *The Crisis of the Old Order, 1919–1933*, vol. 1 of *The Age of Roosevelt* (Boston: Houghton Mifflin, 1957), pp. 147–52.

120. James T. Patterson, "Transformative Economic Policies: Tax Cutting, Stimuli, and Bailouts," in *The Presidency of George W. Bush: A First Historical Assessment*, ed. Julian E. Zelizer (Princeton, NJ: Princeton University Press, 2010), pp. 114–38; Nelson Lichtenstein, "Ideology and Interest on the Social Policy Home Front," in Zelizer, *Presidency of George W. Bush*, pp. 183–93; Kevin M. Krause, "Compassionate Conservatism: Religion in the Age of George W. Bush," in Zelizer, *Presidency of George W. Bush*, pp. 227–51; Jean Edward Smith, *Bush* (New York: Simon and Schuster, 2016), pp. 162–63, 390–92.

121. The Patient Protection and Affordable Care Act, Pub. L. No. 111–148, 124 Stat. 119–1025 (2010).

CHAPTER 13: THE PENDULUM OF GREAT AWAKENINGS

1. Frank Lambert, *Inventing the "Great Awakening"* (Princeton, NJ: Princeton University Press, 1999), pp. 32–43.

2. Alan Heimert, *Religion and the American Mind: From the Great Awakening to the Revolution* (Cambridge: Harvard University Press, 1966), pp. 160–61.

3. Edwards went on to play a major role in the Awakening, becoming among its most important theologian. (William G. McLoughlin, *Revivals, Awakenings, and Reform: An Essay on Religion and Social Change in America, 1607–1977* [Chicago: University of Chicago Press, 1978], p. 71; Heimert, *Religion and the American Mind*, pp. 59–94.)

4. "The separate and sporadic stirrings of religion fostered by Edwards, Frelinghuysen, the Tennent brothers, and their respective followers were finally consolidated into the Great Awakening when George Whitefield came from England to tour the Middle Colonies and New England in 1739 and 1740." (Cedric Cowing, *The Great Awakenings and the American Revolution: Colonial Thought in the 18th Century* [Chicago: Rand McNally, 1971], p. 59.)

5. Thomas S. Kidd, *George Whitefield: America's Spiritual Founding Father* (New Haven, CT: Yale University Press, 2014), pp. 24–28.

6. Lambert, *Inventing the "Great Awakening,"* pp. 93–94.

7. Kidd, *George Whitefield*, pp. 36–45.

8. Ibid., pp. 45–47.

9. Cowing, *Great Awakenings and the American Revolution*, p. 59.

10. Lambert, *Inventing the "Great Awakening,"* pp. 95–98; Kidd, *George Whitefield*, p. 65.

11. Kidd, *George Whitefield*, pp. 67–68.

12. Ibid., pp. 65, 67.

13. Lambert, *Inventing the "Great Awakening,"* pp. 105–107; Kidd, *George Whitefield*, p. 68.

14. Heimert, *Religion and the American Mind*, pp. 40–49; Kidd, *George Whitefield*, pp. 62–63.

15. Lambert, *Inventing the "Great Awakening,"* p. 112.

16. Benjamin Franklin, *The Autobiography and Other Writings on Politics, Economics, and Virtue* (Cambridge: Cambridge University Press, 2004), pp. 87–88; see also Lambert, *Inventing the "Great Awakening,"* p. 120.

17. Franklin, *Autobiography*, pp. 87–88.

18. McLoughlin, *Revivals, Awakenings, and Reform*, p. 61.

19. Patricia U. Bonomi, *Under the Cope of Heaven: Religion, Society, and Politics in Colonial America* (New York: Oxford University Press, 2003), p. 125.

20. Lambert, *Inventing the "Great Awakening,"* pp. 185–88; Bonomi, *Under the Cope of Heaven*, p. 151.

21. Heimert, *Religion and the American Mind*, pp. 139–44, 157–58.

22. Bonomi, *Under the Cope of Heaven*, pp. 119–125.

23. Ibid., pp. 157–58.

24. Heimert, *Religion and the American Mind*, pp. 450–53; Thomas S. Kidd, *God of Liberty: Religious History of the American Revolution* (New York: Basic Books, 2010), pp. 76–95, 115–46; Bonomi, *Under the Cope of Heaven*, pp. 210–11; Bryan LeBeau, *Religion in America to 1865* (New York: New York University Press 2000), pp. 58–63.-

25. Heimert, *Religion and the American Mind*, pp. 360–400, 512–17; Bonomi, *Under the Cope of Heaven*, p. 186; Frank Lambert, *"Pedlar in Divinity": George Whitefield and the Transatlantic Revivals, 1737–1770* (Princeton, NJ: Princeton University Press, 1993), pp. 214–25; J. C. D. Clark, *The Language of Liberty, 1660–1832: Political Discourse and Social Dynamics in the Anglo-American World* (Cambridge: Cambridge University Press, 1994), p. 310.

26. Kidd, *God of Liberty*, pp. 97–114; McLoughlin, *Revivals, Awakenings, and Reform*, pp. 96–97.

27. Sydney E. Ahlstrom, *A Religious History of the American People* (New Haven, CT: Yale University Press, 1972), pp. 364–366. "The churches reached a lower ebb of vitality during the two decades after the end of hostilities than at any other time in the country's religious history." (Ibid., p. 365.)

28. "A colonial people almost congenitally exercised with religious questions—and possibly exhausted by or in reaction against the Great Awakening—became preoccupied for forty years chiefly with the problems of politics." (Ibid., p. 365.)

29. Ibid., pp. 429–54; Keith J. Hardman, *Charles Grandison Finney, 1792–1875: Revivalist and Reformer* (Syracuse, NY: Syracuse University Press, 1987), pp. 6–13; LeBeau, *Religion in America to 1865*, pp. 92–95.

30. It's hardly an accident so many critical events of religious history and activism, from the founding of the LDS church to the Seneca Falls Convention, took place at this time in the religious and cultural hotbed of western New York state.

31. Whitney R. Cross, *The Burned-Over District: The Social and Intellectual History of Enthusiastic Religion in Western New York, 1800–1850* (New York: Octagon Books, 1981), pp. 185–207.

32. Paul W. Glad, *The Trumpet Soundeth: William Jennings Bryan and His Democracy, 1896–1912* (Lincoln: University of Nebraska Press, 1960), p. 5.

33. Cross, *Burned-Over District*, pp. 40–2; Richard Carwardine, *Evangelicals and Politics in Antebellum America* (New Haven, CT: Yale University Press, 1993), p. 2.

Revivalism "wiped out theological obstacles to interdenominational cooperation." (Glad, *Trumpet Soundeth*, pp. 5–6.)

34. Ahlstrom, *Religious History of the American People*, pp. 491–509; see also Cross, *Burned-Over District*, pp. 30–32 (on Shakers), pp. 138–50 (on LDS), pp. 287–90 (Adventists), pp. 333–40 (Oneida Community); LeBeau, *Religion in America to 1865*, pp. 118–27.

35. Glad, *Trumpet Soundeth*, p. 7.

36. Ahlstrom, *Religious History of the American People*, pp. 388–402; Cross, *Burned-Over District*, pp, 43–44.

37. Ahlstrom, *Religious History of the American People*, pp. 597–614.

38. LeBeau, *Religion in America to 1865*, 109–13; Ahlstrom, *Religious History of the American People*, pp. 488–90.

39. John R. McKivigan, *The War against Proslavery Religion: Abolitionism and the Northern Churches, 1830–1865* (Ithaca, NY: Cornell University Press, 1984), pp. 20–21; Carwardine, *Evangelicals and Politics in Antebellum America*, p. 3. The First Great Awakening did have some millennial impulses as well, and can be said to have planted the seeds of millennialism in American Protestantism that bloomed during later awakenings. (Heimert, *Religion and the American Mind*, pp. 59–66.)

40. Ben Wright and Zachary W. Dresser, introduction to *Apocalypse and the Millennium: In the American Civil War Era*, ed. Ben Wright and Zachary W. Dresser (Baton Rouge: Louisiana State University Press, 2013), pp. 2–4; Carwardine, *Evangelicals and Politics in Antebellum America*, p. 3. For the importance of the millennial concept of the Kingdom of God in American history, see also H. Richard Niebuhr, *The Kingdom of God in America* (New York: Harper and Row, 1937), pp. 135–98.

41. Carwardine, *Evangelicals and Politics in Antebellum America*, p. 22.

42. Cross, *Burned-Over District*, pp. 233–37; LeBeau, *Religion in America to 1865*, pp. 116–17.

43. Carwardine, *Evangelicals and Politics in Antebellum America*, pp. 6–14.

44. Ibid., pp. 134–39.

45. Cross, *Burned-Over District*, pp. 151–69; LeBeau, *Religion in America to 1865*, pp. 163–76.

46. Harriet Beecher Stowe, *Uncle Tom's Cabin*, Brunswick ed. (Boston: Houghton Mifflin, 1893).

47. Carwardine, *Evangelicals and Politics in Antebellum America*, pp. 137–38.

48. Ibid., pp. 19–150. The Free Soil Party "function[ed] as a religious crusade as much as a conventional political party." (Ibid., p. 150.) Its first political convention functioned almost as a revival meeting with early morning gatherings for prayer and the singing of religious hymns. (Ibid., p. 151.)

49. Ibid., pp. 1, 4.

50. Ibid., pp. 153–57.

51. Cross, *Burned-Over District*, pp. 84–85, 176–79. "Properly, [women] should dominate a history of enthusiastic movements, for their influence was paramount." (Ibid., p. 84; Mary P. Ryan, "A Women's Awakening: Evangelical Religion and the Families of Utica, New York, 1800–1840," *American Quarterly* 50, no. 3 [1978]: 602–23.)

52. Sally G. McMillen, *Seneca Falls and the Origins of the Women's Rights Movement* (New York: Oxford University Press, 2008), pp. 52–54; Sue Davis, *The Political Thought of Elizabeth Cady Stanton: Women's Rights and the American Political Traditions* (New York: New York University Press), pp. 85–88.

Temperance was also from the start a movement highly tied up with anti-Catholicism and anti-immigrant sentiment. (William E. Gienapp, *The Origins of the Republican Party, 1852–1856* [New York: Oxford University Press, 1987], p. 45.)

53. Almost all the major and minor figures of the early women's suffrage movement came out of the abolition and temperance movement and Second Great Awakening. As Whitney Cross wrote in his definitive book on the Burned-Over District, "Elizabeth Cady Stanton, Amelia Bloomer, Susan B. Anthony, Antoinette Brown Blackwell, the Grimke sisters, and others soon to lead the women's rights movement served apprenticeship in the reforms which flourished in western New York." (Cross, *Burned-Over District*, p. 237; see also Daniel Walker Howe, *The Political Culture of the American Whigs* [Chicago: University of Chicago Press, 1979], pp. 160–61.)

Stanton, however, famously came to aggressively reject the religious traditions she rose up from, and was always ambivalent about, if not hostile toward, significant portions of revivalist religious teachings. (Davis, *Political Thought of Elizabeth Cady Stanton*, pp. 5–7.)

54. Ellen Carol DuBois, *Feminism and Suffrage: The Emergence of an Independent Women's Movement in America* (Ithaca, NY: Cornell University Press, 1979), pp. 31–34.

55. Garrison's faction was most supportive of full equality for women, with Garrison openly declaring he wanted women to have the vote. (W. Caleb McDaniel, *The Problem of Democracy in the Age of Slavery: Garrisonian Abolitionists and Transatlantic Reform* [Baton Rouge: Louisiana State University Press], p. 137.)

56. McMillen, *Seneca Falls*, p. 71.

57. Cross, *Burned-Over District*, p. 237.

58. Carwardine, *Evangelicals and Politics in Antebellum America*, p. 17.

59. "From its first lines proclaiming 'the glory of the coming of the Lord' to its final verse assuring that 'He is coming like the glory of the morning on the wave,' 'The Battle Hymn of the Republic' trumpets the millennial faith that echoed in the hearts of men and women, North and South, during an era of apocalyptic turmoil." (Wright and Dresser, introduction, *Apocalypse and the Millennium*, p. 1.)

60. Ahlstrom, *Religious History of the American People*, pp. 733–34.

61. Ibid., pp. 743–46; Michael Kazin, *The Populist Persuasion: An American History* (Ithaca, NY: Cornell University Press, 1994), p. 33.

62. Ibid., pp. 785–87.

63. Walter Rauschenbusch, *Christianity and the Social Crisis* (Louisville: Westminster / John Knox Press, 1991).

64. Ahlstrom, *Religious History of the American People*, pp. 785–87, 800–802.

65. George E. Mowry, *The Era of Theodore Roosevelt, 1900–1912* (New York: Harper and Brothers, 1958), pp. 85–86.

66. Ahlstrom, *Religious History of the American People*, pp. 805–814; McLoughlin, *Revivals, Awakenings, and Reform*, p. 153.

67. Ahlstrom, *Religious History of the American People*, pp. 807–12; 1020–26; 1037–47.

68. Glad, *Trumpet Soundeth*, pp. 15–20.

69. McLoughlin, *Revivals, Awakenings, and Reform*, pp. 145–50; Ahlstrom, *Religious History of the American People*, pp. 747–48.

70. Ahlstrom, *Religious History of the American People*, pp. 815–16.

71. Ibid., pp. 909–10.

72. McLoughlin, *Revivals, Awakenings, and Reform*, pp. 7–10.

73. Ibid., p. 2.

74. For example, see McLoughlin, *Revivals, Awakenings, and Reform*, p. 1.

CHAPTER 14: THE FOURTH GREAT AWAKENING AND THE 1960s

1. John Killick, *The United States and European Reconstruction, 1945–1960* (Edinburgh, UK: Keele University Press, 1997), p. 85.

2. Richard M. Abrams, *America Transformed: Sixty Years of Revolutionary Change, 1941–2001* (Cambridge: Cambridge University Press, 2006), pp. 28–30.

3. Steven F. Hayward, *The Fall of the Old Liberal Order, 1964–1980*, vol. 1 of *The Age of Reagan* (New York: Forum, 2001), pp. 8–11 (regarding America's peace, prosperity, and stability until 1964).

4. Lyndon B. Johnson, "Commencement Address—The Great Society," in *America in the Sixties—Right, Left, and Center: A Documentary History*, ed. Peter B. Levy (Westport, CT: Praeger, 1998), pp. 106–109.

5. Eric F. Goldman, *The Tragedy of Lyndon Johnson* (New York: Alfred A. Knopf, 1969), pp. 165–66; Robert Dallek, *Flawed Giant: Lyndon Johnson and His Times, 1961–1973* (New York: Oxford University Press, 1998), pp. 80–84.

6. Goldman, *Tragedy of Lyndon Johnson*, pp. 138–42.

7. Ibid., pp. 164.

8. Dallek, *Flawed Giant*, pp. 60, 71–74, 111.

9. Robert A. Caro, *Master of the Senate*, vol. 3 of *The Years of Lyndon Johnson* (New York: Alfred A. Knopf, 2002), pp. 365–66, 475–85, 495–99, 599.

10. Ibid., pp. 942–89; Timothy N. Thurber, *Republicans and Race: The GOP's Frayed Relationships with African Americans, 1945–1974* (Lawrence: University Press of Kansas, 2013), pp. 104–108.

11. Doris Kearns, *Lyndon Johnson and the American Dream* (New York: Harper and Row, 1976), p. 148.

12. Caro, *Master of the Senate*, pp. 985–88.

13. Arthur M. Schlesinger Jr., *A Thousand Days: John F. Kennedy in the White House* (Boston: Houghton Mifflin, 1965), pp. 930–31; see also Hayward, *Fall of the Old Liberal Order*, p. 23 (on Kennedy ambivalence on civil rights).

14. Kearns, *Lyndon Johnson*, p. 191; Dallek, *Flawed Giant*, p. 114. As Johnson explained to Kearns, "I knew that if I didn't get out in front of the issue, they [the liberals] would get me. They'd

throw up my background against me, they'd use it to prove that I was incapable of bringing unity to the land I loved so much . . . I couldn't let that happen." (Kearns, *Lyndon Johnson*, p. 191.)

15. Dallek, *Flawed Giant*, p. 118.

16. Ibid., pp. 118–21; Thurber, *Republicans and Race*, pp. 153–70 (on Republican support for 1964 Civil Rights Act). Republican support for the 1964 Civil Rights Act was substantial and essential to the bill's passage. While not every Republican supported the bill, the support of the party as a whole and its leadership in particular were necessary to overcome the considerable legislative power of the Southern segregationist Democrats. Republican objections to government intervention in private actions, however, played a role in limiting the bill's scope in its prohibitions of discrimination by private business owners.

17. Dallek, *Flawed Giant*, pp. 189–211, 226–31, 311–22, 329–34.

18. For perhaps the best balanced discussion of Lyndon Johnson's continuing and horrific personal racism see Caro, *Master of the Senate*, pp. 712–39.

19. Theodore H. White, *The Making of the President: 1968* (New York: Atheneum, 1969), pp. 80–85, 111–45.

20. Robert A. Caro, *Means of Ascent*, vol. 2 of *The Years of Lyndon Johnson* (New York: Alfred A. Knopf, 1990), pp. 80–118, 301–50; Dallek, *Flawed Giant*, pp. 38–41.

21. Caro, *Master of the Senate*, pp. 1018–20.

22. Dallek, *Flawed Giant*, pp. 124, 185–89; Caro, *Master of the Senate*, pp. 653–54.

23. Goldman, *Tragedy of Lyndon Johnson*, p. 166.

24. Terry H. Anderson, *The Movement and the Sixties: Protest in America from Greensboro to Wounded Knee* (New York: Oxford University Press, 1995), p. 32.

25. Ibid., pp. 1–27.

26. Mark Hamilton Lytle, *America's Uncivil Wars: The Sixties Era from Elvis to the Fall of Richard Nixon* (New York: Oxford University Press, 2006), pp. 198–99.

27. Ibid., pp. 334–38.

28. Gary Wills, *Nixon Agonistes: The Crisis of the Self-Made Man* (Boston: Houghton Mifflin, 1970), pp. 322–24 (portrait of the manners and style of the New Left activists at the 1968 convention, from the scraggy beards to the long hairstyles and loose clothes).

29. Anderson, *Movement and the Sixties*, pp. 93–95, 173.

30. Ibid., pp. 89–92.

31. Ahlstrom, *Religious History of the American People*, pp. 1050–54.

32. Anderson, *Movement and the Sixties*, p. 267.

33. Ibid., p. 261.

34. Ibid., p. 268; Lisa McGirr, *Suburban Warriors: The Origins of the New American Right* (Princeton, NJ: Princeton University Press, 2001), p. 243.

35. Lytle, *America's Uncivil Wars*, pp. 201–205.

36. Anderson, *Movement and the Sixties*, p. 172.

37. Lytle, *America's Uncivil Wars*, pp. 240–54.

38. Ibid., pp. 218–33.

39. Ibid., pp. 272–82.

40. Anderson, *Movement and the Sixties*, pp. 124–30, 135–52; Lytle, *America's Uncivil Wars*, pp. 283–87, 304–14.

41. James Miller, *Democracy Is in the Streets: From Port Huron to the Siege of Chicago* (New York: Simon and Schuster, 1987), pp. 191–94.

42. As historian Terry Anderson put it: "The counterculture believed that the nation had become a Steppenwolf, a berserk monster, a cruel society that made war on peasants abroad and at home beat up on minorities, dissidents, students, and hippies. America the Beautiful was no more; it had been replaced by Amerika the Death Culture." (Anderson, *Movement and the Sixties*, p. 251.)

43. Lytle, *America's Uncivil Wars*, pp. 77–80; Anderson, *Movement and the Sixties*, pp. 49–62.

44. Lytle, *America's Uncivil Wars*, pp. 80–88.

45. "The Port Huron Statement," in *The Port Huron Statement: Sources and Legacies of the New Left's Founding Manifesto*, ed. Richard Flacks and Nelson Lichtenstein (Philadelphia: University of Pennsylvania Press, 2015), pp. 239, 242; White, *Making of the President: 1968*, pp. 250–51; Wills, *Nixon Agonistes*, pp. 256–59.

46. Maurice Isserman, *If I Had a Hammer: The Death of the Old Left and the Birth of the New Left* (New York Basic Books, 1987), pp. 202–19; Anderson, *Movement and the Sixties*, pp. 62–66.

47. Tom Hayden, "Crafting the Port Huron Statement: Measuring Its Impact in the 1960s and After," in Flacks and Lichtenstein, *Port Huron Statement*, p. 23.

48. Rachel Carson, *Silent Spring* (Boston: Houghton Mifflin, 1963); Anderson, *Movement and the Sixties*, pp. 347–48.

49. Betty Friedan, *The Feminine Mystique* (New York: W. W. Norton, 2001); Lytle, *America's Uncivil Wars*, pp. 272–82; Anderson, *Movement and the Sixties*, pp. 311–12.

50. National Organization of Women, "Statement of Purpose," in Levy, *America in the Sixties*, pp. 202–204.

51. White, *Making of the President: 1968*, pp. 28–33.

52. Lytle, *America's Uncivil Wars*, pp. 230–39.

53. Anderson, *Movement and the Sixties*, pp. 152–58; Lytle, *America's Uncivil Wars*, pp. 227–30; White, *Making of the President: 1968*, pp. 237–41.

54. White, *Making of the President: 1968*, pp. 250–58.

55. Todd Gitlin, *The Whole World Is Watching: Mass Media in the Making and Unmaking of the New Left* (Berkeley: University of California Press, 1980), pp. 190–92; Lytle, *America's Uncivil Wars*, pp. 344–47.

56. White, *Making of the President: 1968*, pp. 336–37.

57. Goldman, *The Tragedy of Lyndon Johnson*, p. 337.

58. Lytle, *America's Uncivil Wars*, pp. 257–65; White, *Making of the President: 1968*, pp. 301–66; Richard Perlstein, *Nixonland: The Rise of a President and the Fracturing of America* (New York: Scribner, 2008), pp. 320–21; Wills, *Nixon Agonistes*, pp. 324–34; Tom Hayden, *Reunion: A Memoir* (New York: Random House, 1988), pp. 291–326.

59. Anderson, *Movement and the Sixties*, pp. 392–95.

60. The historian Michael Kazin, who identifies strongly with the movement, fittingly said these "young moralists of the 1960s" were acting as "missionaries of a secular persuasion." (Michael Kazin, *The Populist Persuasion: An American History* [Ithaca, NY: Cornell University Press, 1995], p. 197.)

61. Hayden, *Reunion*, p. 505.

62. William G. McLoughlin, *Revivals, Awakenings, and Reform: An Essay on Religion and Social Change in America, 1607–1977* (Chicago: University of Chicago Press, 1978), pp. 193–211 (the counterculture's ethics, embrace of Eastern religion, use of psychedelic drugs, and interest in the occult are all suggestive of the usual course and behavior of an awakening).

63. Theodore H. White, *The Making of the President: 1960* (New York: Atheneum, 1961), pp. 290–93.

64. Caro, *Master of the Senate*, pp. 987–88 (1957 Civil Rights Act); Thurber, *Republicans and Race*, pp. 120–21 (on Nixon's positive relationship with the African American vote in 1960).

65. Richard H. K. Vietor, "Government Regulation of Business," in *The Cambridge Economic History of the United States*, vol. 3, *The Twentieth Century*, ed. Stanley L. Engerman and Robert E. Gallman (Cambridge: Cambridge University Press, 2000), pp. 995–97.

The downturn moreover quickly got worse over the next few years. Where unemployment was 3.5 percent in 1968, it rose to 5.9 percent by 1971. The Dow dropped from 1,000 in 1966 to 578 in 1974. (John Steele Gordon, *An Empire of Wealth* [New York: Harper Collins, 2004], p. 383.)

66. White, *Making of the President: 1968*, pp. 222–26.

67. Dallek, *Flawed Giant*, pp. 221–26; White, *Making of the President: 1968*, pp. 232–41. The urban riots so troubled the nation they, more than any other event of the 1960s, significantly shifted the national mood away from further advancing civil rights. They also caused Johnson to abandon any effort to further advance civil rights and to back away from the issue almost entirely. (See Dallek, *Flawed Giant*, pp. 221–26.)

68. Ibid., p. 38.

69. Ibid., pp. 280–85; William A. Rusher, *The Rise of the Right* (New York: William Morrow, 1984), pp. 196–97.

70. Perlstein, *Nixonland*, p. 277; Kevin P. Phillips, *The Emerging Republican Majority* (New Rochelle, NY: Arlington House, 1969), pp. 461–74.

71. Wills, *Nixon Agonistes*, pp. 264–65; Robert Mason, *Richard Nixon and the Quest for a New Majority* (Chapel Hill: University of North Carolina Press, 2004), p. 27.

72. Mason, *Richard Nixon*, p. 27; Richard Nixon, "A New Alignment for American Unity," radio address, May 16, 1968, available at the Richard Nixon Foundation, https://www.nixonfoundation.org/artifact/new-alignment-american-unity/.

73. Richard M. Nixon, "Acceptance Speech at the Republican National Convention," in Levy, *America in the Sixties*, pp. 245–52.

74. White, *Making of the President: 1968*, p. 220.

75. Thurber, *Republicans and Race*, p. 276 (on Nixon), pp. 46, 73–77 (on Eisenhower's success with the African American vote).

76. Richard Scammon and Ben J. Wattenburg, *The Real Majority: An Extraordinary Examination of the American Electorate* (New York: Coward-McCann, 1970), pp. 180–83.

77. Rowland Evans Jr. and Robert D. Novak, *Nixon in the White House: The Frustration of Power* (New York: Random House, 1971), pp. 323–25; Mason, *Richard Nixon*, pp. 82–85.

78. Mason, *Richard Nixon*, pp. 88–90.

79. Patrick J. Buchanan, *The New Majority: President Nixon at Mid-Passage* (Philadelphia: Girard, 1973), pp. 62–64.

80. Theodore H. White, *The Making of the President: 1964* (New York: Atheneum, 1965), p. 245.

81. Mason, *Richard Nixon*, p. 48.

82. Ibid., pp. 48–49.

83. Mason, *Richard Nixon*, pp. 52–54.

84. Thurber, *Republicans and Race*, p. 127; Wills, *Nixon Agonistes*, p. 380.

85. Evans and Novak, *Nixon in the White House*, pp. 141–76.

86. Ibid., p. 136.

87. Thurber, *Republicans and Race*, p. 133 (on Republican disappointment in 1960); Phillips, *Emerging Republican Majority*, p. 468 (on no longer needing to win African American support) ("Substantial Negro support is not necessary to national Republican victory in light of the 1968 returns. Obviously, the GOP can build a winning coalition without Negro votes.").

88. As he told his aide William Safire: "You're not going to solve this race problem for a hundred years. Intermarriage and all that, assimilation, it will happen, but not in our time." (William Safire, *Before the Fall: An Inside View of the Pre-Watergate White House* [New York: Doubleday, 1975], p. 237.)

89. Mason, *Richard Nixon*, p. 104 (on Nixon's 1970 campaign and race). The most notorious evidence of this sort of cynicism was campaign operative Lee Atwater, who described it this way in an interview: "By 1968 you can't say 'n*****'—that hurts you, backfires. So you say stuff like, uh, forced busing, states' rights, and all that stuff, and you're getting so abstract. Now, you're talking about cutting taxes, and all these things you're talking about are totally economic things and a byproduct of them is, blacks get hurt worse than whites." (Rick Perlstein, "Exclusive: Lee Atwater's Infamous 1981 Interview on the Southern Strategy," *Nation*, November 13, 2012.)

90. Wills, *Nixon Agonistes*, p. 265.

91. For example, see Matthew B. Lassiter, *The Silent Majority: Suburban Politics in the Sunbelt South* (Princeton, NJ: Princeton University Press, 2006); Joseph A. Aistrup, *The Southern Strategy Revisited: Republican Top-Down Advancement in the Deep South* (Lexington: University Press of Kentucky, 1996); Dan T. Carter, *From George Wallace to Newt Gingrich, Race in the Conservative Counter-Revolution, 1963–1994* (Baton Rouge: Louisiana State University Press, 1996); Byron E. Shafer and Richard Johnson, *The End of Southern Exceptionalism: Class, Race, and Partisan Change in the Postwar South* (Cambridge, MA: Harvard University Press 2006); Alexander P. Lamis, *The Two-Party South* (New York: Oxford University Press, 1988).

92. Few segregationist Democrats, of course, actually switched to the Republican Party in 1964 or 1968. The most powerful Southern segregationist politicians mostly remained proud Democrats throughout their careers, including Wallace, many into the 1980s. The old Democratic Solid South, for example, had been slowly trending Republican since Eisenhower but didn't become a Republican bastion until the boomers fully replaced older generations in the 1990s—almost thirty years after the awakening began.

93. See Jonathan Haidt, *The Righteous Mind: Why Good People Are Divided by Politics and Religion* (New York: Vintage, 2012), pp. 330–66.

94. Grant Wacker, *America's Pastor: Billy Graham and the Shaping of a Nation* (Cambridge, MA: Belknap, 2014), pp. 37–50; Daniel K. Williams, *God's Own Party: The Making of the Christian Right* (New York: Oxford University Press, 2010), pp. 12–15.

95. Steven P. Miller, *Billy Graham and the Rise of the Republican South* (Philadelphia: University of Pennsylvania Press, 2009), pp. 7, 19–21; Williams, *God's Own Party*, pp. 15–18.

96. Wacker, *America's Pastor*, pp. 204–47; Williams, *God's Own Party*, pp. 69, 90–91.

97. Steven P. Miller, *The Age of Evangelicalism: America's Born-Again Years* (New York: Oxford University Press, 2014), pp. 29–22, 40–49.

98. *Newsweek*, October 25, 1976.

99. Laura Kalman, *Right Star Rising: A New Politics, 1974–1980* (New York: W. W. Norton, 2010), pp. 271–74; Williams, *God's Own Party*, pp. 159–94; McGirr, *Suburban Warriors*, pp. 255–57; Miller, *Age of Evangelicalism*, pp. 58–59.

100. Miller, *Age of Evangelicalism*, pp. 53–56; Williams, *God's Own Party*, pp. 111–20.

101. Williams, *God's Own Party*, pp. 159–94.

102. Erling Jorstad, *Evangelicals in the White House: The Cultural Maturation of Born-Again Christianity, 1960–1981* (New York: Edwin Mellen, 1981), pp. 46–47 (noting statistical evidence for a sudden burst of enthusiasm for evangelical Protestantism in the 1970s); see also Miller, *Age of Evangelicalism*, pp. 9–31; McGirr, *Suburban Warriors*, pp. 241–42.

103. Miller, *Age of Evangelicalism*, p. 103.

104. McGirr, *Suburban Warriors*, pp. 255–57; Miller, *Age of Evangelicalism*, pp. 102–106.

105. Randall J. Stephens and Karl W. Giberson, *The Anointed: Evangelical Truth in a Secular Age* (Cambridge, MA: Belknap, 2011), pp. 180–223; Miller, *Age of Evangelicalism*, pp. 102–106, 130–35.

106. McGirr, *Suburban Warriors*, pp. 254–55.

107. Jorstad, *Evangelicals in the White House*, pp. 50–59.

108. Miller, *Age of Evangelicalism*, pp. 106–16; Williams, *God's Own Party*, pp. 235–44.

109. Walter H. Capps, *The New Religious Right: Piety, Patriotism, and Politics* (Columbia: University of South Carolina Press, 1990), pp. 158–84.

CHAPTER 15: THE END OF THE INDUSTRIAL ERA AND THE AMERICAN CENTURY

1. Daniel Patrick Moynihan, "Of 'Sons' and Their 'Grandsons,'" *New York Times*, July 7, 1980, p. 15.

2. John Killick, *The United States and European Reconstruction, 1945–1960* (Edinburgh, UK: Keele University Press, 1997), p. 7.

3. Richard M. Abrams, *America Transformed: Sixty Years of Revolutionary Change, 1941–2001* (Cambridge, UK: Cambridge University Press, 2006), pp. 28–29.

4. Henry Luce, "The American Century," *Life*, February 17, 191, p. 61–65; Andrew J. Bacevich, "*Life* at the Dawn of the American Century," in *Short American Century*, pp. 1–14.

5. Killick, *United States and European Reconstruction*, p. 7.

6. John Steele Gordon, *An Empire of Wealth: The Epic History of American Economic Power* (New York: Harper Collins, 2004), pp. 377–78; Angus Maddison, *The World Economy* (Paris: OECD Development Centre, 2006), pp. 261–64.

7. Killick, *United States and European Reconstruction*, p. 85; Abrams, *America Transformed*, p. 30; Louis Galambos, "The U.S. Corporate Economy in the Twentieth Century," in *Cambridge Economic History of the United States*, vol. 3, pp. 948–57.

8. Maddison, *World Economy*, pp. 261–64; Taylor Jaworski and Price V. Fishback, "Two World Wars in American Economic History," in *Oxford Handbook of American Economic History*, vol. 2, ed. Louis P. Cain, Price V. Fishback, and Paul W. Rhode (Oxford: Oxford University Press, 2018), p. 404; Moses Abramovitz and Paul A. David, "American Macroeconomic Growth in the Era of Knowledge-Based Progress: The Long-Run Perspective," in *The Cambridge Economic History of the United States*, vol. 3, *The Twentieth Century*, ed. Stanley E. Engerman and Robert E. Gallman (Cambridge, UK: Cambridge University Press, 2000), pp. 70–71.

9. Emily S. Rosenberg, "Consuming the American Century," in *The Short American Century: A Postmortem*, ed. Andrew J. Bacevich (Cambridge, MA: Harvard University Press, 2012), pp. 45–52.

10. Barry Eichengreen, "U.S. Foreign Financial Relations in the Twentieth Century," in *Cambridge Economic History of the United States*, vol. 3; Gordon, *Empire of Wealth*, pp. 377–78.

11. Abrams, *America Transformed*, p. 28.

12. Claudia Goldin, "Labor Markets in the Twentieth Century," in *Cambridge Economic History of the United States*, vol. 3, p. 565.

13. Maddison, *World Economy*, pp. 132, 261–64; Abramovitz and David, "American Macroeconomic Growth," pp. 70–71.

14. John DiIulio to Ron Suskind, October 24, 2002, available at *Esquire*, May 22, 2007, https://www.esquire.com/news-politics/a2880/diiulio/. The letter served as the primary source of an explosive article *Esquire* published in its January 2003 issue: Ron Suskind, "Why Are These Men Laughing," *Esquire*, January 2003.

15. "War therefore is an act of violence intended to compel our opponent to fulfil our will." (Carl von Clausewitz, *On War*, trans. Col. J. J. Graham, vol. 1 [London: Routledge and Kegan Paul, 1962], p. 2.) This is why Clausewitz famously said, "War is a mere continuation of policy by other means." (Ibid., p. 23.)

16. "Tactics is the theory of the use of military forces in combat. Strategy is the theory of the use of combats for the object of the War." (Clausewitz, *On War*, p. 86.)

17. The current consensus is that most voters who label themselves political "independents" are in reality soft and discontented partisans wishing to communicate, by rejecting a party label, their disagreement with their party's positions and public associations. (For example, see Bruce E. Keith et al., *The Myth of the Independent Voter* [Berkeley: University of California Press, 1992], pp. 169–77.)

CHAPTER 16: AMERICA UNRAVELING

1. John Kenneth White, "Sound Work in a Tough Environment: Obama's Governing Achievements," in *Debating the Obama Presidency*, ed. Steven E. Schier (Lanham, MD: Rowman and Littlefield, 2016), pp. 24–25.

2. Barack Obama, "Keynote Address at the 2004 Democratic National Convention, July 27, 2004, Boston, MA," in *An American Story: The Speeches of Barack Obama*, David Olive (Toronto: ECW Press, 2008), p. 103; Barack Obama, "Remarks on Super Tuesday, February 5, 2008, Chicago, IL," in Olive, *American Story*, p. 247.

3. Obama, "Remarks on Super Tuesday," p. 247.

4. Erika Schneider, "The Politics of Tagging: Shepard Fairey's Obama," in *The Iconic Obama, 2007–2009: Essays on Media Representation of the Candidate and New President*, ed. Nicholas A. Yanes and Derrais Carter (Jefferson, NC: McFarland, 2012), pp. 97–108.

5. James Carviou, "New Media's Impact on Elections: An Interview with Obama Girl Creator Ben Relles," in Yanes and Carter, *Iconic Obama*, pp. 189–93.

6. Michael E. Ruane and Aaron C. Davis, "D.C.'s Inauguration Head Count: 1.8 Million," *Washington Post*, January 22, 2009; Jonathan Alter, *The Promise: President Obama, Year One* (New York: Simon and Schuster, 2010), pp. 100–109.

7. Steven Erlanger and Sheryl Gay Stolberg, "Surprise Nobel for Obama Stirs Praise and Doubts," *New York Times*, October 9, 2009.

8. Stanley A. Renshon, *Barack Obama and the Politics of Redemption* (New York: Routledge, 2012), pp. 16–25, 230–58.

9. Christine Trost and Lawrence Rosenthal, "The Rise of the Tea Party," in *Steep: The Precipitous Rise of the Tea Party*, ed. Lawrence Rosenthal and Christine Trost (Berkeley: University of California Press, 2012), pp. 1–16.

10. Jonathan Chait, *Audacity: How Barack Obama Defied His Critics and Created a Legacy That Will Prevail* (New York: Custom House, 2017), pp. 11–163, 184–91.

11. John D. Graham, *Obama on the Home Front: Domestic Policy Triumphs and Setbacks* (Bloomington: Indiana University Press, 2016), pp. 66–135; Eric Rauchway, "Neither a Depression nor a New Deal: Bailout, Stimulus, and the Economy" in *The Presidency of Barack Obama: A First Historical Assessment*, ed. Julian Zelizer (Princeton, NJ: Princeton University Press, 2018), pp. 30–44; Paul Starr, "Achievement Without Credit: The Obama Presidency and Inequality," in Zelizer, *Presidency of Barack Obama*, pp. 45–61.

12. Jeremi Suri, "Liberal Internationalism, Law, and the First African American President," in Zelizer, *Presidency of Barack Obama*, pp. 195–211.

13. Graham, *Obama on the Home Front*, pp. 135–205.

14. Ibid., pp. 124–27, 269–305; David Fitzgerald and David Ryan, *Obama, US Foreign Policy and the Dilemmas of Intervention* (London: Palgrave Macmillan 2014), pp. 92–105.

15. Lahnee J. Chen and Andrew Reeves, "Turning Out the Base or Appealing to the Periphery? An Analysis of County-Level Candidate Appearances in the 2008 Presidential Campaign," *American Politics Research* 39, no. 3 (May 2011): 535; Michael Peress, "Securing the Base: Electoral Competition Under Variable Turnout," *Public Choice* 148, no. 1–2 (July 2011): 87–89.

16. Chen and Reeves, "Turning Out the Base or the Appealing to the Periphery?" p. 538; Costas Panagopoulos and Peter W. Wielhouwer, "The Ground War 2000–2004: Strategic Targeting in Grassroots Campaigns," *Presidential Studies Quarterly* 38, no. 2 (June 2008): 348–50, 359–60; Peress, "Securing the Base," p. 88; Donald P. Green and Alan S. Gerber, *Get Out the Vote: How to Increase Voter Turnout* (Washington, DC: Brookings Institution Press, 2015), pp. 1–10; Eitan D. Hersh, *Hacking the Electorate: How Campaigns Perceive Voters* (New York: Cambridge University Press, 2015), pp. 13–26.

17. Seth J. Hill, "Changing Votes or Changing Voters? How Candidates and Election Context Swing Voters and Mobilize the Base," *Electoral Studies* 48 (August 2017): 142.

18. Hersh, *Hacking the Electorate*, pp. 13–14, 35–44, 66–76, 151, 169–76; Dennis W. Johnson, *Campaigning in the Twenty-First Century: A Whole New Ballgame?* (New York: Routledge, 2011), pp. 79–85; Dennis W. Johnson, *Democracy for Hire: A History of American Political Consulting* (New York: Oxford University Press, 2017), pp. 329–33.

19. Geoffrey Kabaservice, *Rule and Ruin: The Downfall of Moderation and the Destruction of the Republican Party, from Eisenhower to the Tea Party* (Oxford: Oxford University Press, 2012), pp. 363–88; Christine Todd Whitman, *It's My Party Too: The Battle for the Heart of the GOP and the Future of America* (New York: Penguin, 2005), pp. 10–13.

20. Kenneth S. Baer, *Reinventing Democrats: The Politics of Liberalism from Reagan to Clinton* (Lawrence: University of Kansas Press, 2000), pp. 253–75; Dylan Loewe, *Permanently Blue: How Democrats Can End the Republican Party and Rule the Next Generation* (New York: Three Rivers, 2010), p. 171.

21. Claire Suddath, "A Brief History of Blue Dog Democrats," *Time*, July 28, 2009, http://content.time.com/time/politics/article/0,8599,1913057,00.html.

22. "Coalition of the ascendant" is a term journalist Ronald Brownstein coined to describe Barack Obama's electoral coalition in the 2008 and 2012 elections. According to Brownstein, it consisted of "young people, minorities, and college-educated whites." (Ronald Brownstein, "How Obama Won: Marrying Old and New Democratic Coalitions," *Atlantic*, November 12, 2012, https://www.theatlantic.com/politics/archive/2012/11/how-obama-won-marrying-old-and-new-democratic-coalitions/264884/.) This idea of this "coalition of the ascendant" delivering the Democratic Party future majorities through demographic change became popular in Democratic Party circles, and it continues to have a great hold on Democratic Party thinking.

23. "Millennials in Adulthood: Detached from Institutions, Networked with Friends," Pew Research Center, March 2014, http://www.pewresearch.org/wp-content/uploads/sites/3/2014/03/2014-03-07_generations-report-version-for-web.pdf; "Millennials: A Portrait of Generation Next," Pew Research Center, February 2010, http://www.pewresearch.org/wp-content/uploads/sites/3/2010/10/millennials-confident-connected-open-to-change.pdf; see also "The Generation Gap in American Politics," Pew Research Center, March 1, 2018, http://www.people-press.org/2018/03/01/the-generation-gap-in-american-politics/; "The Whys and Hows of Generations Research," Pew Research Center, September 3, 2015, http://www.pewresearch.org/wp-content/uploads/sites/4/2015/09/09-3-2015-Generations-explainer-release.pdf.

Nor is this simply a factor of age, as other generations were more "conservative" leaning at the same stage of life. ("A Different Look at Generations and Partisanship," Pew Research

Center, April 30, 2015, http://www.pewresearch.org/wp-content/uploads/sites/4/2015/04/04-30-2015-Party-ID-and-generations-release.pdf.) Research suggests, however, that while millennials indeed do take more liberal positions than older generations as a whole, a portion of the effect isn't due to differences in the attitudes of the cohort, but to their different racial makeup. (Vladimir Enrique Medenica, "Millennials and Race in the 2016 Election," *Journal of Race Ethnicity and Politics* 3, no. 1 [March 2018]: 72–73.)

24. "Millennials in Adulthood"; "How Young People View Their Lives, Futures, and Politics: A Portrait of 'Generation Next,'" Pew Research Center, January 9, 2007, http://www.pewresearch.org/wp-content/uploads/sites/4/legacy-pdf/300.pdf; Hannah Fingerhut, "Millennials' Views of News Media, Religious Organizations Grow More Negative," Pew Research Center, January 4, 2016, http://www.pewresearch.org/fact-tank/2016/01/04/millennials-views-of-news-media-religious-organizations-grow-more-negative/.

25. This now commonly accepted view of generational cohorts sharing common characteristics due to their common life experiences is usually credited to Karl Mannheim and his foundational theory of generations, first set out in his 1928 essay "Das Problem der Generationen," later published in English in 1952 as "The Problem of Generations." (Karl Mannheim, "The Problem of Generations," in *Essays on the Sociology of Knowledge*, vol. 5 of *Collected Works of Karl Mannheim*, ed. Paul Kecskemeti [Abingdon, UK: Routledge, 2000], pp. 276–322.)

26. Richard Fry, "Millennials Projected to Overtake Baby Boomers as America's Largest Generation," Pew Research Center, March 1, 2018, http://www.pewresearch.org/fact-tank/2018/03/01/millennials-overtake-baby-boomers/.

27. Susan B. Glasser, "The Man Who Put Andrew Jackson in Trump's Oval Office," *Politico Magazine*, January 22, 2018, https://www.politico.com/magazine/story/2018/01/22/andrew-jackson-donald-trump-216493.

CHAPTER 17: WHAT HAPPENS NEXT

1. "The Debt to the Penny and Who Holds It," TreasuryDirect, last updated October 25, 2018, https://treasurydirect.gov/NP/debt/current.

2. *Financial Report of the United States Government* (Washington, DC: Secretary of the Treasury, 2017), https://www.fiscal.treasury.gov/fsreports/rpt/finrep/fr/17frusg/02142018_FR(Final).pdf.

The treasury reports spending as $4.5 trillion for accounting purposes when including additional accrued costs.

3. Barry Blom et al., *The Budget and Economic Outlook: 2018 to 2028* (Washington, DC: Congressional Budget Office, April 2018), https://www.cbo.gov/system/files?file=115th-congress-2017–2018/reports/53651-outlook.pdf.

4. For further discussion of these potential downsides and dangers a debt crisis might create, see for example: Andrew J. Yarrow, *Forgive Us Our Debts: The Intergenerational Dangers of Fiscal Irresponsibility* (New Haven, CT: Yale University Press, 2008), pp. 70–80.

CHAPTER 18: THE PARTY OF THE AMERICAN DREAM

1. James Truslow Adams, *The Epic of America* (New York: Blue Ribbon Books, 1931), p. 404.

2. Gordon S. Wood, *Empire of Liberty: A History of the Early Republic, 1789–1815* (New York: Oxford University Press, 2009), pp. 84–85.

3. Thomas Wolfe, *You Can't Go Home Again* (New York: Harper and Brothers, 1940), p. 741.

INDEX